AF352735

Recent Titles from the Moral Traditions Series

David Cloutier, Andrea Vicini, SJ, and Darlene Weaver, Editors

The Structures of Virtue and Vice
Daniel J. Daly

The Aesthetics of Solidarity: Our Lady of Guadalupe and American Democracy
Nichole M. Flores

Radical Sufficiency: Work, Livelihood, and a US Catholic Economic Ethic
Christine Firer Hinze

Tragic Dilemmas in Christian Ethics
Kate Jackson-Meyer

The Fullness of Free Time: Leisure and Recreation in the Moral Life
Connor Kelly

Beyond Biology: Rethinking Parenthood in the Catholic Tradition
Jacob M. Kohlhaas

Beyond Virtue Ethics: A Contemporary Ethic of Ancient Spiritual Struggle
Stephen M. Meawad

Growing in Virtue: Aquinas on Habit
William C. Mattison III

Reenvisioning Sexual Ethics: A Feminist Christian Account
Karen Peterson-Iyer

Tomorrow's Troubles: Risk, Anxiety, and Prudence in an Age of Algorithmic Governance
Paul Scherz

Wealth, Virtue, and Moral Luck: Christian Ethics in an Age of Inequality
Kate Ward

ON TEACHING AND LEARNING CHRISTIAN ETHICS

D. STEPHEN LONG

GEORGETOWN UNIVERSITY PRESS/WASHINGTON, DC

The publisher is not responsible for third-party websites or their content. URL links were active at time of publication.

Library of Congress Cataloging-in-Publication Data

Names: Long, D. Stephen, 1960– author.
Title: On teaching and learning Christian ethics / D. Stephen Long.
Description: Washington, DC : Georgetown University Press, 2024. | Series: Moral traditions series | Includes bibliographical references and index.
Identifiers: LCCN 2023014345 (print) | LCCN 2023014346 (ebook) | ISBN 9781647124137 (hardcover) | ISBN 9781647124144 (paperback) | ISBN 9781647124151 (ebook)
Subjects: LCSH: Christian ethics—Study and teaching. | Christian ethics— Catholic authors.
Classification: LCC BJ1249 .L58 2024 (print) | LCC BJ1249 (ebook) | DDC 241—dc23/eng/20231116
LC record available at https://lccn.loc.gov/2023014345
LC ebook record available at https://lccn.loc.gov/2023014346

∞ This paper meets the requirements of ANSI/NISO Z39.48-1992 (Permanence of Paper).

25 24   9 8 7 6 5 4 3 2   First printing

Printed in the United States of America

Cover design by Brad Norr
Cover art, "Sisyphus," by Adam James Stoner
Interior design by BookComp, Inc.

For Lilette, whose courage inspires

CONTENTS

PREFACE

This book attempts to answer a common question I receive when people ask me, "What do you do for a living?" When I answer that I am a professor, the next question is almost always the same. Whether in an airplane, during a bicycle ride, in the company of strangers or acquaintances, and even once during life-saving surgery, the follow-up is, "So what do you teach?" Answering is not easy, because I teach a discipline that few recognize: moral theology. I sometimes answer that I teach theology and ethics; the "and" is significant. My primary subject matter is how theology relates to ethics and vice versa. This answer may seem straightforward, but satisfactorily describing either of these disciplines is no simple task. Initial descriptions would be that theology is the study of who God is, how we might know, and what difference it makes. Ethics is the study of human action as it relates to good, bad, and evil, or right and wrong.

Ethics, at least as taught by the Greeks, predates Christian theology. It does not predate Christianity's primary source in Judaism, and any adequate account of moral theology must acknowledge its sources in both older traditions. Christian theology adopted themes from philosophical ethics as early as the New Testament; references to the virtues are plentiful throughout Scripture and into the patristic era. The ancient traditions of ethics and Christian theology, however, came together in a new way at the end of the sixteenth century, as part of the Thomistic renaissance in Catholic theology, which generated the distinct discipline "moral theology" (*theologia moralis*). Thomas Aquinas himself did not use this term, but he did refer to "moral science."[1] Moral theology became a subdiscipline within Christian theology after the Council of Trent (1545–63).[2] Moral theology is one of two systematic theological disciplines within Catholic theology, the other being speculative or dogmatic theology.[3] I prefer the term "moral theology" to "Christian ethics," but the two can be used synonymously.[4] Much more needs to be said about both disciplines—and will be. For now, what matters is that moral theology brings the two disciplines of ethics and theology together. It assumes that ethics cannot be done well if it excludes theology.

Over the years, I have discovered that explaining moral theology takes more time than most people have patience, so I often shorten my answer to either "I teach theology" or "I teach ethics." Each of these answers can lead to an uncomfortable conversation. If I give the first, it potentially creates an awkward discussion about religion. Persons explain how they were raised religious but no longer find it compelling, or how they are religious, assuming that how I teach theology will support their view of religion. Sometimes it is met with the conversation-stopping "Oh," followed by silence. And on rare occasions, it is met with a militant atheism enlightening me on why religion poisons everything, as if those of us who teach theology have never confronted atheisms new or old, or the self-perceived cogency of atheists' arguments for God's nonexistence.

If I say that I teach ethics, responses markedly differ. Awkward conversations about ethics seldom follow; a militant antiethics seems nonexistent. Instead, responses are more along these lines: "Well, that is important. God knows this society needs ethics" or "At least you will always have work." No one has ever asked "Ethics? What is that?" There seems to be an assumption that people know what ethics is and that teaching it is a good and honorable vocation. Perhaps this assumption will prove as time bound as previous assumptions about theology. Much of Western culture, especially in the academy, agrees with Nietzsche that gods die. They become useless. Yet it has not yet agreed with him that ethics also dies. "The twilight of the idols" is affirmed; "beyond good and evil" awaits affirmation. Nietzsche predicted this when he proclaimed, "Those who reject God, cling all the more firmly to ethics."[5] He did not mean it as a compliment. Perhaps a next stage in Western culture will produce a militant antiethics, and one day soon people will respond to my answer that I teach ethics as some do when I say that I teach theology; but that day has not yet arrived, and I am skeptical that it will. The pursuit of goodness is too baked into what it means to be human.

As someone who teaches moral theology, when pressed to explain what I do, I find it unsatisfying to answer either that I teach ethics or that I teach theology. It is safer, at the moment, to say I teach ethics, but this is at most a partial answer. It is riskier to say I teach theology, but this leaves out the important place ethics has in moral theology. This book is, in some sense, what I would say if I had the opportunity to explain more fully what moral theology is, how it relates theology and ethics, and how one goes about learning and teaching it. What theology brings to ethics is an understanding of the moral life as a gift that seeks to participate in divine perfection. The gift character of ethics is found in the central role of the theological virtues of faith, hope, and love. They recalibrate the discipline of ethics; charity gives form to all other virtues through its infusion by the Holy Spirit. Yet this is to get ahead of the conversation. What theology brings to ethics first requires considering what ethics is.

Like all modern academic disciplines, ethics justifies itself in the university by having a distinct domain to which properly trained professionals bring their expertise. A major contention of this work is that approaching ethics from this perspective makes it difficult to teach or learn it well. In fact, I am less convinced that I know what I am doing when I teach ethics than when I teach theology. That teaching or learning ethics is more difficult to discern than teaching or learning theology may surprise. Theology's role in the modern university frequently gets questioned; many scholars think that it has little to no purpose, except for the possibility of the kind of training that occurs in professional schools such as seminaries. Conversely, ethics' role in the modern university is seldom questioned. There is broad agreement that it should be taught across the curriculum. As someone who teaches both theology and ethics, and who teaches in both a seminary and a school of humanities, I find this unsettling and slightly amusing. I think I know what I am doing when I teach theology. It has a clear subject matter— God and all things as they relate to God. There are well-worn paths that a teacher can traverse to guide students into arguments about who God is, how we would know or not know, and how God and creation relate. Even if God does not exist, the discipline that addresses "God" has a coherence to it often lacking in ethics. If this is true, how does one go about teaching or learning ethics?

First, a caveat—the title of this work, *On Teaching and Learning Christian Ethics*, should not mislead readers; this book is not on pedagogy but on something more basic. Before learning or teaching Christian ethics, what ethics is should be sufficiently identified so that it can be, like other academic disciplines, taught and learned; that is easier said than done. Ethics is now an academic discipline, like chemistry, history, accounting, and so forth. I have made a living teaching it for more than three decades and do not consider those decades a waste of my, or my students', time. Nonetheless, after three decades of teaching ethics, I am still uncertain how to teach it because of the confusion about what it is and whether the academic practice of teaching it gets to the core of what it is. I am not confused *that* it is, even if I find setting forth *what* it is to be difficult.

Learning and teaching ethics is never a solitary affair. I owe a debt of gratitude to many persons who read and commented on all or portions of the manuscript for this book. The two anonymous reviewers were immensely helpful, and anyone who has sent out a manuscript for review knows that does not always happen. Thank you. Others assisted me with sources and information. Luke Bretherton, Michael Budde, Brian Clark, Shandon Klein, Peter H. Sedgwick, Daniel Lightsey, Sylvester Tan, and Tyler Womack helped with the latter. Through the support of Southern Methodist University's provost, Elizabeth Loboa, and funding from the Maguire Chair, I was able to have two symposia on early drafts. Jacob Goodson provided extensive philosophical commentary on the first part of the manuscript in the fall semester of 2020. A day-long symposium was held in the fall semester of 2022. John Berkman, Jonathan Tran, Alida Liberman, and Rob Miner read the manuscript with care and offered me substantive written feedback. Dallas Gingles and Margaret Watkins also participated with insightful critiques. They saved me from many (I am sure not all) errors. Doctoral students in Southern Methodist University's Graduate Program in Religious Studies (GPRS) attended and commented on the work then and later. Our ongoing conversations enriched the work. Working with such able students has made me a better teacher and scholar. Thanks especially belong to Zach deMoya, Lindsey Johnson Edwards, Noemi Vega Quiñones, and Danny Sebastian. We could not have held the symposium without the administrative prowess of Pamela Hogan from the GPRS. Three graduate assistants worked with me at different times on this project and deserve particular mention: Justin Bronson Barringer, Brian Clark, and Danny Sebastian. Stanley Hauerwas read the manuscript and offered suggestions that strengthened it. His friendship and mentorship for over forty years have been invaluable.

I was able to try out these ideas in some traditional and not-so-traditional places. The Affirmation Sunday School Class of Highland Park United Methodist Church, led by Dana Harkey; the New Life Class at University Park United Methodist Church; and the Dallas Rotary Club welcomed me to discuss teaching and learning ethics. Christopher Insole extended an invitation to present an essay, "A Theological Redemption of Autonomy," at the 2022 Rome Seminar, Redeeming Autonomy: Agency, Vulnerability, and Relationality. I am grateful to him for the invitation to discuss autonomy and use it as an opportunity to discuss F. D. Maurice. Several people offered me insightful comments, including Benjamin DeSpain, Jennifer Herdt, Karen Kilby, Vincent Lloyd, and Charles Mathewes. Abigail Cutter, Jacob Goodson, and Jackson Lashier invited me to Southwestern College to present the Parkhurst Lecture on Maurice's Christian Socialism. In the audience was a Methodist bishop who had studied with H. Richard Niebuhr, who had advised him to read Maurice's *Moral and Metaphysical Philosophy*. He is the only person I came across who has also read that massive tome.

I am grateful to Al Bertrand; David Cloutier; Andrea Vicini, SJ; and Darlene Fozard Weaver for their assistance in publishing with Georgetown University Press. I find it fitting that I do so. Not only am I able to carry on the Southern Methodist tradition of publishing moral theology with Georgetown established by my friend and colleague Charlie Curran, but I owe a tremendous debt to the Jesuits, who saved my teaching vocation on two different occasions. When I was about to give up finding a teaching position, the theology faculty at Saint Joseph's University in Philadelphia offered me my first position. When I was disillusioned with teaching, Marquette University brought me on and revived my vocation. I am indebted to these institutions—as well as to Southern Methodist University and to its Provost's Office—for supporting my vocation to teach, learn, and research Christian ethics.

NOTES

1. Aquinas, *Summa Theologiae*, II-II, 45.2 resp. Unless otherwise noted, English translations of the *Summa Theologiae* come from Freddoso, "New English Translations." Latin citations come from "Corpus Thomisticum," corpusthomisticum.org.
2. Mahoney, *Making of Moral Theology*, vii.
3. Grisez, *Christian Moral Principles*, 3–6.
4. See my chapter "Moral Theology" in *Oxford Handbook of Systematic Theology* for a discussion as to why I prefer the term "moral theology" to "Christian ethics"; Long, "Moral Theology."
5. Nietzsche, *Beyond Good*, 533.

INTRODUCTION
Clarifying Ethics

This book is, in part, a historical narration about how "ethics" became an academic discipline and why I find this problematic. The historical narration has the purpose of expanding what is meant by "ethics" as academic study beyond reductive accounts that arose in the mid–nineteenth century—accounts that are still hailed as progress when it is uncertain to me that they have accomplished much. This argument should neither lead readers to conclude that ethics should not be taught nor that it should only be taught as moral theology, excluding moral philosophy. Even reductive accounts of ethics have something to teach us, but an account of what constitutes well-lived lives teaches us more.

Dominant strands of ethics as an academic discipline lop off too much of ordinary life to accomplish anything more than teaching about theories and theorists of ethics rather than accomplishing what teaching and learning ethics should accomplish, which is to make us better people than we would be otherwise. As an academic discipline, ethics has been in search of a method, system, or procedure that will give it precision, so that an individual knows what they ought to do. This quest has not been without merit; it clarifies that ethics has been, and continues to be, an important and worthwhile endeavor. Learning theories and theorists of ethics remains an important task, one that I hope to take the reader through in what follows. In this sense, this work participates in the search for clarifying what ethics is—but with a twist. It questions if ethics can consist of isolated, independent subject matter divided from metaphysics, politics, theology, or everyday sources of life, such as families, neighborhoods, nations, religious institutions, friendships, and more. When ethics becomes an independent discipline, it will inevitably incline toward theory, without giving attention to what matters most for learning and teaching ethics—life. Ethics' possible focus on system, method, and procedures means that it loses attention to actual lives. If ethics concerns a life lived well, then emphasizing systems at the expense of lives inhibits learning or teaching it well. A second issue inevitably arises when ethics is isolated as its own internally coherent discipline; it becomes primarily what human persons achieve or accomplish through the application of such systems, methods, or procedures, and that means overlooking an essential feature of the moral life: that it comes as a gift as much as an achievement. For theologians, of course, ethics is a life lived well within the conditions of a broken and unjust world that requires gifts because the brokenness cannot be fixed through the sources internal to human persons, although those internal sources cannot be neglected.

THE CRUX OF THE MATTER: INFUSED AND ACQUIRED VIRTUES, F. D. MAURICE, AND HENRY SIDGWICK

Two persons and two definitions of ethics form the structure of the argument that is made here. Even when they are not being discussed, they are always in the background. These definitions are the accounts of virtue given by Aristotle and Augustine:

> Aristotle: Virtue, then, is a state that decides, consisting in a mean, the mean relative to us, which is defined by reference to reason, that is to say, to the reason by reference to which the prudent person would define it. It is a mean between two vices, one of excess and one of deficiency.[1]
>
> Saint Augustine: Virtue is a good quality of the mind, by which one lives rightly, which no one uses badly, which God works in us without us.[2]

These two definitions appear contradictory. The first takes the measure of the virtuous life to be the reason present in the prudent person. For Aristotle, human nature is not naturally virtuous, but contains what is necessary, in potentiality, to live well. "Internal" sources suffice. The second takes the measure of the virtuous life to be God. The scandalous aspect of this measure is that it is not only God but God who works in us without us. An "external" source suffices.[3] Anyone who reads that second definition and does not bristle, raising challenging questions, would be less than earnest about the moral life. Are we not free? Does God evacuate our agency? How can we be held responsible for actions worked in us without us? Is a God who acts in us without us immoral? These are good questions that should trouble virtuous persons. If they cannot be answered, moral philosophy should proceed without theology. As I explain in the pages to come, I think they can and have been answered, and I look to Thomas Aquinas and F. D. Maurice as sources for the answers. When Aquinas introduces his discussion of virtue with Augustine's definition, he adds that God does not do this work in us without us without our consent.[4] Yet this does not completely resolve this question. If God's work depends on our consent, then how is it done without us? How would consent not be an intentional human act?

The extent to which Aquinas is Aristotelian in his understanding of virtue continues to be controversial among Thomists. The difficulty is that he works with an Aristotelian understanding, never explicitly rejects it, and overlays or integrates it with a very different Augustinian understanding of the virtuous life as a gift of grace. In the mid–nineteenth century, Maurice recognized a tension in Aquinas's thought and sought not so much to alleviate it as to keep it from being reduced to a contradiction that required us to side either for natural, acquired virtue arising from "pagan" wisdom or for supernatural, infused virtue arising from Christian revelation. The sources of moral theology, Maurice argued, in Thomistic fashion, can be both. They are both because the Wisdom by which the brokenness of creation is redeemed is the same Wisdom by which it is created. The task of the moral theologian is to "dig," or unearth, the common source of these diverse moralities. The difficult task of teaching and learning ethics, especially as it includes moral theology, is to unearth the common source and practice of these two definitions without losing what is wise and true in both. For Aristotle, the good life is an achievement brought about by persons cooperating in activities over a complete life. For Augustine and those who follow him, including Aquinas, ethics concerns gifts that God works in us, drawing us into divine perfection.

Just as these two definitions of ethics frame everything that follows, even when they are not explicitly referred to, so the relationship between two significant Cambridge moral philosophers, Maurice (1805–72) and Henry Sidgwick (1838–1900), does so as well. Maurice and Sidgwick both held the prestigious Knightbridge Chair at Cambridge. Established in 1683, it was originally known as the "Professorship of Moral Theology or Casuistical Divinity." Its ninth holder, William Whewell, added the term "Moral Philosophy," so when Maurice received it in 1866, it had the awkward designation "Professorship of Moral Theology, Casuistical Divinity, and Moral Philosophy." Sidgwick inherited the title but simplified it to "Professorship of Moral Philosophy." Moral theology and casuistical divinity disappeared.

But more than its name changed. Sidgwick's effort to provide scientific precision to the inherited discipline led to the bracketing of theological and metaphysical concerns for teaching and learning ethics. This bracketing became a major source for the distinction between "is" and "ought" that was emphasized by G. E. Moore (1873–1958) in his so-called naturalistic fallacy. Ethics, Sidgwick argued, can gain precision if it abstracts from what is and attends exclusively to what ought to be. But he fought no rear-guard action against theology or metaphysics. They were irrelevant, an unnecessary imposition into the scientific study of ethics, but he did not explicitly seek to deny them.[5] It comes as no surprise that two Hegelian philosophers who were contemporaries of Sidgwick, T. H. Green (1836–82) and F. H. Bradley (1846–1924), offered sharp criticisms of Sidgwick's approach. They denied the is/ought distinction, as did Maurice before them, and considered it naive to pursue ethics without attention to metaphysics, religion, and theology. Green and Bradley still have their defenders, but neither of them had the influence on the discipline of ethics that Sidgwick did. His approach became the source and standard for much of the modern discipline.

Leading philosophers credit Sidgwick's 1874 publication *Methods of Ethics* with beginning the modern discipline. J. B. Schneewind refers to it as "the prototype of modern moral philosophy" that established "new standards of precision in wording, clarity in exposition, and care in argument."[6] John Rawls notes, "It is the first truly academic work in moral philosophy which undertakes to provide a systematic comparative study of moral conceptions, starting with those which historically and by present assessment are the most significant."[7] Thomas Hurka states, "With its concern for precise statement and rigorous argument, it reads very differently from earlier writing on ethics and is arguably the first philosophical work in a distinctively 'analytic' style."[8] Martha Nussbaum describes it as "an important work in part because of its systematic ambition and rigorous argumentation."[9] Sidgwick is rightly heralded as initiating the modern academic study of ethics, not only surpassing the influence of his Hegelian critics but also generating a sharp distinction between moral philosophy and theology that informs the teaching and learning of ethics to this day. Before Sidgwick, only moral theologians held the Knightbridge Chair. After him, none would.

Seminaries and Church-related institutions still teach moral theology, but it is seldom, outside those contexts, assumed to be important for teaching or learning ethics. What Sidgwick bracketed out came to be consistently ignored. Reputable moral theologians require training in moral philosophy; they should know Sidgwick. Reputable moral philosophers receive no training in moral theology; they seldom know Maurice. I find this to be a loss; a moral theologian like Maurice has much to teach us. But Sidgwick did not abandon moral theology without cause; good reasons existed for him to ignore it. As I show below, theology sought to maintain its privileged place in the academic teaching of ethics by way of authority and coercive power. It became a reactionary force, anxious and fearful. Maurice and Sidgwick acknowledged the viciousness of this fearful and coercive theology; together, they fought it.

Maurice was the last significant theologian who held the Knightbridge Chair. He was its eleventh holder, and he was also Sidgwick's friend and a fellow Cambridge Apostle. The transition from Maurice to Sidgwick speaks volumes about the transition that had taken place, was taking place, and would continue to take place in the teaching and learning of ethics in the English-speaking world. The utilitarian philosopher Barton Schultz, who wrote an extensive intellectual biography of Sidgwick, explains Maurice as a "mysterious figure . . . who though virtually unread today, was a gigantic force during the Victorian period and in many ways stood behind both Sidgwick and J. S. Mill, as a powerful voice pleading the limitations of utilitarianism."[10] Schultz is both correct and incorrect about Maurice. He overstates Maurice's intellectual influence on Sidgwick and Mill. Although other kinds of influence were present, Mill and Sidgwick left Maurice's deep theological convictions behind. For them, Maurice pointed backward to Samuel Coleridge and the eighteenth century, whereas they, like Jeremy Bentham, represented the progress that had been made from the eighteenth into the nineteenth centuries.[11] Part II of this book returns to Maurice to consider how forgetting his work diminishes the discipline of ethics. I argue that reading Maurice assists us in understanding well the gift character of the moral life and its implications for political economy. Sidgwick was less resistant to the disciplining of human agents by capitalism than Maurice, who feared it worked against the centrality of the infused virtues. Maurice's Christian Socialism, for all its faults, holds forth better promise for bringing the gift character of the moral life, brought about by the infused virtues, together with concrete economic practice.

The transition from Maurice to Sidgwick is momentous for too many reasons to name at this point. It suffices for now to recognize the uncontested fact that Sidgwick played a central role in the modern developments of ethics as a scientific discipline. Part I of this book, "Teaching Moral Philosophy in Conversation with Moral Theology," focuses on moral philosophy and how developments in it since the nineteenth century have diminished any role for the infusing of virtue. It examines Sidgwick's central role (chapter 1), and two influential responses to it by John Rawls and G. E. M. Anscombe (chapter 2). In one sense, these three figures are exemplars of textbook typologies of ethical theories: utilitarianism (Sidgwick), deontology (Rawls), and virtue (Anscombe). However, one of this book's purposes is to reject the usefulness of such a typology, a purpose with which Rawls and Anscombe would have agreed. Rawls and Anscombe were critical of Sidgwick's ethics, but for different reasons and with different consequences. Sidgwick considered, but rejected, an earlier approach to ethics found in Aquinas and Aristotle, which he referred to as "perfectionism." Rawls follows him in rejecting it; Anscombe retrieves Aristotle, Aquinas, and virtue, pointing in the direction of a perfectionist ethics. Given Ludwig Wittgenstein's influence on her, this should come as no surprise. Many philosophers and theologians who have been influenced by Wittgenstein have maintained a perfectionist approach to ethics—one that is open to the infusing of virtue. They are noted along the way. Although Rawls and Anscombe were both influenced by Wittgenstein, they took his work in different paths. Chapter 3 charts this path, pointing toward the infusing of virtue in their moral philosophy.

The selection of Anscombe and Rawls as crucial philosophers for teaching and learning ethics might seem odd. Anscombe was not primarily a moral philosopher but focused on metaphysics and action theory. Yet her 1958 criticisms of "Modern Moral Philosophy," her work in translating and explaining Wittgenstein, and her 1957 publication *Intention* opened new possibilities for ethics that were taken up by philosophers such as Cora Diamond and Alasdair MacIntyre. Stanley Cavell, Rawls's colleague at Harvard, forged a similar path toward an "ethics of perfection" and encouraged his colleague to recognize its importance for his moral philosophy. Yet Rawls did not seem convinced. Rawls is best known as a political philosopher, but his political philosophy grew out of his interest in moral philosophy. He taught it to generations of students at Harvard, and he trained many influential philosophical ethicists. He shared with Anscombe and Cavell a Wittgensteinian influence. Anscombe and Rawls overlapped at Oxford, and although we have no evidence of their interaction, Rawls knew and addressed her work and that of her husband, Peter Geach. What divides them, and perhaps divides the teaching and learning of ethics, is their response to Sidgwick. Utilitarians like Schultz and Peter Singer view Sidgwick as their "spiritual godfather" and see him providing a "demanding ethic" to guide modern thought.[12] Rawls rejected Sidgwick's utilitarianism but affirmed his attempt at precision in ethics, finding it a source for his "reflective equilibrium." Anscombe harshly criticized Sidgwick, especially what she referred to as his "consequentialism," identifying it as a corrupt theory of human action.

Sidgwick argued for ethics' independence, especially from theology and metaphysics, but also from psychology and politics. The independence of ethics does not mean that it lacks connection to each of these disciplines; he recognized that it does. But, he thought, if we are to make progress in the scientific precision of ethics, each of these disciplines, which are primarily concerned with what is, must be bracketed out to focus on an ethical method for guiding action that will be concerned with what ought to be. There is a certain irony here, because Sidgwick was undoubtedly haunted not only by theology but also by faith. As John Maynard Keynes, whose father was one of Sidgwick's early students, put it, "He never did anything but wonder whether Christianity was true and prove that it wasn't and hope that it was."[13] Sidgwick gave us the first independent ethics, something that could be taught and learned on its own merits without attention to any other discipline.

Central to my argument in part I of this work is that this effort to isolate a distinct domain for ethics is what makes figuring out what we are doing when we teach or learn ethics so difficult. How does one isolate a domain of human action available to the ethicist that would make for a coherent discipline that would differ, or differentiate it, from sociology, biology, political science, economics, or even theology? The domain for ethics is usually identified as voluntary human action, but that is what each of these disciplines (biology excepted) pursues as well. What makes its pursuit in ethics different from their pursuits? The difficulty I find in teaching moral theology has less to do with theology's marginal role in the university; it is what makes teaching theology enjoyable, even subversive. Because theology is seldom welcome in the university, theologians cannot be complacent in setting forth what it is and does. We are constantly considering and responding to critical scrutiny. Teaching ethics differs. Because it is more than welcome, it does not receive the same critical scrutiny as theology and seldom needs to justify its place, and this means it can too easily become complacent, refusing to interrogate itself. Ethicists might be laboring under a false assumption that they oversee distinct subject matter that is isolatable from other academic disciplines. The difficulty in teaching moral theology is figuring out what ethics is, or even if there is such a thing, so that it can be related to theology. In this regard, Maurice remains a wise and reliable guide for teaching and learning ethics as a discipline that is attentive to ordinary life.

Maurice's moral theology takes on a central role in part II of the book, "Teaching Moral Theology in Conversation with Moral Philosophy." Although he was, at one time, a mentor to Sidgwick, Maurice never lived to see, or respond to, the changes Sidgwick brought to the teaching and learning of ethics. The theological virtues of faith, hope, and charity were the foundation for Maurice's approach to ethics; he referred to them as the true "cardinal" virtues. Chapters 4 and 5 draw attention to the richness of Maurice's teaching on ethics, including his critical appropriation of Aquinas's moral theology. Aquinas's moral theology, I argue, is often used for a reactionary, antimodern or postliberal political or ethical project. Maurice's use of Aquinas differs. Writing when he did, he predated that reactionary use and offers a more sober interpretation of Aquinas than one that requires him to stand as a bulwark against all things modern.

Maurice thought that he identified a tension at the heart of Aquinas's virtue ethics between his Aristotelian understanding of virtue as the actualization of a potentiality intrinsic to human beings based on the standard of the reasonable person and Augustine's teaching that virtue is "what God does in us without us." What makes Maurice fascinating is how he reconciles this tension without abandoning either Aristotle or Augustine by offering an account of human agency centered on the Incarnation as the practical exemplification of the Trinity in everyday life. Chapter 6 sets forth Maurice's resolution to the relationship between the acquired and infused virtues and makes a case for why the infused virtues should still matter for religious and nonreligious persons alike. Aquinas, I argue, offers something quite similar by framing the acquired virtues in terms of the theological virtues in the *Summa Theologiae*.[14] Aquinas's moral theology offers a corrective to aspects of modern moral philosophy as Anscombe identified and critiqued them, but it need not lead to the wholesale dismissal of modern political or ethical thought. Chapter 7 cautions that retrieving Aquinas can lead to an unfortunate reactionary politics. Maurice's Christian Socialism and MacIntyre's politics of resistance chart a different path.

I should say something about the language I use throughout the book, especially for the terms "theological virtues," "infusing virtues," and "infused virtues." The theological virtues are faith, hope, and charity. They are infused by the Holy Spirit, and in turn they infuse the "natural virtues." I use "infused" and "infusing" synonymously, but I prefer "infusing." "Infused" has too much of a sense of something cultic, if not occultic. It could convey a sense that these virtues are zapped into us from the beyond. "Infusing" instead conveys an ongoing activity, akin to what occurs in everyday life. From the billions of cells that are daily replaced, to the food and water we take in to sustain life, to the communication that occurs through our most intimate activities, life is an ongoing activity of infusing. Maurice understood that the infused virtues are not something in us, but, by means of being creatures of a charitable God, we are in them. The act of creation is the infusing of goodness correlative with being, an act that influences the virtues of faith, hope, and charity in ordinary life. They are both inescapable and yet become the source of our acts only through consent. We live into them as they are the basis for our lives. This image fits well with Aquinas's act of creation as God *"semper eis esse dando"* (always giving being to them). With a common source in gifts, the religious life of faith bears an inevitable connection to the natural, moral life. As Rowan Williams puts it, "The supernatural is not something inserted into the natural and breaking its integrity; it is never 'cut off from its natural base.' Its distinctiveness is not in some sort of 'territorial' difference from finite acts and substances but is simply to do with the degree to which the unconditioned is allowed to transform the finite from within."[15] But citing Maurice, Aquinas, and Williams gets us ahead of the argument. We will return to these claims in part II of this work, but there is much to do between now and then.

ETHICAL AUDIENCES AND SOURCES

I imagine three potential readerships for this book. These readers are not simply persons whom I hope will read it; they are people whom I have in mind as I write it. In this sense, they are as much sources as readers. The first and most likely are moral theologians and Christian ethicists. Yet Christian ethics is not only for Christians or theologians. The doctrine of creation is an essential locus within Christian theology. Everything that is not God is creature. Ethics concerns creaturely action that is available to anyone who reflects well on how to pursue what is good or right and avoid what is evil, bad, or wrong. Christianity has a distinct interpretation of ethics, but ethics predates Christianity and was pursued by philosophers and ordinary people intending to living well; most Christian ethicists, whether ancient or modern, find much of this reflection useful. Moral theologians take note of, and learn from, both ancient and modern ethics. They are sources of wisdom. Aquinas affirmed Aristotle's teaching on friendship and found secular analogues to the infused virtues. When Christian ethics is done well, philosophers, including secular ones, should be able to recognize what Christian ethicists are doing, even when their approaches differ. Likewise, when philosophical ethics is done well, theologians should be able to recognize what philosophers are doing, even with their different approaches.

A second readership is philosophical ethicists. I am not naive; philosophers will most likely not read this book, but every theologian should write as if philosophers were looking over their shoulder. Philosophy is an indispensable source for moral theology.[16] Theology includes more than philosophy; it draws on reason and revelation. For theologians, faith has epistemic value, even as faith seeks understanding. Seeking understanding is intrinsic to faith or it would be fideism, a vice and not a virtue. Faith opens one to mystery that requires investigation. Mystery does not foreclose the search for knowledge; it expands it. It recognizes, with Saint Paul, Saint Anselm, and Wittgenstein that even if all our questions would find their answers, a riddle would remain: we see through a glass enigmatically.[17] Was not this what Aristotle finally meant by that perplexing word "metaphysics"? Faith seeking understanding is neither a method nor concern that one expects philosophers to adopt qua philosophers (unless, perhaps, they are philosophers of religion). Yet Anscombe argued that philosophy cannot be done well without some kind of faith.[18] Even a philosopher like Rawls, who lost his religious faith, still found a reasonable faith necessary for his moral and political constructivism. Clearly, not all faith is the same. The epistemic value of Christian faith assumes that God is a unique "object" unlike any other, so the methods used to know any other object will not suffice to know God. God is not an object in the world to be indicated; God exceeds human comprehension; God is that than which nothing greater can be conceived. Language never directly, or univocally, applies to God; yet by faith, we can speak well of God, even if as an enigma. Knowledge of God reasonably requires something more than reason alone, pure, or practical. Faith is that "something more." The wisdom found in recognizing the uniqueness of faith can assist in knowing other things well. Faith is not epistemic with respect to any or every object. One does not have "faith" per se in climate change; it either exists or it does not. We look to climatologists to garner evidence to convince us one way or the other. Yet evidence never eliminates insecurity. Judgments must be made; unless the future is known without reserve, known from some God's-eye view, such judgments cannot exclude faith, should not exclude hope, and are best when guided by charity.

If faith is epistemic, then it must have its reasons. Reasons are, like language, publicly accessible. Moral theologians write for other theologians, but they should also write for philosophers and expect their work to be intelligible to them and open to their criticisms. Theologians should seek to learn from, and be heard by, philosophers even if the latter has become something of a Sisyphean task. Theologians and philosophers share a knowledge of ethics that requires studying and learning a common set of arguments and literature. We both read and interpret authors such as Plato, Aristotle, David Hume, Immanuel Kant, Frederick Douglass, Mill, Moore, Sidgwick, Anscombe, Philippa Foot, Iris Murdoch, Rawls, James Baldwin, and Virginia Held. We examine virtue, principles, duties, consequences, practical reasoning, human agency, and the like. Theologians have other topics that are seldom pursued by philosophers, such as infused virtues, gifts, beatitude, and revelation, and authors such as Philo, John Chrysostom, Augustine, Aquinas, and Julian of Norwich. Yet the purpose of ethics should not be merely to learn arguments and authors. Ethics is about ordinary life. Its concern is to instruct people—both teachers and learners—not so that they might become professional ethicists but better people. On this point, there is still much to learn from Aristotle, who taught us that ethics is not so much about theory but about practical reasoning pursued by prudent people. They are the measure of virtue. This is why MacIntyre finds that "plain persons" are almost always tacit Aristotelians in their moral practice (even though they may be less than prudent). Ethics is learned from wise exemplars who become its measure.

An even more important readership for ethics than trained philosophers and theologians are ordinary persons, people who live and act as moral agents in the world and who seek to be, as we all should, better people, ever striving for perfection. Not only must ethics address ordinary persons; it also finds in their concerns and actions an important source for ethics.

That ethics should address the concerns of ordinary persons has been universally recognized, but how it should do so has differing views. Is the purpose of ethics education to affirm, correct, clarify, or debunk the moral convictions of ordinary persons? Should the readership for ethics primarily be the first two groups already mentioned, trained philosophers and theologians who possess the background to understand and contribute to an increasingly specialized field of study, and perhaps to those few students who seek this specialized knowledge? Should ethics address ordinary persons engaged in practical activities in life because they already have practical wisdom concerning the good life that the specialized professional might miss? Some form of these questions has haunted ethics since Aristotle. I would venture, however, that once it became a scientific discipline, the readership for ethics shifted. It attended less to ordinary life and more to the province of experts.

In his intellectual history about Sidgwick, Schneewind identifies this transition well. The "professionalization" of philosophy takes hold in England in 1876, resulting in the philosophical journal *Mind*. Schneewind names "Bain in Scotland, Green at Oxford, and Sidgwick at Cambridge" as "the first of a new breed of philosopher" who made this transition possible. What brings them together, he states, was the following: "Unclerical, independent of formal allegiance to any set creed, they saw philosophy as an academic discipline dealing with problems defined and transmitted by a group of experts who were the best available judges of proposed solutions." Schneewind evaluates this transition favorably. Because of their "detachment" from "practical affairs," philosophy regained its "ancient ideal of the love of wisdom for its own sake."[19] Is this an adequate judgment? Schneewind's description might characterize Sidgwick, at least in his *Methods* but less so perhaps in his *Practical Ethics*. It is less adequate in characterizing Green. Schneewind neglects Green's desire to become a deacon in the Church of England. I also have some reservations that the detachment Schneewind affirms returns philosophy to its ancient love of wisdom. Ancient philosophical ethics was traditionally associated with practical wisdom. The early Sidgwick emphasized morality as a science overseen by experts, making it much more a theoretical than a practical discipline. He explicitly rejected Aristotle's understanding of it as a practical discipline in favor of a theoretical one. His focus was on the "methods" of ethics. As is shown below, he went as far as to suggest that not everyone should be taught moral philosophy because some of its teachings will be misunderstood and potentially misused. He affirmed an "esoteric" morality. It was not a discipline for ordinary life or plain persons. Whether, as Sissela Bok suggests, this "youthful arrogance" changed later in his work needs to be explored.[20]

Sidgwick professionalized ethics. He reformed the teaching of moral science at Cambridge, formed "ethical societies," and sought to teach ethics with scientific precision. Perhaps a similar scientific precision finds precedent in Kant's moral philosophy, but Kant did not abstract ethics from metaphysics or theology.[21] Kant's moral proof for the existence of God maintained more of a place for religion in ethics than did Sidgwick. Sidgwick was influenced by Kant and spent considerable time studying Kant's ethics and metaphysics. He lectured on them in a course on metaphysics in 1899–1900 and had planned on writing a book titled *Kant and Kantism in England* but decided against it.[22] He preferred Kant to Johann Fichte, Friedrich von Schelling, or G. W. F. Hegel. In 1866 he wrote, "I am coming more and more to the opinion that the whole 'Identitäts-philosophie' (Fichte, Schelling, and Hegel) is a monstrous mistake, and that we must go back to Kant and begin again from him. Not that I feel prepared to call myself a Kantian, but I shall always look on him as one of my teachers."[23] Sidgwick's ethics were not Kantian; he was a utilitarian, but his utilitarianism was troubled by "heroic self-sacrifice." It was what attracted him to Jesus and to Kant's moral philosophy. In his preface to the sixth edition of *Methods*, he stated that this concern motivated him to reread Kant's ethics and incorporate his categorical imperative, particularly its universality, into Mill's ethics. It led him to assimilate Kant to Mill's utilitarianism via "'disinterested' or 'extra regarding' impulses to action not directed toward the agent's pleasure."

Sidgwick also claimed to be following Aristotle and Kant by beginning with "commonsense morality."[24] Yet Kant sought a critical examination of practical reason in order to serve everyday life. Heinrich Heine was not that far off when he "invented his tale" that Kant wrote his second critique, the *Critique of Practical Reason*, to give his servant Martin Lampe his faith back.[25] Like Sidgwick, he was interested in method and defined his as moving "analytically from common knowledge to the determination of its supreme principle and then synthetically from the examination of this principle and its sources back to common knowledge."[26] It is unclear that Sidgwick had an interest in Kant's final step. His late publication *Practical Ethics* included his lectures to the Cambridge Ethical Society. The "aim" of such a society, he acknowledged, was the construction of a "Theory or Science of Right." Trained philosophers played a key but not an exclusive role in constructing such a theory; it also required consulting the "morality of common sense" that was found in persons in practical vocations such as lawyers, clergy, and businesspersons. The morality of common sense was not to be confused with the "worldly morality" that made up the mass of humanity, who want "not simply to realize the good life in virtue of its supreme worth to humanity, but to realize it as much as they can while keeping terms with all their appetites and passions, their sordid interests and vulgar ambitions."[27]

Did ethics become a discipline for scientific experts more so than ordinary persons after Sidgwick? Any answer is confusing; philosophers themselves seem conflicted. W. D. Ross appears to side more with Aristotle and Kant than Sidgwick; Ross claimed to write ethics for plain persons rather than for professional experts. However, it is not always clear who the audience is for his ethics. As Anthony Skelton notes, "Ross sometimes writes as though what he cares about is the opinions of the 'thoughtful and well-educated.' . . . At other times, he suggests that what he cares about is the opinions of the 'plain man.'"[28] Ross wrote influential works on both Aristotle and Kant and addressed this question of audience in both. Kant, Ross argues, "equally emphasized two things: (1) that ordinary human reason has in its possession all the data for forming true moral judgements, and does not need to learn them from science or from philosophy; but (2) that this intellectual innocence cannot usually maintain itself against the solicitations of passion, but is easily led into a dialectic in which it seeks to compromise with inclination."[29] Ross thought Kant never fully answered how ordinary human reason and moral philosophy worked together. He wrote,

Does [Kant] mean (1) that the common rational knowledge of morality is mistaken, and that we must abandon it, first taking refuge in a popular moral philosophy, and then seeing the error of this and advancing to metaphysic of morals and to critique of pure practical reason? Or does he mean (2) that the common rational knowledge of morality is correct but does not go deep enough, and that the same is true of popular moral philosophy?[30]

Ross identified a similar problem in the work of Aristotle, referring to it as Aristotle's "paradox." In order to do good, we must first be good, but we cannot be good without first doing good.[31] Ross thinks Aristotle has a way out of this paradox, but he has put his finger on an issue that did not vex Sidgwick as much as it did Aristotle, Kant, and Ross. Can ethics be taught if those being taught are not already, in some sense ethical? And if they are already ethical, what good could teaching ethics accomplish? Sidgwick was less concerned with this question because his audience, with some noted exceptions, was the educated Cambridge philosopher and professional. As an academic discipline, ethics became too centrally concerned with training ethicists rather than making people better human beings. These two objects of teaching ethics are not the same, and learning the former can be done without the latter.

More so than Ross, Alasdair MacIntyre questions Sidgwick's endeavor. Due as much to his Marxism as his Aristotelianism, MacIntyre critiques moral philosophy when the distinction between moral philosophy and "everyday moral judgments and activities" mimics natural science or the legal profession and views the task of moral philosophy to make a "second order commentary" on those judgments and activities. For the Aristotelian view, he states, the two are "inseparable" because they are asking a similar question "What is my good?" or "What is *the* good for human beings?"[32] For this reason, he has called into question the "academic teaching of ethics in general," suggesting that it "has little or nothing to do with the formation of moral character and is ineffective as an instrument of moral transformation."[33] MacIntyre's audience is "plain persons," but appealing to them is not an appeal to "common sense," which he refers to as "a graveyard of past philosophies."[34] In fact, MacIntyre does not pit practice and theory against each other but writes, "It is central to my argument that the practice of the moral life by plain persons always presupposes the truth of some particular theoretical standpoint and that, when confronted by rival claims to her or his moral allegiance, the plain person's reflective practical choices will implicitly at least be a choice between theoretical standpoints."[35] For MacIntyre, the theoretical standpoint adopted by plan persons will inevitably be an Aristotelian or Thomistic one.[36]

If either philosophical or theological ethics cannot speak to, and learn from, ordinary persons, then it has lost touch with what matters most. Ethics should be more than a guild in which professionals speak to each other. There is a place for professional guilds and trained ethicists. No one should apologize for being educated in the discipline of ethics. Yet if, as Aristotle taught, ethics assists us in becoming good people, then there will be a populist element to it, in that it arises from, and is for, "the people." Populism takes different forms. Luke Bretherton divides them between democratic and authoritarian.[37] Authoritarian populism is reactionary, resisting self-critique, dismissing education, and falsely assuming that what the authoritarian populist thinks is what all right-thinking people should think if they had not been deluded by education or other "elitist" means. It has no ability to reflect critically on embedded contexts. Populism can lead to *herrenvolk* democracy, a form of democracy in which the majority race or religion assumes that it alone speaks for "the people" and all other people pose a threat to the ordinary or plain person.[38] The populist element in ethics must distance itself from any *herrenvolk* assumption; one way that it does so is by its openness to reasonable and critical deliberation, something that a truly prudent person embodies.

The third readership and source for this work, ordinary persons, is just as important as the first two. By that term, I mean people who do not spend their lives as scholars reading and writing about ethical arguments and their authors. Ethicists should strive to speak and listen to these readers more than any other, but that is a difficult task. Friedrich Nietzsche said about Kant that he wanted to prove that the morality of the common person was correct, but he wrote in such a way that the common person was unable to understand it. This malady does not afflict Kant alone; it is a malady that afflicts all moral theologians, philosophers, and even Nietzsche himself. Nearly every ethicist seeks to address, and learn from, this third type of reader, but the task is difficult.

I would be delighted if this book reached a general readership—welders and nurses, parents and grandparents, factory workers and administrators, anyone who is interested or should be in ethics, and that should include everyone, especially all those people I meet in diverse contexts who ask me what I do and are pleased to discover that I teach ethics. Moral theologians are uniquely positioned to speak to these readers because many of us are still rooted in the Church, a community that we share with a diversity of people that is present in rural, urban, and suburban geographies across racial and class diversities. While this, unfortunately, has become a liability in many universities, it should be construed otherwise. That we are rooted in the Church does not mean we fail to distinguish between the university and the Church; their vocations differ. Yet speaking to and from the Church within the university provides an audience and resource for our work that is unavailable to philosophers. When philosophers abandoned religious institutions, they neglected an essential source for ethics. The Church also provides readers other than those from the modern university's main collaborative partners: the state and the corporation. Is it any surprise that professional ethics too often serves them? I would be delighted if professional ethicists and moral theologians collaborated and attended to ordinary people. That task may be the most difficult of all. My point is not that ordinary persons, people who do something other than research and teach for a living will, or should, take up this book and read it. I hold no expectations that factory workers will spend their limited breaks reading this book rather than hitting the vending machines for caffeine and sugar (I speak from my limited experience). My hope is that an ethics based on the infused virtues speaks well to, and from, these readers so that it will make a difference in all the diverse ways that ethics is taught and learned both inside and outside the university.

NOTES

1. Aristotle, *Nicomachean Ethics*, 1107a1–5. English translations of Aristotle's *Nicomachean Ethics* come from the translation by Terence Irwin, second edition, 1999.
2. Augustine, *De Libero Arbitrio*, II, 19. "Virtus est bona qualitas mentis, qua recte vivitur, qua nemo male utitur, quam Deus in nobis sine nobis operatur."
3. An astute reader might question if this internal/external distinction makes sense. I would agree and therefore put those terms in scare quotes. What is "internal" always begins as "external" in human being. Aristotle and Thomas Aquinas use these terms; but as F. D. Maurice argues, they are problematic.
4. Aquinas, *Summa Theologiae* (hereafter, *ST*), I-II, 55.4 ad 6.
5. In other words, he was no A. J. Ayer.
6. Schneewind, *Sidgwick's Ethics*, 1.
7. Rawls, "Foreword," v.
8. Hurka, *British Ethical Theorists*, 4.
9. Nussbaum, "Epistemology," 28.
10. Schultz, *Henry Sidgwick*, 46.
11. Sidgwick, *Miscellaneous Essays*, 137.
12. Schultz, *Henry Sidgwick*, 105.
13. Quoted by Williams, "Point of View," 279.
14. *ST*, II-II, questions 1–170.
15. Williams, *Christ*, 226–27.
16. I recognize that not all theologians agree with this statement. I think it is necessary to avoid fideism but will not make that argument here. I attempted to make it in Long, *Speaking of God*.
17. The citations here are Saint Paul, 1 Cor. 13; Saint Anselm, *Monologion* 65; and Wittgenstein, *Tractatus* 6.4132–6.5.

18. Anscombe, *Faith*, 3.

19. Schneewind, *Sidgwick's Ethics*, 6.

20. Bok, "Introduction," to Sidgwick, *Practical Ethics*, xiii.

21. Kant may rightly be interpreted as abstracting ethics from *Christian* theology. Nonetheless, as Christopher Insole has ably demonstrated, his work depends on a "philosophical religiosity"; Insole, *Kant and the Divine*, 2.

22. Ward, "Editorial Note," v.

23. Sidgwick and Sidgwick, *Henry Sidgwick*, 151.

24. Sidgwick, *Methods of Ethics*, xix–xxii.

25. Beck, "Translator's Introduction," xviii.

26. Kant, *Critique*, 8–9.

27. Sidgwick, *Practical Ethics*, 22.

28. Skelton, "William David Ross."

29. Ross, *Kant's Ethical Theory*, 36.

30. Ross, 6.

31. Ross, *Aristotle*, 201.

32. MacIntyre, "Plain Persons," 136.

33. MacIntyre, *Ethics*, 17–20.

34. MacIntyre, "Plain Persons," 150.

35. MacIntyre, 149.

36. MacIntyre, 138.

37. Bretherton, *Christ*, 434.

38. McCarraher, *Enchantments*, 588.

PART I

TEACHING MORAL PHILOSOPHY IN CONVERSATION WITH MORAL THEOLOGY

1

TEACHING AND LEARNING ETHICS

The beginnings of teaching ethics could be traced to Socrates, Plato, Aristotle, or Moses, or perhaps to the creation of the discipline of *theologia moralis* at the Council of Trent. Yet none of these persons or traditions understood ethics as a distinct, autonomous discipline. Perhaps Adam Smith or David Hume could be heralded as providing an independent ethics, but they were also economists whose ethics was linked to, if not dependent upon, their economics. Another potential originator of an independent ethics would be Immanuel Kant, but Kant still referred to the "metaphysics of morals" and correlated ethics to his philosophical religiosity. The person who most explicitly structured ethics as a scientific discipline that could stand on its own was Henry Sidgwick.

SIDGWICK'S ETHICAL VOCATION

Sidgwick sought to make ethics scientific by clarifying the domain over which it worked. To do so, he bracketed out other disciplines that claimed to render it intelligible. During his time in England, professors who taught moral philosophy also taught moral theology, and it was assumed that the latter would be taught consistent with the Church of England's Thirty-Nine Articles of Religion. Sidgwick desired an academic position, and he knew that he would be unable to teach moral theology in good conscience on those terms. Initially, rather than pursue what he considered to be his vocation, moral philosophy, he decided in the early 1860s to learn Arabic, write a history of Islam, and seek an "Arabic professorship." The questions of moral philosophy, however, never left him. Even his "resolution to read theology" was for the purpose of his "moral improvement."[1] Rather than becoming an Islamic scholar, Sidgwick developed the science of ethics.

In 1862, while Sidgwick was a student, two new "triposes" were introduced at Cambridge. One was in "natural science" and the other in "moral science." A tripos allowed for an undergraduate examination in a field that would confer a bachelor's degree. Sidgwick was a leader in garnering support for the moral science tripos.[2] It did not attract many students. According to Sidgwick, the reason was that it competed "with the prestige of the older subjects of classics and mathematics, and with the more obvious professional utility of these and other subjects, such as theology, science, and engineering." The purpose of the new moral science tripos was primarily to prepare students to teach ethics.[3] Under Sidgwick's guiding hand, ethics became a specialized, scientific discipline alongside other respectable academic disciplines.

Sidgwick was the first nonordained holder of the Knightbridge Chair; he followed two moral theologians, F. D. Maurice and T. R. Birks. Sidgwick and Maurice were friends; the older Maurice was a mentor of sorts. At one point in his life, Sidgwick was attracted to Maurice's theology. In June 1862, he wrote to his friend H. G. Dakyns, telling him that he had gone through a change, giving up his "materialism and skepticism and come round to Maurice and Broad Church again." A few months later, he changed his mind, writing, "My conversion ended in smoke."[4] Maurice did not lead Sidgwick to convert, but his influence led him to support women's education and become involved in the "cooperative production" movement.[5] Together, they opposed subscription to the Thirty-Nine Articles for students.

Maurice and Sidgwick were, along with the economist Alfred Marshall, members of the Grote Society, which was dedicated to moral science and named after John Grote, the tenth holder of the Knightbridge Professorship. As mentioned above, the term "Moral Philosophy" had been added to the title when William Whewell held the chair immediately before Grote. Maurice mentioned the title change in his lectures on conscience at his inauguration as the Knightbridge Professor. While he concurred with Whewell's addition of "moral philosophy," he would also continue to treat "casuistry" as an essential element of morality.[6] For Maurice, casuistry meant that ethics was primarily a practical discipline, but casuistry was less a method for adjudicating cases of conscience and more about attending to the ordinary actions by which people live. For instance, casuistry meant that you could not look only at Bentham's ethical theories but also had to look at his life. History and biography were more important for moral action than one's theories. How Bentham lived, says Maurice, contradicted his theory. If a theory could not be lived, especially by its author, then it lacked practical wisdom.[7]

Sidgwick did away with the name "casuistry" from the chair, but he attempted to retrieve it for the ethical societies. Yet he meant something different by it, something related to his avowal of an "esoteric morality" in his *Methods*. The morality of common sense laid down general principles, such as truth-telling, that might need to be questioned given one's vocation. Although he does not affirm deceit per se, he thinks casuistry requires considering that "barristers must be allowed to urge persuasively for their clients'" false claims, a "clergy" person can possibly be virtuous without "exactly believing the creeds he says or the articles he signs" (although he changed his mind later on, rejecting what he called "pious fraud" because he thought it did more harm than good), a physiologist can torture animals, and a general can use spies. There is a danger here, he notes, that "in the esoteric morality of any particular profession or trade, ordinary morality will be put aside altogether."[8] It is a danger that might nonetheless need to be risked.[9] In an 1888 address, he stated that, on utilitarian principles, "I find exceptional cases in which I have to approve of unveracity."[10]

Upon Grote's death, Sidgwick contemplated applying for the vacant Knightbridge Chair, but he decided against it because Maurice was a candidate.[11] But when Maurice died on April 1, 1872, the chair became open, and Sidgwick decided to proceed with his candidacy.[12] He worried that a theologian, J. B. Pearson, rather than a philosopher would be elected. In private correspondence, Sidgwick threatened to leave Cambridge if that occurred. Pearson was not elected, but the Reverend T. R. Birks, an evangelical theologian, was. Sidgwick did not follow through on his threat to leave. He expressed his pleasure that Birks had been elected rather than Pearson, but his comments are confusing. He preferred Birks to Pearson, but he made contradictory judgments about Birks. In one letter he calls it a "catastrophe" because it may "crush [moral philosophy] under the Heel of Theology." But in another letter, he stated, "it is not as bad as it looks" because Birks was the "best philosopher" who had been considered.[13]

After Birks's death in 1883, Sidgwick was elected Knightbridge Professor, holding the chair until his death in 1900. In 1896, while Sidgwick held it, the title was changed to Knightbridge Professor of Moral Philosophy. This change in the name of the chair during Sidgwick's professorship speaks to a shift in the relationship between moral philosophy and theology that occurred in the nineteenth century. They not only became distanced, but theology was also viewed as something that lacked precision, privileged authority over reason, and prevented moral philosophy from coming into its own.

Sidgwick knew theology well; it was present early in his life. His father was the Reverend William Sidgwick, a Church of England priest.[14] His sister was married to their mother's cousin, the archbishop of Canterbury, E. W. Benson, who mentored Sidgwick before his studies at Cambridge, where his influence "waned."[15] Sidgwick wrote about this change, stating, "In my second year at Cambridge, I began to fall under different influences, which went on increasing till I was definitely enlisted as an 'Academic Liberal.' . . . This led inevitably to a profound change in my relations to E. W. B."[16] He then rejected orthodox, Anglican theology, refusing to subscribe to the Thirty-Nine Articles, and thus was required to surrender his Trinity College fellowship in 1869. It was his bold stance in this situation that contributed to the 1871 Act of Parliament, which abolished religious tests completely.[17] He regained his fellowship in 1885.[18] Sidgwick remained a theist and had a lifelong interest in parapsychology. He insisted that the Cambridge Ethics Society should not conceive itself in "conflict" or "competition" with the Christian churches and thought they had a genuine role to play in ethics.[19] Yet he could not affirm the basic doctrines of Christianity. Here is the best he could muster: "Thus Christianity will soon come to have a purely ethical import, and the divine sonship of Jesus, so far as it is still affirmed, will only be affirmed in the sense of unique consciousness of the relation existing, essentially or ideally, between the human spirit and the divine."[20] Science had disproven Christianity, but he felt it was a loss and sought to rescue as much of it as he could. Ethics would proceed without it. Christianity would endure only as it supported ethics.

In 1886, Sidgwick published his *History of Ethics*. This work was originally an encyclopedia article, and he introduced it by stating that he had "taken pains to keep Ethics as separate as I conveniently could from Theology and Metaphysics, and also from Politics: this separation, however, is naturally less complete in some parts of the subject than in others—e.g., in dealing with the mediaeval period, the relations of Ethics to Theology are necessarily more prominent than in the modern period."[21] His history provides insight into why he thought theology and ethics needed to be separated. As long as ethics was related to theology, it could not have scientific precision.

Sidgwick's *History* remains an insightful work on the development of ethics. It takes a threefold form: "Greek and Greco-Roman Ethics," "Christianity and Medieval Ethics," and "Modern, Chiefly English Ethics." Although he finds much to affirm in the first two forms, his sympathies clearly lie with the third. Like his *The Principles of Political Economy*, which was published three years later, Sidgwick does not hide his preference for English scholarship. It was Hobbes, he argues, who first presented an "independent ethics" free from "revelational theology." He did so because the religious wars had proven that theology could not serve as a foundation for ethics. Just as

Hobbes turned to the "natural law" to provide a new foundation for ethics, distancing it from theology, Adam Smith provided a new footing for economics by identifying "natural liberty."[22] If the "statesmen" did not unnecessarily interfere with the economy, then "Nature herself" would provide "ample provision."[23]

Surprisingly, Sidgwick traced the origin for an independent ethics before Hobbes to Thomas Aquinas. In the same year that he was working on his *History of Ethics*, Sidgwick wrote in his diary that reading Gass's *Christliche Ethik* made him "wonder" during what age he might have been a Christian. He mused that it would have been the thirteenth century if he could have been a pupil of Aquinas.[24] But what interested him in Aquinas was not theology or the infused virtues; what interested him was Aquinas's incorporation of Roman jurisprudence into theological ethics. It "gave the starting-point for independent ethical thought in the modern world."[25] Ironically, as will be shown in part II, one tradition of a Catholic retrieval of Thomism pits it, unlike Sidgwick, against the modern world. Both Sidgwick and this reactionary use of Aquinas, however, emphasize the natural or acquired virtues and neglect the theological and infused ones.

Sidgwick's affirmation of Aquinas differs from Maurice's. It is not the gifts and infused virtues that matter; but, with Aquinas, ethics was on its way to becoming a discipline primarily concerned with obligation. The form was there, but not yet the substance. The substance awaited the resolution of two significant problems that neither Greek nor Christian ethics had resolved but English ethics eventually did. The difficulty with the Greeks, especially Plato and Aristotle, was their inadequate account of voluntary action, generating this twofold problem. First, they lacked the concept that the will could directly choose evil. If the good were known, then it was motivating, such that evil resulted not from an evil choice but from insufficient knowledge of the good. Second, they emphasized character at the expense of voluntary action. Sidgwick wrote, "the 'voluntariness' which Aristotle attributes to the acts of a vicious man does not exclude complete determination of them, from moment to moment, by formed character and present external influences; and hence does not really amount to 'free agency' in the modern philosophical sense."[26] An external influence, even that of a formed character, contradicts voluntary action, for it must arise from internal or immanent sources. This concern, as is shown below, gave rise to his understanding of virtue as a quality of "right conduct" rather than of "character." Resolving these problems is essential for the discipline of ethics because, as Sidgwick had previously argued in his 1874 book *Methods of Ethics*, the domain of ethics is voluntary action.

Sidgwick found Aristotle's ethics less than satisfactory. His *eudaimonia*, and his "whole discussion of ethics," is characterized by a "looseness" that refuses a "completely scientific treatment."[27] His emphasis on "formed character" prevented him from founding ethics upon "free agency." His ethics lacked scientific rigor and failed as a guide for conduct. Aristotle's practical syllogism did not permit "a distinct general idea" for "right action." He also demonstrated inadequate concern for benevolence. Benevolence is one of the three essential virtues that Sidgwick names, the other two being practical wisdom and justice. In a caricatured but still pervasive interpretation, Sidgwick argued that Aristotle's ethics failed to regard the interest of others independent of their benefit to oneself. This lack, he wrote, "strikes a modern reader" as a "defect."[28] In these criticisms, three crucial elements for Sidgwick's independent ethics emerge. First, it has its own specific domain, the voluntary action of individuals. Second, ethics must have a method that guides that action into right conduct. And third, benevolence, or action done for the benefit of another qua other, is at the heart of right ethical conduct. Aristotle did not have these three elements in his ethics, so it has little to contribute to modern ethics.

Sidgwick rejected Aristotelian virtue. Robert Todd makes a compelling case that Sidgwick "clearly helped make philosophy at Cambridge inhospitable to the study of ancient philosophy." Instead of ancient philosophy, "natural science" became the "principal route to philosophy."[29] This judgment does not require dismissing a positive role for Aristotle in Sidgwick's work; he acknowledges the influence of books II through IV of the *Nicomachean Ethics* in the sixth edition of *Methods*.[30] Schultz agrees in part with Todd's judgment. He writes, "Although there is some truth in the claim that Sidgwick's notion of the Moral Sciences Tripos made the classics less significant in the undergraduate philosophy curriculum, this does not do justice to the extraordinary importance of Plato and Aristotle in Sidgwick's own philosophical work, or to the way they shaped his larger Apostolic vision of the educational enterprise."[31] Yet what he takes from Aristotle is a form of "inquiry," and that is too generic to claim Aristotle's "extraordinary importance" for him. The criticisms that Sidgwick makes of Aristotle's ethics, his efforts to shift ethics away from ancient philosophy at Cambridge, and his explicit statement inverting Aristotle's priority of practice to theory for the sake of method all show a rejection of previous ethical teaching.[32]

Despite Sidgwick's affirmation of Aquinas, he fares no better than Aristotle. Both have an ethics of perfection, but Aquinas is incapable of answering how it is attainable because of his inability to synthesize these two difficulties:

1. The old pagan difficulty of reconciling the proposition, that will or purpose is rational desire always directed towards apparent good, with the freedom of choice between good and evil that the jural view of morality seems to require;
2. The Christian difficulty of harmonizing this latter notion with the absolute dependence on divine grace which the religious consciousness affirms.[33]

Rather than the will as rational desire, Sidgwick's ethics will follow Kant and find the source of the will in a pure practical reason independent of inclination. Moreover, Aquinas's doctrine of grace as an external principle of action worked against the freedom of choice that Aquinas's recognition of Roman jurisprudence required. For Sidgwick, Duns Scotus saw and corrected the first problem by dividing the will from reason. Scotus is viewed as a necessary transition to the more Kantian view of the will.[34] The second problem was never addressed until ethics became independent from theology, something that Hobbes initiated and that Sidgwick continued in his *Methods*.

The continuities that Sidgwick finds with previous understandings of the moral life in thinkers like Aristotle and Aquinas are outweighed by the advances he attributes to modern moral philosophy. At most, Aquinas inchoately recognized the seeds of what would germinate in Hobbes, Locke, and Sidgwick, an ethics focused on voluntary action oriented toward what ought to be done without attention to the historical embeddedness of the agent who acts. A method could secure right action. Sidgwick's *History of Ethics* was published twelve years after his *Methods of Ethics*, but the history he narrates leads to his *Methods*.

SIDGWICK'S *METHODS OF ETHICS*

Although ethics has been taught since the ancient Greek philosophers, it seldom had clear boundaries in antiquity or the Middle Ages. As W. D. Ross noted, "Aristotle never speaks of 'ethics' as a separate science, but only of 'the study of character' or 'our discussions of character.'" Aristotle's "practical science" includes metaphysics, ethics, and politics.[35] Likewise, John Rawls reminds us that the "great utilitarians, Hume and Adam Smith, Bentham and Mill, were social theorists and economists of the first rank; and the moral doctrine they worked out was framed to meet the needs of their wider interests and to fit into a comprehensive scheme."[36] None of these thinkers could have written Sidgwick's *The Methods of Ethics*.

Methods is no easy read, not because it is difficult but because it is dull and plodding. This has been a common assessment. Sidgwick's contemporary, F. H. Bradley, found it meandering and incoherent. He wrote, "I can find no unity of principle which holds its parts together."[37] Alfred North Whitehead remarked that Sidgwick's *Methods* was so boring that after reading it, he never read another book on ethics.[38] When John Rawls lectured on it, which he regularly did, he told his students, "It can easily seem dull and tiring." He gave them this advice: "You won't find it entertaining. Take it a little bit at a time."[39]

Sidgwick most likely would not have been offended by these sentiments. As he was completing *Methods* in 1874, he wrote to his friend Dakyns, "It bores me very much, and I want to get it off my hands before it makes me quite ill."[40] After its publication, he wrote this to C. H. Pearson (although he never sent the letter): "It is essentially an attempt to introduce precision of thought into a subject usually treated in a too loose and popular way, and therefore, I feel cannot fail to be somewhat dry and repellent."[41] Bernard Williams attributes the book's boringness to its Englishness but also finds that it has a redeeming feature: "One might say indeed that the overwhelming Englishness of this book extends even to a similarity to a cricket match, which has the very sophisticated feature that one can only appreciate the significant detail of the monotony that lies before one at a given time because one understands remote and hypothetical moments of excitement which might grow from it."[42] Sidgwick identifies previous methods tacitly used in commonsense views of morality, showing their limits, and assessing them on their ability to guide right action with precision.

A responsible investigation of teaching and learning ethics, inquiring as to what its subject matter is, would be negligent if it did not pass through Sidgwick's *Methods*, assessing it and its affirmers and dissenters. *Methods* sets a new standard for teaching, learning, and researching ethics, one that is often affirmed for its post-Christian approach to ethics and the development of an independent ethics that promoted a method focused on what ought to be done independent from what is. He influenced G. E. Moore's nonnaturalist ethics, his distinction between is and ought, and his identification of a "naturalistic fallacy." As significant as his influence on Moore is, Sidgwick's influence on subsequent philosophers cannot be ignored. His work represents a great divide; either it is affirmed and his methods are extended, or it is critiqued and an alternative path in teaching and learning ethics is charted.

Despite his later work primarily being in political philosophy, John Rawls is one of the most influential moral philosophers of the twentieth century. Although Rawls is deeply indebted to Sidgwick, Rawls rejects his utilitarianism and extends his methods originally, with a view he refers to as Kantian constructivism. G. E. M. Anscombe faults Sidgwick for his understanding of human agency. Her "Modern Moral Philosophy" and *Intention* counter Sidgwick's *Methods*, setting a different direction for teaching and learning ethics, one taken up by Alasdair MacIntyre, among others. MacIntyre refers to Sidgwick's project as "falsifying history" by placing his modern concept of "morality" upon philosophers who had no such concept, seeking to rationalize the "morality of plain persons" through "principles" known primarily to the ethical scientist for the purpose of a "rational consensus," but one that eludes their efforts and turns out to be as "dubious" as the theology that Sidgwick thought he had "discredited."[43] Anscombe's colleague and sometimes philosophical opponent, Bernard Williams, does not take Anscombe's path but finds Sidgwick's ethics to be an elitist exercise in defense of British colonialism.

I have already suggested to readers that I find Sidgwick's approach to ethics reductive and thereby disorienting. It takes attention away from ordinary moral life and lops off too much of what constitutes it to elucidate a well-lived life. For this reason, I make a case here for the path charted by Anscombe, which is an alternative to Sidgwick—one that opens up the possibility of reconsidering moral theology along the lines of Maurice. For this argument to be more than an assertion, a careful reading of Sidgwick and Rawls is first necessary, one that shows their strengths and limits. Sidgwick's *Methods* cannot be ignored; it is too important for the discipline of ethics. He lays its foundation with the methods he delineates, the definition of ethics he gives, the ends he sets forth, and the distinctions he makes. As dull and plodding as the book can be, a careful analysis of *Methods* is necessary to understand why ethics today is taught as it is, why some oppose teaching it, and how the infusion of virtues, with its concomitant understanding of gift, became problematic in the transition from Maurice to Sidgwick.

Sidgwick begins *Methods* by acknowledging that his "immediate object—to invert Aristotle's phrase—is not Practice but Knowledge."[44] Is *Methods*, then, an exercise in constructing an independent ethical theory? Schultz suggests otherwise. Although *Methods* can give that impression, it should be read in context with the work of the previous Knightbridge chairs—Whewell, Grote, and Maurice—who limited their analysis to the "moral realm" to see if it "provided independent grounds for religious belief of some sort."[45] Yet the previous chairs did not bracket out theology, as Sidgwick did; nor did they claim that they were applying the same scientific approach to ethics that had been successful in physics. Sidgwick claims to do so by attending "not to the practical results to which our methods lead, but on the methods themselves."[46] The inversion of Aristotle from practice to knowledge occurs by means of a method.

The purpose of Sidgwick's work is to investigate as impartially as possible the different methods used to determine right action. He begins with definitions of "method" and "ethics." Method is "a rational procedure by which we determine what individual human beings 'ought'—or what is 'right' for them—to do, or to seek to realise by voluntary action."[47] Ethics is "the science or study of what is right or what ought to be, so far as this depends upon the voluntary action of individuals."[48] The emphasis on the "right" and "ought" is central to his claim for scientific precision. It allows ethics to be primarily about evaluative judgments rather than factual or descriptive ones. How things *are*—which might be the subject matter for theology, metaphysics, economics, or politics—need not be engaged if the domain of ethics is restricted to what *ought* to be. In this, Sidgwick originates a tradition of ethics that views it as sui generis. Sidgwick will view the right or ought as an irreducible principle.

Methods is divided into four books and a concluding chapter. The first book provides an overview. Drawing from the "common sense of morality," Sidgwick suggests that ethical action has two possible ends, "Happiness" and "Perfection or Excellence of human nature."[49] This distinction between happiness and perfection or excellence can be confusing. The prior tradition of ethics, from Aristotle to Aquinas, did not separate them. Sidgwick does, and he interprets happiness as the increase of pleasure because it provides, he argues, more precision in ethical decision-making.[50]

Sidgwick's three main books—egoism (book II), intuitionism (book III), and utilitarianism (book IV)—discuss a variety of methods showing the limits and strengths of each and their corresponding ends. Sidgwick never rejects these methods outright but builds upon them, finally fastening upon utilitarianism as the method that guides action with the most precision but with support in intuitionism. Egoism is similar to utilitarianism. It guides action by quantifying pleasures and pains, such that the agent "chooses the one which he thinks will yield him the greatest surplus of pleasure over pain."[51] The crucial difference is that egoism seeks the good of the individual, whereas utilitarianism seeks the general good. Sidgwick divides egoism into four methods: empirical hedonism, objective hedonism, doing one's duty, and deductive hedonism. Empirical hedonism assumes "commensurability of Pleasures and Pains" with "determinate quantitative relations."[52] Egoism is primarily a form of hedonism, something Sidgwick does not dismiss outright.[53] In fact, one of his students, Edgeworth, is credited with assisting in the "marginalist revolution" in economics. Edgeworth could be said to have originated econometrics, applying mathematics to economics and suggesting that utility could be measured by a "hedinometer."[54] Attempting to find precise measurements for utility offers no contradiction to Sidgwick's methods.

It would provide the clarity and precision he seeks; but for Sidgwick, empirical egoism offers no such precise measurements because it individuates pleasure without aggregating it.

After identifying the limitations of empirical egoism, Sidgwick next examines objective hedonism, which is more in line with "common sense in our pursuit of happiness." Rather than looking at the empirical reality of pleasure and pain, it looks to the "objective conditions and sources of happiness." Objective hedonism has its own set of problems. Common sense cannot provide an adequate account of these conditions because it gives "at the best an estimate true for an average or typical human being." Yet the "average" human being is not the best standard to determine happiness because the "mass of mankind" spend their days working to ward off starvation rather than being afforded the leisure that brings happiness. Moreover, common sense too often perpetuates the "idols of the tribe," malign influences that one imagines will bring happiness when they cannot.[55] Looking to the social conditions and sources for happiness rather than happiness itself is too fraught with problems for Sidgwick to give it much credence.[56] Empirical hedonism remains more promising than objective hedonism in guiding right action, even with its limitations.

The fulfillment of duty is a third possibility. The method here is moral rules that arise from a source such as conscience, with the assumption that fulfilling those rules brings happiness. It is the latter assumption that makes doing one's duty fit within egoism. While fulfilling duties generally brings happiness, it does not do so in every situation. In fact, one's "vices" can be as useful to others as one's virtues.[57] Nor is happiness coincident with fulfilling duty.[58] The person who reasons practically to fulfill their individual duty or happiness, which is one version of practical reasoning, and one who does so for the sake of the greatest good, which is another, will find the two forms of reasoning at odds. This problem of the duality of practical reason runs throughout *Methods*. The practical reasoning involved in the fulfillment of duties stands in contrast to that which seeks happiness, either of oneself or the greater good. As Kant recognizes, doing one's duty and happiness are not correlates. Kant resolves this problem theologically. If doing what is right does not make one happy in this life, then God must bring about a proper proportion between virtue and happiness in the next. Sidgwick returns to this problem in the final chapter of *Methods* and considers Kant's solution, but he cannot appeal to theology or metaphysics without losing what he seeks to accomplish: ethics' independence. Instead, he leaves the problem unresolved and states that ethics cannot be fully rationalized because doing what is right might not make one happy.

A fourth possibility, deductive hedonism, would use the scientific method to give a more solid foundation for the causes of pleasure and pain drawn from psychology, biology, or evolution. Sidgwick discusses Herbert Spencer's work as an example. If such an ethic were possible, it would move from what is to what ought to be.[59] Before moving on to a different set of methods under "Intuitionism," Sidgwick summarizes the argument so far:

> We seem, then, forced to conclude that there is no scientific short-cut to the ascertainment of the right means to the individual's happiness: every attempt to find a "high priori road" to this goal brings us back inevitably to the empirical method. For instead of a clear principle universally valid, we only get at best a vague and general rule, based on considerations which it is important not to overlook, but the relative value of which we can only estimate by careful observation and comparison of individual experience.[60]

Empirical hedonism is the most promising method within egoism. Sidgwick builds on its promise when he discusses utilitarianism, but he first addresses a method that he calls intuitionism, which is concerned with the end of perfection or human excellence.

Plato, Aristotle, Samuel Clarke, Joseph Butler, and Immanuel Kant are Sidgwick's exemplars for intuitionism.[61] It is "the view of ethics which regards as the practically ultimate end of moral actions their conformity to certain rules or dictates of Duty unconditionally prescribed."[62] Intuitionism takes diverse forms, and Sidgwick is not always consistent in what he means by it. Whewell's claim that the intellect intuits first principles from which moral rules could be derived is one example of it, one that Sidgwick rejects. Sidgwick also places an ethics of perfection under intuitionism, something he likewise questions, especially the version found in T. H. Green. Another version of intuitionism assumes that moral properties are nonnatural, which is usually self-evident, so that the duties or virtues necessary for action are readily available to any human person qua human knower.[63] While he found intuitionism wanting, Sidgwick accepts elements of it. He finds utilitarianism to be a principle that nearly everyone intuits and uses at some point, including Whewell and Green, so he does not think that he needs to counter their intuitionism with utilitarianism. Instead, utilitarianism incorporates the best of intuitionism, without its problems. One way that Sidgwick accomplishes this incorporation is through a revised understanding of "intention."

Intuitionism and utilitarianism are often distinguished, Sidgwick notes, in that utilitarianism is supposedly concerned with the state of affairs brought about in the world, while intuitionism focuses on "intentions and motives."[64] He labels this common distinction a "misunderstanding," and he refuses to concede that intention is the exclusive domain of intuitionists. Intention is as important for the utilitarian method, and for "moralists of all schools," as it is for the intuitionists. Everyone agrees that "moral judgments" are primarily based on intentions; but in a move that calls down the ire of G. E. M. Anscombe, he then describes intention as "the effects which [the agent] foresaw in willing the act." Intention consists of the foreseen consequences of a voluntary act. Sidgwick writes, "What we judge to be 'wrong'—in the strictest ethical sense—is not any part of the actual effects, as such, of the muscular movements immediately caused by the agent's volition, but the effects which he foresaw in willing to act; or, more strictly, the volition or choice of realizing the effects as foreseen."[65] Intentions are consequences agents foresee that their acts will bring about. They are like mental future events that are willed. For instance, the death of innocents in a bombing campaign may not be the effects that the person who ordered it intended if the foreseen effects, the state of affairs brought about, was something like the end of the war or saving the greatest number of people possible.

Neither Rawls nor Anscombe accepts this theory of human action, and both reject it because of Wittgenstein's philosophy. Intention fits within forms of life that render it intelligible. Rawls places voluntary actions within a pluralistic, democratic context that privileges right over good, but within a necessary minimal theory of the good that challenges Sidgwick's utilitarianism.[66] Anscombe is more thorough in her criticism of Sidgwick. His theory of action and philosophy of mind are sources behind the corruption of moral philosophy that prevented the English-speaking world from recognizing that the dropping of the atomic bomb in World War II was an act of murder. The origins for her *Intention*, and especially her discussion of the multiple descriptions involved in the act of someone pumping water and poisoning members of a syndicate involved in killing others, were her response to Sidgwick.[67]

Once the foreseen effects of a voluntary act define intention, Sidgwick states that there is no dispute on the role of intention in ethics between intuitionists and utilitarians.[68] This is not so, however, with motives. Intuitionists have not maintained the proper distinction between intention and motive. "Ordinary language" misleads because it seldom distinguishes them. For the sake of "exact moral or jural discussion," intention must be identified as foreseen consequences of actions, while motive is what moves the actor. Sidgwick gives the example, drawn from Bentham, of a judge who rightly judges a criminal as guilty but does so from a malicious motive. The judge has a right intention but a bad motive. Motives and intentions differ, and both contribute to an act's moral worth, but the precision he seeks for ethics locates moral worth primarily in the intention as foreseen consequence and the state of affairs brought about. Sidgwick draws two conclusions from this distinction between intention and motive. First, motives can make actions "better or worse," but judgments of right and wrong are appropriate to intentions and not motives. The value of the intention will be found in whether it promotes the greater good.[69]

His second conclusion depends on the bifurcation of intentions between an interior and exterior direction. Interiorly, they can affect the motive of the agent, and this direction should be "morally prescribed." In other words, the intention of bringing about the best consequences should affect the motivation. However, "the primary—though not the sole—content of the main prescriptions of duty" are found in its "external effects."[70] Intention focuses on the rightness of an action; motive focuses on the goodness of the will that moves the agent who acts. Sidgwick's distinctions significantly influence the later development of ethics. Judgments of what is *right*, which become the primary domain for the discipline of ethics, are correlated with intentions understood as the foreseen consequences of actions. Judgments of *good* are correlated with motives and are given a secondary role.

Sidgwick then examines virtue and duty within the intuitionist method. Duty is "broadly convertible with Right conduct," or "those Right actions or abstinences, for the adequate accomplishment of which a moral impulse is conceived to be at least occasionally necessary." Virtue is more complex. In his *History of Ethics*, he critiques Aristotle's emphasis on formed character because it lacks voluntariness and thus does not contribute to a scientific ethic. Sidgwick makes an identical criticism of T. H. Green, whom he accuses of a "determinist view" of freedom, in contrast to his own "libertarian view." Green's understanding of "volition," he writes, "seems clearly not 'free' in any important sense: since it is determined by the agent's 'character'—i.e., by his 'habitual' or 'steady' direction of himself, by a concentration of his faculties towards the fulfilment of certain purposes; and the particularity of his character must be attributed, as we have seen, to its past history."[71] Given Sidgwick's definition of ethics, the method adopted, and his understanding of intention, neither Aristotle's ethics of character nor Green's ethics of perfection offers the precision he seeks, but Sidgwick does not abandon the language of virtue. He sets forth a positive account of it that does not conflict with libertarian freedom and fits with his preferred method. Virtues are "qualities exhibited in right conduct," which he explicitly contrasts with virtue as a "quality of character."[72] He finds it useless to consider virtue as a "quality of 'character' rather than of 'conduct'" expressed in "the moral law in the form,

'Be this,' instead of the form 'Do this.'" The former, unlike the latter, gives us no guide for right action.[73] If he had read Maurice's work, he would have known that he was explicitly contradicting him as well as Green. Maurice begins ethics with the question "Who or What am I?" Being precedes doing. Sidgwick disagrees. The question "What ought I to do?" is more important than "Who am I?" because the former can be given a specific answer and the latter cannot. If ethics is to gain scientific precision, the question Maurice asks must give way to Sidgwick's.[74]

Virtues and duties are related for Sidgwick, but virtue goes beyond duty. Virtues fulfill duties but also exceed duties, in that they call forth actions that we would not expect the ordinary person to achieve in carrying out duties. The wealthy who live abstemiously and give generously are virtuous, but we would not promulgate such generosity as a duty.[75] Virtue is more, not less than, nor fundamentally different from, duty. They are both forms of obligation. They overlap but answer different questions. Duty addresses "what others blame or forbear" someone for doing or not doing; virtue addresses what someone "ought to do or forbear." In other words, duty has a "laxer standard" than virtue. Virtue also depends on voluntary actions; and thus most moralists of virtue, Sidgwick states, would likely agree with Kant "that a good will is the only absolute and unconditional Good."[76]

Sidgwick continues his "empirical investigation" of intuitionism by setting forth "the virtues . . . in the order of their importance."[77] The most important virtues are practical wisdom, benevolence, and justice. Practical wisdom "is a tendency to discern, in the conduct of life generally, the best means to the attainment of any ends that the natural play of human motives may lead us to seek." It contrasts with "technical skill."[78] Practical wisdom is the overarching virtue in intuitionism because it deliberates about means. Benevolence and justice form the content of the virtues and duties. The prominent role given to "benevolence" in this list of virtues is significant. Benevolence as a completely other-regarding virtue is unknown to the Greeks or the Medievals. It is a duty, which, "according to Kant and others . . . is not strictly the affection of love or kindness, so far as this contains an emotional element, but only the determination of the will to seek the good or happiness of others." Sidgwick accepts this moral prescription but prefers the term "happiness" to that of the "good."[79]

Justice, Sidgwick states, "denotes a quality which it is ultimately desirable to realise in the conduct and social relations of men; and that a definition may be given of this which will be accepted by all competent judges as presenting, in a clear and explicit form, what they have always meant by the term, though perhaps implicitly and vaguely."[80] Determining right action based on the virtues (or duties) of justice and benevolence is not easy. Benevolence exceeds but does not contradict justice. Justice is morally obligatory, but Sidgwick questions if the intuitional method provides sufficient clarity to determine the role of benevolence in ethics. The question is whether intuitionism can provide "the right rules of distribution of services and kind acts, in so far as we consider the rendering of these to be morally obligatory."[81]

In the last two chapters of the book, both on intuitionism—"Philosophical Intuitionism" and "Ultimate Good"—Sidgwick returns to the question of whether it offers adequate precision to know what to do. He asks if it provides "intuitive propositions of real clearness and certainty" and answers no.[82] Self-evident principles are "sham axioms." He refers to the cardinal virtues as examples. The ancient cardinal virtue of wisdom, he states, can be placed in this summary form: "It is right to act rationally." Although this appears to give information, it does not. It is a useless tautology, as are the other cardinal virtues. They "can only be defended" if they are construed as "definitions of the problem to be solved and not as attempts at its solution." Plato and Aristotle provide no method for discovering virtues, only vague indications of their "whereabouts."[83] Their accounts of the virtues give insufficient guidance for action.

In his final chapter, on the ultimate good, Sidgwick refers to a distinction that he previously made between "two different forms" of ethics. Ethics can take the form of (1) a consideration of "moral laws or rational precepts of conduct" or (2) "the good, or 'true good' of man and the method of attaining it." The first, he notes, "seems most prominent in modern ethics." The second, the ultimate good, is "practically useful" only when it serves to provide "directive rules of conduct."[84] Sidgwick returns to this distinction as he transitions from intuitionism to utilitarianism, claiming that for "the moral consciousness of modern Europe," right conduct and the good are often divided because right conduct does not bring the ultimate good understood as "well-being." The virtuous life makes no one happy when "combined with extreme pain."[85] What is right and what is good have been divided because there is no guarantee, especially when the good is understood as happiness that depends in some sense on material things, that doing what is right leads to happiness and well-being. For Sidgwick, virtue assumes cooperation between duty and well-being, but happiness always has an element of competitiveness, and this means that doing one's duty and being happy are often at cross-purposes. Many people look to a "supernatural" source to bring duty and happiness into unity, but Sidgwick has sworn off invoking theology or metaphysics; so this avenue, which Kant himself took, is unavailable for him. Instead, Sidgwick suggests that ethics can bring the good and the right, intuitionism and utilitarianism, together as much as is possible in this life by interpreting the universal good as universal happiness, and happiness as increased pleasure. Intuitionism sought self-evident principles that would guide action to right conduct and attain the good, but the principles remained vague and the good elusive. Utilitarianism is more promising. He concludes the book on intuitionism by stating, "I am finally led to the conclusion . . . that the Intuitional method rigorously applied yields as its final result the doctrine of pure Universalistic Hedonism—which it is convenient to denote by the single word, Utilitarianism."[86]

Utilitarianism provides the precision that Sidgwick seeks. It sets forth "objectively right conduct, under any given circumstances" as "that which will produce the greatest amount of happiness on the whole; that is, taking into account all whose happiness is affected by the conduct." The "all" here makes it preferable to the various methods of egoism. The "greater amount of happiness" is then defined as "the greatest possible surplus of pleasure over pain, the pain being conceived as balanced against an equal amount of plea-sure, so that the two contrasted amounts annihilate each other for purposes of ethical calculation." Utilitarianism allows for quantitative comparison.[87] Sidgwick buttresses his case by appealing to economics, especially in terms of marginalism: "As political economists have explained, the means of happi-ness are immensely increased by that complex system of co-operation which has been gradually organized among civilized men," where it is best "to let each individual exchange such services as he is disposed to render for such return as he can obtain for them by free consent." He makes exceptions to these "services" when it comes to the reproduction and care of children, to persons with special needs, and to friendship. They should have "no market price," but are properly understood as natural exchanges based on contracts.[88] He then suggests that there are "two competing views of an ideally just social order," one he calls "individualistic" and the other "socialistic." Utilitarian-ism adopts the individualistic and insists on the freedom of each person "to provide for his own interests."[89] Having freed ethics from theology, Sidgwick makes it nearly identical to marginalist economics.

The utilitarian method works with existing morality, reshaping and guid-ing action as much as it can with the precision made available by it. It does not create morality "de novo." It may, however, conflict with common moral views. For this reason, it might need to institute its principles secretly. In what has become a somewhat infamous passage, he writes,

Thus, on Utilitarian principles, it may be right to do and privately rec-ommend, under certain circumstances, what it would not be right to advocate openly; it may be right to teach openly to one set of persons what it would be wrong to teach to others; it may be conceivably right to do, if it can be done with comparative secrecy, what it would be wrong to do in the face of the world; and even, if perfect secrecy can be reasonably expected, what it would be wrong to recommend by private advice or example.[90]

The "plain man," he states, would surely "repudiate the general notion of an esoteric morality." If it were widely known and promulgated, it would have unfortunate consequences. Thus, he concludes not that esotericism should be eschewed in morality but that the "esoteric morality should be kept esoteric."[91]

In his final chapter, Sidgwick discusses the relations among the three broad methods he has assessed. Utilitarianism absorbs what is best in the previous methods without taking on board their limitations. A presumed "antithesis" between intuitionism and utilitarianism should be "entirely discarded," because the self-evident principles that were most compelling in the intuitionist method "are not only not incompatible with a Utilitarian system, but even seem required to furnish a rational basis for such a system."[92] He made the point previously that all virtues and duties are aspects of benevolence, and benevolence points to utilitarianism.[93] Likewise, the egoist should be a universal hedonist, because "his own greatest happiness can be best attained by so doing."[94]

One problem remains that he has discussed throughout *Methods*: "The inseparable connexion between Utilitarian Duty and the greatest happiness of the individual who conforms to it cannot be satisfactorily demonstrated on empirical grounds."[95] Here is his statement of a "dualism of practical reason." Utilitarianism implies that it might be my duty to sacrifice my own interests for the sake of the greater good and that such a sacrifice should be "compensated." As Schultz acknowledges, this dualism is Sidgwick's truthful attempt to remain impartial and not fit everything within a system. It also emerges once ethics proceeds in a post-Christian society without recourse to theology. Yet the pressing question that haunts Sidgwick is if the universe is hospitable to ethics if there is no God, and he lacks confidence that he can answer this question affirmatively. If not, then ethics may not be fully rational.[96] One way to resolve this problem is theologically, by positing a God who rewards duty and virtue and condemns vice in the afterlife. God could be useful as the one who sorts it all out in the end. Maurice's doctrine of judgment was thought to be insufficient on just this point; it cost him his job at King's College because he denied that eternal punishment fit with the Triune God. Kant gave God this primary role as judge in his attempt to reconcile duty and happiness. Sidgwick recognizes that turning to theology to reconcile morality and happiness would undo his system; it would lose the independence of his ethics. Rather than saving ethics theologically, Sidgwick acknowledges that "it would seem necessary to abandon the idea of rationalising [morality] completely."[97] Duty and happiness cannot be reconciled.

SUMMARY AND EVALUATION OF SIDGWICK'S *METHODS*

Sidgwick's *Methods* gave rise to a modern independent discipline of ethics in a post-Christian society. It takes the following shape. The domain for ethics is voluntary action seeking the right or ought. The "right" takes priority over the "good." Right concerns intention as foreseen consequences. Good concerns motives for these intentions, which are not easily accessible to observation. The ends of action are defined in terms of happiness or perfection/excellence, but Sidgwick leads the way (following Mill) in arguing that happiness, especially in terms of promoting pleasure and diminishing pain, provides more precision in guiding action than perfection/excellence. A typology of methods is constructed of egoism, intuitionism, and utilitarianism. The independence of ethics is based on a sharp is/ought distinction. The ethicist strikes the posture of an impartial spectator who offers various methods—as rational procedures—for guiding action, privileging theory over practice.

Sidgwick never argues that the methods he assesses are the only ones available. He acknowledges that "God's will," "self-realization or self-development," and "life according to nature" provide methods as well, but he "brackets" them because they assume theology or metaphysics and seek to discover what is.[98] For Sidgwick, if ethics is to be an independent discipline, then it should only concern itself with what ought to be. Ethics concerns the "ought" and leaves what "is" to other disciplines. Each discipline has its division of labor. He explains why he finds theology and metaphysics to be a problem based on this strong is/ought distinction. He writes, "The introduction of these notions [theology, metaphysics] into Ethics is liable to bring with it a fundamental confusion between 'what is' and 'what ought to be,' destructive of all clearness in ethical reasoning."[99] When ethics works from its own proper domain, what ought to be, it will be able to guide action. If it gets concerned with what is, then it will depend upon something other than ethics for its intelligibility. Sidgwick bequeaths to the discipline of ethics this sharp distinction, which then requires bracketing metaphysical, theological, and even political claims about what is.

How successful was Sidgwick's attempt to clarify the boundary within which ethics pursues its investigation? Schneewind does not exaggerate when he concludes his history of Sidgwick's ethics by stating, "Sidgwick gave the problem of ethics the form in which they have dominated British and American moral philosophy since his time."[100] Sidgwick gives the dominant form whereby ethics is taken up within analytic philosophy, but it is not the exclusive form. In one sense, Sidgwick's *Methods* proves to be a fork in the road. Philosophers convinced that ethics has its own unique domain and is primarily concerned with the guidance of voluntary action to do what is right take up Sidgwick's project. Moral theologians, obviously, cannot follow Sidgwick unless they intend to cease being theologians, for Sidgwick has bracketed theology from ethics a priori. Such an ethics would be a temptation to render theology irrelevant not because of any argument against it but because of a method that will supposedly give scientific precision. Moral theologians are not the only ones who question the dominance of Sidgwick's method.

Many moral philosophers likewise reject the way Sidgwick sets up a system of modern ethics. It will fall to four women philosophers—Philippa Foot, G. E. M. Anscombe, Iris Murdoch, and Mary Midgley—to reorient moral philosophy away from the is/ought distinction. Philippa Foot sees the post-Holocaust images of devastation and says to her mentor, Donald Mac-Kinnon, "Nothing is ever going to be the same again."[101] Moral philosophy needed something more than a domain limited to the "right" or "ought" to address the concrete, historical, material present in these images. The so-called naturalistic fallacy, which asserts that evaluative judgments of good cannot be derived from factual statements of true or false, was inadequate. Mac Cumhaill and Wiseman explain Foot's opposition to the fact/value split: "Philippa's point is a simple and elegant extension of Wittgenstein's: our evaluative language does not peel off the world, leaving behind a stripped-out, valueless scene that we might call 'reality' or 'nature.' Rather, an evaluative description makes sense only when it is located in a pattern of human life."[102] These women have opened new possibilities for learning and teaching ethics. Maurice's criticism of the is/ought distinction nearly a century earlier bears a striking resemblance to their approach to ethics. It is no surprise that they all looked to virtue and an ethics of perfection.

What divides philosophers and theologians post-Sidgwick is whether ethics should be its own independent discipline or whether it always requires something more than ethics for its intelligibility, something that Maurice thought was necessary. He found this "something more" in all moral philosophy and theology. For instance, in discussing the teachings of Socrates, he reminds the reader of his "attending daemon." "The longings and movements of his spirit," Maurice states, "had a divine source and were subject to a divine impulse." For this reason, he concludes that Socrates "acknowledged the need of something besides philosophy in order that he might realise the meaning of philosophy."[103] For Sidgwick, despite his devoted attention to parapsychology, this "something more" prevents ethics from becoming what he desires it to be, a discipline that needs nothing more than the "ought" for its intelligibility. The crucial question is if the "ought" can function as an independent domain for a self-sufficient discipline called ethics. Another way to put this question is to ask if there *is* no ought without some *is*.

Sidgwick was the inheritor of nineteenth-century trends. Some of those trends were salutary, such as the reaction against a mandated moral theology that required subscription to the Thirty-Nine Articles to teach moral philosophy. Maurice and Sidgwick led the way to challenge subscription. As a result, human freedom and inquiry advanced; progress was made. Another trend was the attempt to advance ethics by providing it with scientific precision. Mathematics, physics, chemistry, biology, and other scientific disciplines had made remarkable progress in the preceding decades. Ethics, as a science of human action, so it was thought, could likewise benefit by taking up similar methods, assuming that method and a narrowed domain make for such progress. The more this narrows, and the specified domain for ethics predominates, the more the larger frame disappears that renders good human action intelligible. Any careful observer of the history of ethics would be hard-pressed to discover the same progress in it as has been made in physics or biology.

Part of the frame that disappears is the recognition that ethics is inevitably linked to politics—not politics in the modern sense of nation-states with determinate borders secured and controlled by a state with a monopoly on the use of violence, but politics in the Aristotelian sense of a deliberative body seeking the good in common that contributes to human flourishing. Here, too, Sidgwick significantly shifted from Maurice, whose work, for better and worse, constantly referred to the importance of "nation." Ethics is not pursued in some neutral realm by an impartial spectator; it always assumes a social ordering, within which human actions become possible and sometimes impossible. The ought cannot be had without an "is" because, as Karl Polanyi noted, human action is always "embedded" in natural, biological, and social contexts. Likewise, the Hegelian philosopher Gillian Rose questions the "neo-Kantian paradigm" that begins by assuming its object, in this case ethics, and then asks what are the transcendental conditions that make it possible. Then a method emerges that obscures the relationship between the assumed objects and the categories that supposedly explain it.[104] This schema loses the complexity of the "object" and its relations, obfuscating rather than clarifying. It should come as no surprise that some of the strongest challenges contemporary to Sidgwick came from the Hegelians, T. H. Green and F. H. Bradley.[105]

THE HEGELIAN CRITICS

Sidgwick's contemporaries, the Hegelians Green and Bradley, took issue with his ethical theory, just as he took issue with theirs. Green and Sidgwick were classmates at Rugby. They traveled together, and Sidgwick referred to him as a "valued friend." Green was married to Charlotte Symonds, the sister of John Addington Symonds, who was a close friend of Sidgwick.[106] Symonds found Sidgwick's *Methods* to be nothing short of revolutionary, writing to him that "on the method of Ethics will depend upon the future of the human race. . . . We beat about the bush so long because we have not found the scientific starting-point of ethics."[107] Sidgwick found the right starting point. Symonds shared his homoerotic poetry with Sidgwick, who advised him not to publish it, not because he did not share his commitment to liberating sexual norms but because he thought it would do more harm than good.

In 1862, Green discussed with Sidgwick the possibility that he might take deacon's orders in the Church of England. Sidgwick states, "I was horrified by his idea of deaconising."[108] Sidgwick neither understood Green's attraction to the Anglican Church nor to Hegelianism. He wrote, "I should like to get at this Oxford *Hegelianism* and see what it means. I used to talk with Green, but I did not draw much."[109] He referred to Hegelianism as a "monstrous mistake" and insisted that "we must go back to Kant and begin again from him." After making this judgment, he acknowledged that he had "not yet managed to read any Hegel." He read Hegel years later and found him beneficial, in that he sets forth an "essentially and fundamentally rational Universe."[110]

The differences among Green, Bradley, and Sidgwick are differences that hearken back to Hegel's criticism of Kant's ethics. Green, like Hegel, approved much in Kant's philosophy, especially his emphasis on freedom; but Kant's division between freedom and nature, predicated as it was on the noumenal/phenomenal distinction, rendered freedom too impractical, too devoid of historical situatedness. As John Rawls notes, Hegel shifts ethics from *Sollen* to *Sittlichkeit*, from a focus on what-ought-to-be to our embedded social and political contexts.[111] This distinction creates a division in teaching and learning ethics. For those who follow Sidgwick and a Kantian emphasis, the history of learners matters less than providing them with a guide, procedure, or method for right, individual action. For those who follow Hegel, even those who follow the path from Hegel to Marx, this emphasis on method or procedure and the priority of the right is mistaken. It overlooks that ethics presumes a social context. In this sense, Green and Bradley's criticisms are not peculiar; they fit well with an alternative way of thinking about ethics found among Hegelians such as Gillian Rose, who identified the problem beginning with the Kantian method of ethics. Method is a form of "positivism" that gives "validity" to the method, thereby "suppressing the social and historical preconditions of its own possibility."[112] Her response to this positivism is not to find a different method but to dispense with it altogether. She writes, "There can be no question of changing from Kant's method to a different method, for all 'method,' by definition, imposes a schema on its object."[113] If she is right, Sidgwick's method of ethics looks in the wrong direction for ethical wisdom. Bradley and Green said as much during Sidgwick's day.

Bradley wrote a small monograph titled *Mr. Sidgwick's Hedonism* that reviews and criticizes *Methods*. His main criticism is that Sidgwick misidentifies "the Good." He writes, "The cardinal point in my opinion is that the Good must be a whole, and that hence a mere aggregate is not the Good. The true End is not put together out of counted units, but the Hedonistic End is a mere addition of particulars."[114] Green makes a similar criticism of Sidgwick in his *Prolegomena to Ethics*, stating that "a greatest possible sum of pleasures is a phrase to which no idea really corresponds." Because the Good cannot be such a sum, it is not the idea "which really actuates" utilitarians. Instead, their key idea is a "state of existence" in which all human beings "live as pleasantly as it is possible for them."[115] Green affirms what he thinks is the utilitarians' actual idea and lauds the social reforms they produce—reforms that he does not consider result from the proposed ethical method.

Green and Bradley deny that pleasure could be an ultimate good. Green does not deny a place for pleasure, but he finds utilitarians confused about its role. His ethics of perfection assume capacities that could be realized. The desire to realize those capacities is satisfying and brings about pleasure. Yet to reduce the satisfaction of desire in the realization of capacities to pleasure and assume that it is the ultimate good is to confuse the ultimate good of perfection with pleasure. Green states, "Because there is pleasure in all satisfaction of desire, men have come to think that the object of desire is always some pleasure; that every good is a pleasure."[116] Green also denies that the "sum of pleasures" is itself a pleasure that could be usefully applied in the way that Sidgwick's universal hedonism demands. Nor can pleasures be compared, given their different intensities and durations. Nor can they be differentiated from the diverse conditions that make them possible; these conditions are not themselves pleasures. Green writes,

> Now according to all strictly Hedonistic theories the difference between objects willed is, according to this sense of the terms, extrinsic, not intrinsic. The motive to the persons willing is supposed to be in all cases the same, viz., desire for some pleasure or aversion from some pain. The conditions of the pleasures which different men desire, or which the same man desires at different times, are of course most various; but it is not the conditions of any pleasure but the pleasure itself that a man desires, if pleasure is really his object at all.[117]

Green critiques utilitarianism for neglecting these diverse conditions. Sidgwick dismisses Green's criticism, stating that distinguishing pleasure and the conditions for it is "too violent a paradox to need refutation." Perhaps the most significant difference between them is that Bradley and Green refuse to divide ought from is.[118] Green differentiates his ethics from utilitarianism because they ask different questions. Green thinks the more expansive and significant question is, "What ought I to be?" Utilitarians ask, "What ought to be done?"[119]

Green died young, just before his forty-sixth birthday, and before *Prolegomena* appeared. He and Sidgwick never had the opportunity to clarify or resolve their differences. Sidgwick's ethics caught the wave of the analytic turn dominating Western philosophy, Green's ethics, along with moral theology, languished. Moral philosophers who still read Sidgwick and Green continue to disagree over who misunderstood whom more, and whose criticisms were compelling. For Schneewind, Green's ethics are less compelling than Sidgwick's. His incorporation of theological and metaphysical themes prevents him from making the transition Sidgwick made. As Schneewind puts it, Green was more interested in making an apology for Christianity, whereas Sidgwick sought truth.[120] Schultz would agree, and sees in Green something similar to "the old Maurice and Platonic soaring toward the form of the Good, apprehended in this world only through a glass darkly."[121] Brink offers a different "assessment" that, in his own words, "contrasts with the more unreservedly favourable assessment offered by J. B. Schneewind."[122] Brink finds Sidgwick's "dismissive attitude toward all non-hedonic conceptions of eudaimonism and perfectionism" to be "quite breathtaking." He dismisses them because they "appeal to metaphysical and contestable conceptions of the good." Yet he never offers a counterargument to these conceptions; he only asserts the self-evident character of pleasure as the ultimate good.[123]

Interestingly, Alfred Marshall, Sidgwick and Green's contemporary, found Green to have the more satisfactory ethics. In 1884, Marshall was elected "professor of political economy," at a time when economics was housed within the moral sciences. As chair of the Board of Moral Science, Sidgwick was charged with explaining to him the expectations for his lectures. Marshall was not pleased, and Sidgwick reported their uncomfortable encounter: "I had produced on him the impression of a petty tyrant 'dressed in a little brief authority' (Chairman of the Board of Moral Science) who wished to regulate, trammel, hamper a man who knew more about the subject than I did. I tried to explain and we parted friends." After further correspondence, Marshall, whom Sidgwick refers to as an "old friend," told Sidgwick that his academic career was constrained by "overregulation," through his focus on administering the moral sciences tripos. This focus was the reason Sidgwick had only a handful of students, while T. H. Green's classroom was full. Green ignored examinations but sought "to teach them the truth about the universe and human life."[124] For Marshall, Green aimed higher than Sidgwick. Marshall viewed Sidgwick as overly bureaucratic and concerned more with administration than pursuing the questions Green pursued.

More than a century later, Bernard Williams made a related criticism of Sidgwick's utilitarianism:

> Utilitarianism emerges as the morality of an élite, and the distinction between theory and practice determines a class of theorists distinct from other persons, theorists in whose hands the truth of the Utilitarian justification of non-Utilitarian dispositions will be responsibly deployed. This outlook accords well enough with the important colonial origins of Utilitarianism. This version may be called "Government House Utilitarianism."[125]

Schultz questions these criticisms, referring to Marshall's "infamous invidious comparison of Sidgwick to Green," and countering Williams's judgment.[126] He interprets Sidgwick along "semi-socialist" lines, and while he acknowledges that he might be considered "'the last of the Benthamites,' he nonetheless goes far toward burying the 'Benthamite' defense of laissez-faire, and is certainly not as complacent or conservative as the term 'Government House' utilitarian suggests."[127] Yet Schultz is inconsistent in his defense of Sidgwick. After a discussion of Sidgwick's failures on questions of race and class, arguing that they are "certainly no better, than J. S. Mill's," he acknowledges that if Sidgwick held to such opinions, and it appears that he did, it provides evidence for "Government House Utilitarianism" in service to colonialism.[128] Sidgwick also affirms his friend C. H. Pearson's racist work, *National Life and Character*.[129] Pearson was one of Maurice's students, which raises the question of whether Maurice is as implicated as Sidgwick in developing an ethics for racist and colonialist measures, a question that I address in part II of this book. Schultz considers Sidgwick's colonialist and racist views to be a "great mystery": "The great mystery is how he could have been so alienated and so skeptical and yet remain so supremely confident in the moral mission of English civilization, which in the end he prized mainly for its political institutions and greater emphasis on science."[130] Perhaps the mystery is not that great? The reason for it might be found in his affirmation of Adam Smith's "natural liberty."

Sidgwick published a lengthy work in 1883 titled *The Principles of Political Economy*. The preface was written by J. N. Keynes, the father of John Maynard Keynes. The senior Keynes had been Sidgwick's student and then colleague in Moral Science.[131] *Principles* was divided into two parts: the "science" and the "art" of political economy, a division that tracked Sidgwick's emphasis on a theory/practice distinction. The science of political economy concerns the "ideal situation," and the art the application of the ideal situation in practice. The ideal is "competition perfectly free and active." It presumes the "natural liberty" identified by Adam Smith and perpetuated by nearly every British economist. Sidgwick defends this ideal against the socialists. They mistakenly interpret Ricardo's labor theory of value to imagine that workers have not received the full remuneration of their labor.[132] Insofar as their remuneration was based on market competition, they received their due. He affirmed the division of labor and paying wages based solely on the market rate. He viewed the market wage as disciplining workers to avoid improvident marriage and vicious actions. Nonetheless, Sidgwick recognized that the ideal could not always be actualized in politics, and thus the "art" of political economy remained important.

Sidgwick concludes this lengthy work with the chapter "Economics and Private Morality," where he discusses the duty or virtue of justice. He defines justice as making "claims to wealth or service" that are "precise in nature." Because they are precise, their "nonfulfillment . . . is liable to strong censure, if not legal enforcement."[133] Less strict claims are better described as "fair" or "equitable" than just. He classifies both sets of claims by their "sources," which largely depend on "custom" or "contract." Contract offers precise obligations, but custom only provides "quasi-moral obligations." Of course, Hegel thought that custom, or *Sitte*, was the source of a just ethical life rather than an abstract right based on contract. For Sidgwick, contract has the precision to guide action to the "ought," and he sees it being fostered by the modern discipline of economics. He writes, "There seems no doubt that the influence of economic discussion has tended to invalidate all quasi-moral obligations founded on customs pure and simple, substituting for customary terms of exchange conditions determined by definite agreements freely entered into."[134] Contracts freely entered into bear a strong resemblance to Sidgwick's definition of ethics in *Methods*: "the science or study of what is right or what ought to be, so far as this depends upon the voluntary action of individuals."[135] Define the idea of the right in terms of the increase of pleasure and the diminishment of pain, place them on a balance sheet, and little difference exists between Sidgwick's ethics and his economics. It also fits well his criticism of Green's understanding of freedom from his "libertarian" defense. The Hegelian approach to ethics asks which social forms our ethics assumes and gives rise to. Sidgwick's ethics never poses this question, but it undoubtedly serves well the marginalist economics that was becoming entrenched in the nineteenth century. In narrowing what constitutes ethics, Sidgwick narrowed its constituency.

This judgment sides with Williams and Brink against Schultz and Schneewind. It seems justified, given Sidgwick's statement correlating his utilitarianism, his esoteric morality, and colonialism. Schultz brings our attention to a statement Sidgwick made on the duty of civilized nations: "For it is their legitimate business on utilitarian principles—of civilizing the world, they have to commit acts which cannot but be regarded as aggressive by the savage nations whom it is their business to educate and absorb."[136] They will be educated and absorbed by performing labor that the "civilized nations" lack motivation to do. Manual labor will primarily be performed in the future by non-European races.[137] Sidgwick explicitly stated that his "utilitarian principles" led to these conclusions. With them, he sided with Pearson.

Schultz argues that Sidgwick's utilitarianism mitigates some of the worst tendencies that he points out in Sidgwick's ethics. He views them as the exception. As is shown in the next chapter, G. E. M. Anscombe disagrees. She charges Sidgwick with introducing a corrupt sense of moral agency based on "consequentialism" that justifies committing acts that others will recognize as aggressive, such as killing the innocent for the sake of a perceived greater good. Anscombe does not critique him for utilitarianism but consequentialism; the difference between the two matters. Schultz has no time for Anscombe or MacIntyre's criticism of Sidgwick; he is as dismissive of them as Sidgwick was of Green. He acknowledges that Sidgwick conceives "intention" as "foreseeable consequences" and states, "In this connection, mention might also be made of how Sidgwick construes the notion of an 'intention' as extending to cover all the foreseeable consequences of one's actions (a point that, while it does not trouble utilitarians, has much provoked Catholic defenders of the so-called doctrine of the 'double-effect')." The troubled Catholic defenders are Anscombe and MacIntyre: "It certainly provoked G. E. M. Anscombe, anyway; her tirade on 'Modern Moral Philosophy' took Sidgwick as the kind of 'corrupt mind' emblematic of the failings of all modern moral theory. This tradition of abuse has been carried on by Alasdair MacIntyre in his *Three Rival Versions,* . . . though with little gain in plausibility."[138]

For Anscombe, the difficulty with consequentialist reasoning resulted in the mass murder carried out by Truman at the end of World War II. Is such a judgment warranted against Sidgwick? In an address to the Cambridge Ethical Society on the ethics of war, Sidgwick made a similar controversial statement about the need for "civilized nations" to "absorb" the "semi-civilized nations." He wrote,

> For the nations most advanced in civilization have a tendence—the legitimacy of which cannot be broadly and entirely disputed—to absorb semicivilized states in their neighborhood as in the expansion of England and Russia in Asia, and of France in Africa. As, I say, the tendency cannot be altogether condemned, since it often seems clearly a gain to the world on the whole that the absorption should take place; still it is obviously difficult to define the condition under which this is legitimate, and the civilized nation engaged in this process of absorption cannot be surprised that other civilized nations think that they have a right to interfere and prevent the aggression.[139]

Such a war of aggression for the purpose of imperial expansion would not seem to fit any criterion of a just cause. Sidgwick does not address the traditional concern of *jus ad bellum*; nor does he discuss the justice necessary to prosecute a war (*jus in bello*), although he does suggest something like the principle of discrimination.[140] Laying the indiscriminate bombing of World War II at the feet of Sidgwick would certainly be inappropriate. Yet this would not invalidate the appropriateness of Anscombe's concern about whether consequentialist reasoning can legitimate illegitimate intentional means, or whether it can even acknowledge that there could be any. Consider these moral judgments that Sidgwick made: (1) He justified an esoteric morality for those responsible for implementing policies that might be considered questionable to those in whose name they were implemented. (2) He refused subscription out of conscience, even when it cost him his fellowship. (3) He admonished clergy to avoid pious fraud by telling the truth to the laity about doctrines that they no longer held. (4) He counseled and prevented Symonds's homoerotic works from publication because it would do more harm than good. (5) He defended, albeit with caution, colonial and imperial wars of aggression. Schultz argues that Sidgwick's "moral rigorism" and "consequentialist reasoning" dissolve any apparent contradiction between judgments 2 and 4.[141] Rigorism about consequentialism gives a criterion that justifies present actions, even apparently contradictory ones, based on their "gain" for the world. If that is the case, then Anscombe's criticism seems justified.

NOTES

1. Sidgwick and Sidgwick, *Henry Sidgwick*, 121.
2. Sidgwick and Sidgwick, 135.
3. Sidgwick and Sidgwick, 303–4.
4. Sidgwick and Sidgwick, 79–81.
5. Sidgwick and Sidgwick, 205.
6. Maurice, *Conscience*, 21–22.
7. Maurice, 45.
8. Sidgwick, *Practical Ethics*, 12–13.
9. Sidgwick stated this in his 1888 address to the Cambridge Ethical Society and is included in his *Practical Ethics*. Bok claims that this work shows that he moved away from his earlier claims about "esoteric morality" that were founded upon a "youthful arrogance," but his use of that very term for the kind of casuistry suggests otherwise. On this point, I find Bart Schultz's judgment more compelling when he writes, "Sidgwick may have had a reputation, during his lifetime for saintly honesty and candor. But he did not deserve it"; Schultz, *Henry Sidgwick*, 713. Unfortunately, Schultz repeatedly, and without adequate evidence, attributes Sidgwick's occasional duplicity to Maurice's influence.
10. Sidgwick, *Practical Ethics*, 73.
11. Sidgwick and Sidgwick, *Henry Sidgwick*, 152.
12. Sidgwick and Sidgwick, 261.
13. Sidgwick and Sidgwick, 262–65.
14. Sidgwick and Sidgwick, 1.
15. Schneewind, *Sidgwick's Ethics*, 22; Schultz, *Henry Sidgwick*, 36.
16. Sidgwick and Sidgwick, *Henry Sidgwick*, 11.
17. Sidgwick and Sidgwick, 219.
18. Sidgwick and Sidgwick, 400.
19. Sidgwick, *Practical Ethics*, 65.
20. Sidgwick, 95.
21. Sidgwick, *History of Ethics*, vi.
22. Sidgwick, 159–60.
23. Sidgwick, *Principles of Political Economy*, 16–19.
24. Sidgwick and Sidgwick, *Henry Sidgwick*, 446.
25. Sidgwick, *History of Ethics*, 145.

26. Sidgwick, 68–69.
27. Sidgwick, 58.
28. Sidgwick, 66.
29. Todd, "Henry Sidgwick," 21–25.
30. See Schultz, *Henry Sidgwick,* 175.
31. Schultz, 57.
32. I previously noted that Sidgwick offered a more Aristotelian understanding of the relation between theory and practice in his 1888 address to the Cambridge Ethical Society, when he stated that "the aim of such an Ethics Society, in the Aristotelian phrase, is not knowledge but action"; Sidgwick, *Practical Ethics,* 5. That statement was not accompanied by a retraction or correction from his previous claim in *Methods.* Because a modern, scientific ethics guides human action through a proper theory, I do not find a fundamental shift in Sidgwick as Bok did from his earlier to his later work. He never begins with practice (*techne* or *praxis*), explains its significance for an Aristotelian ethics, and how *theoria* relates to it through *phronesis.* His method remains the same through his published addresses to the Ethical Societies—utilitarianism. He uses it to show what actions ought or ought not be done.
33. Sidgwick, *History of Ethics,* 146–67.
34. Sidgwick.
35. Ross, *Aristotle,* 195.
36. Rawls, *Law of Peoples,* xvii.
37. Bradley, *Sidgwick's Hedonism,* 58.
38. Quoted by Williams, "Point of View," 280.
39. Rawls, *Lectures on the History of Political Philosophy,* 379.
40. Sidgwick and Sidgwick, *Henry Sidgwick,* 287.
41. Sidgwick and Sidgwick, 295. We return to Pearson, *National Life,* in part II. A friend of Sidgwick and undergraduate student of Maurice, he became notorious for supporting white supremacy because of his liberalism.
42. Williams, "Point of View," 280.
43. MacIntyre, *Three Rival Versions,* 28, 177, 186–89.
44. Sidgwick, *Methods of Ethics,* viii.
45. Schultz, *Henry Sidgwick,* 155.
46. Sidgwick, *Methods of Ethics,* viii.
47. Sidgwick, 1.
48. Sidgwick, 4.
49. Sidgwick, 9.
50. As is argued in chapter 3, Sidgwick's distinction proves fateful for modern ethics. The most influential inheritor of Sidgwick's *Methods,* John Rawls, also distinguishes happiness and perfection, rejects them both, and expands them with a Kantian constructivism. Rawls's Harvard colleague, Stanley Cavell, defends perfectionism against Rawls's criticism and argues that Rawls needs it for his own position. Perfection becomes the path less traveled except for a few philosophers influenced by Nietzsche, Emerson, or Wittgenstein. Thomas Hurka works fully within Sidgwick's approach to develop an ethics of perfection that is a "free standing morality" that can accept the fact/value distinction and give guidance for action with a quantitative method. It bears little relation to Cavell's approach and questions whether theology provides any significant knowledge at all; Hurka, *Perfectionism,* 20, 84. He writes, "Perfectionist writing about knowledge often

concentrate on its most rarefied forms, such as theology (if that is indeed knowledge), philosophy, and physics, but outside these abstract domains are many bodies of knowledge with some generality and some intrinsic worth"; Hurka, 120. The perfectionist path taken by moral theology offers a completely different direction than Hurka's. His perfectionism follows modern economics closely and assumes marginal rationality. Moral theology cannot adopt such a quantitative approach. Infusing virtue concerns grace's perfecting work as a gift that cannot, as F. D. Maurice put it, be measured.

51. Sidgwick, *Methods of Ethics*, 121.

52. Sidgwick, 123.

53. Sidgwick finds the method of empirical egoism unsatisfying because (1) it leads to a paradox in which directly aiming for pleasure often diminishes it, and (2) the quantitative method necessary for it cannot be accomplished individually. Individuals lack precise measurements for "definite degrees of pleasure and pain"; Sidgwick, *Methods of Ethics*, 140–47.

54. Screpanti and Zamagni, *Outline*, 146–47, 187, 204; also see Schultz, *Henry Sidgwick*, 538.

55. Sidgwick, *Methods of Ethics*, 151–52.

56. This criticism divides Sidgwick from his friend T. H. Green, who criticized Sidgwick for refusing to distinguish pleasure from the conditions and sources that gave rise to it. Sidgwick did not find that distinction helpful for ethics.

57. Sidgwick, *Methods of Ethics*, 168.

58. Sidgwick, 162.

59. In his posthumously published lectures on Spencer, he refers to his ethics as "naturalistic," but he does not find that deductive hedonism yields a satisfactory account of these causes; Sidgwick, *Ethics of T. H. Green*, 8.

60. Sidgwick, *Methods of Ethics*, 195.

61. While acknowledging that Kant "nowhere clearly describes rational intuitionism," Rawls disagrees that Kant fits within intuitionism. He would reject it as heteronomous because it assumes a given moral law rather than a moral law that we construct for ourselves out of pure practical reason; Rawls, *Lectures on the History of Moral Philosophy*, 235. Rawls's criticism is important because it allows him to separate Kantian constructivism as a method that is other than intuitionism and is not ordered to the end of perfection. As will be shown, Allen Wood offers a contrary interpretation of Kant.

62. Sidgwick, *Methods of Ethics*, 96.

63. For a good discussion of intuitionism that traces it back to Samuel Clarke (1675–1729), see Rawls, *Political Liberalism*, 91–92.

64. "Character" and "disposition" are sometimes included in the intuitionists' focus on the agent's "state of mind," but Sidgwick dismisses them because they "cannot be known directly"; Sidgwick, *Methods of Ethics*, 201.

65. Sidgwick.

66. Like Anscombe, he expresses concern that a utilitarian ethic could directly target the innocent; but as we shall see, in the end he sides with Michael Walzer's supreme emergency.

67. Anscombe, *Intention*, 34–46.

68. Sidgwick, *Methods of Ethics*, 202.

69. Throughout his work, Sidgwick consistently affirms that that the end justifies the means. In an 1897 address to the Cambridge Ethical Society on "public morality," he discusses Machiavelli's claim that the "end justifies the means." He confesses that as a utilitarian he cannot join with those who "reject it as anti-moral." Means only gain their justification

from the ends they serve. The problem with Machiavelli is not that the end justifies the means but that the end he seeks lacks universality. Sidgwick states, "The end must always ultimately justify the means—there is no other way in which the use of any means whatever could possibly be justified. Only it must be a *universal end*; not the preservation of any particular state; . . . but the happiness or well-being of humanity at large—or, rather, of the whole universe of living things, so far as any practical issue can be raised between these two conceptions of the universal end (Sidgwick, *Practical Ethics*, 37).

70. Sidgwick, *Methods of Ethics*, 204.

71. Sidgwick, *Ethics of T. H. Green*, 21.

72. Sidgwick, *Methods of Ethics*, 217–22.

73. Sidgwick, 393.

74. The second part of this work will suggest that Maurice's question is more revelatory of ordinary moral life than Sidgwick's.

75. Sidgwick, *Methods of Ethics*, 220.

76. Sidgwick, 221–22.

77. Sidgwick, 230.

78. Sidgwick, 231.

79. Sidgwick, 239.

80. Sidgwick, 264.

81. Sidgwick, 245. As is shown below, in his *Principles of Political Economy*, p. 583, Sidgwick argues that contracts rather than customs provide the necessary rules for such distribution.

82. Sidgwick, *Methods of Ethics*, 373.

83. Sidgwick, 374–75.

84. Sidgwick, 3.

85. Sidgwick, 392.

86. Sidgwick, 406–7.

87. Sidgwick, 411–13.

88. Sidgwick, 435–38.

89. Sidgwick, 444.

90. Sidgwick, 489–90.

91. Sidgwick. Schultz is rightly critical of this esoteric morality in Sidgwick but also sees it as "most personal and revelatory." He associates it with Sidgwick's homoerotic longings and the "epistemology of the closet" that he, his brother, and his friends were forced into. He also blames it on F. D. Maurice, interpreting it as a "philosophical expression of Mauricean paternalism." For some reason, Schultz consistently interprets Maurice as duplicitous in his theological convictions and contributing to Sidgwick's defense of an "esoteric morality." It completely misrepresents Maurice and detracts from Schultz's otherwise splendid biography of Sidgwick; Schultz, *Henry Sidgwick*, 270–73.

92. Sidgwick, *Methods of Ethics*, 496.

93. Sidgwick, 430–31.

94. Sidgwick, 498.

95. Sidgwick, 503.

96. Schultz, *Henry Sidgwick*, 206, 212, 222, 238.

97. Sidgwick, *Methods of Ethics*, 508.

98. Those three possibilities fit well Sidgwick's lectures on the ethics of T. H. Green (self-realization), J. Martineau (God's will), and Herbert Spencer (nature)—posthumously published as *The Ethics of T. H. Green, Herbert Spencer, and J. Martineau*.

99. Sidgwick, *Methods of Ethics*, 79.

100. Schneewind, *Sidgwick's Ethics*, 422.

101. Lipscomb, *Women Are up to Something*, 4; Mac Cumhaill and Wiseman, *Metaphysical Animals*, 144–45.

102. Mac Cumhaill and Wiseman, *Metaphysical Animals*, 197.

103. Maurice, *Kingdom of Christ*, 41–42.

104. Rose, *Hegel*, 49.

105. It should also come as no surprise that a philosopher of ancient ethics, Julia Annas, finds Bradley a much better guide to ethics than Sidgwick. While critical of Sidgwick's approach to ethics, she states, "Bradley's own brilliant account of ethics owes much to the leading idea of ancient ethics; but it has been uninfluential in the mainstream of analytical moral philosophy"; Annas, Morality, 4n5. Brink says the same about Green, referring to his *Prolegomena to Ethics* as a "neglected classic in the history of ethics"; Brink, "Introduction," xiii. Bradley also had an influence on Mary Midgley and Iris Murdoch. Both taught him in their courses; Mac Cumhaill and Wiseman *Metaphysical Animals*, 273.

106. Brink, "Introduction," xviii.

107. Schultz, *Henry Sidgwick*, 445.

108. Sidgwick and Sidgwick, *Henry Sidgwick*, 104; Gouldstone, *Rise and Fall*, 48.

109. Sidgwick and Sidgwick, *Henry Sidgwick*, 102.

110. Sidgwick and Sidgwick, 151, 159, 238.

111. Rawls, *Lectures on the History of Moral Philosophy*, 333.

112. Rose, *Hegel*, 35.

113. Rose, 48–49.

114. Bradley, *Sidgwick's Hedonism*, 19.

115. Green, *Prolegomena*, 442.

116. Green, 439.

117. Green, 178.

118. Green begins the *Prolegomena* with a book on the metaphysics of knowledge. He could be misunderstood as offering a nonnaturalistic ethics. Ethics, he wrote, requires a "principle which is not natural." His nonnatural principle is confusing because it is both immanent and transcendent to nature at the same time. The principle is a "self-distinguishing consciousness" that is both beyond and within nature. He toyed with referring to it as "supernatural" but thought this would be "misleading" because it only has a place "*within* nature." Despite his expressed intention as a moral philosopher to avoid "theological language," about which he was, unlike Sidgwick, unsuccessful, the self-consciousness necessary for ethical agency was best described as "nature as it is in God"; Green, 60–62. This self-consciousness reflects the influence of Kant's metaphysics on Green. It provides the acting person unity over time, allows them to differentiate themselves from the objects around them, and renders judgment possible. Green wrote, "If there is such a thing as a connected experience of related objects, there must be operative in consciousness a unifying principle, which not only presents related objects to itself, but at once renders them objects and unites them in relation to each other by this act of presentation; and which is single throughout the experience"; Green, 37. Green referred to this as "the spiritual principle in knowledge and nature" and built his ethics upon it. Sidgwick found such metaphysical speculation irrelevant for ethics. For Green, it was necessary because this subject possessed capacities capable of being realized over time.

119. Green, 435; Brink, "Introduction," lx.

120. Schneewind, *Sidgwick's Ethics*, 402.

121. Schultz, *Henry Sidgwick*, 346.
122. Brink, "Introduction," cv n.72.
123. Brink, xcix. On these questions, Brink finds that Green "compares favourably with Sidgwick": (1) Whether pleasure or self-realization "provide a better measure of what makes a life go well?" (2) "Which standard has better resources to explain why one has reason to pursue one's own good, so conceived?" (3) Which of them "provides a better account of the moral bonds among associates?" (4) Which attends better to a concern "for the good of others?" See Brink, "Introduction," civ.
124. Sidgwick and Sidgwick, *Henry Sidgwick*, 394.
125. Williams, "Point of View," 291.
126. Schultz, *Henry Sidgwick*, 493.
127. Schultz, 520.
128. Schultz, 317.
129. Schultz, 654.
130. Schultz, 668.
131. Sidgwick and Sidgwick, *Henry Sidgwick*, 307.
132. Sidgwick, *Principles of Political Economy*, 24, 67, 157.
133. Sidgwick, 582.
134. Sidgwick, 583.
135. Sidgwick, *Methods of Ethics*, 4.
136. Schultz, *Henry Sidgwick*, 673.
137. Schultz, 636.
138. Schultz, 752n94.
139. Sidgwick, *Practical Ethics*, 57.
140. Sidgwick, 58.
141. Schultz, *Henry Sidgwick*, 457.

2

RAWLS AND ANSCOMBE,
SIDGWICKIAN DISSENTERS

By turning ethics into a modern academic discipline with a distinct domain and method overseen by professionals, Henry Sidgwick changed what it meant to teach and learn ethics. Whether this shift is resisted, adopted, or adapted, it is now built into studying and learning ethics. This chapter begins with two sections comparing two influential English-speaking approaches to ethics, those of John Rawls and G. E. M. Anscombe. For different reasons, both became central for learning and teaching ethics, and both were indebted to Sidgwick. Rawls affirms Sidgwick's methods, and he regularly cites it in his teaching and publications as signaling a momentous and lasting shift. In her "Modern Moral Philosophy" Anscombe identifies it as momentous, but for a different reason. Sidgwick reconceived the philosophy of action that led to "consequentialism." His work had dire consequences for modern moral philosophy. Rawls affirms the "modern" in this expression; Anscombe rejects it. Rawls looks forward, seeing the Reformation and the marginalization of Medieval moral theology as a decisive gain for modern moral philosophy that provides the conditions for Sidgwick's scientific method. Anscombe looks backward to Aristotle and Aquinas for an alternative understanding of human action that counters Sidgwick.

The first section of this chapter, "Sidgwick and Modern Moral Philosophy," examines their different evaluations of the changes Sidgwick brought to the discipline of ethics and why they differ in their evaluation of the term "modern." Readers should not be misled by Anscombe's polemic in "Modern Moral Philosophy."[1] She, like Rawls, is a modern philosopher. She affirms analytic philosophy, which "is more characterized by styles of argument and investigation than by doctrinal content." Because it lacks doctrinal content, it can readily be used by Catholic thinkers. She states, "It ought not surprise anyone that a seriously believing Catholic Christian should also be

55

an analytic philosopher."[2] Her critique of "modern" has a focused target: Sidgwick's philosophy of human action. Rawls does not object to Sidgwick on this ground and finds his methodical precision an advance, but he explicitly dissents to the utilitarian content of Sidgwick's approach. His work, from *A Theory of Justice* to *Political Liberalism*, supplements Sidgwick's methods, first with Kantian constructivism and then with political constructivism.

The chapter's second section, "Countering Sidgwick's Ethics," shows how both Anscombe and Rawls offer alternatives to Sidgwick. Because Anscombe makes room for an ethic of infusing virtue more so than Rawls, her work is carried over in the chapters that follow in ways than Rawls's is not. The final two sections—"The Right and the Good" and "Moral Constructivism: Between Theory of Justice and Political Liberalism"—seek to offer a charitable interpretation of Rawls's revision of Sidgwick's ethics and also point out its limitations. Unlike Anscombe, Rawls continued to work with Sidgwick's differentiation and prioritizing of right and good. What distinguished him from Sidgwick is the addition of a method that he referred to as "moral constructivism." He later shifted it to "political constructivism," but the basic features remained.

Although Rawls and Anscombe differed in their evaluation of Sidgwick's approach to ethics, their approaches share a surprising overlap. Perhaps this is less surprising than it should be. They were both at Oxford in the early 1950s. Both disagreed strongly with Sidgwick's utilitarianism and were concerned about the hold it had on modern ethics. Both were influenced by Wittgenstein, Rawls through his work with Norman Malcolm, first at Princeton in his undergraduate years and then during his first teaching position at Cornell University from 1953 to 1959, after he returned from his Fulbright Fellowship in Oxford. While at Cornell, he taught Christian ethics, among other topics. Anscombe was Wittgenstein's student, translator, and literary executor. Friedrich Waismann, Wittgenstein's student, was Anscombe's doctoral supervisor.[3] Both Rawls and Anscombe were fundamentally concerned with the virtue of justice and the forms of life necessary to sustain it. Both had a central place for the virtue of faith, but the objects of their faith differed considerably. Both had youthful conversions to Christianity; Anscombe's stuck, Rawls's did not.

I know of no evidence that Rawls and Anscombe met in person, but if they had it would not be surprising. Rawls had a Fulbright Fellowship in Oxford from 1952 to 1953, studying philosophy, especially the work of R. M. Hare.[4] Anscombe had been given a research fellowship at Somerville College, Oxford, in 1946; was made an official teaching fellow in 1964; and did not leave Oxford for Cambridge until 1970, receiving a chair in philosophy.[5]

Anscombe was lecturing at Oxford on the *Philosophical Investigations* during Rawls's fellowship.[6] She led her protest against Truman in 1956 after Rawls left Oxford, but he alludes to it in his published work. In a famous radio address on the BBC in 1957, she challenged Oxford Moral Philosophy, including the philosophers with whom Rawls had studied during his Fulbright, such as Hare. Rawls also challenged Hare's work, as is shown below, and he sides with Peter Geach (Anscombe's husband) against Hare, but he makes no reference to her controversial radio address. Anscombe accused the Oxford moral philosophers Hare and P. H. Nowell-Smith of furthering the already moral corruption of youth through a "moral earnestness" that permitted evil actions if they furthered good future outcomes, relating this to the "massacre of the Japanese" in World War II.[7] Rawls fought the Japanese in World War II. He refers to Anscombe's argument in *Laws of Peoples*, and he expresses some sympathy for it, but he finally sides with Walzer's "supreme emergency."[8] Anscombe and Rawls reacted against the so-called naturalistic fallacy that G. E. Moore set forth and claimed to have found in Sidgwick. Anscombe did so in a 1958 essay, "On Brute Facts." Rawls cites her essay favorably in his *Theory of Justice*, appealing to her distinction between brute facts and institutional facts to support justice as fairness.

Anscombe does not fit easily within political or cultural types. She strongly objected to World War II because the British were fighting it unjustly. In 1956, while only holding a research fellowship at Oxford that afforded her few faculty protections, she spoke out against Oxford awarding Harry Truman an honorary degree and led the opposition to doing it during the faculty's vote. She favorably cited the controversial economist Joan Robinson (F. D. Maurice's great-granddaughter), who had defended the cultural revolution in China. She was close friends with the atheist Philippa Foot, who stated that she owed "everything to her," despite her "Catholic intransigence."[9]

Eighty-seven years after Sidgwick was elected to the Knightbridge Chair at Cambridge, Anscombe was elected professor of philosophy at that same institution. Bernard Williams then held the Knightbridge Chair, its name having changed yet again, shortened to "Philosophy." In 1972, two years after her appointment, Williams and Anscombe had a public disagreement over her controversial essay "Contraception and Chastity," which had been published in *The Human World*. Anscombe defended the Catholic Church's teaching on contraception, going so far as to argue that contraception invalidated marriage, rendering it little more than concubinage; Williams rejected her argument. It should also be noted that in a 2002 interview, right before his death, Williams was asked, "Which of your teachers and contemporaries most influenced you?" His response was Gilbert Ryle, David Pears, and Elizabeth Anscombe. She taught him "that being clever wasn't enough" and "conveyed a strong sense of the seriousness of the subject." He demurred that she had not influenced him in "other ways!"[10]

Rawls is not easily categorized either. His concept of "justice as fairness" was first presented as a moral system but later shifted to a political philosophy. Although primarily a political philosopher, he regularly taught and trained leading moral philosophers at Harvard. His relationship with faith and its implications for his political and moral philosophy continue to be debated. Some see his earlier theological convictions as still evident in his later work; others think they make little to no difference, and are not even worth mentioning. Some argue that democratic socialism is the logical consequence of his theory of justice; others interpret him as a conventional thinker, affirming the status quo. Friedrich Hayek stated that he and Rawls "had no basic quarrel."[11] Although Rawls joined the Mont Pèlerin Society in 1968 at Milton Friedman's invitation, he let his "membership lapse" when *A Theory of Justice* was published in 1971.[12] Katrina Forrester notes that his redistribution principle was more Keynesian than neoliberal. In 1984 Rawls began to lecture on Marx. Edmundson claims that democratic socialism best fits his justice as fairness.[13]

Their inability to be categorized, their common shared influences, and the significant influence that they both had on ethics make a comparison between Rawls and Anscombe fruitful for any adequate consideration of how to teach and learn ethics post-Sidgwick—but especially important are their very different takes on what Sidgwick accomplished. For Rawls, Sidgwick's *Methods* makes significant ethical advances; for Anscombe, it misleads and provides theoretical and "respectable" cover for an emerging murderous society that has no qualms about directly intending to kill the innocent. In what follows, these initial comparisons are further elaborated in examining how their work relates to Sidgwick's methods and modern moral philosophy and how they counter Sidgwick's approach.

SIDGWICK AND MODERN MORAL PHILOSOPHY

John Rawls may be one of the most influential philosophers in the English-speaking world of the twentieth century, perhaps behind Ludwig Wittgenstein (if such comparisons make any sense), who influenced both him and Anscombe. Although best known for his political and social philosophy, he regularly taught philosophical ethics, allowed those lectures to be published, trained many of the leading philosophical ethicists working today, and throughout his political philosophy acknowledged that it always contained a moral conception. Forrester's historical narrative on the "remaking of political philosophy" identifies the sea change that Rawls, at the age of fifty, created with his 1971 book *A Theory of Justice*. She writes, "It was widely acclaimed as the most important work of philosophy since Henry Sidgwick's *The Method of Ethics* of 1871."[14] The noted Kantian scholar Allen Wood states, "The study of ethics in the analytic tradition owes a great deal to Rawls and his followers. In some respects, it could even be called chiefly their product."[15] He credits Rawls and his students with reviving the study away from expressivism and utilitarianism. He disagrees with their "Kantian constructivism," and develops a version of Kantian ethics more faithful to Kant, yet Wood acknowledges that neither Rawls nor his students aimed to be faithful interpreters of Kant. They revived ethics from its moribund state. Rawls's vast influence on contemporary philosophical ethics cannot be denied; it was an influence that built on Sidgwick's *Methods* a century after its publication.

Rawls wrote the foreword to the 1981 publication of Sidgwick's *Methods*, claiming it was "the first truly academic work in moral philosophy." For Rawls, Sidgwick set the discipline of ethics on a promising trajectory. For three decades at Harvard, he began his course on philosophical ethics with Sidgwick's *Methods*. It framed his teaching. Barbara Herman claims that his lecture course "had a profound influence on the approach to philosophical ethics of many generations of students, and through them, on the way the subject is now understood."[16] Rawls distributed his ethics notes each year, and Herman, with Rawls's approval, collected, edited, and published them. Rawls also regularly lectured on Sidgwick in his "Political Philosophy" course. Samuel Freeman, another Rawls student, edited and published those lectures. He acknowledged Sidgwick's influence. Rawls, he stated, "regarded Sidgwick's comparative method in *The Methods of Ethics* as providing a pattern for moral philosophy to emulate."[17]

In 1980, nine years after the publication of his influential *A Theory of Justice* and thirteen years before his revisions of his explanation of justice as fairness in *Political Liberalism*, Rawls gave the John Dewey Lectures at Columbia University on "Kantian Constructivism in Moral Theory." The term "moral theory," he stated, refers to Sidgwick's achievement, which brought "moral theory" into "moral philosophy." As was noted in the previous chapter, Sidgwick explicitly affirmed the primacy of theory against Aristotle in the preface to *Methods*, and Rawls understands this as an advance in ethical knowledge. His third lecture "looked back" to Sidgwick's *Methods* and began by paying homage to *The Methods of Ethics*, calling it "the outstanding achievement of modern moral theory." What did Sidgwick accomplish? He provided the first "systematic and comparative study of moral conceptions, starting with those which historically and by current estimation seem to be the most important," and thus brought a rigorous attention to "moral theory" into moral philosophy that had previously been lacking. Through Sidgwick's "influence" on Moore, his systematic approach subsequently "defined much of the framework of subsequent moral philosophy."[18] Sidgwick also advanced the method of reflective equilibrium that was central to Rawls's own method.[19] Sidgwick was decisive in the transition from ancient or classical to modern moral philosophy.

Rawls never abandoned the central role that Sidgwick's *Methods* had for his own work. He began his lectures on moral philosophy by quoting Sidgwick's distinction between "modern moral philosophy" and "classical moral philosophy" from book I of *Methods*, based on the distinction between the good and right: "The chief characteristics of ancient ethical controversy as distinguished from modern may be traced to the employment of a generic notion [of good] instead of a specific one [such as rightness] in expressing the common moral judgments on actions" (the brackets are Rawls's).[20] Modern moral philosophy emphasizes what is right to do, whereas the classical tradition emphasized the "ideal good" as "attractive . . . rather than as a dictate, or an imperative of reason."[21] Rawls affirms this distinction and also privileges right over the good, something he consistently did throughout his work. Modern moral philosophy, per Sidgwick, is also "'quasi-jural,'" and such a "legalistic conception" differs from the classical—primarily Greek—position.[22] The advance of modern moral philosophy over classical ethics, then, is twofold. First, it privileges the right over the good; and second, it is jural, concerned with rights and obligations.

Although he sides with Sidgwick in setting forth the advance of modern moral philosophy over its premodern alternatives, Rawls is more sympathetic to Greek ethics than to Medieval moral theology. This represents a change from his undergraduate thesis on theological ethics, in which both were subject to criticism, Plato and Aristotle more so than moral theology. The young, theological Rawls wrote, "I do not believe that the Greek tradition mixes very well with Christianity, and the sooner we stop kowtowing to Plato and Aristotle the better. An ounce of the Bible is worth a pound (possibly a ton) of Aristotle." In his later work, Aristotle holds more promise. He draws on the "Aristotelian principle" that "participating in the life of a well-ordered society is a great good" throughout *Theory of Justice*.[23] Yet Aristotle offers little more than that. In *Theory of Justice*, he agrees with Sidgwick that an ethics of perfection, like Aristotle's, is too imprecise to guide human action to do what is right. In the lectures, he agrees with Sidgwick that Aristotle's ethics is insufficiently modern. Ancient ethics confronted the problem of how to generate the highest moral good independent of Greek civil religion. Aristotle attempted to do this for "individuals" who engage in "the exercise of free, disciplined reason alone," but premodern moral thought went astray in the Middle Ages. Medieval moral thought lost this free exercise of reason. It took the Reformation, the rise of the modern state, and the development of science to make modern moral philosophy possible.[24]

Rawls affirms the form of Sidgwick's ethics but not its content. One consequence was an unequivocal commitment to modern moral philosophy but not to utilitarianism. Sidgwick's weakness resided in this interpretation of Kant, and Rawls will develop, with qualification, a Kantian alternative to Sidgwick that at one point he referred to as "Kantian moral constructivism." Freeman argues that this was a transition in Rawls's philosophy that he later left behind once he moved from moral to political constructivism.[25] His student Christine Korsgaard remains committed to Kantian moral constructivism. As Wood notes, it is one of the most influential developments of Kant's ethics in the modern era.

The kind of acclaim that Forrester gives to Rawls's 1971 publication, Donald Davidson also gives to Anscombe's 1957 *Intention*, referring to it as "the most important treatment of action since Aristotle." Nonetheless, her criticism of modern moral philosophy does not endear her to modern moral philosophers. For Anscombe, Sidgwick's definition of ethics and theory of human action are mistaken. She finds Sidgwick's influence on modern moral philosophy corrupting, and for this reason it should be "laid aside" until philosophers obtain a better "philosophy of psychology."[26] When she turned her attention to modern moral philosophy in the 1950s, she did not see the progress that Rawls did. She saw nonsense, and Sidgwick's ethics were the source of that nonsense because of his faulty psychology, which led to an impoverished theory of action and intention.

In her 1958 essay "Modern Moral Philosophy," Anscombe claims that a "startling change" occurred in ethics from J. S. Mill (1806–73) to G. E. Moore (1873–1958), due to Sidgwick's reshaping of the discipline. The difference is the extent to which actions such as "murder or theft" can be "calculated" based on their "consequences." Anscombe did not find Mill's utilitarianism compelling, referring to it as "stupid," because no single "principle of utility" exists under which actions can be placed.[27] However, she argues, Mill did not determine the morality of actions like murder or theft based on their consequences. What changed between Mill and Moore was Sidgwick's delineation of his understanding of human action.[28] He defines intention as "foreseen consequences of one's voluntary action."[29]

Anscombe coins the term "consequentialism" and is known for her work on intention, but the extent to which she challenged the academic discipline of ethics can be missed or misunderstood. She is no divine command theorist; nor does she reject modern philosophy. She unapologetically takes up the analytic approach from Frege and Wittgenstein and was central to its promulgation. Nor does she reject an ethics of obligation for something called a virtue ethic. What she opposes is identifying some special domain of action called "moral" and then finding its source in a faulty philosophy of mind that sets forth mental states like an "intention" as that which distinguishes moral from nonmoral acts. Intention as "foreseen consequences" cannot exist outside the mind because consequences that are foreseen are nonexistent. Anscombe refuses to accept the boundary Sidgwick has drawn around ethics; it is why she rejects the term "moral" when it is used adjectivally to qualify "obligation" or "duty." She challenges the idea that the terms "moral" obligation or "moral" duty do any work in modern debates, suggesting that they be excised from our vocabulary until we arrive at an "adequate philosophy of psychology."[30]

An "adequate philosophy of psychology" refers to one of Anscombe's main philosophical interests. Like her mentor Wittgenstein, she found the Cartesian philosophy of mind deeply misleading. In her 1961 essay "War and Murder," one that Rawls cites favorably, she attributes mistaken understandings of intention to Sidgwick and Descartes. Anscombe learned from Wittgenstein that Descartes's philosophy of mind generated unnecessary problems that philosophers then attempted to resolve, and by doing so they obfuscated ordinary human action. The point of philosophy was not to resolve illusory problems but to recognize the nonsense in them so that they would no longer present obstacles to seeing what was before us.

Nonsense is not the same as falsity. Since the seventeenth century when Cartesian psychology made intention "an interior act of the mind which could be produced at will," the principle of double effect has been abused, exacerbating much nonsense.[31] A Cartesian philosophy of psychology led to a causalist theory of action, whereby intention as an inner, mental state became the cause of voluntary actions, providing them with their "moral" aspect. The acting person has an intention that is more or less private, which then issues forth in action. Because it is private, it is not necessarily exhibited in the action itself. In this sense, it gives the agent too much authority to describe the performed action, an authority that can in its consequences either diminish or intensify moral responsibility.

Anscombe coined the term "consequentialism," but she did not use it in terms of the well-known typology of moral theories, such as deontology–virtue–consequentialism, the last of which usually encompasses teleological and utilitarian theories. For instance, she critiques W. D. Ross's pluralistic deontology for being consequentialist. Some overlap exists between her use of consequentialism and the textbook chart of ethical theories, but she means something more. The foreseen consequences of an action become the matter of a putatively interiorized mental intention that can *either* excuse responsibility for what is done *or* make any good action performed morally irresponsible. The example of Harry Truman illustrates the former. He sets in motion the bombing of Hiroshima and Nagasaki by targeting civilian populations. The justification for the action is based on the foreseen consequence that he is saving one million American soldiers who otherwise would have died in an invasion. The action is no longer directly killing the innocent, because his "intention" is saving life; and given that it is a private mental state, who are we to judge it otherwise? If he says that is what he is doing, then that is his intention, and that is the morally relevant consideration. In this case, the foreseen consequence excuses a morally reprehensible action. It diminishes Truman's responsibility for the deaths of innocent civilians.

We can also imagine the possibility in which intention as foreseen consequence demands too much responsibility. Anscombe explains this in a disagreement with Philippa Foot in her 1967 essay, "Who Is Wronged? Philippa Foot on Double Effect: One Point." Foot generated this quandary: A patient needs a "massive dose" of medicine to save his life. A physician begins to administer it but is interrupted by the appearance of five new patients, each of whom only need one-fifth of that dose to be restored to health. Surely, it is better, she argues, to let the one patient die to save the others. Anscombe has little time for such quandaries, because they often assume that intention is little more than foreseen consequences, and little was present to stop them from extending ad infinitum. One becomes responsible not only for one's actions but also for every possible future consequence. Rather than understanding a physician's obligation to treat the single patient before them, potential foreseen consequences can be hypothesized without limit. For example, what happens if once the physician begins to administer one-fifth of the dose to five patients, then ten patients arrive, each of whom could be restored with one-tenth of the medicine, and then twenty with one-twentieth, thirty with one-thirtieth, and so on. Such quandaries place such high demand on ethical responsibility that at any time you administer the dose you have potentially wronged others through possible foreseen consequences that you omitted acting upon. Because the *moral* aspect of an act is found in those foreseen consequences, a good action could seldom, if ever, be identified.

For Anscombe, if the physician gives the single patient before her the full dose, she has wronged no one. If she gives five doses to the others, she has wronged no one. She has not directly intended to kill one at the expense of five or five at the expense of one, and setting forth the quandary this way overlooks the importance of intention by substituting foreseen consequences for it. She writes, "When I do action *A* for reasons *R*, it is not necessary or even usual for me to have any special reason for doing-action-*A*-rather-than-action-*B*, which may also be possible."[32] If neither *A* nor *B* is illicit, then doing either is permitted, and doing *A* for reason *R* does not make the agent responsible for omitting *B*.

The difficulty with such quandaries is what consequentialism can justify. If we say surely it is better to let one die rather than five, then on what basis do we say as much? And why would we not also be justified in saving the medicine for people in future generations who might need it by letting the five die now? If we do not, are we responsible for every future possibility? Would every action be judged by possible foreseen consequences such that no action could ever be good or right? Anscombe is not denying that there are tragic instances in which doing one good action will prevent someone from doing a different good action. Life raises unpalatable options. What she denies is that we can muddle through by thinking of intention solely as foreseen consequences and then calculate future possible results to determine what is the moral course of action now.

Anscombe offers another example of this in a discussion of someone harboring fugitives. Imagine that we live during the time of the Fugitive Slave Act in the United States, when it was required by law to turn slaves in, even in free states, to the slave patrols because they were the property of another. For Anscombe, it is good to tell the truth and it is bad to "betray the unjustly persecuted fugitive," but she thinks that in this situation it is "sufficiently obvious" that the latter is worse so one should lie and protect the fugitive. She writes, "To betray the fugitive, we will suppose, is a gravely wicked thing to do. Telling the pursuers he is there *is* betraying him. So in this case telling the truth is a wicked act—more than telling the lie that he is not there." She addresses an obvious objection: "Aren't we going by consequences?" And she answers no, explaining herself by adding a third nefarious person who knows you are in this tragic situation. This person attempts to extort a different lie from you. Lie for the purposes of X, or he will turn in the fugitive. In this case, if you do not lie, are you betraying the fugitive? Anscombe thinks not. She writes, "If you are a consequentialist you will hold that you are responsible for all the consequences of your acts and omissions and therefore that you are responsible for the capture of the fugitive if he was caught because you refused to tell the lie demanded by the person who betrayed him—just as much as if you betrayed him."[33] In this case, you did not intend the betrayal of the fugitive in the same way that you would have in the other because you are not responsible for the nefarious person's betrayal.

Substituting foreseen consequences and private, mental causation for intentional action has contradictory results for ethical action. On one hand, it so limits responsibility that nearly any action can be justified: "I was not killing the innocent; my intention was to save others." On the other hand, it so expands responsibility that no action could be morally justified: "I thought I was saving the person before me, but I was harming countless others." Some quandary can always be presented that attributes an omission to the act done, jeopardizing its goodness or rightness. In essence, there would be no "stopping modals." One could always say "but what about . . ." or "what about a possible world in which . . ." and thus nothing would be absolutely prohibited—not even murder. As Roger Teichmann recognized, this means that you can always be "at fault for not preventing something."[34]

Although Descartes's philosophy of mind provided the seeds for the problems associated with intention in modern moral philosophy, Sidgwick's ethics brought it to fruition. Like Rawls, she rejects his utilitarianism, but her critique of consequentialism is something more than that. Sidgwick loses an adequate understanding of a human action. What ought to be no longer finds a home in what is. Ethics does not exist in the world that actually is.

COUNTERING SIDGWICK'S ETHICS

In her essay "On Brute Facts," published the same year as "Modern Moral Philosophy," Anscombe undoes an element in Sidgwick's ethics that Moore identified as an essential advance. Recall that for Sidgwick, if ethics is to be an independent discipline, it takes as its primary concern "what ought to be" and leaves "what is" to other disciplines. This permits a special domain for the concept "moral." Anscombe uses an everyday example of being supplied with potatoes by a grocer to question if this distinction means anything. If not, it would be another example of philosophical nonsense.

If a grocer supplies you with potatoes, is it appropriate for the customer to say, "You must not jump from an 'is'—as, that it really is the case that I asked for the potatoes and that you delivered them and send me a bill—to an 'owes.'"[35] Of course, "preventing factors" could emerge that qualifies the "is"; the exchange occurs in the context of a film rather than the ordinary institution of buying and selling; but the problem with identifying preventing factors is that they can be multiplied without limit. It adds little to our concept of obligation if we add to the basic exchange every conceivable preventing factor so that we qualify the relationship with a proposition, such as "you supplied me potatoes and I owe you for them, unless we were acting in a play or x or y or z." None of these preventing factors changes the fact that, within the institutional fact of buying and selling, having been supplied with potatoes by a grocer for potatoes requested by the customer, the customer owes the grocer. Nor is there any reason to state all the possible preventing factors to identify what counts as the *moral* obligation in this context. As Anscombe puts it, "Every description presupposes a context of normal procedure, but this context is not even implicitly described by the description."[36] The normal context within which the action occurs is an "institutional fact." It limits possible preventing factors. Rawls draws on Anscombe's institutional fact early in *A Theory of Justice* to explain a key element in his understanding of justice as fairness, the "basic structure of society."[37]

Anscombe's "On Brute Facts" concerns obligations. Obligation is an essential concept in her ethics that requires it first be understood within a language game, such as a customer ordering potatoes from a grocer. Once it is understood, then, as Anscombe states, both the delivery of the potatoes and the obligation to pay are "brute facts." The obligation arises from participation in this particular language game, but that does not lessen its brute facticity. To ask what about the exchange makes it a *moral* obligation adds nothing to what makes it an obligation in the first place. Fulfilling the obligation constitutes a practical truth founded upon the practical knowledge entailed in selling and buying groceries. Intention is practical knowledge in that the agent knows what they are doing without observation. Someone intentionally buying groceries does not need to observe themselves doing so in order to know that they are buying groceries.

The performance of such practical knowledge results in practical truth. Something is brought about that did not previously exist. Anscombe thought that Aristotle's practical knowledge and practical truth had been misunderstood and neglected in contemporary philosophy because of its preoccupation with contemplative or theoretical truth. The latter is primarily concerned with reasoning to truth, whereas practical reasoning ends in action. Practical knowledge, as Anscombe puts it, is "the cause of what it understands," while theoretical knowledge attends to objects that can be known.[38] Both theory and practice are involved in reasoning, but they take different forms. Practical reasoning assumes a means–end ordering that takes the form of desire or wanting something, whereas theoretical reasoning takes the form of justification. Anscombe demonstrated this distinction by jumping on a table during a lecture.[39] Practical reasoning addresses the question "Why?" Why are you jumping on a table? Her answer: to demonstrate the difference between practical and theoretical knowledge. In her desire to explain practical knowledge, she effectuated the truth of jumping on the table. She was the cause of what is known and did not need to observe it to know that she did it. Jumping on the table is not the only way to achieve this end; the end does not mandate the means. Theoretical reasoning would show that she was successful because she was now standing on the table. It would be observational.[40]

Rawls also rejected the naturalistic fallacy, although he is much less obvious about it than Anscombe and did not offer as precise an account of practical reasoning and practical truth as did Anscombe. P. MacKenzie Bok sees Rawls working against Moore, and by implication Sidgwick, by opposing the naturalistic fallacy. The early Rawls "developed a 'naturalistic' view of ethics" to "refute the emotivist or noncognitivist theories of A. J. Ayer, R. M. Hare, and C. L. Stevenson."[41] Bok refers to Rawls's philosophy as a "liberal naturalism" that attempted to ground ethics in nature without any appeals to science, theology, or metaphysics.[42] To set forth this naturalistic ethic, Rawls turned to Wittgenstein's language games. Bok writes, "For Rawls and others, Ludwig Wittgenstein's later arguments offered a key resource for normative naturalism that skirted metaphysics. Wittgenstein argued that concepts could only be understood inductively, through their use in a given frame."[43] Forrester makes a similar argument. Because of Wittgenstein's influence during his time at Cornell working with Malcolm as well as his time at Oxford, Rawls "joined a transatlantic community of ethical theorists, which included Richard Brandt, Roderick Firth, William Frankena, Stephen Toulmin, and Kurt Baier, in their search for a naturalistic, objective foundation for ethics that took Wittgenstein as inspiration." According to Forrester, Rawls read Anscombe and Foot and was influenced by their use of "Wittgenstein's naturalistic understanding of the person" situated within "the conventions of human life." Rawls already held to an "interpersonal ethic" grounded in a Hegelian understanding of "recognition." "Soon," she writes, "he used Wittgenstein to explain that morality was social, defined by its use—there in the world to be discovered not chosen."[44] Given Rawls's explicit avowal of a Kantian moral constructivism, Forrester's claim here would seem, at first blush, to misinterpret his work. Yet, as we shall see, it is, like most things Rawlsian, complex. His moral constructivism rejects moral facts, but his justice as fairness assumes a thin theory of goodness that cannot be chosen because it is necessary for the purpose of rational choice in the original position.

Bok's and Forrester's intriguing interpretation finds continuities between the theological interests of the early Rawls and his later moral and political philosophy. Bok states that "his writings on Christian ethics and on philosophical metaethics intertwine in one continuous moral project. That project centered on seeing persons as embedded in a community of universal mutual recognition."[45] William Edmundson thinks that Rawls reacts against his earlier theological convictions more strongly than Bok and Forrester do. Rawls's worry that justice as fairness might be "religious, as well as moral and philosophical in the comprehensive sense" led him to make significant revisions to justice as fairness from *A Theory of Justice* to *Political Liberalism*. Does Rawls have a continuous project from his early theological considerations that extends through his teaching Christian ethics in the 1950s and into his later political philosophy, or does his worry that a residual comprehensive religious or moral framework lingers in his work prompt the revisions in *Political Liberalism*? Evidence exists for both interpretations, so judging between them is complicated. His thin theory of goodness in *A Theory of Justice* suggests a nonmetaphysical naturalism, but the moral constructivism that he affirms between it and *Political Liberalism* suggests otherwise.

THE RIGHT AND THE GOOD

Rawls prioritizes the right over the good. Agreeing with Sidgwick, he finds this prioritization to be an advance that modern moral philosophy makes over ancient and Medieval moral philosophy and theology. As we shall see in the work of Peter Geach, distinguishing right from good is something that did not happen before modern developments in ethics. If they cannot be distinguished, one could not be privileged over the other. Rawls, like Sidgwick, distinguishes and prioritizes, but he never dismisses the importance of goodness. Good and right are the "two main concepts of ethics," and the question of "ethical theory" depends upon their relation.[46] The good functions both negatively and positively in Rawls. Negatively, it illumines the problems present in teleological theories that hold diverse accounts of the good but share the subordination of the right to it by first establishing the good and then determining the right as what maximizes it. He identifies four such theories. Perfectionism sets forth the good as human excellence, eudaimonism as happiness, hedonism as pleasure, and utilitarianism as satisfaction of rational desire.[47] Because justice as fairness is nonteleological, he rejects each of these accounts of the good, but he spends less energy discussing or critiquing the first three than he does utilitarianism. Although he refers to an "Aristotelian principle," he makes little effort to lay out exegetically, and then counter, an ancient or Medieval ethics of perfection or excellence (*eudaimonia*). They have been superseded. They still pose a risk to a proper political order, but it is the utilitarian good as satisfaction of rational desire that Rawls works most ardently against.

Positively, justice as fairness requires a "thin theory" of goodness for the sake of the principles that construct the basic structure of society. Rawls acknowledges that his two principles assume a minimal theory of goodness. As his definitions of the two principles given here show, they assume accounts of goodness:

First Principle:
Each person is to have an equal right to the most extensive total system of equal basic liberties compatible with a similar system of
liberty for all.
Second Principle:
Social and economic inequalities are to be arranged so that they are
both:
(a) To the greatest benefit of the least advantaged, consistent
with the just saving principle, and
(b) Attached to offices and positions open to all under conditions of fair equality of opportunity.[48]

These two principles are unintelligible without ethical terms such as "rights, liberties, equality, and opportunities." They are primary goods, to which Rawls adds "income and wealth," and later "self-respect," grounded in the "moral worth" of persons.[49] If persons in the original position have no desire for these goods, then their choices could not be rational. These goods are not chosen but make possible rational choices that prioritize right. This thin theory of goodness cannot take precedence over the right, but it can be "congruent" with it.[50]

Along with prompting persons in the original position to make rational choices with respect to the first principle, the thin theory of goodness is also necessary so that the "least advantaged" who are to benefit can be identified. If Rawls has a naturalistic ethics, it is found in these primary goods; but they are thin. He avoids any account of human flourishing or perfection that the basic structure of society should seek to serve. Such thick notions of goodness have a place for individuals in their life plans or for associations within the liberal state but not in the basic structure itself.

Rawls's thickest notion of the good is the "comprehensive account" needed for establishing "the moral worth of persons." It is his "third main concept of ethics," along with the right and the good.[51] Moral worth is not a matter of peoples' roles nor their performance of such roles, but of "broadly based properties" that would be desirable in any role performed.[52] These broadly based properties include the rationality necessary to make proper choices in the original position based on the thin theory of the good. In an easily missed but intriguing footnote, Rawls sides with Peter Geach against R. M. Hare on their midcentury public disagreement over good and evil. Conversations from his Oxford days remained with him.

Rawls does not offer a lengthy analysis or evaluation of the disagreement between Geach and Hare. His argument is subtle. He raises a possible objection to moral worth based on rational properties: "Some philosophers have thought that since a person qua person has no definite role or function, and it is not to be treated as an instrument or object, a definition along the lines of goodness as rationality must fail."[53] Rawls develops "goodness as rationality" much earlier in *A Theory of Justice*, acknowledges that he "borrowed" his understanding of it from Geach, refers to it as a "descriptive theory," and states, "It is helpful to think of the sense of 'good' as being analogous to that of a function sign."[54] Geach refers to the good as a function. Now, Rawls notes that "some philosophers" reject this definition. Who are these philosophers? He only cites Hare and refers to his April 1957 essay "Geach on Good and Evil." Hare's essay responds to Geach's "Good and Evil," published in December 1956 in the journal *Analysis*, which accused the Oxford Moralists, especially W. D. Ross, of a moral theory that permitted judicial killing of the innocent. His criticism is not as strident as Anscombe's radio address a few months later in February 1957—"Does Oxford Moral Philosophy Corrupt the Youth?"—which also took aim at Hare, nor is it as hard-hitting as her "Modern Moral Philosophy," published the next year, which accuses Hare of permitting the judicial killing of the innocent. Yet before her criticisms of the Oxford moralists, Geach made his own. After publishing his essay, Geach invited Hare to respond. He did, and published the essay to which Rawls refers. Hare dismisses Geach's criticism.

Geach begins "Good and Evil" with a distinction between an attributive and predicative use of good, making an analogy from the use of red. The attributive "red book" and the predicative "this book is red" make sense. We can say "x is a book" and "x is red" because red can be used attributively and predicatively. We know red separately from a red book. However, good and bad cannot be so used; they can only be used attributively. To divide up "a good person" into "x is a person" and "x is good" misuses language. Geach writes, "There is no such thing as being just good or bad, there is only being a good or bad so-and-so."[55] If good were a nonnaturalistic property, as the Oxford moralists suggest, then it could be predicative and the division would make sense, but "nobody has ever given a coherent and understandable account of what it is for an attribute to be nonnatural." Good is a function that has "primarily descriptive force," as in a "good book."

For Geach, once we acknowledge that good is attributive with a descriptive force that assumes a function, then it cannot be used primarily for "commendation," as the Oxford moralists suggest, for then it would need to be predicative. A good x would be equivalent to "x is good because it is commended." The x matters little; its commendation does the work, but if we do not know what x is and whether it is good, it makes no sense to commend it. Take as an example (mine, not Geach's) that x is a good violinist. One must first know what a good violinist is before the statement makes sense. It makes no sense to say x is a violinist and x is good. Rather than conceiving goodness as commendatory or expressive of preferences, Geach locates the use of the term under "the *ratio* of 'want,' choose,' 'good,' and 'bad'"—"*quidquid appetitur, appetitur sub specie boni.*" Geach is explicitly thinking in concert with Aristotle and Aquinas, especially their understanding of practical reasoning that takes the form of desire. The good is what someone wants, often in specific contexts. If you seek to cut an apple and want a knife, then someone will choose a sharp knife. If he wanted to cut an apple and had the choice between a sharp or dull knife and chose the dull one, then his action would be irrational. To this point, Rawls would agree. If we are forming a just political society, then we must have a thin theory of goodness that will permit rational choices for the construction of that society. Geach thinks that he can move from a good knife to a good human being, and on this point Rawls objects because this would require something more like an ethics of perfection, which is a comprehensive moral framework. Geach recognizes that moving from a good knife to a good human being is not easily done, but it is the only way to make sense of our use of the term "good." If we are to say, "x is a good person," then we must be using the term attributively. The difficult but necessary step in moral philosophy is to venture forth with an account of what a "good person" is; and this the Oxford moralists, like Rawls, resist—not only Hare but also Ross. They do so by wrongly distinguishing between and then confusing right and good.

To elucidate this confusion, Geach turns to Ross's *The Right and the Good.* Between chapter 2 of that work, "What Makes Right Acts Right?" and chapter 3, "The Meaning of Good," Ross placed an appendix, "On Punishment." He lays out three prima facie rights that the state possesses to punish. The state has the right (1) to punish the guilty; (2) "in the last resort, of inflicting injury on any of its members when the public interest sufficiently demands"; and (3) to keep its promise to punish certain crimes. Based on these prima facie rights, Ross concludes that "there may be cases in which the prima facie duty of punishing the guilty, and even that of not punishing the innocent, may have to give way to that of promoting the public interest."[56] For Geach, Ross's distinction between right and good, as well as his understanding of good, mislead him, so that "*the* right act may be the judicial killing of the innocent."[57]

Ross confuses "morally good action" with intention and "*the* right act" with the object or state of affairs that the action produces. Like Sidgwick, this permits intention to be understood as foreseen consequences. Thus, if the state recognizes that the judicial execution of the innocent (the object or state of affairs brought about) is necessary for the sake of the "public interest," then the morally good action of intending the preservation of the public interest would issue in *the* right act of killing the innocent; but for Geach, the latter is nonsense. Geach puts it like this: "When Ross would say that there is a morally good action but not a right action, Aquinas would say that a good human intention had issued in what was, in fact, a bad action; and when Ross would say that there was a right act but not a morally good action, Aquinas would say that there was a bad human act performed in circumstances in which a similar act with a different intention would have been a good one."[58] Geach rejects Ross's distinctions. They bifurcate a human act into pieces that render it unintelligible. For Geach, like Aquinas, there is no distinction between right and good.

Hare is not impressed with Geach's argument. He defends good as commending, denies that it is descriptive, and discusses "functional words" only to dismiss them: "A word is a functional word if, in order to explain its meaning fully, we have to say what the object it refers to is *for*, or what it is supposed to do." This instrumentalizes the good, rendering it something other than moral. Geach's position works only for functional words, and therein resides its problem. The functional use of good "is normally an indication that the context is *not* a moral one" (with some exceptions, like "good example"); but "good man" or "good human action," as functional, is not moral.[59] Hare then chides Geach for failing to affirm the is/ought distinction and claims that Geach, like Plato and Aristotle, confuses them. They have not learned the lesson of Sidgwick and Moore. Hare quotes Aristotle's principle: "*Nature (sive Deus) nihil facit inane*" and thinks that this Aristotelian principle led to his justification of slavery and the subjugation of women.[60] In other words, function words lack morality because they turn human beings into instruments to be used based on their putative nature.

When it comes to understanding the meaning of good, Rawls sides with Geach, providing evidence for Bok's and Forrester's interpretation that his ethics is naturalistic. Yet his affirmation of Geach on the good remains within a distinction between right and good laid out by the Oxford moralists that Geach thought his argument required rejecting. Why does Rawls only go part way with Geach? Because he must have a thin theory of the good so that he can develop, as Bok puts it, "a normative naturalism that skirted metaphysics." He refuses the difficult work of addressing what the function of a good human being is. For Rawls, philosophy cannot and should not address this question; or, put better, political liberalism must not address this question, or it will propagate the "fact of oppression." Rawls's "normative naturalism" must be the thinnest possible account of what human nature is—a rational chooser seeking rights, liberties, equality, opportunities, income, and wealth. The thickest his normative naturalism gets is that this rational chooser has moral worth because of the broadly based properties that enable them to be rational choosers.

Perhaps we should not ask philosophy to tell us what a good human life is. Modern moral philosophy certainly forgets this question, or finds it too difficult, contentious, and politically fraught to raise. Yet is this thin concept of good sufficient? Is it what we mean when we utter statements like "Harriett Tubman was a good human being?" It does not seem wrong to view her as a "rational chooser seeking rights, liberties, equality, opportunities, income and wealth," but it also does not seem to get at what we intend to say. It seems too mediocre a description to explain her excellence in liberating the enslaved. It may be unfair to use Tubman as an example. After all, if Rawls's two principles had been in force, her work might not have been necessary. Yet could Rawls's principles make room for the prison abolitionists working today? Joshua Dubler and Vincent Lloyd argue that this movement requires "higher ideals of justice," more like what is found in Martin Luther King Jr.'s vision of the beloved community. Rawls discusses abolitionism, as is shown below, and he acknowledges that it puts questions to his moral philosophy. For Rawls, Christian abolitionism is a comprehensive ethics and thus is limited to a nonpublic realm. Its claims, he acknowledges, can be made publicly; but they need to be translated into public reasons. Perhaps this is the best we can do within the moral or political constructivism of political liberalism. But is it enough? Anscombe and Maurice offer something more: an ethics of perfection that makes better sense of an abolitionist ethics. It requires an infusion of virtue, a gift that brings about more than we can choose for ourselves.

MORAL CONSTRUCTIVISM: BETWEEN THE THEORY OF JUSTICE AND POLITICAL LIBERALISM

Forrester's claim that Rawls's naturalistic ethics is discovered and not chosen seems to falter on the "Kantian moral constructivism" that he affirmed in the decade after the publication of *A Theory of Justice*. Once again, he sets his affirmation of a Kantian moral theory within the context of Sidgwick's *Methods* and what it lacks, arguing that Kantian constructivism is the best ethical theory for justice as fairness. For Rawls, because it is a less familiar theory than Sidgwick's division of "utilitarianism, perfectionism, and intuitionism," Kantian constructivism is not widely understood, and this "impedes the advance of moral theory."[61]

Rawls refers to moral constructivism as a pure proceduralism that does not begin with moral facts or a "search for moral truth." He writes, "Kantian constructivism holds that moral objectivity is to be understood in terms of a suitably constructed social point of view that all can accept. Apart from the procedure of constructing the principles of justice, there are no moral facts."[62] If there are no moral facts or practical moral truths before the construction of the procedure, then how is Rawls's ethic naturalistic? "Kantian moral constructivism" is not nonnaturalistic, but it does not seem to look to anything in nature other than procedures for its ethical theory, and that would seem to make it something other than Kantian, since Kant's ethics was not a pure proceduralism. Allen Wood interprets the expression "'Kantian constructivism in ethics' as an oxymoron, whose interest ought to lie exclusively in its shock value." For Kant, the moral law does not result from a procedure (Wood is critical of Rawls's "categorical imperative procedure"), nor from any voluntary human agency. It is "a practically necessary command of practical reason, grounded ... absolutely, in the nature of things, independently of how any being should choose to look at the matter. It binds us not because we have willed it, but through the objective value or absolute worth of rational nature that grounds it."[63] Rawls's turn to Kantian moral constructivism post *A Theory of Justice* does not abandon his thin theory of goodness; he continues to refer to primary goods that allow for moral persons in the original position to be "agents of construction."[64] Yet it is hard to see how to square even this thin theory of goodness with a "pure" proceduralism. If the proceduralism assumes good that is intrinsic to nature, then ethics cannot be constructivist. If ethics is constructivist, then even the thin theory of goodness should be a matter of choice or the purity of the procedure would be in doubt.[65]

A naturalistic ethics is more difficult to reconcile with Rawls's constructivism, given his explicit rejection of naturalism as a justification for this ethical theory at the end of *A Theory of Justice*.[66] Yet his "thin theory of the good" absorbs a variety of positions that are not easily reconcilable when he suggests that it would find "wide agreement, with many variations" in diverse thinkers such as Aristotle, Aquinas, Kant, Sidgwick, F. H. Bradley, Josiah Royce, J. O. Urmson, and Philippa Foot.[67] Would that he told us more how these thinkers, several of whom explicitly rejected the work of the other, such as Bradley and Sidgwick, found agreement. The relation between his thin theory of good and moral constructivism through the 1970s and 1980s is confusing—perhaps because it was also developing. By the 1990s, Freeman was certainly correct. It shifted to political constructivism. Edmundson is likewise correct, and this shift signals his increasing attempt to ensure that justice as fairness excludes any comprehensive moral or religious doctrine, an exclusion that likewise makes it difficult to take Rawls at his word that democratic socialism may be the politics best suited for it. As I hope to show, socialism fits better with a moral or religious view that acknowledges the infused virtues than Rawls's framework permits. Rawls's thin theory of goodness bears strong similarities to *homo economicus*, who primarily seeks a negative liberty for the sake of opportunity for income and wealth.

The original purpose of Rawls's *Theory of Justice* was to offer a Kantian alternative to Sidgwick's utilitarianism. In his 1971 preface, he states that Sidgwick's methods resulted in a "forced choice" between utilitarianism and intuitionism, alternatives that he found unpalatable. He intended to present a "superior" moral conception of justice that "is highly Kantian in nature."[68] What follows appears to be a comprehensive, systematic moral conception that is more compelling than Sidgwick's utilitarianism, except that Rawls later says that is not what it is, and that can be confusing. What began as a "systematic moral conception" turned into a "political conception," and neither was intended to be "comprehensive" or necessarily Kantian. The ground under Rawls's feet kept shifting. His initial concern about the comprehensive moral theology of the Middle Ages expanded into a concern about Kant and Mill's moral theories. No comprehensive doctrine of morality, not even Kant's, can be the basis for the pure proceduralism of his later political constructivism.

Political Liberalism is Rawls's mature expression of his alternative to Sidgwick's utilitarianism. His introduction to the 1993 published version sets forth the same argument that begins his lectures on moral philosophy: "Three historical developments" gave rise to modern "moral and political philosophy": the Reformation, the modern state with its central administration, and the rise of science. He identifies a twofold contrast between the modern period and Medieval Christianity. First, Medieval Christianity is absolutist and intolerant, and the modern period is pluralistic and tolerant. Medieval Christianity is identified as (1) "authoritarian," (2) "a religion of salvation," (3) based on "doctrine," (4) overseen by "priests," and (5) "expansionist." The modern era overcame these traits.[69] Second, the people of the Medieval Christian world were certain about "moral obligation in divine law" because "their moral theology gave them complete guidance."[70] Apart from his undergraduate thesis, which directly addressed Christian ethics, and despite having taught Christian ethics well into the 1950s, this is one of the few references Rawls makes in his published work to moral theology. It is obviously not affirmative. He does not substantiate these claims, and he gives us no idea who these moral theologians were that offered complete guidance. Aquinas's claim that the virtue of faith permits executing heretics could be cited, and it is discussed in part II of this book. Rawls's concern is not without justification, but his judgment conflicts with that of Sidgwick, who found both ancient and Medieval moral thought too vague to give adequate guidance, a judgment Rawls elsewhere echoes in affirming the importance of the transition that Sidgwick's scientific treatment makes for modern moral philosophy.

Rawls's contrast between an authoritarian, moral theology in the Middle Ages and a tolerant, pluralistic modern moral philosophy is little more than an aside in his work. Justice as fairness does not depend on it. Yet avoiding Medieval moral theology was one reason he emphasized that justice as fairness was not to be considered a comprehensive moral doctrine. In the introduction to *Political Liberalism,* Rawls explains the significant shift that occurred in his thinking over the past decades:

> Note that in my summary of the aims of *Theory,* the social contract tradition is seen as part of moral philosophy and no distinction is drawn between moral and political philosophy. In *Theory* a moral doctrine of justice general in scope is not distinguished from a strictly political conception of justice. Nothing is made of the contrast between comprehensive philosophical and moral doctrines and conceptions limited to the domain of the political.[71]

These distinctions came to be "fundamental" in Rawls's later work. How did a position, justice as fairness, that began as a "systematic moral conception" offering an alternative to utilitarianism and intuitionism, turn into a "strictly political conception"? It began as "highly Kantian"; but in Rawls's later work, it does not require Kantian "autonomy" or any "comprehensive doctrine" so it can be available to all reasonable citizens, whether they are Kantians or not.[72] Justice as fairness is, he tells us, "of course, a moral conception," but it is not a comprehensive one. Neither is it "applied moral philosophy." It is a "freestanding view" that can be adopted by any citizen who holds a reasonably comprehensive doctrine because it is not one.[73] If justice as fairness is considered a comprehensive doctrine, Rawls argues, then it could not be the objective, universal, neutral arbiter of rights *sub specie aeternitatis.* (Of course, one of the most important questions to put to Rawls is whether justice as fairness has the objective, universal, and neutral character that he suggests.)

Rawls's transition requires a distinction between the "public justification" for the political conception that differentiates it from the nonpublic justification found in comprehensive doctrines. Because truth and goodness are inevitably linked to comprehensive doctrines, the political conception of justice will eschew any foundation in truth or goodness and only seek what is "reasonable."[74] Reason, then, becomes increasingly differentiated from goodness and truth. If that is the case, practical reasoning could not take the form that Anscombe assumed, the form of desire or wanting that requires a good object capable of being desired. If reason is intrinsically related to desire, and desire is always for something that at least appears to be good, then Rawls's reason must be Kantian, at least in that it can be lopped off from desire. His desire to avoid comprehensive doctrines, even when justified, leads to problematic judgments.

Rawls recognizes that his thin theory would have difficulty incorporating abolitionist religion, and he seeks to make an exception for some comprehensive doctrines. Religious and moral comprehensive doctrines can be "introduced in public political discussion at any time, provided that in due course, proper political reasons . . . are presented that are sufficient to support whatever the comprehensive doctrines introduced are said to support."[75] For instance, abolitionists or civil rights advocates are permitted to state their theological convictions in the public realm, but they cannot ask that they be upheld as law or policy until they are presented as something that is available to all reasonable people. The public realm includes an overlapping consensus of comprehensive doctrines, but they are provisional until set forth in terms of public reasonableness. Rawls's political liberalism cannot work if it is a comprehensive moral or religious doctrine because the whole point of justice as fairness is to secure a public realm that permits comprehensive doctrines without privileging or establishing them. When comprehensive doctrines wield state power, they are dangerous. However, for Rawls, they are not so dangerous that they should be rendered private, as the Enlightenment attempted; for that would make political liberalism into a privileged comprehensive doctrine that polices other doctrines. Instead, they are "nonpublic."[76]

Rawls intends something very specific about his use of "political" and its corresponding public reason. The domain of the political is nonvoluntary. (The oddness of a nonvoluntary social contract theory of the state is discussed below.) Citizens primarily enter it by birth and exit by death. Unlike associations or churches, the consequences of voluntarily exiting the domain of the political are dire. A citizen would lose the protection of political power. And "political power," he states, "is, of course, always coercive power backed by the state's machinery for enforcing its laws."[77] Because the political is defined by coercive power backed by potential violence, every comprehensive doctrine that would seek to garner that power for itself will be oppressive. Yet Rawls seems untroubled by his assumption that there is a neutral use of state violence that serves justice as fairness as something other than a comprehensive doctrine. Rawls consistently notes that "reasonable persons think it unreasonable to use political power, should they possess it, to repress other doctrines that are reasonable yet different from their own."[78] It is not unreasonable, however, to use "political power" to repress unreasonable doctrines, which makes the distinction between reasonable and unreasonable immensely significant, especially when reason has become divided from any desire for what is good. Nonetheless, some of these unreasonable doctrines are obvious. One example he offers is that "while churches can excommunicate heretics, they cannot burn them."[79] This, of course, is wise counsel, but it did not require constitutional democracies for the Church to adopt this counsel since it stopped the practice in the seventeenth century. That the Church held to this practice should not be excused or forgotten. Any who seek to retrieve it, and they are still with us, should be kept to the margins of society. Rawls offers a different ecclesial history and states that the Church's "persecuting zeal" did not come to an end until Vatican II.[80] Another example he gives is the fourteenth-century papal bull by Boniface VII, *Unam sanctam.* Rawls writes, "Thus if it is said that outside the church there is no salvation and hence a constitutional regime cannot be accepted, we must make some reply." It would be an "unreasonable" doctrine. He continues, "This reply does not say that the doctrine *extra ecclesia nulla salus* is not true. Rather, it says that it is unreasonable of any citizen or citizens as members of associations, to insist on using the public's (coercive) political power—the power of citizens as equals—to impose what they view as the implications of that doctrine upon other citizens."[81] One might think that this concern for an alliance between coercive, potentially violent power and Medieval Christianity would prompt Rawls to be wary about the nation-state's use of violence. The latter is less of a concern for him because political liberalism is not a comprehensive doctrine.

Political liberalism permits coercive state measures both internally and externally. Internally, the state uses coercive power to prevent comprehensive doctrines from being imposed. Could it justifiably use external coercion against other states that permit comprehensive doctrine—for instance, Islamic states or those that have established churches? Rawls's answer is ambiguous. He clearly finds liberal democratic societies to be more reasonable and peaceable than other forms of society: "Though liberal democratic societies have often engaged in war against nondemocratic states, since 1800 firmly established liberal societies have not fought one another."[82] The key expression in this statement is "firmly established," and it seems to work tautologously. Firmly established liberal democratic societies do not war against other firmly established democratic societies; so if they do so war, then they are not firmly established. Thus, the US Civil War and the two world wars are not evidence against this claim. They were not wars between "firmly established" democratic societies. Nor is the fact that the United States has been at war since its founding, with the exception of seventeen years. Rawls mentions US state violence against "Allende in Chile, Arbenz in Guatemala, Mossadegh in Iran, and, some would add, the Sandinistas in Nicaragua." These wars of a liberal democratic society against other democratic societies, however, are not evidence against his judgment, because they reflect "the great shortcomings of actual, allegedly constitutional democratic regimes."[83] In other words, the United States does not live up to the ideal theory represented by justice as fairness. This ideal theory gives Rawlsians something of an unassailable position that permits comparisons between ideal and actual, historical states.[84] And the ideal theory does not prohibit historical claims, such as that "since 1800" liberal democracies have not warred against each other. When counterevidence emerges, then the problem is not actual historical performance but the concession that actually existing states fall short of the ideal.

Rawls acknowledges that not all societies are filled with "reasonable liberal people." Reasonable liberal societies are one among four others that he typologizes: "decent peoples," "outlaw states," "societies burdened by unfavorable conditions," and "benevolent absolutisms."[85] The "peoples' territory" in the first two societies is an "asset" that can be protected by limiting immigration and repelling aggressors. Reasonable, well-ordered societies have a prima facie duty to not intervene against other societies, even those that are not well ordered, except for outlaw states. Liberal societies "go to war" only with "unsatisfied societies or outlaw states."[86]

Has Rawls well described the violence, or lack thereof, of modern nation-states? Is his concern that the source of violence, unrest, and oppression arises from comprehensive moral doctrines allied with state power well founded? The comparison between what is, modern constitutional democracies, and what no longer exists, Medieval Christendom, is less than convincing. It provides justification for modern states' uses of violence by setting them against uses of violence that are no longer operating. State power is to be used, but the end that it serves is difficult to identify. It cannot be used for the sake of what is true or good, for that would require a comprehensive doctrine. Can it be used as neutrally, as Rawls assumes? These are autobiographical questions for Rawls. After he lost his faith during World War II—amid its carnage, total warfare, and genocide—Rawls feared inquisitions and the "fact of oppression" that inevitably results from allowing one comprehensive doctrine to dominate through the means of state power.[87] Faith remains essential for him, but its object shifts to the progressive advance of constitutional democracies. The story of this transition is told in the next chapter.

ABOLITIONIST CHRISTIANITY AND THE GIFT OF FAITH

How should moral theologians respond to Rawls's proposal? Moral theologians critical of Constantinianism might welcome parts of it. For adherents of nonestablishment versions of Christianity, Rawls's concern makes some sense. Nonestablished or free churches share a similar concern about linking the Church to state power. A "faith" imposed or privileged by the threat of force cannot be faith as an infused virtue because it does not flow freely. Power backed by violence cannot infuse faith, but only fear or involuntary compliance. Sidgwick and Maurice were correct to oppose subscription for this very reason; imposing subscription upon the university by fiat easily led to coercive practices that undermined faith. As is shown in part II of this book, Maurice distinguished between a confident faith that does not seek power over others and a fearful one that does. Sidgwick opposed subscription for the sake of a more secular moral philosophy, Maurice for the sake of moral theology. The free church tradition goes further than Rawls (or Maurice) in opposing violence.

Faith, as will be shown below, is necessary for Rawls. But it is primarily an immanent power to achieve a progressive development of constitutional democracies. Consider it to be more than this; consider faith as a gift that generates a political society such as a church, and it has the potential to turn into a dangerous, comprehensive doctrine. For Rawls, comprehensive doctrines are the source of violence. Limit their political power and violence diminishes; but a monopoly on the use of violence remains the defining feature of modern constitutional democracies, and this violence can be used against both external and internal enemies. Rawls has nothing to say about any possible abolition of violence; his immanent faith cannot conceive it. He also has little to say about the resources that go into militaries and policing. For free church traditions, the problem with violence is not allying it with goodness or truth but violence itself, a problem that is resolved by sources outside immanent human power in Christ's cross, resurrection, ascension, and the gift of the Spirit, who infuses new possibilities into creation. Anabaptists and Quakers, for instance, refuse to identify politics with the means of violence. They directly apply moral theology to politics. Likewise, abolitionist Christianity directly applies, calling for an end to the state-sanctioned practice of enslavement. Current versions of abolitionist Christianity call for the abolition of prisons and policing based on religious practices and theological convictions, without translating them into terms acceptable for justice as fairness.[88] The liberal Protestantism of Martin Luther King Jr. and the Civil Rights Movement demonstrated the power of a nonviolent, abolitionist Christianity.

Rawls attempts to incorporate theopolitical movements like abolitionist Christianity and the Civil Rights Movement within political liberalism, but he sees them as provisionally political or as "nonpublic"; it is not always clear how this differs from considering religious movements as private. On one hand, a theopolitical argument could be part of an overlapping consensus for the justification of political liberalism. On the other hand, Rawls writes, "Political liberalism does not dismiss spiritual questions as unimportant, but to the contrary, because of their importance, it leaves them for each citizen to decide for himself or herself," which supposedly does not privatize but refuses to politicize.[89] To make spiritual questions matters of individual decision seems to differ little from the Enlightenment's privatization of religion. Many religious people could not conceive of their convictions and practices as decisions made as individual citizens. This denies the central role for "communion," a common sharing in thought and deed.

A significant weakness of political liberalism is its ability to hear and incorporate perfectionist moral theology, such as that found in the Sermon on the Mount. Stanley Cavell identifies a similar weakness in its inability to incorporate Emersonian perfectionism. Rawls had some connection to the free church tradition and its perfectionist inclinations. His Quaker friend, Roderick Firth, who was in a conscientious objector work camp during World War II, brought him to Harvard.[90] With Firth, Rawls "took part in a Washington antiwar conference in May 1967. In the spring term of 1969, he taught a course 'Problems of War'" on the US war in Vietnam and whether it was justified.[91] He seemed open to the kind of questions that Firth's Quakerism raised, but because Rawls took as the object of faith the progressive political goals of constitutional democracies, he did not think Anabaptists should hold office. Quakers, he writes, cannot "in good faith, in the absence of special circumstances, seek the highest offices in a liberal democratic regime."[92]

Because "reasonable pluralism" is a "permanent condition of democratic society," no single "comprehensive doctrine" can dominate without the use of coercive state power. He calls this relationship between state power and a comprehensive doctrine "the fact of oppression." His single historical reference for its justification is the Inquisition. He writes, "Let us call this the fact of oppression. In the society of the Middle Ages, more or less united in affirming the Catholic faith, the Inquisition was not an accident; its suppression of heresy was needed to preserve the shared religious belief." This moral fact is seldom investigated but is assumed. It matters for political liberalism because it holds the fact of oppression at bay. His justice as fairness, with its overlapping consensus, guards against the return of inquisitions. His concern arises from his religious autobiography.

NOTES

1. For a judicious discussion of the polemics of *Modern Moral Philosophy*, see Chapell, "Anscombe's Three Theses."
2. Anscombe, *Faith*, 66.
3. Mac Cumhaill and Wiseman, *Metaphysical Animals*, 101.
4. Pogge, *John Rawls*, 16.
5. Teichmann, *Philosophy*, 31–32.
6. Forrester, *In the Shadow*, 18.
7. Anscombe, *Human Life*, 161–67.
8. Rawls, *Theory of Justice*, 105n31. Walzer cites Anscombe's "Mr Truman's Degree" and refers to it as "one of the best defenses of the immunity of noncombatants" in his 1971 essay "World War II." Thanks to John Berkman for pointing me to Walzer's essay.
9. Quoted by Teichman, "Gertrude," 35.
10. Williams, "Mistrustful Animal," 81.
11. Quoted by Forrester, *In the Shadow*, 14.
12. Forrester, 109.
13. Edmundson, *John Rawls*, 76.
14. Forrester, *In the Shadow*, 104. It is a point hardly worth mentioning, but *Methods* was first published in 1874. The significance of both works and their importance for teaching and learning ethics still stand.
15. Wood, *Kantian Ethics*, x.
16. Herman, "Editor's Foreword," xi.
17. Quoted by Rawls, *Lectures on the History of Political Philosophy*, xi.
18. Rawls, "Kantian Constructivism," 554–55.
19. Rawls, *Law of Peoples*, 44–45.
20. Rawls, *Lectures on the History of Moral Philosophy*, 1–2.
21. Rawls, 1.
22. Rawls, 2.
23. Rawls, *Law of Peoples*, 500.

24. The identical argument is placed at the beginning of Rawls, *Political Liberalism*, 5–6.
25. Freeman, "Burdens."
26. Anscombe, *Human Life*, 169.
27. Anscombe used the term "stupid" as something of a philosophical term. It signifies achieving something for which you worked, such as the implementation of majority will or pleasure as the criterion for ethics, only to realize that it was not something you could have wanted all along. See Anscombe, *Ethics*, 129. In this sense, it is similar to how Wittgenstein uses the term "nonsense." Both have a therapeutic aim.
28. Although I am confident that Allen Wood would find Anscombe's ethics unpalatable, he seems to agree with her assessment of a change from Mill because of Sidgwick. He writes, "Kant and Mill have little sympathy for Sidgwick's fanatical desire to reduce all imprecision and indefiniteness to an absolute minimum"; Wood, *Kantian Ethics*, 64.
29. Anscombe, *Intention*, 11; Anscombe, *Human Life*, 183.
30. Anscombe, *Human Life*, 169.
31. Anscombe, *Ethics*, 59. Anscombe made a similar argument in her 1982 address—"Action, Intention, and Double Effect"—to the American Catholic Philosophical Association upon receiving the Aquinas Medal. She stated, "Ever since the seventeenth century, a false and absurd conception of intention has prevailed, which derives from Cartesian psychology; according to this conception an intention is a secret mental act which is producible at will"; Anscombe, *Human Life*, 247.
32. Anscombe, *Human Life*, 251.
33. Anscombe, *Faith*, 164.
34. Teichmann, *Philosophy*, 114.
35. Anscombe, *Ethics*, 22.
36. Anscombe, 23.
37. Rawls, *Theory of Justice*, 49n2; see also Forrester, *In the Shadow*, 31.
38. Anscombe, *Intention*, 87; Campbell, "On Anscombe," 9.
39. Schwenkler, *Anscombe's Intention*, 206n5.
40. For two helpful discussions of the importance of practical knowledge and truth in Anscombe, see Schwenkler, *Anscombe's Intention*, 117–201; and Campbell, "On Anscombe."
41. Bok, "To the Mountaintop," 156.
42. The view that Wittgenstein's approach is naturalistic arose with Hilary Putnam's and David Pears's interpretations. They distinguish among psychological, linguistic, minimal, and liberal naturalism. Naturalism can be reductive and lead toward atheism or nonreductive and suggest, as Mikel Burley does, that the natural instincts Wittgenstein describes are not somehow "secular" before they were "religious." If these interpretations are correct, then it makes sense that a reductive, liberal naturalism from Wittgenstein could have significantly influenced Rawls. See Burley, "Wittgenstein," 58–64.
43. Bok, "To the Mountaintop," 156. Bok shows how Rawls did not do this alone but with a group of American analytic philosophers who developed this version of naturalism in a way that was different from British developments. She states, "The particular version of liberal naturalism shared by Rawls's group of 1950s analytic ethical theories has been overlooked"; Bok, 156n11.
44. Forrester, *In the Shadow*, 8–9.
45. Bok, "To the Mountaintop," 155.
46. Rawls, *Law of Peoples*, 21.
47. Rawls, 22–23.

48. Rawls, 266.

49. Rawls, 54, 349.

50. Rawls, 496–505.

51. Rawls, 349.

52. Rawls, 382–83.

53. Rawls, 384.

54. Rawls, 356n8.

55. Geach, "Good," 35.

56. Ross, *Right*, 64.

57. Geach, "Good," 41. As they found Ayer and Hare unconvincing, the four women—Anscombe, Foot, Murdoch, and Midgley—did not find Ross compelling either. Murdoch referred to his ethics as "shallow stupid milk & water ethics"; quoted by Mac Cumhaill and Wiseman, *Metaphysical Animals*, 44.

58. Geach, "Good," 42.

59. Hare, "Geach," 107, 109.

60. Hare, 110n2.

61. Rawls, "Kantian Constructivism," 515.

62. Rawls, 519.

63. Wood, *Kantian Ethics*, 46, 76.

64. Rawls, "Kantian Constructivism," 526.

65. Rawls's student Christine Korsgaard takes up constructivism as central to the constitution of moral agency. For her, "normative concepts are not . . . the names of objects or of facts or of the components of facts that we encounter in the world. They are the names of the solutions of problems, problems to which we give names to mark them out as objects for practical thought"; Korsgaard, *Constitution*, 322. Another student, Samuel Freeman, likewise makes constructivism central to Rawls's project. Constructivism is not skepticism; moral principles can be "true, universally valid, and so on," but this only arises from "correct reasoning" that adopts "an objective point of view," which is a "deliberative procedure." Freeman understands Rawls's moral constructivism as transitional and as replaced by political constructivism; Freeman, "Burdens," 7–9.

66. Rawls, *Theory of Justice*, 506–7.

67. Rawls, 351n2.

68. Rawls, xvii–xviii.

69. Rawls, *Political Liberalism*, xxiv–xxv. Although Rawls does not explicitly name pluralism and tolerance at this point, he does so when he notes the second contrast. Here he simply notes that the contrast is "obvious."

70. Rawls, xxvi.

71. Rawls, xvii.

72. Rawls, 98.

73. Rawls, *Justice as Fairness*, 26, 181–82.

74. Rawls, *Political Liberalism*, xxi–xxii.

75. Rawls, *Theory of Justice*, 152.

76. Mulhall and Swift claim that Rawls's overlapping consensus, present in *Political Liberalism* but not in *A Theory of Justice*, makes no advance on the earlier position because the account of reasonableness is circular. Religious associations and others can advance their arguments as long as they are reasonable; but what makes them reasonable is that they fit with political liberalism and do not make political or public claims for religion. However,

they defend Rawls on the question of nonpublic goods, which is how he defines religious goods. Political liberalism assumes a variety of public accounts of reason, and thus diverse associations would have their own "public" reason, but it would not necessarily be political because it would not be allied with state power. Within their associations, these diverse publics are free to use their comprehensive accounts for the purposes of ethical and theological deliberation; but when they advance their cause in the political realm, it will require doing so within a larger public defined by reasonable pluralism. Mulhall and Swift, *Liberals*, 179, 231–33.

77. Rawls, *Justice as Fairness*, 182.

78. Rawls, *Law of Peoples*, 16; Rawls, *Political Liberalism*, 60ff.

79. Rawls, *Justice as Fairness*, 11.

80. Rawls, *Theory of Justice*, 21.

81. Rawls, *Justice as Fairness*, 183–84.

82. Rawls, *Theory of Justice*, 51.

83. Rawls, 53.

84. Rawls explains the relation between ideal and nonideal theory thus: "For until the ideal is identified, at least in outline—and that is all we should expect—nonideal theory lacks an objective, an aim, by reference to which its queries can be answered"; Rawls, *Law of Peoples*, 90.

85. Rawls, *Theory of Justice*, 4.

86. Rawls, 48.

87. Fabian Wendt raises to my mind an appropriate criticism of Rawls by distinguishing the metalevel of public justification that Rawls seeks with a primary level of comprehensive doctrines. He argues that a public justification could arise with a comprehensive liberalism that does not seek to stand above the fray at some metalevel. The assumption that public reason liberalism can be a "mediator" rather than another "sectarian party" leads to this perhaps false search for the metalevel. Wendt notes, "But one may continue asking why it is so important to avoid sectarianism"; Wendt, "Rescuing Public Justification."

88. See Dubler and Lloyd, *Break Every Yoke*.

89. Rawls, *Theory of Justice*, 127.

90. Bok, "To the Mountaintop," 169.

91. Pogge, *John Rawls*, 19.

92. Rawls, *Theory of Justice*, 105. What would he say about the early days of the state of Pennsylvania?

3

FAITH, PERFECTION, AND HOPE
IN MORAL PHILOSOPHY

Faith, hope, and charity are unavoidable; without them, we would be less than human. They are intrinsic to being because of its gift character. We have faith in what we cannot see but long for, whether it be the construction of a just society or the realization of the reign of God, in which violence, domination, and oppression are abolished. Hope arises out of the dissatisfaction with the world as it is and the desire for the one that should be, but without knowing how it is we can get from one to the other. At the foundation of all, of course, is charity. To love and be loved, to seek love and give love, germinate faith and hope. As we will see in part II of this book, Maurice thought that the Reformers missed something when they made faith more basic than charity. It caused them to overlook the gifted character of our lives. Of course, there are different degrees and kinds of faith, hope, and charity. They are addressed in part II. This chapter first examines the role faith had in Rawls's work and raises a question about the adequacy of faith's object. Different objects lead to different kinds of hope, and contrasting expectations of what charity might yet bring about. Rawls lost his religion while serving in World War II, but he did not lose faith. As the second section of this chapter shows, Rawls's faith migrated to a different object. Once she became Catholic, Anscombe never lost her faith. The third section examines how the "object" of her faith provided a more critical perspective, for better or worse, on that in which Rawls placed faith. It also led to a perfectionist ethics (discussed in the fourth section), something that Rawls rejected and that, according to his colleague Stanley Cavell, diminished his political ethic. The difference between that in which Rawls and Anscombe placed their faith is best demonstrated in their ethics of violence and what could be hoped for (covered in the fifth and final section).

RAWLS LOSING HIS RELIGION

Like Sidgwick, Rawls lost his Christian faith. While Sidgwick lost it during his college education, Rawls did not lose his until after college and three years of military service in the Pacific during World War II.[1] Sidgwick's life was suffused with the Christian tradition, his father being an Episcopal priest and his brother-in-law no less than the archbishop of Canterbury. Rawls was not quite as inundated with Christianity. He attended an Episcopal boarding school, although he described his family background as "conventionally religious." Faith became more central during his last two years as an undergraduate at Princeton, so central that he had planned on attending Virginia Theological Seminary and studying for the Episcopal priesthood.[2] Those plans changed after the war, and unlike Sidgwick, whose memoirs are full of wrestling with Christian faith, Rawls seldom mentions it. In the 1990s, Rawls wrote "On My Religion." He did not publish it or make it public. Joshua Cohen and Thomas Nagel suggest that it was written for "family and friends," and they decided, with permission from Rawls's executors, to publish it after his death.[3] It provides insight into his brief, consistent, and caricatured criticism of Medieval Christianity and why he feared comprehensive moral and religious doctrines.

Rawls names several events that exacerbated his loss of faith while he was serving as a solider in the Pacific in World War II. One was a sermon he heard by a Lutheran pastor who claimed that God aimed their unit's bullets at the Japanese but "protected us from theirs." Rawls "upbraided" the chaplain for such a bad doctrine of providence. A second was the loss of his friend Deacon to mortar rounds. A third was finding out about the Holocaust occurring in Germany. He wrote, "How could I pray and ask God to help me, or my family, or my country, or any other cherished thing I cared about, when God would not save millions of Jews from Hitler?" He could not square God's will with "the most basic ideas of justice." He concludes, "Thus, I soon came to reject the idea of the supremacy of the divine will as also hideous and evil." Rawls's quest for justice led him to abandon his faith and his planned study of theology. Rather than enrolling in a seminary, he pursued philosophy.[4]

Rawls's experiences led him to study the Inquisition shortly after the war by reading Henry Lea's history and Lord Acton's review. Harsh judgments seldom appear in Rawls's works, so his condemnation of Medieval Catholicism stands out. For Rawls, it necessarily led to the Inquisition, and that provides the "fact of oppression," one of the historical conditions that must be overcome by modern democratic societies. His study of the Inquisition was also instrumental in his final rejection of Christianity. He wrote, "I came to feel the great curse of Christianity was to persecute dissenters as heretics from the early days of Irenaeus and Tertullian." This contrasted with Greek and Roman religion. It was a "civic religion, and it served to instill loyalty to the *polis* or the Emperor especially in time of war and crisis," but it allowed "many different religions" to exist and "flourish."[5] The Christian Church, however, justified its repression based on the need for "true belief." If your eternal salvation was at stake, then heresy would logically be a capital crime. It is why he could never accept "papal infallibility," even when restricted to "matters of faith and morals," for those are the matters about which we need a reasonable pluralism.[6]

Rawls concluded that when Christianity "is taken seriously," it will have "deleterious effects on one's character" because it individuates persons and views each one as either saved or damned.[7] The Inquisition leads to the Holocaust, and that is why Christianity, or any comprehensive moral or religious doctrines, must be kept from political power. Not even Dietrich Bonhoeffer escapes this judgment.[8] After these denunciations of Christianity, Rawls turns to the work of Jean Bodin for a Catholic faith that tolerates diverse religions. He interprets Bodin favorably but questions his unwillingness to tolerate atheism. For Bodin, God is necessary for "right and justice." Bodin argues, like Kant, that if there is no judgment, there can be no final justice. F. D. Maurice was accused of neglecting this teaching; Sidgwick avoided it, and Rawls dismissed it. For Rawls, it is a limitation in Bodin that he still clung to it. Yet should this desire for justice be so readily dismissed? Terry Eagleton wonders if we can have hope without something like it.[9] (I return to this discussion below.) Rawls seems unmoved by the pull of such a hope. Having dismissed it for how it exacerbates the fact of oppression, Rawls then makes a theological argument that resembles Plato's *Euthyphro*: "If we say that God's will is the source of all being, and of moral and political values, then the denial of God's existence entails the denial of those values. But if we say that the ground and content of those values is God's reason, or else known to God's reason, then God's will serves only a subordinate role of sanctioning the divine intentions now seen as grounded on reason."[10] If divine willing is the source of morality, then Bodin would be correct. If divine reason is its source, and even God is subject to justice, then Bodin is still correct, but God becomes inessential for justice; reason suffices. Rawls then states that divine reason would be both like and unlike ours. However, he only explores how it is like ours and skips over how it might be unlike. Insofar as it is like ours, divine reason is bound by the same logical inferences, practical reasoning, and so on as we are. Whether God exists or not would not affect the "basic judgments of reasoning" that we hold in common. Goodness as rationality would not be affected if God does or does not exist. Rawls does not conclude that faith should be rejected but that people of faith must tolerate nontheists and atheists and vice versa. He writes, "Nontheism is compatible with religious faith; and even atheism is to be tolerated, for what is punishable in religion is not beliefs but deeds."[11] Rawls neglects the possibility that reason arises from something basic like charity, a position central to Maurice, who would agree with Rawls that defining God solely in terms of willfulness is unconscionable. This omission is surprising because Rawls evidenced awareness of something along these lines in his undergraduate thesis.

Rawls's reflections on his religion in the 1990s take a very different approach to faith than his 1942 undergraduate thesis at Princeton University. Eric Gregory, a moral theologian who teaches at Princeton, was looking up undergraduate theses from famous alumni in 2007 and unearthed Rawls's "A Brief Inquiry into the Meaning of Sin and Faith: An Interpretation Based on the Concept of Community." The thesis is fascinating because it showed how the theologically minded early Rawls opposed the social contract tradition that he would later make famous and, as Gregory notes, "dramatically changed the landscape of twentieth-century moral and political philosophy."[12]

Too much should not be made of an undergraduate thesis written by a young man who has not yet endured the life-changing events Rawls was about to face as a soldier or gone through the rigors of a philosophy graduate program and then spent years teaching and writing, clarifying his central moral and political ideas. Placing the thesis within the context of his later published work, however, is illuminating. Some interesting continuities exist between his early engagement with moral theology and his long, careful, and comprehensive engagement with moral philosophy. Perhaps the first and most significant is his emphasis on community, its fragility, and the need for something solid to sustain it. This concern drives his undergraduate thesis and shapes his moral theology. Sin is understood as a loss of community and faith as its restoration. He grounds community in the doctrine of the Trinity. Because the human creature is made in the image of God and God is in God-self "perfect community," this "pattern" in human "nature is the reflection in man of God Himself."[13] Rawls's "justice as fairness" is also concerned with sustaining communities: it is about forging the political structures within which associations and communities can flourish without imposing their comprehensive doctrines on others through state power. Rawls came to see Christianity as a comprehensive doctrine that too easily leads, as he thought all comprehensive doctrines did, to the destruction of the very conditions that would allow it to flourish.

A second significant continuity is his criticism of the good as attractive and the concomitant role of desire in the moral life. His staunchly Protestant moral theology already dismissed any ethics that begins with the good. In one sense, his undergraduate thesis could be read as an extended critique of Thomas Aquinas's understanding of the will as rational appetite. Following rather closely the Swedish Lutheran theologian Anders Nygren's *Eros and Agape*, Rawls finds eros to be a Greek import into Christian theology from Plato and Aristotle that must be discarded. Augustine and Aquinas were adversely affected by the Greeks. They turn God (and the good) into a naturalistic object of desire. Plato, Aristotle, Augustine, and Aquinas, he writes, "failed to distinguish between natural and personal relations." The consequence is that they lost the personal and communal nature of Christian ethics and "consider ethics a matter of relating persons to proper objects, such as the Form of the Good, Truth, or God, who is conceived by Augustine and Aquinas as the most desirable object."[14] The good as desirable distorted Christianity, which is why he wrote what I quoted above, that Christianity should "stop kowtowing to Plato and Aristotle" and retrieve Scripture. Any role for the Bible disappears in the later work, but the subordination of the good to the right was already there.

A third significant continuity is the importance of faith. In his undergraduate thesis, Rawls rejects faith as belief and is critical of the emphasis on "dogma" in the early centuries of Christianity. It distracted from the personal aspect of faith, which should be more central to Christianity.[15] His later, published criticisms of Medieval Christianity, with its insistence on faith as belief in authorized dogmas, was also a criticism already present in the Protestant Christian ethics of his 1942 thesis.[16] He asks, "What is faith," and he answers, "Faith is the spiritual disposition of the whole of a personality which is fully integrated into community and thereby rooted in the source which sustains it. Faith is the perfect relation of person to person."[17] Once constitutional democracies become the object of reasonable faith for Rawls, this statement could be transposed into his later work with little loss. Its appeal to "the perfect relation of person to person" could also provide evidence for Cavell's sympathetic critique that Rawls's liberalism is an unacknowledged form of perfectionism. Compared with the statement in the later "On My Religion" that his nontheism is "compatible" with faith, along with his discussion of Kant's "reasonable faith" in his *Lectures on the History of Moral Theology* (examined below), the place for faith in his undergraduate thesis and those later statements does not significantly differ. What changes is not the place for faith in ethics and politics but "the source which sustains it." Faith no longer takes as its source and object God but the progression of history that led to constitutional democracy. Yet even in his undergraduate thesis, faith was directed more toward interpersonal relations than to God.

A REASONABLE (A)THEOLOGICAL FAITH

Rawls's affirmation of faith occurs in his *Lectures on the History of Moral Philosophy* when he takes up a familiar problem in Kant, one Sidgwick only partially addressed in his final chapter in *Methods*, that though happiness is seldom proportional to virtue in this life, if ethics is to be rational, it must be. For this reason, Kant posited the possibility of an afterlife. Because his method could not lead to this conclusion, Sidgwick acknowledged that morality might not be completely rational. For Kant, as for Bodin, a doctrine of divine judgment holds forth hope for a just proportionality. Rawls has no time for this argument and finds it to be a lingering influence from Kant's pietist theology and a remnant of Leibniz's "idea of the highest good."[18] The problem, as Rawls sees it, is a contradiction between Kant's realm of ends and Kant's account of the highest good, which assumes that happiness should be proportionate to moral worth. Rawls affirms the realm of ends because it is consistent with moral or political constructivism, but he rejects the highest good because it inevitably raises the question of the proper proportionality between virtue and happiness that leads to theology. If the idea of the highest good is discarded, then the realm of ends will not be troubled by theology.

Rawls takes up what Kant failed to do and reworks an application of the categorical imperative to the modern, secular situation as a realm of ends that no longer needs the highest good and its tacit theological underpinnings. He laid out what he calls the CI—categorical imperative—procedure in four steps. First, the agent's maxim is conceived as "rational and sincere." Second, the maxim is generalized, resulting in a "universal precept." The third step "transforms the universal precept into a law of nature," and the fourth step, which he calls the "most complicated," adds the law of nature to existing laws. We then "think through as best we can what the order of nature would be once the effects of the newly adjoined law of nature have had sufficient time to work themselves out."[19] This fourth step is significant for Rawls's later discussion of Kant's "reasonable faith."

Two sections—"The Content of Reasonable Faith" and "The Unity of Reason"—bring Rawls's lectures on Kant to their end. These sections cannot but remind the reader of Sidgwick's failed effort to unify reason and morality in the closing section of his *Methods*. Rawls has no need, as he puts it, to "dispense happiness in proportion to virtue." All he is after is to "authorize penalties and punishments of various kinds, as these are necessary . . . for a stable social world."[20] Thus, he rejects the problem of proportionality between virtue and happiness based on an ill-conceived attachment to the "highest good" because it is unnecessary for justice. He states, "Matching happiness with virtue cannot, then, be part of the moral law as it applies to us by way of the categorical imperative and the CI procedure that interprets it for us. It is for these reasons that, in my presentation of Kant's doctrine, I use the secular ideal of a possible realm of ends that can be (in good part) realized in the natural world."[21] Whether it makes people happy has become irrelevant.

Any shred of Kant's philosophical theology must be removed from his moral philosophy, but Rawls still affirms the need for Kant's "reasonable faith." He interprets it in terms of the fourth stage in the CI procedure, thinking through what the order of nature is, as it results from the procedure. His defense of Kant's reasonable faith abandons Kant's postulates of God and immortality. They are no longer necessary, or at least are made "weaker" because "the object of the moral law is the secular ideal of a possible realm of ends." But we still need Kant's third postulate, freedom.[22] The "order of nature and social necessities" can provide its ground for us rather than postulating God as its source.[23] Here is where faith and the fourth stage of the CI procedure come together. The "order of nature" that becomes the source of a "reasonable political faith" is disclosed in historical progress. Rawls writes, "In our social unsociability that drives us to competition and rivalry, and even to seemingly endless wars and conquests, we may not unreasonably hope to discern a plan of nature to force mankind, if it is to save itself from such destruction, to form a confederation of constitutional democratic states, which will ensure perpetual peace and encourage the free development of culture and the arts."[24]

The "free development" of the arts should not be lost on the reader. Politics should no more be ordered to culture and the arts than it should be to religion. Both are forms of a perfectionist ethic that Rawls considers and rejects. Constitutional democracies are not ordered to such ends but are the conditions for the "free development" of them. If we have Kant's "reasonable political faith" in a secular realm of ends, then we do not need religious beliefs or perfections such as truth, goodness, or beauty to sustain hope. We only need a reasonable faith that discerns the "plan of nature" from our proper procedure.[25]

Rawls does more in this section than simply exegete Kant's moral philosophy. If that were the case, he would not need to point out what he considers to be contradictions in Kant's work from his philosophical theology that need to be reworked. Nor would he rework them. By doing so, Rawls is defending a version of constructivism and linking it to the plan of nature. It is this "reasonable faith" in the "possibility of freedom" that allows us to assume, in practice albeit without "theoretical proof," the unity of reason.[26] Faith remains present in Rawls's work, but its object becomes the historical progression toward constitutional democracy and the natural laws that contribute to it. It is also that in which he placed his hope. It should be relatively uncontroversial that Rawls's project does not work without this reasonable political faith. He says as much in his lectures.

Bok's claim that Rawls's "writings on Christian ethics and on philosophical metaethics intertwine in one continuous moral project" seems to be warranted, in part, given the essential role he gives to faith. The early Christian ethics and later metaethics bear a family resemblance. Faith remains, but its source is radically changed, and that leads to a significant disruption within the continuity. This resemblance, however, assumes that "faith" has an elasticity to it that maintains the same, or a similar, form, despite its source or object. In how many contexts can "faith" be projected until the term becomes so equivocal that it no longer makes sense? Only if such an elastic projection is granted could the early moral theologian Rawls and the later political philosopher be read as engaged in a common project. I would not discount such a possibility. F. D. Maurice finds the theological virtues to be the source of creaturely being; he is not surprised to find them present in nearly every religion, culture, and philosophy. Weithman interprets Rawls in this vein: "I shall try to show the religious aspect of Rawls's work using a condition of religiosity that he himself endorsed." It is a condition that does not require "theism" but "justice as fairness tries to answer some of the questions traditional religion also tries to answer."[27] Likewise, Reidy thinks we miss something if we fail to see the religious character of Rawls's work (something Nagel also identifies). He appears to agree with Bok, suggesting that Rawls lost his Christian theism but held to a form of fideism, his "non-orthodox, non-theistic fideism."[28] For Reidy, Rawls's work is misunderstood because readers miss the religious and Wittgensteinian commitments underlying it: "In the 1990s Rawls characterized his life's work as addressed to a question 'essentially religious in nature': Can human nature be redeemed? It is perhaps, then, no surprise that reading his work against the background of his, eventually non-theistic, religious commitments and concerns helpfully casts it in a new light."[29] Theologians might be excused for asking philosophers to clarify "non-theistic religious commitments," but the inevitability of faith is no surprise. The question is not if faith is necessary to sustain hope for humanity's redemption; the question is in what should one place one's faith?

Is the progress of constitutional democracies sufficient as a source for faith? Rawls's faith in the progressive histories that lead to modern constitutional democracies may be the best interpretation of his nontheistic religion. If so, then Rawls's "religious commitment" embodies well what Sheldon Wolin refers to as "the migration of the holy" from the Church to the state.[30] There may be a less religious way to read Rawls.

The revisions from *A Theory of Justice* to *Political Liberalism* suggest that Rawls feared justice as fairness would be understood along religious lines as though it depended upon a moral or religious comprehensive doctrine. Here I find myself more in agreement with Edmundson than those who interpret Rawls as a religious thinker. Edmundson stated,

> In light of his posthumously published senior thesis, a likelier surmise is that Rawls came to recognize his 1971 conception of a well-ordered society to be too continuous with his youthful—and aggressively Christian—conception of a community of faith. Rawls emphatically does not want a well-ordered society to turn out, under the microscope of analysis, to be a secularized community bonded and stabilized by a controversial religious conception of society.[31]

Edmundson takes Rawls at his word; he is a thoroughgoing secular atheist. But he also argues that Rawls's preoccupation with avoiding comprehensive doctrines may have kept him from fully embracing the socialism that best fits his theory of justice. Socialism, like religion, is "frequently" considered a comprehensive doctrine. Or, as Stanley Cavell suggests, socialism is a version of perfectionism. Maurice's moral theology, with its perfectionist ethics, led him to embrace a version of socialism that was unavailable to Rawls.

ANSCOMBE'S CATHOLIC FAITH

Unlike Sidgwick and Rawls, Anscombe did not abandon her Christian faith. She converted to Catholicism while in high school and remained a devoted Catholic throughout her life. Her conversion concerned her parents, who sent her to an Anglican priest to dissuade her, but he confirmed her convictions.[32] The Catholic faith gave Anscombe a critical perspective on modern, progressive developments that was unavailable to Sidgwick or Rawls. Such a critical perspective could exacerbate a reactionary traditionalism that views every modern development as civilizational decline, and there are theologians and philosophers who put her work to this purpose. Yet such a use seems to overlook too much of her life's work and friendships—especially with Wittgenstein, Philippa Foot, and Iris Murdoch—to be a convincing trajectory of her work. Murdoch referred to her "ruthless authenticity." She must have made quite an impression on her, because Murdoch also wrote about their "three-day 'courtship,'" which most likely had more to do with Murdoch's romantic inclinations than Anscombe's.[33]

Both Rawls and Anscombe were preoccupied with justice, but their approaches differed.[34] Rawls constructed an ideal theory that had an overarching systematic coherence. His methodical approach to justice as procedural shows Sidgwick's influence. Anscombe intentionally eschewed system.[35] Rawls placed a "reasonable faith" in modern, progressive developments that led to constitutional democracies. Anscombe found the modern world declining more and more into a murderous society, especially in its proclivity to kill the innocent through consequentialist reasoning. Rawls wrote in favor of a political order that would find a place for religious people without allowing them to impose their comprehensive moral and theological doctrines on that order. Anscombe was devoutly, even "intransigently," Catholic, but she never sought to gain the levers of political power for her Catholic positions. She was no culture warrior. She wrote both for a general public and a Catholic one. Her hope for Catholics was that they would recognize when the society within which they resided advocated murder and avoid its injustice while living inevitably within it. The broader society had become what Augustine feared. "Take away justice, said St. Augustine, and what are governments but Mafias? That is the situation we are in; and we ought to regard ourselves, as we do not, I fear, as separate."[36] Despite this significant difference, Rawls's work poses little objection to Anscombe's counsel. She never argued that Catholicism should function as a comprehensive moral doctrine imposed by state power. In fact, given her criticism of modern state power, which was much more thoroughgoing than Rawls's, she could not have argued for it.

For Anscombe, murder was normalized in World War II with the intentional bombing of civilians and foolish calls for unconditional surrender.[37] Modern political orders had become little more than illicit syndicates willing to kill the innocent for the sake of some supposed greater, future good. Modern moral philosophy was complicit in promulgating the injustice of the state's war-making excesses. One should not place faith in it or concede it an unquestionable allegiance. Anscombe places faith in the Catholic Church. Rawls seems particularly troubled by the Catholic Church and views it as a vestige of Medieval theology. He sides with the Reformers and seeks to limit the Church's public authority for fear that if such authority is conceded, the Inquisition will logically follow. Ironically, Rawls's ethics would be more prone toward claiming the levers of state power to keep moral theology at bay than would Anscombe's claim that those powers guard against Rawls's secular ethics. As Chantal Mouffe has argued, Rawls's "'well-ordered society' . . . tends to erase the very place of the adversary, thereby expelling any legitimate opposition from the democratic public sphere."[38] Anscombe was an adversary.

Like Rawls, Anscombe's experiences with World War II deeply affected her philosophical vocation. In 1939, while an undergraduate at Oxford, she wrote a pamphlet with Norman Daniel, "The Justice of the Present War Examined," arguing that the British government's "vague" and "unlimited" intentions in responding to Germany's invasion of Poland meant that the war lacked any justifiable end, and without that it would lose any appropriate means. The assertion that the British were building a new order in Europe meant unlimited war. If that were the case, she stated forthrightly, Catholics could not participate in it: "If the choice lies between our total destruction and the commission of sin, then we must choose to be destroyed." Her pamphlet was presented as the "Catholic view," which alarmed the local archbishop, who asked her to withdraw copies from circulation. She complied, perhaps.[39] Given these convictions, her opposition to Oxford's conferral of an honorary degree on Harry Truman, whom she regarded as a war criminal for intentionally killing noncombatants, comes as no surprise. She initiated a "formal protest," which was voted on by the Oxford faculty. Jenny Teichman explains what happened: "It seems that word got round, so that very many dons turned up to the meeting, some in order to support Mr. Truman, others to foil what they suspected of being a mysterious plot concocted by mysterious females." Three persons voted with Anscombe—Philippa Foot, Margaret Hubbard, and the historian M. R. D. Foot, who was a decorated soldier.[40]

PACIFISM, SUPREME EMERGENCY, AND INTENDING EVIL FOR THE SAKE OF THE GOOD

Although they differed over the morality of modern, constitutional states, Anscombe agreed with Rawls, in part, in raising questions about pacifism. Anscombe's approach to the morality of war was complex. She was a member of the Catholic peace organization Pax, whose members considered themselves "just-war pacifists" as opposed to "absolute pacifists."[41] She was an avid reader of Dorothy Day and the *Catholic Worker*.[42] Her husband, Peter Geach, was a conscientious objector in World War II. She was by no means hawkish about war and must have been open to some forms of nonviolence, but her 1961 essay "War and Murder" expressed concern about pacifism's baleful influence since the world wars. Pacifism, she argued, only made sense with "universal conscription," which she described as a "horrid evil." Without conscription, pacifism is just a "private view" that had become buttressed by a "sentimental" and "false" view of Christianity. "According to this image," she wrote, "Christianity is an ideal and beautiful religion, impracticable except for a few rare characters. It preaches a God of love whom there is no reason to fear; it marks an escape from the conception presented in the Old Testament, of a vindictive and jealous God who will utterly punish his enemies," a God whose "only triumph is in the cross." For this sentimental version of Christianity, war and property are viewed as necessary compromises with the world. Once they are rendered such, they are no longer bound by moral precepts.[43] This sentimentalized pacifism exacerbated the "universal forgetfulness of the law against killing the innocent" because it lost the power to discriminate between legitimate targets and the innocent.[44] She opposes pacifism as a form of consequentialism and views it as paving the way for obliteration bombing. The logic of her argument makes sense. If a sentimental pacifism holds everyone equally guilty before hostilities break out, then when that pacifism becomes unsupportable and abandoned, it will be tempted to fail to distinguish among persons after embracing war.[45]

For Anscombe, pacifism wrongly turns the counsels of the Sermon on the Mount into precepts available to everyone.[46] Maurice is an obvious counterexample to Anscombe's concern about the counsels. He was no pacifist; his son and grandson were generals. However, he rejected the Catholic distinction between counsels and precepts and the differing virtues that sustained that distinction. Because we are created in the image of God, who is the Incarnate One, we should expect the self-giving love of the Son to be mirrored in creation. He turned the theological virtues and beatitudes into "precepts available to anyone," without underwriting the sentimentalized Christianity that Anscombe rejects in "War and Murder."

Anscombe's "War and Murder" is more a criticism of sentimental versions of Christianity than a careful analysis of pacifism. She acknowledged that the life of a soldier or ruler was most likely a "vicious life," but this was not because warfare and ruling were themselves vicious activities. They could be virtuous. She gives as an example using violence to suppress slavery; it would be virtuous. The reason that such activities were most likely vicious in the modern era was because warriors and rulers would inevitably acquiesce in the intentional killing of the innocent.[47]

Faith played a significant role for both Rawls and Anscombe, but its very different sources and objects for them led to radically distinct views of politics. For Anscombe, faith is found in the "divine promises," and they alone are what allow us to know "that the Church cannot fail." She writes, "Those, therefore, who think they must be prepared to wage a war with Russia involving the deliberate massacre of cities, must be prepared to say to God: 'We had to break your law, lest your Church fail. We could not obey your commandments, for we did not believe your promises.'"[48] If the choice comes down between intending to kill the innocent or losing the nation, then Christians should be prepared to lose the nation. This was not a deontological commitment to divine law but a sign of hope. Losing the nation would not lose the object of faith. Rawls, following Walzer, could not go this far. Their different objects of faith have significant implications for politics and ethics.

Rawls and Walzer were aware of Anscombe's argument. Walzer commented on it in his 1971 essay "World War II: Why Was This War Different?" and Rawls in his 1999 *The Law of Peoples*. Walzer cites Anscombe's "Mr Truman's War" favorably, and with Anscombe he questions the British bombing of cities. In response, however, he suggests this possibility: "But it does seem to me that the more certain a German victory appeared to be in the absence of a bomber offensive, the more justifiable was the decision to launch the offensive." He initially rejects this argument but then states, "suppose that civilization itself is really at stake." When so much is at stake, he finds himself moving toward Churchill's decision to bomb cities:

> Should I wager this determinate crime against that immeasurable evil? . . . If this is right, and my perception of evil not hysterical or self-serving, then surely I must wager. There is no option; the risk otherwise is too great. My own action is determinate, of course, only as to its immediate consequences, while the rule which bars such acts looks to the future but I dare say that there will be no future or no foreseeable future for civilization and its rules unless I accept the burdens of criminality.[49]

Because the future depends upon the continuity of civilized nations, criminal acts may be warranted, but their burden should be accepted. What exactly it would mean to accept a burden of criminality is unclear. Should Churchill and Truman have stood trial as war criminals? Is this how Walzer can both agree and disagree with Anscombe with what is obviously a consequentialist argument?

Rawls also refers to Anscombe's position and compares Walzer's "supreme emergency exemption," which permits targeting the innocent in war under exceptional circumstances, with the "Catholic doctrine" that rejects it. Anscombe represents the Catholic position. Rawls writes, "See the powerful essay by G. E. M. Anscombe, 'War and Murder,' . . . . This was written to object to Oxford's decision to award an honorary degree to President Truman in 1952." Although he disagrees with the Catholic doctrine, he "agrees with Anscombe in the particular case of Hiroshima."[50] Nonetheless, he follows Walzer's supreme emergency that allows setting aside the principle of nondiscrimination when the object of a reasonable faith—constitutional democracies—is at stake. The British bombing of civilian German cities was permissible because "the nature and history of constitutional democracy and its place in European history were at stake."[51] Because her faith resided elsewhere than in the historical progress of reason culminating in the modern nation-state, Anscombe did not have as much a stake in the nation-state's survival. No "supreme emergency" could arise whereby intentional killing of the innocent would be justified. It was the consideration of such a possibility that misled Sidgwick, Hare, and Ross. Rawls's and Walzer's ethics did not challenge Sidgwick's transition in understanding intentional action as foreseen consequences. A realist ethics that seeks to preserve constitutional democracies cannot abide perfectionist inclinations. It appears always to turn to consequentialism.

THE PATH NOT TAKEN: PERFECTION AND INTENTION IN LEARNING AND TEACHING ETHICS

Rawls's acceptance of a supreme emergency, permitting the killing of innocents under extraordinary circumstances for the sake of constitutional democracies, and Anscombe's rejection of such a possibility highlight their different approaches to ethics, especially concerning what Cavell called the "perfectionist tradition." Rawls appears outside it, Anscombe within it. This judgment, however, disagrees with Cavell's own. He did not consider Rawls's ethics to be opposed to perfectionism; in fact, political liberalism requires a perfectionist ethics if it is to fulfill its promise and be something other than merely conforming with convention.

Both Cavell and Rawls taught ethics at Harvard. Rawls's course was sometimes called "Ethics" and sometimes "Moral Psychology." He structured it, reflecting Sidgwick's influence and his criticism of it, according to four types of moral reasoning: "perfectionism, utilitarianism, intuitionism, and Kantian constructivism."[52] Cavell taught a section of Harvard's core course known as "Moral Reasoning" and titled it "Moral Perfectionism."[53] He taught it, in part, to correct Rawls's misinterpretation of perfectionism as a form of teleology that maximized excellence. Rawls interprets perfectionism in a strict and a moderate form. The first takes it as the sole teleological principle for ordering society and seeks to maximize excellence in the arts, culture, or science. Nietzsche is Rawls's primary exemplar. The moderate version is Aristotle's; his perfectionism is a species of intuitionism, in which perfection is one "standard among several." The latter converges better with justice as fairness; but in the end, Rawls rejects both because perfection is not a "principle of justice" but value.[54] It works against the original position by refusing to distribute goods equally, assuming that those more capable of achieving excellence should have the distribution of basic goods in their favor: "Now the criterion of perfection insists that rights in the basic structure be assigned so as to maximize the total of intrinsic value."[55] For Rawls, then, moral perfectionism "resembles classical utilitarianism."[56] Once perfectionism becomes akin to utilitarianism, Rawls presents it, as he did the content of Sidgwick's ethics, as an alternative to his own Kantian constructivism. The moderate view is more difficult to argue against because there is no single value that is maximized. Echoing Sidgwick's criticism of Aristotle, Rawls states that the principles of moderate perfectionism are "imprecise as political principles."[57] Justice as fairness requires more precision, so that, for instance, no one is burdened unnecessarily with supporting forms of excellence that they might find objectionable. For this reason, Rawls affirmed that no one should be taxed without consent for culture, arts, and universities; they are provided by the "exchange branch."[58]

Cavell, unlike Anscombe, shared Rawls's commitment to "contractarian liberalism."[59] He expressed "admiration" for his colleague's work, and especially "for its accomplishment in establishing a systematic framework for a criticism of constitutional democracy from within."[60] Cavell's moral perfectionism, like Rawls's justice as fairness, challenges it from within, or so he explicitly stated; but he also troubles any easy distinction between "within" and "without." Contract liberalism assumes that human consent constructs political order. In one sense, the "virtues" of liberalism have a similar form to Augustine's definition. The social contract is what democracy works in us without us. That is to say, our mere birth within constitutional democracies assumes that we have taken them on. The social contract tradition would add to this what Aquinas added to Augustine's definition, but not without our consent. Yet unlike our consent to the infused virtues, how we consent to constitutional democracies is not easily adjudicated. As Rawls also noted, citizenship in a democratic state is nonvoluntary. How can there be consent without voluntariness? If consent is an intentional action, as I argue in the second part of this book, then it at least assumes voluntary action. Mulhall explains the difficulty well. Consent is assumed by everyone who participates in democratic society, even if the question of how they consented "remains unanswered." Because this question cannot be answered, neither can the question of how one might withdraw consent.[61] The paradox is that citizens are within constitutional democracies by their consent, but they have no means to withdraw that consent, and thus be "without." Cavell's work on Thoreau and Emerson brings this question to the fore more so than Rawls's principles permitted because they both worried that a significant modern ethical and political problem was conformity. Emersonian perfectionism represents an unwillingness to conform to the principles that society establishes. When necessary, it withdraws consent. For Rawls, the principles provide the moral justification for consent and withdrawal, but this misses the fact that discontent with constitutional democracies cannot be resolved by principles and appeals to contracts. They prevent seeing what perfectionism shows. Necessary, conformed consent cannot be an adequate basis for politics or ethics. Perfectionism challenges and possibly corrects this problem.

Cavell's "direct quarrel" with Rawls's justice as fairness arose from "its implied dismissal" of Emersonian perfectionism. It was implied because Rawls addressed Emerson only indirectly. Emerson influenced Nietzsche, and Rawls's criticism of him as undemocratic and elitist was also a tacit criticism of Emerson, but this criticism misunderstands Emersonian perfectionism. Rather than "inherently undemocratic, or elitist," Cavell wrote, "I find Emerson's version of perfectionism to be essential to the criticism of democracy from within."[62] It accomplishes what Rawls's justice as fairness attempts, democracy as something other than mere conformity. Readers might find this surprising because when Cavell sets forth "features" for the "concept of perfectionism," they include what would appear to be the elitism Rawls rejects. Perfectionism is "a transformation of the self which finds expression in the imagination of a transformation of society into something like an aristocracy where what is best for society is a model for and is modelled on what is best for the individual soul, a best arrived at in view of a new reality, a realm beyond, the true world, that of the Good, sustainer of the good city, of Utopia."[63]

If Rawls read or heard this, which according to Cavell he may have, he might have considered himself justified in excluding perfectionism from the just society because of its elitism.[64] Mulhall raises the obvious question that surely Rawls would have raised, "Is not the idea of such perfectionism inherently elitist?"[65] How should we read "something like an aristocracy" in Cavell's criterion for perfectionism as a criticism from within constitutional democracy? Mulhall also assists with the answer. Cavell understands this aristocracy less in terms of a "virtuous few" who merit rule over others because of their superior virtue, and more in terms of an "attainable self in each reader."[66] As such, it democratizes perfectionism and makes possible a judgment against conformist versions of democracy because of the goal perfectionism sets forth, even if it is unattained.

Cavell's perfectionist ethics addresses what he thinks Rawls neglects, a second aspect of the "conversation of justice." Rawls's ideal conditions are the first aspect of the conversation of justice; they generate the founding principles in the original position. Cavell agrees that Rawls's two principles set forth the democratic ideal of justice. The conversation on justice should begin here, but then it should move to a second aspect: actual citizens deliberating the extent to which their justice measures up to the ideal.[67] For Rawls, basic principles and reflective equilibrium suffice for both conversations. For Cavell, they only suffice for the first; the second requires "reflective judgment." Reflective equilibrium without judgment configures moral deliberation from a "derivation in a principle, something more universal, rational, objective, say a standard, from which it achieves justification or grounding." It would be like asking for a rule that would let you know how to go on, but this is what Cavell learned from Wittgenstein is impossible. There are no rules, no standard of justification, and no universal basis that can ensure a priori that we can move from the ideal situation to the actual one. Such rules work in chess or baseball, but they do not work in the moral life. Reflective judgment takes place when justification in terms of principles or rules comes to an end. It is, Cavell writes, "the expression of a conviction whose grounding remains subjective—say myself—but which expects or claims justification from the (universal) concurrence of other subjectivities."[68] It is potentially universal, but only as a claim advanced that others may or may not accept. Reflective judgment is more akin to an aesthetic, and I would add theological, judgment.[69] It summons the yet unattained self and society that could not be satisfied with what-is even if what-is can be made consonant with the principles set out in the first conversation on justice.

Kant and Wittgenstein show the way to reflective judgment; Kant does so in the *Critique of Judgment* and Wittgenstein in the "scene of instruction" in *Philosophical Investigations* §217, a pivotal text for Cavell's perfectionism. Wittgenstein writes, "If I have exhausted the justifications I have reached bedrock, and my spade is turned. Then I am inclined to say: 'This is simply what I do.'" Before this scene, Wittgenstein had been assessing what it means to obey a rule. Rules seek certainty. If we had clear rules, we would know how to go on from the ideal to the actual without the "whirl of organism" that constitutes everyday life. If we could only get others to understand and see the rule, they would know what to do next; we would have a way of proceeding "beyond reproach," something Cavell charged Rawls with seeking.[70] We would have the kind of transparency and certainty philosophers—but also politicians, lovers, neighbors, teachers, judges, and everyone, to some extent—seek from others. Given our desire for transparency and certainty, coupled with what we think rules might accomplish, we are "inclined to say: 'This is simply what I do.'" I follow the rule.

What is this inclination? Is Wittgenstein suggesting, as Kripke seemed to think, that once justification ends there is nothing but acting "blindly," obeying the rule even when we cannot discern its justification?[71] It might seem so. In §219, Wittgenstein states, "'All the steps are already taken' means: I no longer have any choice. The rule once stamped with a particular meaning traces the lines along which it is to be followed through the whole of space. . . . When I obey a rule, I do not choose. I obey the rule *blindly*." But he then refers to this understanding of rule following as a "mythological description." Kripke interprets it as a skeptical solution to skepticism. We follow the rule of the community, although we have no justification for it.[72] For Cavell, Kripke misheard Wittgenstein's voices. Wittgenstein did not say that we are "inclined" to act, but "to say." Being inclined to say is less a reason and more a temptation to act—one that might need to be resisted, especially if rules cannot accomplish what we think they can. We would be "inclined to say" such a thing if we were looking for the right rule or the right algorithm by which we know how to act with certainty and thus avoid the skepticism that inevitably results when a student misunderstands a teacher, or a teacher misunderstands a student. When no such rule arises, then we are inclined to say, "Just do it!" That may, on occasion, be a reasonable thing to say, but the expectation about another rule alleviating the misunderstanding of a rule, not so much. For Cavell there is no evading possible misunderstandings. Skepticism is not defeated by following rules that bring certainty because no such rules exist. Rules do not determine our future course of action logically or causally.

Wittgenstein directs us to criteria, not rules. Criteria, states Cavell, are Wittgenstein's "insight" into knowledge: "All our knowledge, everything we assert or question (or doubt, or wonder about . . .) is governed not merely by what we understand as 'evidence' or 'truth conditions' but by criteria."[73] Criteria are the ordinary conditions that permit understanding something as well as we can. He gives three steps for how this works. First, we have a concept or a "phenomenon" that we want to understand, such as "pain, expecting, knowledge, understanding" or, in the discussion above, "obeying a rule." Second, we "remind ourselves of the kind of statements we make about it."

Finally, "We ask ourselves what criteria we have for (what we go on in) saying what we say."[74]

Let us apply Cavell's criteria and reflective judgment to Rawls's principles. First, we have a conversation about justice that posits the original position and the veil of ignorance. It is a helpful imaginative exercise that we understand is mythological. We never had and never will have such an actual conversation. Yet it is generative. It creates two principles: "Each person is to have an equal right to the most extensive total system of equal basic liberties compatible with a similar system of liberty for all" and "Social and economic inequalities are to be arranged so that they are to the greatest benefit of the least advantaged, consistent with the just saving principle, and attached to offices and positions open to all under conditions of fair equality of opportunity." These two principles generate the fair distribution of goods without any account of what constitutes a good life, human flourishing, excellence, or perfection.

Now let us suppose someone who considers themselves, rightly or wrongly, excluded from this way of life. Perhaps they say, "Your veil of ignorance, like justice, is blind, and that is the problem. It cannot see the inherited inequalities of race, gender, class, or religious discrimination that must first be remedied through conditions of redistribution that will appear, on your principles to be unjust. Justice, like injustice, should acknowledge it has a history."[75] Or perhaps they might say, "Your system only works within the mythical construction of Westphalian states with their clear border markers."[76] Or: "As a baptized Christian (or member of the Islamic umma), I cannot consent to the primacy of relations among citizens that your principles assume. My primary role is not that of citizen. I have obligations to those that exceed the category of national citizen." Or, to use a trivial example that Rawls himself repeatedly uses: "I am a surfer; it is my excellence. Society should be structured so that I have the liberty to surf." Less trivially, replace surfer with musician, artist, scientist, novelist, parent, clergy, monk, pacifist, radical democrat, socialist, or community organizer and discern if the principles permit someone to justly pursue such a way of life, if they let us know how to go on. Rawlsians might respond, "Of course, the principles permit these forms of life as associational, individual, or nonpublic pursuits. Let me explain again how the principles work, clarifying them one more time." It is at this point that the conversation breaks down. It forces objectors to present who they are through the principles Rawlsians know before the conversation takes place. It also refuses to deliberate and judge about what makes for a good life, evaluating each of these claims to excellence. It may not be good to structure society for the vocation of surfing, but what would it mean to structure it so that parents could stay home with newborns, musicians could compose and perform, and epidemiologists can study what might never occur but could? It is unclear that Rawls's principles could accommodate these pursuits, or if he would have the ability to hear how they might justify themselves.

We might not find a way to go on with such a conversation. The Rawlsian might say, "You are being intransigent. I clearly demonstrated how the principles make sense of your particular objection." The non-Rawlsian might reply, "You lack imagination. Your principles have made you see the world as if it were a contract when it is so much more." Cavell acknowledges this potential breakdown in conversation; it is what can happen with our ordinary communication: "Nothing that I have said denies that the scene of instruction ends in a crisis—there is anxiety over whether teacher and child will to go on together. It strikes me as a crisis of consent." It is a "political crisis" concerning what Emerson called "conformity." "The scene thus represents the permanent crisis of a society that conceives of itself as based on consent."[77] Anyone who does not agree with the Rawlsian terms of the conversation might be considered unreasonable, ill-informed, and possibly outside the bounds of a constitutional democracy. If so, then the conversation on justice will be halted; and, at its worst, the proper authorities will be called. Are they not always waiting in the wings? Yet, even when this crisis is reached, we are not without hope. The rational desire for perfection requires us to go on. It acts as an ideal that untidies the putative certainty of rules and principles. For Cavell, perfectionism is necessary for hope; it is why the conversation on justice requires it, if democracy is to be more than conformity.

Anscombe's philosophy can accommodate Cavell's moral perfectionism, even if it does so outside the structure of contractual liberalism. Ethics can never be a discipline isolated from others such as politics, metaphysics, literature, philosophy of mind, or theology; nor does that mean it should be collapsed into them. It cannot do this, because ethics is not about voluntary action aimed at what *ought* to be done. It is about intentional action, and intention requires that we acknowledge actions have histories that provide adequate descriptions to the relevant sense of the questions "Why?" Why did you do that? Why are you doing that? Why do you plan to do that? These histories fit within the "texture of being" (Cora Diamond) or "whirl of organism" (Cavell) that never stand still, as if a snapshot, or a brain scan, or an algorithm, could provide proof positive of the intention. Intentions are forms of communicating with others. Like Anscombe's "total orientation of a human life," perfectionism assumes that there is a truth about one's being that requires intentional action that brings with it constant discovery and attention. Perfectionism is this search for truth. It is archeological—or, in Maurice's terms, "digging"—rather than constructing. It is established "on a concept of truth to oneself."[78] The search for what is good cannot be divided from the investigation of what is true. Practical and theoretical reasoning involve each other. This perfectionism is not a "competing theory of the moral life," one more method to be placed alongside utilitarianism, intuitionism, and Kantian constructivism for students to choose as their method. Ethics does not work this way. Perfectionism is "a dimension or tradition of the moral life that spans the course of Western thought and concerns what used to be called the state of one's soul, a dimension that places tremendous burdens on personal relationships and on the possibility or necessity of the transforming of oneself and of one's society."[79] It aims toward a transformation that often seems unlikely; it requires hope, not optimism.

HOPE, OPTIMISM, AND ETHICS

At its best, Rawls's political liberalism is aspirational; it sets forth a hopeful vision of what democracy might be, and that would make it a form of perfectionism. As Rawls acknowledges, a property-owning democracy or democratic socialism best secures justice as fairness. Yet neither of these forms of society is readily found among current constitutional democracies. Rawls's ideal is capable of critiquing existing societies and calling them to embody their best possibilities; but to do so, it needs some account of what those best possibilities are, and that is what is lacking. Instead, it assumes faith in what has already transpired that led to constitutional democracies and seeks to protect it against something like a perfectionist vision. It too easily falls into conformity to convention.

Faith in human reasonableness leads to a moral or political constructivism that has the potential to limit violence as best we can. Nation-states are to be protected within limits; but when they face a possible demise, then those limits can be neglected for the sake of a "supreme emergency." Because the modern nation-state has become the source of that faith, it cannot be jeopardized. As I noted above, Rawls argues that pacifists, like Quakers, should not hold public office.[80] Yet Quakers are not alone in this exclusion; strict just warriors like Anscombe are also questionable as public office holders—for such officers might need to intentionally kill the innocent to save the republic. Anscombe admitted that she is unwilling for her or her Catholic compatriots to do so. For Rawls, if the republic is lost, the source for a reasonable faith goes with it. His reasonable faith finds its source in a fragile object that depends on our consent for its sustenance without explanation of how that consent works. That implied consent might require actions such as killing the innocent to preserve the nation-state. Rawls has backed into the very account of human action that Anscombe argued defined much of English-speaking ethics since Sidgwick, an account that she named "consequentialism" and derided for its inability to hold fast the command not to murder. Their differences over just-war teaching reveal their differences over the virtues of faith and hope, and then by implication, charity.

Rawls's faith in the historical rise and progress of constitutional democracies is his basis for hope. Yet it is unclear if his hope is hope or optimism, at least as Eagleton distinguishes them. Optimists place faith in progress. They incline toward a kind of conservatism "because their faith in a benign future is rooted in their trust in the essential soundness of the present."[81] Hope is more demanding. It recognizes that things are not as they should be and that getting from where we are to where we should be is no inevitable result of historical progress. Hope requires more than optimism. Faith comes prior; it "reveals what one may legitimately hope for." Hope is the "future tense" of faith. Faith and hope are rooted in charity.[82] Love for neighbors, even enemies, imagines and projects a future where domination, misery, and injustice are not normalized.

For Eagleton, the virtue of hope is not limited to Christian faith. He chides Peter Geach for grounding hope in the "Christian gospel" alone and states, "It is hard to believe that one's eager expectation of a square meal is rendered null and void by the fact that it is not grounded in the death and resurrection of Jesus."[83] Surely, he is correct if grounding hope in the Christian Gospel is limited to Christian persons. Maurice and Aquinas find the hope present in the Gospel also intrinsic to creaturely being. Neither are hope, faith, and charity add-ons to a human nature complete without them, as if the acquired virtues alone suffice for moral or political action. They are an inevitable aspect of existence. Because the Gospel asserts that in Christ all things are made, the theological and infused virtues, along with the gifts that accompany them, have creaturely instantiations as much as redemptive ones. They are ordinary features of life, just like birth, labor, and caring for others. How seldom do philosophical ethicists, or moral theologians for that matter, write or teach as if someone gave us birth? The very condition for our ability to act occurs because someone else labored, and is laboring, on our behalf. Virginia Held makes this point in her "ethics of care" by noting, "Every human being has been cared for as a child or would not be alive."[84] Each human creature exists not because we come ready made with the resources to achieve true happiness on our own behalf but because we received something from others when we did not have such resources. Life exists through the infusing of virtue that we did not, and could not, yet acquire with our own immanent resources. Eagleton states something similar, reminding us that grace perfects nature, a nature that "cannot transcend itself in virtue of its own powers."[85] This grace is a divine gift and at the same time cannot be alien to human nature, which is why Geach's understanding of hope would be misguided if it ties hope too exclusively to Jesus as redeemer and over-looks that he is also the one through whom all things were made.

If there is hope, it is not grounded in nature or history and inevitable progress. Too much death, sorrow, and destruction have already taken place for either optimism or hope located exclusively in nature or history. What hope is available to those whose lives are, or were, mired in misery? Defend-ers of global capitalism are awash in optimism. Bill Gates tells us that "by almost any measure, the world is better than it has ever been." Hans Rosling, a Swedish professor of public health, gave a TED talk on the United Nations' poverty reduction goals titled "The Best Stats You've Ever Seen." What is the good news? According to the adjusted statistics for these goals, only 1,327 million people live in extreme poverty.[86] Let that sink in for a minute. The *good* news is that only 1,327 million of God's creatures live on this Earth in *extreme* poverty, and this is what is acceptable after the goals shifted from poverty reduction of 3.25 percent to 1.25 percent. According to Hickel, this "good news story" serves the strategy of neoliberalism's structural adjust-ment programs as the best way to progress toward poverty reduction. Would it not seem morally perverse to counsel hope to the millions of persons who live in this misery now, telling them that the future is bright because the structural adjustment programs are giving us the best stats that we have seen? Optimism is not hope.

Let us assume a socialist future in which the redistribution of wealth nar-rows global inequality so that the basics of food, shelter, clothing, health care, and education are accessible to all. A radical break with the present leads to a longed-for future. Such a radical hope should be included in the practice of Christian communities, even if it seems that there is very little possibility of getting there from here. Pentecost and its sharing of goods demands it. Nonetheless, even a possible socialist future would be insufficient to counsel those currently living in misery to be optimistic. Hope requires more than that. Kant, somewhat, understood what hope required when he recognized that justice required a proportion between happiness and virtue, which if not realized now must be after death. Sidgwick and Rawls walked away from that recognition. Eagleton acknowledges it when he writes, "No historical event, not even a nuclear holocaust or ecological catastrophe, can shipwreck the fact that history for the Gospel lies in the embrace of the resurrection.

Because of the risen Christ, hope, so to speak, has already happened." He then reminds us that even a great philosopher of hope like Ernst Bloch could not affirm this hope because of his atheism. Eagleton chides Christians for claiming hope exclusively, and he chides Marxists for abandoning the past and present by reducing hope to future projects. "It is striking how few Marxists appear to have asked themselves whether even the most resplendently emancipatory future could outweigh this saga of sorrow."[87] If there is no God, perhaps there is only optimism? If there is only optimism, morality will be reduced to sentimental progress.

No one would accuse Anscombe of optimism. She was incapable of placing trust in the "soundness of the present." Given their inability to resist unjust killing, modern nation-states were not an object or source of hope. Her Catholic ethic is a version of perfectionism, one that generates an ethic of justice, unlike those of Rawls and Cavell, that is external to democratic structures. It does not reject them, but it assumes that they alone are insufficient for a good life. Ethics begins not with principles but the orientation of a human life, by which I take her to mean what is good, excellent, or perfect. Her 1968 essay "You Can Have Sex without Children" finds contemporary moral theology "developing unhealthily" because it leads moral theologians to be primarily concerned with permissible and impermissible acts. Moral theology begins with wrong questions, such as, Can we fulfill the vocation of marriage if we refuse bringing children into the world because of poverty? Focusing on "specific kinds of actions" should be, at most, she argues, a "peripheral" matter. Moral theology should begin elsewhere, with a "sound philosophy of action and intention, which would have to bring this subject matter into connection with the total orientation of a human life and with the virtuous and vicious habits of human beings."[88] This beginning point assumes that human life has an "orientation" within which virtues and vices become intelligible. Rules and permissible or impermissible specific actions, even virtues, only make sense once that "total orientation" is acknowledged.

For Anscombe, hope arises not within a modern understanding of human agents who construct themselves and their politics. It arises from the gift of being. She gives us an understanding of human agency that necessarily leads to a broader approach for teaching and learning ethics than Sidgwick's methods bequeathed us. Because being is itself a divine gift, human action qua action is good, just as being qua being is good. She refuses to distinguish human action from moral action, stating, "All human action is moral action. It is all either good or bad (It may be both)."[89] To be able to act at all, to exercise one's powers, is a good creaturely gift. What makes it bad is that something is missing from the action that should be present, an omission, or something is present that should not be, a bad intention. Good and bad are not opposites; nor are they either-or. Teaching and learning ethics, then, is not about determining if you are a teleologist or deontologist. Anscombe refers to them as "non-existent beasts."[90] The problem with these "ideal abstractions," which is what Broad called them when he set them forth, is that they refer generically to human actions by categorizing them in terms of consequences or duties or some such thing.[91] Yet human actions are always specific, and this specificity makes them subject to moral descriptions.

Something more than just being an action makes it "specifically good or specifically bad." Generic action is writing a name on a piece of paper. Yet we never come across someone who is simply writing their name on something. We hardly have any criteria to make sense of such a generic action. If we did, and we asked why they were writing their name, and they responded "for no particular reason" or "I did not realize that I was," we would find ourselves confronted with a species of nonsense. We would seek further explanations. How can you take pen in hand, put ink on paper, see it is your name, and either not realize that you are doing it or doing so for no reason? Perhaps they could provide further explanations, but whatever those explanations would be, they would be something more than those original responses. Moral descriptions will specify some good or bad under which these actions occur, such as I was signing a contract.[92] It is that specification that gets at what we mean by ethics, not whether it fits with teleology or deontology. In truth, Anscombe says, we are all a bit of both, even Kant.[93] An act's specificity comes from ends, circumstances, and an agent's purpose or purposes. It cannot be bifurcated solely into one of these and treated generically. Once we specify its goodness or badness, the term "moral" adds nothing to it. No difference exists between "good human action" and "moral human action." What permits action to fall under goodness or badness is how it fits within the "total orientation" of a good life.

Anscombe was not, per se, a theologian. She did not write on the doctrine of God or any specific Christian doctrines. She did not lay out with any thoroughness what the human orientation is or how natural happiness and supernatural beatitude relate. It would be inaccurate to refer to her as a moral theologian. She was an analytic philosopher who incorporated elements of moral theology into her philosophical analyses. To be more precise, she was a philosopher of human action, who, like Wittgenstein, offered a therapy for what misleads us into nonsense. The term "Anscombian ethics" would be as nonsensical as what she considered to be Kant's teaching on autonomy or self-legislation, as if my left hand could give my right hand an obligation that it had to fulfill.[94] If she is considered as originating a school of ethical theory or creating shifts in ethical method analogous to those of Sidgwick or Rawls, then her work would be misunderstood. Good action already exists in the world because it is a necessary feature of being itself. Philosophy helps us see what is there so that we can describe what is going on. Her approach fits better with F. D. Maurice's claim that we "dig" or unearth the good. It is there to be found. The virtue of faith is necessary for such a discovery because it approaches what is not yet seen with the hope that it may come into view. For Anscombe, faith is necessary not only for theology but also for a philosophy of knowledge; it was an early concern of hers, even before she wrote about ethics.

Anscombe's daughter, Mary Geach, suggests that she turned to ethics when Philippa Foot was on leave from Somerville College at Oxford to the United States and asked Anscombe to cover her course on ethics. In preparation, Anscombe read works in modern moral philosophy, and she recognized the same faulty understanding of human action that led Oxford to celebrate Truman's indiscriminate killing. She then turned her attention to providing a better understanding of human action, culminating in her 1957 work *Intention*.[95] Whether this story is too simple, as John Berkman suggests, it is the case that if Oxford had not decided to honor Truman, Anscombe may never have turned her attention to ethics.

Anscombe concludes that the academic discipline of ethics since Sidgwick was misguided and that conclusion will always make her work controversial within the academic discipline of ethics. Unlike those who work in the wake of Rawls and his more immanent criticism of Sidgwick, Anscombe and those who work in the wake of her critique challenge the very idea that teaching ethics as a self-coherent academic discipline with its own unique domain is salutary. It is too misguided to be of service to students who seek to be better people, and especially to those who lack awareness that they should so seek.

We know why Anscombe thinks modern moral philosophy is misguided; that much is clear and has already been pointed out, but she only offers indirect insight into how it became such and only hints at how, or if, it could be remedied. She clearly does not argue that the academic discipline of ethics had such a strong hold over people that it misled them into thinking and acting in a corrupt manner. She disagrees with the accusation that moral philosophy "corrupts the youth." For such an accusation to be correct, the accuser would need to demonstrate that youth and others would have had better ethical lives if they had not been taught moral philosophy. What is taught in modern moral philosophy does not significantly differ from "the highest and best ideals of the country at large."[96] It was not because Truman was a Sidgwickian that he felt no moral compunction about directly targeting the innocent. It was because Sidgwick mirrored ideas already present in Western culture, as did W. D. Ross, R. M. Hare, Nowell-Smith, and others. Hume recognized, and promulgated, the corrupting ideas with his distinction of "is" from "ought," but he also clarified the problem. We have the "survival" of the language of obligation, the ought, without the social context for its intelligibility, the is. The ordinary term "ought" became "invested" with something new, "moral force." Anscombe, however, never gives us a genealogy of these ideas in the way that Alasdair MacIntyre attempts in *After Virtue*; but it would not have been possible without Anscombe opening the way.

The genealogy Anscombe provides in "Modern Moral Philosophy" is to lay the problem at the feet of the Reformers. They gave up "divine law" as something that was intended to be obeyed, and emphasized "man's incapacity to obey it, even by grace; and this applied not merely to the ramified prescriptions of the Torah, but to the requirements of the 'natural divine law.'"[97] Anscombe offers no remedy to fix ethics by recovering a divine command ethics that makes sense of "ought"; that is a bad and hasty misreading. She is describing how "ought" survived as a "concept outside the framework that made it a really intelligible one."[98] "Ought" supposedly becomes more precise and scientific as we move from Hume through Sidgwick and into the academic discipline of ethics; but Anscombe finds this inaccurate and distracting. It would be like having the discipline of criminology without knowing anything about criminal law, courts, and judgments. The use of "ought" comes to mean moralists pontificating with earnest emotion that once the term "moral" is employed, we enter another dimension, the moral zone. Anscombe rejects this. There is no such dimension, no such zone, no domain overseen by professionals that will either corrupt ordinary people or keep them from corruption. The corruption predates the philosophical ideas.

Locating the corruption within a supposed faulty understanding of divine law, human agency, and a doctrine of grace brought about by the Reformation is woefully inadequate. It repeats teachings from the Council of Trent that few continue to take seriously as dividing Catholics and Protestants. Just as Rawls revealed a lack of depth in understanding Medieval theology, it is unclear that Anscombe had much understanding of Protestant theology. Her claim that Protestants rejected human capacity to obey the divine law "even by grace" is, quite frankly, a howler.[99] If anything, many Protestant traditions intensified the human capacity to obey divine law through grace by denying that its performance was set aside for those who live by the counsels rather than the ordinary faithful, who are only called to live by precepts, a distinction Anscombe affirmed. Nor is it adequate to conceive, as she does, that the Council of Trent was sufficient to resolve this apparent dispute by authoritatively promulgating that Christ is both legislator and mediator.[100] At most, Anscombe's genealogy would fit the radical Lutherans, a minor off-shoot of Protestants.

Anscombe's claim is unusual in that she is normally more careful in her judgments; but here, her claim invites a reactionary traditionalism. If only we did not have the Reformation, the Enlightenment, and modernity, then we would still have the contexts within which terms such as "obligation" are intelligible. Then the remedy for corrupt moral practice becomes "overcoming" whatever is placed at the origins of the corruption. As in all such reactionary discourse, the remedy too easily colludes with what it opposes, requiring its mischaracterization for the sake of its own identity. Reactionary traditionalism is not concerned with tradition, which is why so often yesterday's radical (libertarian, capitalist, utilitarian, atheist) becomes today's conservative.[101] Despite Anscombe's impoverished interpretation of Protestantism, her work is not best understood as a version of reactionary traditionalism, although it has been, and most likely will continue to be, used as such. She does not seek to preserve a threatened position of supremacy over others. Perhaps it is because she was a British Catholic, but she never sought to use the state apparatus to enforce Catholic teaching. She did not fear the loss of something that did not exist. At her best, she identified a problematic modern understanding of human agency but offered insufficient attention to its genealogy. Nor is it reactionary to suggest that diverse traditions of thought from Catholic accounts of pure nature to Protestant doctrines of grace, Enlightenment notions of the free, autonomous, agent, and capitalist conceptions of instrumental rationality exacerbated, or reflected, a corrupt view of agency that lost the ability to recognize, let alone oppose, unjustly killing innocents. Her criticisms of modern moral philosophy were not sweeping generalities, as if everything from the Reformation on was corrupt and needed to be dismantled, but were analytically precise. The problem lay with a shift in what was meant by intention.

If there is a remedy for what ails modern moral philosophy to be found in Anscombe's work, it is her *Intention*, as a counter to Sidgwick's limiting the domain of ethics to voluntary action. Intentional action and voluntary action are not identical. Intention is acting under a description with a relevant sense of an answer for why one was so acting. The relevant sense would be one that offers reasons for action that would be neither senseless nor nonsense. Take her example: You walk into a room to discover someone spreading out the green books from their library on the floor. Their actions are voluntary; no one is compelling them. Given the specificity of their action, it would seem to be intentional. What would be the intention? The best means to discover the intention would be to ask, "Why?" "Why are you doing that?" They could respond, "No particular reason" or "I just thought I would." Such responses, she notes, could be "intelligible," "strange," or "unintelligible" in different contexts. For instance, asking someone who is tapping their finger on a table why they are doing so might be met with an intelligible use of the response "No particular reason." Tapping your finger for no particular reason makes sense. It fits within the "texture of being" available to us, something we can understand. We have criteria that let us know how to go on with such an answer. But such a response in terms of placing only the green books from the shelves on the floor would be unintelligible. It is not the kind of thing that one does "for no particular reason." No criteria exist by which we could make sense of it.

Drawing on Wittgenstein, she addresses this question by distinguishing two forms of unintelligibility or senselessness. The first is what Wittgenstein referred to as "a form of words is being excluded from the language." The syntax of the form of words is correct; they have a certain sense. We are not confused by them, but they are senseless. Let me give an example drawing on, and supplementing, an example from Stanley Cavell. I can say "feed the kitty," and I can project the use of a similar form of words to say "feed the meter." I could come upon people doing both actions, and when I ask what they are doing, they could respond with such expressions and be perfectly intelligible. They make sense. If, however, I come upon someone writing numbers on a page and I ask what they are doing, it would be senseless for them to say "I'm feeding the quadratic equation." A proper response would be "That makes no sense." The form of words would be excluded. Quadratic equations are not the sort of things that normally, using ordinary language, can be fed.

This first use of senselessness does not help us with the green book example. In this case, it is not a form of words that is being excluded. "Feed the quadratic equation" is not like "For no particular reason." We understand what someone is saying when they say the latter words. What we do not understand is the person who utters them.[102] What is being excluded is the form of life within which it would be intelligible voluntarily to lay out green books on the floor for no particular reason. The action may be voluntary, how could it be otherwise, but it could not be intentional. There is no adequate answer to the question "Why?" in the relevant sense that makes for intentional action. Without a persuasive telling of the reasons for acting, there can be no making sense of intentional action.

Infusing virtue assumes an answer can be given to the question "Why?" Questions such as "In what do you have faith?" "For what do you hope?" and "What do you love?" can be answered with "nothing in particular" in theory but seldom in practice. Practical reasoning can hardly get going without assuming some kind of faith, hope, and love. Answering those questions is as important, and the basis for, addressing the question "What is a life lived well?" It connects the infusing of virtue with intentional action and redeems it from some kind of cultic secret that Kant rightly warned against.

Here we have three different versions of hope. The first is Rawls's, interpreted by Cavell. Hope expresses a desire for the perfection of constitutional democracy. It brings an internal critique that acknowledges its failures and summons it to what it could, but has not yet, attained. Cavell's interpretation resembles my claim above that Rawls's work is aspirational, pointing at its best to democratic socialism, but is unable to affirm it because he inordinately fears comprehensive moral and religious doctrines. It cannot achieve its potential without giving way to reflective judgments.

The second version of hope is Cavell's. Perfectionism calls both the individual soul and society to take a continual journey to the good that cannot rest satisfied with the way the world is while simultaneously finding delight in the way it is. In his 1985 essay "Hope against Hope," Cavell, like Eagleton, addressed the difference between hope and optimism. The latter refuses to recognize the "mortal danger" that the tragic rains down on existence. (The mortal danger noted in this essay was nuclear destruction based on the end-times theology "endorsed" by then President Ronald Reagan.) Emersonian perfectionism recognizes the danger but refuses to submit to despair, for to do so is to "fear" life. Cavell sides with Emerson's "(American) faith," which is "not optimism." Instead, he affirms, "Our moral and religious natures *must* aspire to the perfection for which they have been created and they *must* understand themselves as capable of changing in the direction of perfection; and this perfection has in view the goal and end of moral struggle."[103] It is hope that causes him to quarrel with Rawls's dismissal of perfection. Constitutional democracy, even on Rawls's terms, requires it. Rawls was incorrect to view perfectionism as positing human excellence and then seeking to maximize it. In fact, neither Nietzsche nor Emerson thought that the excellence present in contemporaneous versions of art, science, and culture was such that it should be maximized. Cavell also critiques Rawls for focusing on Nietzsche, dismissing his perfectionism and never attending to other perfectionists such as George Bernard Shaw and the socialists William Morris, John Ruskin, and Thomas Carlyle.[104] I would add F. D. Maurice to this list. Perfectionism is not a threat to constitutional democracy; it refuses to "excuse" it "for its inevitable failures" or withdraw from them.[105]

And the third version of hope is Anscombe's. Hope is a gift of the Holy Spirit. Like faith, it is an inescapable aspect of existence. A good life is not to be found in a complete, virtuous life achieved over a lifetime, as it was for Aristotle. A good life is a gift that can give an answer to the questions that the infused virtues pose. Here is where her Christianity recalibrates ethics. Virtues do not set the ends for the Christian life. Anscombe writes, "Virtues, however, may be means rather than ends. Indeed, Christians *must* regard them as such, for we have an end proposed to us, namely the vision of God, and participation in the life of God, which is not a state or practice of moral virtue. And we don't even think it is attained by the practices of the moral virtues—only that the failure to practice them greatly endangers its attainment."[106] Participation in the divine life comes as a gift received in faith. Faith, however, is not only for the religious; it has a secular analogue. Faith is, she states, "important not only for theology and for the philosophy of religion. It is also of huge importance for the theory of knowledge. The greater part of our knowledge of reality rests upon the belief that we repose in things we have been taught and told."[107] Testimony is an inevitable feature of learning. It assumes faith. This faith is not a blind faith in authority, whether secular or religious. It is "coming to see."

Like Wittgenstein, Anscombe also draws on a scene of instruction, a teacher imparting wisdom to a student. It only works if there is faith, but not faith in the teacher or necessarily in what the teacher is saying. Instead, she puts it like this: "In teaching philosophy we do not hope that our pupils will *believe us*, but rather that they will *come to see* that what we say is true—if it is."[108] Faith hopes that the truth of our endeavors comes to be seen. Truth matters. If there were no truth, faith and hope would be nothing more than sentimentality and optimism. Since Hume, she fears, truth has become "indifferent" for the philosopher. If so, then that prohibits the kind of reflective judgment Cavell ventured. Reason as slave to the passions "cannot give you ends or judge for or against ends."[109] It does not make a claim. Against this indifference to truth, she defends "connatural knowledge." It is the virtue of the just person who knows, for instance, that selling poor women powdered milk to make money, as the Nestlé Company did, is wrong. Such knowledge is not only about having the proper information, but it also requires the practical wisdom that links such information to "good inclination, the inclination toward good ends." Why do some come to see this, and others miss it? Can we account for it by luck or contingency? It requires more than that. Anscombe writes,

> It belongs with a just way of looking at things; and *it* can't be called
> a good of fortune. The spirit of such knowledge is what is called a
> gift of the Holy Ghost; the light of it a light that is there to enlighten

everyone who comes into the world. I do not mean that everyone actually has this light on in his mind, for it may have been extinguished or never allowed to come on. It may be there as a mere glimmer, whose sign is the understanding of human language with all its multifarious action and motive descriptions, its machinery for accusing others and excusing oneself.[110]

Why is it that some come to see what others miss, but who might yet see it because others saw it first?

Vincent Lloyd's *In Defense of Charisma* suggests something similar. The transcendentals—the good, true, and beautiful—are always there. They are intrinsic to our humanity but clouded over, turned into an enigma, by "cultural and ideological forces." Our "attunement to them" occurs when charisma exposes them. Charisma, like infusing virtues, does not take us away from our humanity but intensifies it, disclosing its fullness.[111] Perhaps the most appropriate image for infusing virtue is the Transfiguration. It was Irenaeus who looked deeply into that mystery and saw the correlation between glory and humanity: *Gloria Dei, vivens homo* (the glory of God is a human being fully alive), a theological image taken up by Hans Urs von Balthasar and extended by Oscar Romero, *Gloria Dei vivens pauper*.[112] But it was the Apostle Paul who was caught up short by that transfigured presence and came to see that even though we only see in an enigma or a riddle, faith, hope, and love sustain us until the riddle makes sense. Once this occurs, if it occurs, love alone remains.

NOTES

1. As previously noted in this book, Rawls's work on Christian ethics went well into the 1950s, and Bok notes that he still expressed Christian belief during this time, something that Rawls contradicts in his reflection "On My Religion" late in life. Bok thinks it misstates Rawls's public record.
2. Rawls, *Brief Inquiry*, 261; Gregory, "Before the Original Position," 195.
3. Cohen and Nagel, quoted by Rawls, *Brief Inquiry*, 1.
4. Rawls, *Brief Inquiry*, 263. See also Gregory, "Before the Original Position," 195.
5. Rawls, *Brief Inquiry*, 264.
6. Rawls, 265.
7. Rawls.
8. See Rawls, *Law of Peoples*, 22.
9. Eagleton, *Hope*.
10. Rawls, *Brief Inquiry*, 268. By dividing will and intellect in God, Rawls fails to attend to the doctrine of simplicity. Rawls seems concerned, and rightly so, with bad doctrines of divine

sovereignty, many of which emerged in the late Middle Ages. He does not consider that God's freedom to act always depends on God's nature as perfect.

11. Rawls, *Brief Inquiry*, 269.

12. Gregory, "Before the Original Position," 181, 195.

13. Rawls, *Brief Inquiry*, 193.

14. Rawls, 115.

15. Rawls, 124, 170.

16. It is also present in his unpublished essay from Cornell in the mid-1950s "Toleration and Justification," where he wrote, "For a church to seek the elimination of her sister churches in the hope that she herself may be established supreme in the state is to seek the embrace of death. . . . The medieval church was living on borrowed time. Like a person, the Church can gain the world, but lose her soul"; Reidy, "Rawls's Religion," 335.

17. Rawls, *Brief Inquiry*, 123.

18. Rawls, *Lectures on the History of Moral Philosophy*, 314–17. Christopher J. Insole makes a compelling case that Rawls misinterprets Kant here and that Kant already reworked a doctrine of the highest good that significantly differed from previous theological traditions. See Insole, *Kant and the Divine*, 143.

19. Rawls, *Lectures on the History of Moral Philosophy*, 167–69.

20. Rawls, 316.

21. Rawls, 316–17.

22. Rawls, 318.

23. Rawls, 319.

24. Rawls, 320.

25. Rawls, 322.

26. Rawls, 324.

27. Weithman, "Does Justice as Fairness Have a Religions Aspect?" 31. Weithman takes Rawls's "religiosity condition" from his lectures on Kant and cites Rawls's comment on the Second Critique, "the step to religion is taken for the sake of the highest good and to preserve our devotion to the moral law"; Weithman, 32. Yet this seems to overlook his later criticisms of the highest good as a vestige of Leibniz's philosophical theology in Kant that needed to be excised.

28. Reidy, "Rawls's Religion," 331.

29. Reidy, 309.

30. Cavanaugh, *Migrations of the Holy*; Wolin, *Politics and Vision*.

31. Edmundson, *John Rawls*, 182–83.

32. Anscombe, *Faith*, xii.

33. Conradi, *Iris Murdoch*, 273, 284; Mac Cumhaill and Wiseman, *Metaphysical Animals*, 219–23.

34. John Berkman has made a compelling case that Anscombe's interest in justice is the basis for her "Modern Moral Philosophy" and retrieval of virtue; Berkman, "Justice and Murder," 225–71.

35. Teichmann, *Philosophy*, xi.

36. Anscombe, *Faith*, 116, 153.

37. Anscombe viewed abortion as the direct killing of the innocent. Early on, she thought contraception might lessen abortions and if so, the Catholic Church's position should not be "kept up," a position she later rejected; Anscombe, *Ethics*, 82–83. She also acknowledged that abortion was never legally classified as murder; Anscombe, *Human Life*, 264.

38. Mouffe, *Democratic Paradox*, 14.

39. Anscombe, *Ethics*, vii, 75–79; Mac Cumhaill and Wiseman, *Metaphysical Animals*, 65–69. John Berkman has discovered that her pamphlet remained in circulation despite her assertion that it was removed. See Berkman, "Justice and Murder," 246–47.

40. Teichman, "Gertrude," 49.

41. Berkman, "Justice and Murder," 237–42.

42. I would not have known about her admiration for Day and the Catholic Worker apart from my conversations with John Berkman, who discovered this information through interviews.

43. Anscombe, *Ethics*, 55–56.

44. Anscombe, 58.

45. Whether this is an adequate historical record would require much more than what Anscombe suggests here. Is it the case that the indiscriminate warfare of World War II can be traced to pacifists turned warriors? It seems unlikely.

46. Her friend Jenny Teichman, who was also a research fellow at Somerville College, Oxford, in the late 1950s, would publish a much better interpretation of pacifism in which she challenges Anscombe's interpretation. See Teichman, *Pacifism*, 50, 64–66.

47. Anscombe, *Ethics*, 52.

48. Anscombe, 61.

49. Walzer, "Why?" 17, 19.

50. Rawls, *Law of Peoples*, 105.

51. Rawls, 99.

52. Herman, "Editor's Foreword," xii.

53. Cavell, *Conditions Handsome*, xviii.

54. Rawls, *Theory of Justice*, 288.

55. Rawls, 290.

56. Rawls.

57. Rawls.

58. Rawls, 291.

59. In his interpretation of Cavell's work, Stephen Mulhall shows how Cavell's liberalism fits well with Rawls's. Mulhall writes that Cavell's "portrait of the procedures of moral discourse is one which emphasizes the fundamental importance of the individual's right to work out her moral position for herself: ethical debate is primarily an essential part of a process of self-development, and although it is structured in such a way as to permit the possibility of moral community, that community is based upon an agreement to disagree and presupposes that one must confront others on their own terms rather than upon one's own." Along with these aspects of liberalism is also their shared assumption that we live in pluralistic communities that lack the ability to come to agreement on many moral, aesthetic and political controversies. Cavell's liberalism, however, serves the purpose not of affirming atomized individuals but communities. I think the same could be said of Rawls. Mulhall identifies other "ordinary" forms of life that would not fit well contractarian liberalism, including socialism and Christianity. Mulhall, *Stanley Cavell*, 68–73.

60. Cavell, *Conditions Handsome*, 3.

61. Mulhall, *Stanley Cavell*, 259.

62. Cavell, *Conditions Handsome*, 3.

63. Cavell, *Conditions Handsome*, 6–7; see also Mulhall, *Stanley Cavell*, 266.

64. Rawls read Cavell's first and third Carus lectures, which became the first and third chapters of *Conditions Handsome*. They then had "two long and full conversations" about them; Cavell, *Conditions Handsome*, xxii.

65. Mulhall, *Stanley Cavell*, 266.

66. Mulhall, 270.

67. Mulhall, 271.

68. Cavell, *Conditions Handsome*, xxvi.

69. Here I would agree with Peter Dula that Cavell not only questions "the boundaries between philosophy and literature, [but] also questions the boundaries between philosophy and theology." This is not to suggest that the two are the same, only that the boundaries could never be so well defined that everything on this side of some imagined disciplinary line is philosophy and everything on the other is theology. Dula, *Cavell*, 67.

70. See Mulhall, *Stanley Cavell*, 276.

71. Kripke, *Wittgenstein*, 81.

72. See Cavell, *Conditions Handsome*, 69–71.

73. Cavell, *Claim*, 14.

74. Cavell, 29.

75. For a similar argument, see Nichole Flores's criticism of Rawls's liberal aesthetics with its inability to attend adequately either to a religious aesthetic or to persons on the margins of society; Flores, *Aesthetics*, 10, 47–74. Cavell's reflective judgment exemplifies the kind of aesthetics that I find her advocating.

76. See Osiander, "Sovereignty"; and Vergerio, "Beyond."

77. Cavell, *Conditions Handsome*, 76.

78. Cavell, 1.

79. Cavell, 2.

80. Rawls, *Law of Peoples*, 105.

81. Eagleton, *Hope*, 4.

82. Eagleton, 42, 68.

83. Eagleton, 40.

84. Held, *Ethics*, 3.

85. Eagleton, *Hope*, 127.

86. Hickel, *Divide*, 34, 38.

87. Eagleton, *Hope*, 36, 100.

88. Anscombe, *Ethics*, 91.

89. Anscombe, *Human Life*, 209.

90. Anscombe, 232.

91. Broad, *Five Types*, 207–8.

92. Anscombe, 214.

93. Anscombe, 232.

94. Allen Wood acknowledges the power of Anscombe's critique of Kant and attempts to answer it; see Wood, *Kantian Ethics*, 108–9. For Kant, he writes, "The law of autonomy is objectively valid for rational volition because it is based on an objective end—the dignity of rational nature as an end in itself." If it were not for this, Anscombe's criticism would be valid. Kant's self-legislating agent is "absurd" only if we assume statutory and not natural legislation. The latter is based on "objective reasons valid for all rational beings." It is why he considers Rawls and Korsgaard's moral constructivism unable to answer Anscombe's criticism. Contra the constructivists, objectivity cannot arise from a procedure.

95. Anscombe, *Human Life*, xvii.

96. Anscombe, 163.

97. Anscombe, *Ethics*, 31n2.

98. Anscombe, 31.

99. It is interesting, given MacIntyre's later appreciation for Anscombe, that in his 1959 essay "Hume on 'Is' and 'Ought,'" he questions her critique of the Reformers, but not by way of defending them. He wrote, "Miss G. E. M. Anscombe has recently suggested that the notion of a morality of law was effectively dropped by the Reformers; I should have thought that there were good grounds for asserting that a moral of law-and-nothing-else was introduced by them"; MacIntyre, "Hume," 467. This, too, of course, is a reduction of what Protestant moral theologians taught.

100. Anscombe, *Ethics*, 31n2.

101. Corey Robin has traced the "reactionary mind" from Edmund Burke through Donald Trump. What unifies this kind of conservativism, he suggests, is less the specific ideas or practices that are being conserved and more the fear of losing power that one either has or thought one had. Conservatism is a "struggle for supremacy"; Robin, *Reactionary Mind*, 29. Conservatives are reactionary because their power over others is threatened. Robin's argument is highly illuminating, and it explains well the incoherence of conservative movements in the English-speaking world.

102. Anscombe, *Intention*, 26–27.

103. Cavell, *Conditions Handsome*, 130–31.

104. Cavell, xxiii.

105. Cavell, 18.

106. Anscombe, *Faith*, 230.

107. Anscombe, 3.

108. Anscombe, 4.

109. Anscombe, *Human Life*, 59.

110. Anscombe, 62.

111. Lloyd, *In Defense*, 7.

112. Colón-Emeric, *Oscar Romero's Theological Vision*, 20–24.

CONCLUSION TO PART I
Destabilizing the Boundary to Teaching and Learning Ethics

Sidgwick set the agenda for moral philosophy in the analytic tradition. What ethics is, however, and how one goes about teaching it has been challenged. Is ethics' primary concern value, ought, right, good, theoretical or practical, cognitive or noncognitive, natural or nonnatural? Once a domain is agreed upon, if it ever is, then the question of method or procedure arises. Should teachers and learners adopt perfectionism, intuitionism, hedonism—egoistic or utilitarian, contractarianism, deontology, virtue, or some other? Much teaching and learning ethics concerns interminable debates about these domains and methods. To their credit, John Rawls and G. E. M. Anscombe largely avoid such debates and point in more normative directions. Perhaps the reason for this is their common commitment to justice and the influence Wittgenstein had on their approach to philosophy. They differ considerably, however, on Henry Sidgwick's transformation of the discipline of ethics.

Rawls worked within Sidgwick's boundaries; Anscombe destabilized the boundary, and this has implications not only for ethics but also for the relationship between it and theology. Sidgwick's boundary bracketed out theological matters. He did not reject them; nor did he deny their importance. Instead, they were set aside in order to develop a precision guiding method for ethical action. Utilitarianism was this method. Rawls countered it first with Kantian moral constructivism and then with political liberalism. He also bracketed out theological matters; they were not rejected or denied but were considered harmful if allied with state power. Associations and individuals with theological convictions were tolerated, permitted, and even affirmed as long as they presented their convictions within the terms of an overlapping consensus founded on public reasonableness. As Stephen Mulhall noted, this overlapping consensus was a circular argument;

religious claims were acceptable only when they first passed the test of public reasonableness that Rawls laid out as early as *A Theory of Justice*. Morality was a species of political reason, but political reason must remain independent, even transcendent, over comprehensive moral and religious frameworks.

Anscombe finds the distinctions within which both Sidgwick and Rawls work to be unconvincing. For her, the term "moral" adds nothing to "human action." By setting forth a distinction between voluntary and intentional action and by showing the necessity of the latter not only for "moral" but for all actions, she destabilizes Sidgwick's boundaries. Sidgwick's definition of ethics no longer makes sense. It clarifies nothing. How can ethics be "the science or study of what is right or what ought to be, so far as this depends upon the voluntary action of individuals" when voluntary action is an inadequate domain upon which to make the discipline of ethics depend? Ethics also becomes too enamored with "science or study," focusing on methods and theories, assuming that one teaches ethics by taking learners through diverse theories that will assist them to know which voluntary act to perform. Intentional action, practical knowledge, and practical truth forge a better way forward in teaching and learning ethics.

Anscombe's criticisms remain important because they usher in new possibilities for teaching and learning ethics, possibilities that she indicated by noting the gift character of coming to see what should be seen. The theological and infused virtues are another way of naming this gift character. If the infused virtues explain ordinary action well, then Sidgwick's approach misses what matters most. Anscombe pointed out what it misses. She is by no means the only philosopher who evaluated Sidgwick's take on ethics as inadequate. As we have seen, the Hegelians also found it reductive. Likewise, many, if not most, who look to sources before Sidgwick, especially Aristotle and Aquinas, recognize that something shifted with Sidgwick. Julia Annas argues that Sidgwick transformed expectations for what moral theory accomplished. Based on the assumption that "ethics, as it stands, is a mess and needs to be sanitized by scientific methods," the task of ethics became to "identify, systematize and formalize out of our moral thinking certain 'methods' or procedures for coming to ethical conclusions."[1] This led to a misguided attempt at a "hierarchical and complete" ethical system that first seeks to identify the precision guiding principle—whether it be utility, respect for persons, agape, or even virtue—and then use this principle to construct the procedure or method that will guide persons to right action, to what ought to be done.

DOMINANT FEATURES OF MODERN MORAL PHILOSOPHY

My argument has been, and will continue to be, less that these dominant features of teaching and learning ethics are wrong and more that they are too limiting, and that for this reason they inhibit coming to see what a life lived well looks like. This, of course, will require focusing on life more than system, method, or theory. The dominant features that arise from Sidgwick's transformation of ethics are

1. Voluntary action as the domain within which the ethicist works
2. Distinguishing right and good
3. An emphasis on theory, methods, or procedures
4. Asking the question that guides action: What shall I do?
5. Privileging modern over ancient ethics

These features fit together; each leads to the next. Actions are voluntary when they arise from individuals unconstrained by others, by their own characters, by the good, or by God. We saw this in Sidgwick's twofold criticism of Aristotle as well as in his critique of T. H. Green's doctrine of freedom. First, the good as attractive kept them from recognizing the power of the will to choose against it. Second, their emphasis on the stability of character led them to an inadequate understanding of voluntary action. Once this account of human action is in place, then distinguishing right from good, and privileging the former over the latter, naturally follows. If the good is attractive, as Sidgwick notes, it supposedly diminishes the significance of voluntary action. Ethics would be more concerned with identifying the good and asking questions about what it is and how rational desire is ordered to it, as Aristotle does in his first sentence of the *Nicomachean Ethics*: "Every craft and every line of inquiry, and likewise every action and decision, seems to seek some good; that is why some people were right to describe the good as what everything seeks."[2] If ethics begins here, then voluntary action is not, of course, rejected. Aristotle has a place for it as a precondition for virtue, but it does not define ethics.

Demoting the good to motivation, which is often internal to the agent, does away with the question "What is the good your actions inevitably seek?" The quest for the good, which was also a quest for what is right, is replaced by a new interpretation of the "right" as the proper state of affairs brought about through voluntary action. An emphasis on method or procedure becomes the heart of ethics as its task becomes guiding action toward the right. Because the right is not attractive, because it has been differentiated from the good, it is not an object that preexists the agent's voluntary action; it is what the former brings about. The question that makes best sense of this version of ethics is not "What is the good?" or "What is a life lived well?" but "What shall I do?"

Voluntary Action

Voluntary action is essential, but insufficient, in thinking about ethics. Aristotle and Anscombe have a place for it. Yet Anscombe shows its limitations much more than Aristotle. Stanley Cavell likewise recognizes its limitations, and he asks what criteria cause us to ask the question about the voluntariness of an action.

Aristotle identified ἑκούσιον, often translated as "voluntary," as one of the preconditions for virtue. Virtue concerns feelings (πάθη) and actions (πράχεις), and it is the latter that is the reason actions are praised or blamed because they are voluntary (ἑκούσιος).[3] The term ἑκούσιον contrasts with ακούσιον, involuntary. It is involuntary because it is forced; it has an external principle or an "origin from without" rather than being an action internal to the agent.[4] The agent's internal sources make no contribution to involuntary forced actions, and because the agent's contribution matters so much for Aristotle's understanding of virtue, such involuntary actions cannot be praised or blamed.

Ignorance is also a species of involuntary action.[5] However, it is not ακούσιον but οὐχ ἑκούσιον or nonvoluntary. For Aristotle, then, voluntary action is a precondition for virtue, but he is more interested in telling us what it is not, actions not done from force or ignorance, than telling us what it is. In fact, it is one of four preconditions for virtue, including "decision" or "choice" (προαιρέσις), "deliberation" (βούλευσις), and "wish" (βούλησις). Aristotle summarizes these preconditions, stating that "we have found, then, that we wish for the end, and deliberate and decide about things that promote it; hence the actions concerned with things that promote the end are in accord with decision and are voluntary. The activity of the virtues are concerned with these things [that promote the end.] Hence virtue is also up to us, and so also, in the same way, is vice."[6]

Aristotle can sound more like Kant here than Augustine, who defined virtue as what God works in us without us. For Aristotle, as with most modern philosophers, the happiness achieved through the exercise of the virtues primarily results from one's own efforts.

Unlike most modern philosophers, but consistent with theologians, Aristotle considered the possibility that happiness arose from divine action.

He poses a two-part question as to how happiness comes about and considered two possibilities: (1) "Is happiness acquired by learning, or habituation, or by some other form of cultivation?" (2) "Or is it the result of some divine fate, or even of fortune?"[7] He does not rule out the second possibility, and he states that if the gods give us "any gift," it would be happiness; but he passes over this possibility because it would be more appropriate for a "different inquiry." Virtue primarily comes about through some kind of "learning and attention."[8] It is better, he suggests, that it come from us, even if it is something divine.

Anscombe and Cavell did not disagree with Aristotle about the importance of voluntary action but rather critique its central place in modern ethics based on a Cartesian philosophy of mind. This philosophy of mind posits mental states that offer a causal theory of action. Action begins with an intention or belief or desire that becomes the "antecedent of actions." Will becomes the causal power effecting that intention in the world. Anscombe's *Intention* disabuses us of this causal theory of action. Will and intention are not causally but conceptually related.[9] Much like Cavell, Anscombe does not look to individuals and their mental states but examines criteria whereby we use diverse forms of the word "intention," dividing them into three: "an expression of intention," "intentional action," and "intention in acting."[10] She then clarifies these diverse forms of intention, not seeking to determine what intention is or how it is always used, as if there were such a thing, but as Rachel Wiseman puts it, "to describe the look of a human life containing that concept."[11]

Cavell does something similar in discussing action, and he cautions against reading too much into its voluntariness; it is a philosopher's temptation that should be avoided. He writes, "Philosophers imagine, because of a distorted picture of the mind, that the term 'voluntary' must apply to all actions which are not involuntary (or unintentional), whereas it is only applicable where there is some specific reason to raise the question."[12] Like Anscombe, the distorted picture places the origin of action in the mind and generates a false view of action as causal. The mind plans on how it will cause its work in the world, and the will extends outward to achieve it. The world may not be accommodating, so whatever situation is brought about may very well differ from the motive by which the mind initially works. Human action is bifurcated between an interior, perhaps even private, space of the mind and the state of affairs it seeks to achieve. The former could be good and the latter wrong, or the former could be bad and the latter right.

Anscombe problematized this conception with her green books analogy. Placing green books on the floor could only be a voluntary act, but without a reasonable answer to the question "Why?" it cannot be understood as intential. Cavell problematizes the centrality of voluntary action by asking us to consider what the criteria would be whereby we would raise the question "Was that action voluntary?" We seldom go around asking people this question. We assume that they are responsible for their actions without locating some good or right-making property in an antecedent mental state like "voluntariness." We raise the question of voluntariness when there is a specific reason to do so, such as in a criminal proceeding or an ethics review. The criteria whereby we ask the question shows that ethics is more than voluntary action. Consider an example from the world of medicine.

An oncology nurse goes about her daily work offering patients medication to alleviate their suffering. One day she gives a lethal dose of painkillers to a dying patient. When this action is discovered, the hospital authorities investigate and subject her to an ethics review, asking questions such as "Did you know the dose was lethal?" "Did you voluntarily kill the patient with the lethal dose?" Before this act, the nurse was never questioned about the voluntariness of her actions. She had never been brought before the review board when she did what oncology nurses do, seek to cure cancer while alleviating suffering. It would seem odd to question her everyday routine, asking if her actions were voluntary, but not odd to question her on the day her actions exacerbate a patient's unnecessary death. The voluntariness of her action matters in a new way. It answers the question "Why?" differently from her normal routine in seeking to cure patients. It is not only voluntary but also intentional. If she responds, "Yes, I gave a lethal dose of painkillers to kill the patient. I succeeded in my aim, but I did not intend to kill the patient. I intended to do what I always do and sought his cure," then we have the kind of situation that Anscombe attributed to Sidgwick's revised view of intention. She is not responsible for her action because of what she foresaw the consequences of her action to be—the alleviation of suffering. The motive that began her action was good, and that mental state gives her a power of description over her action, taking precedence over the action itself. What ought to be, the alleviation of suffering, is the relevant moral feature and not what is, the intentional death of an innocent.

Only in a troubling, exceptional case do we need to ask about the voluntariness of an action. Before that, its voluntariness lacks the same significance. Yet it would be odd to suggest that ethics concerns those cases in which the question of the voluntariness of an action holds but not when it seems less pressing when the criteria for its use are absent. Surely, the nurse's routine, daily actions are as ethically significant, even if she gives little thought to them. The question of the voluntariness of the action does not identify its ethical significance. When voluntary action alone defines the domain of ethics, something has gone awry, most likely the assumption that some kind of mental event transforms the action into something ethical. We look in the wrong place if we seek to identify a property like voluntariness to make an action ethical. We are not looking at the "form of life" (Wittgenstein), "whirl of organism" (Cavell), or "texture of being" (Cora Diamond) within which actions occur. We look outside these and try to locate an ethical-making property just as an oncologist locates cancer, perhaps finding it in what is "right" to do based on a proper method or procedure rather than what is "good."

Distinguishing the Right from the Good

Firm distinctions between the good and the right are not easy to come by. As Peter Geach has noted, the two terms were once considered synonymous. What differentiates a good human action from a right one? Sidgwick and Ross distinguished them by bifurcating human action. The good addresses questions of motivation, and the right is that which is brought about in the world. It is possible to perform the right action from the wrong motive and, conversely, the wrong action from the right motive. Good as motivation becomes internalized, often opaque, and disconnected from objects that prompt desire. Before Sidgwick's transitions, the good was less subjective, less capable of the distinction that Sidgwick sought. Now "right" becomes a property of actions and "good" becomes a description of will or motive. This distinction makes possible the consequentialism that Anscombe challenged.

To show the problems with this distinction, consider this case. You have a home for rent, and two groups have asked to rent it at different times. Both requests arise from rallies going on in your neighborhood. The first is a Black Lives Matter rally, and the second is a neo-Nazi rally. Convinced that the first is virtuous and the second is vicious, you offer your house without cost to Black Lives Matter but refuse to offer it at any price to the neo-Nazis. Perhaps someone then asks, "You have done what is good, but have you done what is right?" By what criteria might this question make sense? It assumes that a clear distinction can be drawn between them. Right does not ask if it is "morally good" to rent one's home to either party; as Ross puts it, "'Right' does not mean the same as 'morally good.'"[13] It may be that we have a duty, based on the right, not to discriminate against anyone. I am not suggesting that Ross might have a prima facie duty not to rent one's house to Nazis, but that distinguishing right from good lets us ask a different set of questions: What is the right thing to do? What is good? Different answers can be given to both.

If the good and right are not so easily distinguishable—and the good, like the right, is an end that allows persons to cultivate virtues—then a different question arises concerning the case. The primary question is not whether renting one's house to facilitate Nazis or Black Lives Matter protesters is good or evil, right or wrong; the primary question is given that we know supporting the former is evil and the latter good. What kinds of life must we inhabit to direct our actions to what is right and good? If we are asked to debate whether supporting Nazis is good, we have already entered a corrupt conversation from which no good can come. Instead, the question is what virtues we need to achieve good and avoid evil in such a context, and this will require a fuller conversation than the mere binary of good/evil or right/wrong provides. We will need to discuss courage, justice, truthfulness, friendship, proper indignation, and, for Christian ethics, the place of faith, hope, and charity. We may find it appropriate to invite a Nazi to Shabbat to convert them but do nothing to support their projects.[14] Once the discussion occurs in the context of these virtues, then it will also become apparent that how we respond to it will not only effect what occurs in the world but also what it does to us and neighbors near and far.

The priority of the right too easily frees persons from the thorny questions of what is good. The Reagan administration's defense of Bob Jones University's prohibition of interracial dating in the 1970s was not based on moral judgments on the character of the university's administrators who defended and implemented that policy, or on an understanding of the good ordering of human creatures; it was based on the state of affairs that would be permitted by government intrusion into the affairs of a private university. The same is true of the Supreme Court's decision on the Masterpiece Cakeshop. No moral judgment on same-sex marriage was presented. The judgment was based on possible foreseen consequences. If we deny Jack Phillips his religious convictions against gay marriage, then will we not be duty bound to deny other religious or moral convictions, whether we agree with them or not, that motivate a business owner not to provide services for what they consider objectionable practices?

Refusing to distinguish right and good requires understanding and appraising these situations differently. There are not two sides to the moral evaluation of neo-Nazi speech. In order not to be materially implicated in their hatred, a just, wise, and faithful person will resist it. Whether it produces the best possible foreseen consequences, giving neo-Nazis a platform affects those who shelter them, the communities within which they are sheltered, and the persons who will be subjected to their vitriol. Speech-acts are not neutral; they are ethically burdened. Privileging the right over the good, and basing moral philosophy on this privileging, fails to address this reality.[15]

Few ethicists, whether modern or ancient, abandon the good altogether. Rawls has his thin theory of it. However, the ethics of the right, sometimes referred to as an ethics of obligation, is emphasized in modern ethics and was relatively unknown in antiquity. Of course, the ancients knew duty and the importance of principles or rules. Christianity, following its Jewish origins, had an important place for law, as was noted above in discussing Thomas Aquinas. As Alasdair MacIntyre has repeatedly noted, a "morality of the virtues" should not be set against a "morality of rules." Laws are necessary, but it is the person with the virtue of justice who knows how to apply them.[16] For Aquinas, law directs human acts to virtuous ends. If the ends are unknown, the law becomes arbitrary, to be obeyed for its own sake. As an external principle, law is a means and not an end. Martin Luther King Jr. built his protest against unjust laws on this very idea. The end for which law is a means is a vision of the good, a beloved community.

When I tell people that the question "What makes for a good human life?" has become controversial in the university and among many contemporary philosophical ethicists, they often express surprise. How can ethics avoid this question? There are good reasons, and not so good reasons, for this controversy. The good was traditionally a metaphysical or theological concept. In the Middle Ages, it was, along with truth and beauty, one of the "transcendental predicates of being." These predicates were understood to be convertible, so that if something exists, if it has being, it would possess the possibility of being known to be what it is (the true); it could be ordered to its purpose for existing (the good), and knowing and ordering it would bring aesthetic delight (the beautiful). Although they are in reality the same, the transcendentals differ conceptually. The true is the adequation of being to a mind. The good is an appetitive relation to being. Beauty is the sensory delight in being as "duly proportioned."[17]

Thomas Aquinas set forth these transcendentals and their convertibility by drawing on Aristotle and Augustine. Good and being, Aquinas wrote, "are the same in reality" and differ only "conceptually."[18] His argument begins with the first line from Aristotle's *Nicomachean Ethics*: "The good is what all things desire" (*bonum est quod omnia appetunt*). After utilitarianism, Aquinas's understanding of the relationship between the good and desire can easily be misunderstood. For Aquinas, that something is desired does not make it good. Rather, that something is good makes it desirable; its goodness cannot be separated from its desirability. Nonetheless, ethics cannot proceed to an account of the good by listing the many things someone might desire, even if they had the "full information" of what their best possible future holds.

Theory and Practice

The change in the name of the Knightbridge Chair from "Casuistry, Moral Theology, and Moral Philosophy" to "Moral Philosophy" indicates one significant change that Sidgwick brought about in teaching and learning ethics. Theology dropped out, but so did politics, metaphysics, psychology, poetry, and other disciplines. The difference between his definition of ethics compared with Aristotle's indicates another. Recall the two definitions:

> Sidgwick: The science or study of what is right or what ought to be, so far as this depends upon the voluntary action of individuals.
>
> Aristotle: Our present discussion does not aim, as our others do, at study; for the purpose of our examination is not to know what virtue is, but to become good, since otherwise the inquiry would be of no benefit to us.

Should ethics be a study of what ought to be as it depends upon voluntary action, or should it be an examination in becoming better human beings? The former moves in the direction of theory, the latter toward everyday life. The two directions are not necessarily opposed, but neither are they moving toward the same goal.

Sidgwick's theory asks us to address ethical matters as an impartial spectator whose objectivity is grounded outside ethics. Bernard Williams challenges this aspect of Sidgwick's ethics. Sidgwick wrongly thinks that he "can occupy, if only temporarily and imperfectly, the point of view of the universe, and see everything from the outside view." Such an assumption, however, overlooks the "depth or thickness" to our "moral dispositions." Getting "outside" them and evaluating ethics primarily on "actions or states of affairs" neglects the depth dimension to our moral dispositions.[19] In fact, Williams is skeptical that theory can accomplish what Sidgwick wants it to:

> My own view is that no ethical theory can render a coherent account of its own relation to practice: it will always run into some version of the fundamental difficulty that the practice of life, and hence also an adequate theory of that practice, will require the recognition of what I have called deep dispositions; but at the same time the abstract and impersonal view that is required if the theory is to be genuinely a *theory* cannot be satisfactorily understood in relation to the depth and necessity of those dispositions. Thus the theory will remain, in one way or another, in an incoherent relation to practice. But if ethical

theory is anything, then it must stand in close and explicable relation to practice, because that is the kind of theory it would have to be. It thus follows that there is no coherent ethical theory.[20]

Sidgwick fails because he offers a "significant example" of an ethical theory that freed itself from practice.

Alasdair MacIntyre and Bernard Williams have significant differences, but both have questioned the transitions brought about in the teaching and learning of ethics since Sidgwick made the theory of ethics central.[21] For MacIntyre, the contemporary scientific discipline of ethics fails not only to make people better but might also be "insuperably disadvantageous" to the learner because of the clear disciplinary divisions that render it a science. The divide between ethics and economic practice, for instance, has especially contributed to ethics' irrelevance. He states, "It is that those concerned with ethics in the last two hundred years, from whatever standpoint, became insufficiently concerned with money and those engaging with money became insufficiently concerned with ethics."[22] Here, too, is an example of ethical theory freed from everyday practice. Yet MacIntyre rejects any binary choice between theory or praxis; the "practice of the moral life by plain persons always presupposes the truth of some particular theoretical standpoint." Many who would side with Aristotle against Sidgwick recognize a role for theory. As I noted above, Annas insists that ethical practice is not "extraneous to theory." The question of theory and practice is the question of the connection between them, not if we should have one or the other. Do we theorize by standing within practices or by abstracting from them?

Once the significance of intentional action is recognized, then a connection between theory and practice is inevitable. Rather than asking if an action was voluntary, for example,

Did you place the green books on the floor voluntarily?
Of course I did; how could it be otherwise?

The question becomes the relevant reason why you so placed them. Similarly, the question is not if you should act on the basis of increasing utility, performing duties, or attending to virtues, but why you so acted. Relevant reasons require a theoretical construal. Answers might be: "I spent thirty-five years working in the Dutch East India Company" or "As a civil servant in charge of munitions, I had a duty to discharge." Such answers help explain the relation between theory and practice, but they do not yet get at the relevant sense of the question why. More needs to be asked, such as "Why did you so serve, to what end?" If an answer would be "for no particular reason," then it jeopardizes taking moral claims seriously. Answers that require taking the claims seriously will inevitably take the form of "it is good, right, or meet so to do because . . ." and those answers inevitably connect theory and practice, perhaps in a way Williams thought impossible. Asking the right questions is itself a theoretical endeavor to which different answers will arise.

What Ought I Do?

A specific voluntary action is often the answer to the question "What shall I do?" But as many philosophers and theologians have argued, this is not the best question to discover what ethics is about. Cora Diamond distinguishes the question "What shall I do?" from "What makes a good human life?" and finds the latter more appropriate for ethical investigation.[23] The focus on action arising from the question "What shall I do?" avoids attending to the "texture" of human life. Focusing on the evaluation of action alone diverts our gaze from the person who does the acting, with all their longings, hopes, anticipations, fears, relationships, and so on. Ethics is not first concerned with what should be done but more with what someone sees, how they come to see it, and why what they see matters. It is not mere action that is the focus of ethics, but all that which makes for a good human life.

Diamond's two questions provide an important distinction in discerning what ethics is about, but they could also tempt us to distinguish what should not be distinguished, doing and being, practice and theory. It is in doing that we discover who we are. It is in discovering who we are that we know what we ought to do. Yet the distinction between the right and the good and the focus on voluntary action make the question "What shall I do?" come to the fore, and too often we neglect to ask "What makes a good human life?" Many modern philosophers pursue what makes an action *right* without attention to, or investigation about, what makes for a *good* life. The modern moral philosopher Simon Blackburn suggests a similar criticism when he states that a "peculiarity of our present climate is that we care much more about our rights than about our 'good.'"[24] The question "What shall we do?" is not opposed to "What is a good life?" but asking the question of the "ought" without attention to what makes for a good life inevitably results in an unnecessary and unwarranted restriction of ethics, unmooring voluntary action from the contexts that could render it intentional and reducing ethics to useless platitudes, such as "Do your duty" or "Increase utility." One cannot oppose such platitudes, because they say nothing; they are nonsense.

Privileging Modern over Ancient Ethics

Sidgwick and Rawls examined premodern sources for ethics and found them wanting, such that they were of minimal use. Ethics became a modern discipline that privileged the modern over the past, often neglecting the study of the latter. Anscombe did not reverse the binary by privileging the past over the modern; that way lies a reactionary ethics. She refused the binary. She also challenged other binaries—such as fact/value, objective/subjective, is/ought, and theory/practice. These binaries place undue limitations on modern moral philosophy. Their deconstruction opens new possibilities for teaching and learning ethics, possibilities that were nascent in the moral theology Sidgwick left behind. It gains a better hearing once these distinctions no longer hold us captive.[25]

UNMAKING ETHICAL DISTINCTIONS

Academic disciplines in the modern university usually have a distinct subject matter with clearly demarcated boundaries. For some disciplines, this assumption makes sense. Disciplines like chemistry and French history have recognizable domains within which their practitioners work, but the boundaries of ethics are not so easily demarcated. The fact that, unlike most other academic disciplines, we both assume that people already have some knowledge of it and that teaching it will prove beneficial shows how teaching and learning ethics has a uniqueness to it that assumes much more than teaching or learning history, biology, or mathematics. Most educational settings assume

1. Learners already possess some understanding and practice of ethics so that they can be held accountable for their actions even if they never investigated philosophical or theological ethics.
2. Learners should be instructed in ethics.

Learners are accountable for their ethical conduct from the first day that they set foot in a classroom or begin a philosophical or theological investigation into ethics. Ethical living precedes teaching and learning ethics; it precedes teaching and learning any discipline. Wisdom, knowledge, and science cannot be pursued without ethical preconditions. A person could be excused for not knowing what a Grignard reaction is by protesting, "I have not yet had an organic chemistry course." But a person could not be excused for moral failure by protesting, "I have not yet studied ethics." We assume (1) that everyone has some knowledge of it and (2) that specific study can be beneficial. Are these two assumptions contradictory? If learners can be held accountable for ethical behavior without having taken an ethics course, and if the very act of teaching ethics presumes its practice, then why teach ethics? If students need an education in ethics, then why hold them accountable for an ethical failure or assume that ethics is a precondition for the pursuit of knowledge and wisdom?

Ethics, then, is both like and unlike other academic disciplines; yet the modern moral philosophy that seeks to take its place among them adopts distinctions that present ethics as an independent discipline. One distinction is to argue that ethics, unlike more fact-based disciplines, is about values. If it is about values, then a question arises if those values are objective or subjective. Do we abstract from our histories via some method or procedure to avoid subjectivity and gain a "moral point of view," like that of an impartial spectator? Another strategy to affirm ethics' distinctiveness asserts that other disciplines teach what *is* while ethics teaches what *ought* to be. These distinctions fail to attend to the uniqueness of teaching ethics found in the two assumptions listed above. They either tend toward accepting the first without challenging students in terms of the second or they adopt the second and neglect the first. If the domain of ethics is individual voluntary action toward what is right, and we acknowledge that students already arrive with their value convictions in place, then who is the teacher to challenge those convictions? Teaching ethics is reduced to helping students clarify what those convictions are by taking them through possible theories until they discover which ones align with theirs. If the objectivity of values can be acquired through some method, then the first assumption is irrelevant, and the task of the teacher is to guide the student toward that appropriate method regardless of their subjective convictions. Perhaps ethics looks different if we move away from the fact/value, objective/subjective, is/ought, and theory/practice distinctions.

The Fact/Value Distinction

The fact/value distinction is often traced back to David Hume's is/ought distinction. There is, however, a subtle difference between the two. The fact/value distinction was Max Weber's protest against the idea that the scientific view could do for morality and religion what it had done for technology. Lay tracks straight, get the facts right, and a streetcar will take you wherever you would like to go. Perhaps if we had sufficient data or a correct algorithm, we could do the same for the moral life? Weber rejected such a possibility, and he posited the fact/value distinction to make room for values in ethics, aesthetics, and religion. They should not be pursued in the same terms that one would pursue driverless automobiles. They proceed through freedom grounded in the "mystery of personality."[26] Facts are based on determined states of affairs, and values in the free exercise of human agency. While his work was a laudable effort to preserve ethics from scientific reductionism, Weber's distinction diminished the role of ethics. Take, for example, how the fact/value distinction works in economics. Positive economics uses quantitative methods to give us the facts, which are usually correlated with numbers. Normative economics uses qualitative methods to give us the ethical values that we would prefer to see actualized in the world. As important as the latter are, values must be attentive to the facts.

The fact/value distinction predates Hume's is/ought distinction, originating in double-entry bookkeeping, which was "codified" in 1494 by Luca Pacioli, a Franciscan friar, who had been trained in rhetoric.[27] The new discipline of accounting held forth the promise of transparency between a sign and the reality it signified, which would diminish the role for rhetoric or figurative language. Numbers, statistics, and data would not dissimulate. Mary Poovey traces how thoroughly this hoped-for transparency influenced economics, political science, and moral philosophy. It continues to do so, generating the promise and peril of big data.

If we consider the difference between other academic disciplines and ethics to be that of fact versus value, then we are confronted with two problems. First, we readily lose the power of our moral language. An economist's opportunity cost can be given a number. If a family spends $100 going out to eat, and it costs $50 to stay home and fix a meal, then the opportunity cost for dining out is $50. Opportunity costs appear to be facts, the way the world is based on objective judgments, but they mislead. In 1896 Frederick Hoffman worked for Prudential Life Insurance Company. He was a numbers cruncher whose statistical work led to advances in public health. He also used his mathematical skills to demonstrate that Black Americans were "uninsurable."[28] Rather than examining the social and political conditions that led to such an evaluation, he assumed that the transparency of the numbers resulted in the rational conclusion that it was too risky for Prudential Life to insure Black lives. He was just giving the "facts."

Second, because numbers, statistics, and data have compelling persuasive power in much of Western, if not also non-Western, culture, the fact/value distinction tempts us to turn ethics into a data-driven, putatively fact-based endeavor. If ethics is not to be reduced to values, then it must be about facts. Like driverless automobiles, agent-free ethical algorithms might become the future for ethics. How we should behave, or, even more frightening, how we will behave, would be fed into an algorithm, and rewards or punishments would be meted out before we act. Whatever such a world would be, it would not be one where what we mean by ethics has a place. The problem is not that facts should be more accommodating of values or values should be concretized by becoming more factual; the problem is the fact/value distinction altogether. It is an inadequate way of conceptualizing the world because it seeks for something inhuman, a transparency between sign and signified that can occur without the kind of communication that language makes possible.

The Objective/Subjective Distinction

Related to the fact/value distinction is the objective/subjective distinction. If ethics is about values, and values are preferences, then who are we to judge among peoples' diverse preferences?[29] Some people prefer one kind of lifestyle; others prefer something different. No objective criteria exist to determine that one is better than another. Anyone who has taught ethics will recognize this kind of claim; some student inevitably raises it in a course on ethics. While a stream of popular opinion assumes that ethics is—unlike economics, chemistry, or history—a subjective discipline, few moral philosophers or theologians hold this to be the case. Instead, they develop procedures such as Adam Smith's impartial spectator, John Rawls's veil of ignorance, or William Frankena's moral point of view that put forth ethics as objective, even something accomplished *sub specie aeternitatis*.[30] Frankena (1908–94) presented the "moral point of view" in his meta-ethical theory of justification of moral concepts by drawing on David Hume's (1711–76) moral philosophy, and especially what is known as Hume's "general point of view." For Frankena, ethical judgments are justified when they arise from a consensus by agents who are "free, impartial, willing to universalize, conceptually clear, and informed about all possible facts." This consensus is, he notes, "ideal" and not "actual." It also assumes that morality is independent of any specific religious or philosophical tradition; such dependence would impose partiality.[31] The moral point of view provides a source of authority for ethics. It must stand on its own as an independent, objective, universal discipline.[32]

The discipline of ethics cannot be salvaged by turning it into something that it cannot be—a form of reasoning *sub specie aeternitatis*. The possible partiality and subjectivity of ethics is not remedied by abstracting from our subjective agency and turning toward something else, something supposedly universal because it overcomes, or lacks, human embodiment. If ethics assumes what Alice Crary calls the "abstraction requirement," whereby moral objectivity can be had only if one abstracts from subjective endowments, then we once again lose what makes ethics, for better and worse, a human endeavor.[33] We lose life as it is actually lived, and if ethics has little place for that, what good is it? Yet here, too, ethics is tricky. The story of James Rebanks told in *The Shepherd's Life* tells how his location in a "deeply traditioned" form of shepherding provided "an ancient, hard-earned, local kind of freedom that was stolen from people elsewhere."[34] His powerful narrative shows us why we need these forms of life and how modern assumptions about progress and education threaten them. He sees what he can because of his subjective location. But put those same words in the mouth of Derek Black, who was born into a tradition of white nationalists convinced that their heritage was being stolen, and they sound remarkably different. Asking Rebanks to abstract from his traditioned way of life for the sake of an objective ethics would prevent us from seeing the beauty he shares through his writings. Asking Black not to abstract from his would be immoral; it would prevent us from seeing the beauty he shows us in *Rising out of Hatred*.[35] How do we know when we should affirm a traditioned way of life, and when we should abstract from it? These questions pose a temptation to ask for a rule that would turn ethics more into an algorithm than the rhetorically ladened communicative exercise that it is. The philosopher Stanley Cavell helps us resist this temptation by asking to attend to criteria located in forms of life. The question is not if ethics should be objective or subjective but how we "learn to go on" by making ethical judgments with our contingent human endowments.

The Is/Ought Distinction

The attempt to ground ethics in objectivity through the device of an ideal observer cannot be laid at the feet of Hume, but perhaps the is/ought distinction can be. Hume's celebrated, or lamented, passage is found in his *Treatise of Human Nature*:

> In every system of morality, which I have hitherto met with, I have always remarked that the author proceeds for some time in the ordinary way of reasoning and establishes the being of a God, or makes observations concerning human affairs; when of a sudden I am surpriz'd to find that instead of the usual copulations of propositions, *is*, and *is not*, I meet with an *ought* or *ought not*. This change is imperceptible, but is, however, of the last consequence. For as this *ought* or *ought not* expresses some new relation or affirmation, tis necessary that it shou'd be observed and explain'd; and at the same time that a

reason should be given, for what seems altogether inconceivable, how this new relation can be a deduction from others, which are entirely different from it.[36]

Moore found in this distinction the basis for his claim that good is a non-natural property. As noted above, he also traced the distinction to Henry Sidgwick. Philippa Foot rejected the is/ought distinction and recognized that it was more indebted to Moore's interpretation of Hume than it was to Hume himself.[37]

In a 1959 essay, Alasdair MacIntyre likewise questions the is/ought distinction and, like Foot, attributes it to Moore's misreading of Hume. Hume's derivation of morality grounded in interest arises from an appeal to the facts, and that calls into question misinterpretations that distinguish is from ought or facts from norms. Hume never attempted to ground morality solely on moral premises. Ethics is no autonomous discipline.[38] MacIntyre did not oppose Hume because of the is/ought distinction but because of a faulty account of what is natural. More than a half century later, he wrote, "Sentiments that Hume takes to be near universal and natural among humankind Aquinas takes to be symptoms of failure as a rational agent."[39] What he provides in his 1959 essay is a way to read Hume's influential statement in his *Treatise*. Hume tells us that he is "surprised" to see the transition from is to ought, not that such a transition is impossible, or that ethics should only be concerned with the ought. He challenges philosophers and theologians to be more careful in demonstrating how they move from is to ought. In this sense, MacIntyre's later work can be interpreted as answering Hume's challenge without adopting Hume's noncognitivism.

The is/ought distinction has had more deleterious consequences for teaching and learning ethics than any of the other distinctions being examined. Ironically, it was the basis in the mid–nineteenth century for the development of ethics as a scientific, academic discipline. Ethics is about what ought to be and not what is. Do away with this distinction and the foundation supporting that version of ethics crumbles. F. D. Maurice knew about this distinction in the mid 1850s and rejected it.[40]

The Practice/Theory Distinction

I have already discussed the primacy of theory, methods, and procedures in modern moral philosophy; this subsection asks if the distinction between them has salutary consequences, as if ethics teaches the conceptual and theoretical tools to examine practical, subjective judgments, leaving the latter untouched. Such a restricted role for ethics is unsatisfying; it limits it to theoretical and conceptual tools, and that is a sign that something has gone awry. If there is any agreement on ethics, it is this: ethics is primarily a practical activity. Of the distinctions under discussion—fact/value, objective/subjective, is/ought, and theoretical/practical—the only one that has been acknowledged as appropriate for ethics, at least since Aristotle, is that ethics concerns practice more than theory.

Aristotle's identification of ethics as a form of practical reasoning has carried the day from his time to ours. Nonetheless, theoretical reasoning plays a role in ethical practice, even for Aristotle. As argued above, Anscombe found modern philosophy overly concerned with theoretical reason and misunderstanding the practical. She did not, however, argue that one should supplant the other. They take different forms but work simultaneously in the acting person. Likewise, Annas makes a case for the importance of theory for the practice of a good life: "Understanding the process of ethical education is part of virtue ethics. Ethical education is not something 'merely practical' and so extraneous to theory."[41] Teaching has its proper place, as does reading texts about ethics and thinking carefully, as Sidgwick taught us, about the methods and objects of ethics. Yet understanding arguments and authors, as important as it may be, is not ethics. It does not embody virtue. Annas goes on to state, "We don't learn to be virtuous from books, even books about virtue, though these help our understanding."[42] Instead, learning virtue "takes place in an *embedded* context."[43]

If virtue requires embedded contexts, then the classroom can be an inadequate place for teaching and learning ethics, especially if it seeks to distance learners from the embedded contexts that are the basis for the first assumption listed above that learners already possess some understanding and practice of ethics. Robert Skidelsky, drawing on the work of Karl Polanyi, makes a similar point about economics, and thus indirectly shows how ethics, like economics, must assume more than either discipline alone if either is to illumine actual existence. Skidelsky questions if microeconomics can simply be "bolted" onto macroeconomics. The former was constructed to show how markets work, and the latter how they "fail." Microeconomics assumed "well-informed, forward-looking rational agents" who "optimize" their choices subject only to the logic of competitive markets."[44] We wrongly assume that economics can take something like this constructed individual householder who must balance their budget as the basic unit of analysis and then extend it outward. But this is mistaken. It overlooks the role of "society" in economics, something that Marx "understood better than Keynes." Polanyi pointed in the right direction "by his stress on the 'embeddedness' of individual behaviour, its dependence on shared beliefs, norms of behaviour, social biology and institutions; in short, on the shared 'rules of the game' or 'heuristics' which define collective life."[45] Ignore this embeddedness and economics will be predicated upon a false account of human action. He concludes, "All individual choices are made in a collective context, whether of family, community, corporation, religion, class or nation: there are no Robinson Crusoes in the real world."[46] If economics cannot consider these collective contexts, it will fail to give an adequate sense of human action. When Sidgwick was writing and teaching ethics at Cambridge, economics was taught within "moral science." It would not become its own discipline until the early twentieth century. Branching off the teaching and learning of economics from ethics has been a significant loss for both disciplines.

Skidelsky's analysis of economics' faulty understanding of human action has a correlate in ethics, which is not surprising since both are about the same subject matter: human action. The embedded contexts within which ethical agency occurs not only explain the first assumption above but also show why this assumption must be honored in any context in which someone seeks to teach ethics. If professional ethicists consider their first task to be disembedding learners from their previous contexts, then they will cut them off from the places where virtue is learned. But this is what the moral point of view, impartial spectator, or original position invites students to do.[47] Imagine the ethicist inviting students to consider themselves without any knowledge of their past, with no history, all empty x's ignorant of themselves and others. Then, from this ideal beginning, we begin anew, constructing virtuous people and societies.

Ideal thought experiments can be illuminating. They show us what might have been rather than what is; imaginative experiments are rich resources for ethical understanding.[48] It is the transition from these imagined, ideal conditions to ordinary life that raises questions; they form what Cavell refers to as the second conversation about justice, the need for reflective judgments grounded in everyday criteria. Neglect them, and ideal thought experiments too easily function by disembedding students and then reembedding them into nothing but a nonexistent ideal context. They give too much power to theory at the expense of the material, social, and historical conditions that are the stuff from which virtue arises. Virtue cannot be achieved if the ethicist first asks persons to abstract from everything that they learned before entering a laboratory. Williams is correct; such an ethical theory cannot attend to the deep dispositions that ethics requires. However, this may not be the only way to think about theory. It could be conceived as intrinsic to practice.

Derek Black was raised to be the heir to the white nationalist project. He matriculated at a liberal, multicultural university with his family and the white nationalist movement's approval so he could discover and infiltrate the enemy. His civil mannerisms and charm made him popular until he was discovered to be a leading proponent of white nationalism with a radio show propounding its ideas. His fellow students were rightly horrified. Some shunned him; others sought to get him expelled. Matthew Stevenson, a convert to Orthodox Judaism, was also horrified but took a different approach, "one rooted in his own faith."[49] He befriended Black, inviting him to attend Shabbat services. Stevenson's friendship and Derek's relationship with a young woman, Allison, gradually led to an epiphany. He came to the conclusion that his embedded context had misled him. There was no impending white genocide; whites were not victims of racial oppression. Derek wrote a long letter explaining how he had "grown past" the "bubble" in which he had been raised, and he sent it to the enemy of white nationalism, the Southern Poverty Law Center. It caused a national stir. He tells us that his friendships and acquaintances with people who were most "affected" by his previous racism led him to "realize the impact" of his actions and to reject it. It also meant that he would be rejected by the family and movement that he previously loved. Clearly, instruction made a moral difference in his life.

Derek Black was embedded in a vicious context. Friendships within a new context, that of Shabbat meals and a university seeking truth, allowed for his transformation. Friendship has always been an important source for ethics. For Thomas Aquinas, it was one of two external principles found in Aristotle's teaching on virtue that resembled the infused virtues. The other was fortune. Fortune, or contingency, and friendship resemble infusing virtue because they influence us to act well even though they arise from something other than our own resources. They are not sources internal to persons, like passions and reason. They are external. We are not the cause of them, but they cause us to be better than we would otherwise be. Once the argument turns to the infused virtues in part II of this book, contingency and friendship will play an important role in pointing to secular analogues to faith, hope, and love.

The virtue of practical wisdom (*phronesis*) links theory and practice, so that the embedded contexts in which we learn practical reasoning are neither rejected nor uncritically valorized. Ordinary life is never only virtuous; it is often vicious. The question of ethics, "What is a life lived well?" is inadequate if we do not add "in a broken and unjust world."[50] The difference between the social locations of James Rebanks and Derek Black should readily be available to persons with practical wisdom. But is this adequate? Do we not need something more than human beings who are practically wise to know when people inhabit vicious or virtuous ways of life? A central argument in this work has been that the desire for something more misleads us. Ethics is an activity for human beings; it is not necessary for God, angels, or nonrational animals. To seek more is to seek something other than ethics. Does this render theology irrelevant for ethics? It does not if, as Irenaeus put it, the glory of God is a human being fully alive. Nothing could be more practical than the wisdom found in a transfigured life.

What Is Extrinsic/Intrinsic to a Good Life

This observation about a transfigured life leads me to one more distinction between ethics and other disciplines that makes sense of the two assumptions that began this section. Someone who does not know Grignard reactions or French history may be missing out on something important in life, but not knowing them does not make someone a failed human being. However, not knowing ethics, especially in its practical dimension, makes someone a failed human being. Chemistry and history matter, but they are extrinsic to a good human life. Ethical practice is intrinsic to it, even though, as with friendship and the infused virtues, its sources are external. The intrinsically good life always assumes salutary extrinsic conditions.

By seeking scientific precision to ethics, Sidgwick distanced it from its embeddedness in the moral traditions that predated his turn to method. He turned the direction of ethics primarily to the future, to what he imagined were progressive trends, and away from what had preceded him. The transition in the name of the Knightbridge Chair that he and Maurice held symbolizes this new direction. The academic discipline of ethics sidelined theology. In so doing, it lost the ability to see and speak well of an undeniable feature of human action; its exercise is always, in part, gift. The gift character of ethics can only be seen when human actions are considered over a complete life rather than as a discrete, unitary event to accomplish what is right through a voluntary decision disconnected from answers to the question "What is a good life?" or "What is a life lived well?" The question "What ought I do?" assumes an "I" who is always capable of doing something, who thus has agency. The limitations of infancy, illness, disability, incapacity, old age, and death are set aside. But surely ethics has to do with all these realities, even when they do not suppose someone capable of the kind of agency present in Sidgwick's question. Every person's life has its moments when their agency depends on that of others. The movement of our body to its final resting place depends on our friends. Ethics considered over a complete life expands our sense of agency, turning our attention to its social contexts and the gifts received from others.

In his lectures on *Social Morality*, Maurice envisioned the most basic acts of everyday life as gifts. In his ninth lecture on language he wrote, "The power of communicating thoughts, instead of being regarded any longer as any ordinary treasure, should be accepted as an amazing gift."[51] Social morality recognizes this gift character of the ordinary and mundane when it attends to worship and the self-giving sacrifice central to it. "Worship which had such a principle for its ground," Maurice states, "must be emphatically a Eucharist, a thanksgiving for a transcendent gift making all common things look beautiful and amazing, giving a divine character to the earth which they trod, to the food which they ate."[52] Whether someone celebrates the Eucharist is less important than to recognize the practical truth it conveys about ethics; it is not understood well when the focus is on the constitution of our agency from within its own internal sources alone; it is seen better when it is constituted from without. And that brings us, yet again, to the infusing of virtues.

NOTES

1. Annas, *Morality*, 7.
2. Aristotle, *Nicomachean Ethics* (hereafter, *NE*), 1094a.
3. *NE*, 1109b30.
4. *NE*, 111023–5.
5. *NE*, 1110a1.
6. *NE*, 1113b5–10.
7. *NE*, 1099b10.
8. *NE*, 1098b20.
9. Wiseman, *Anscombe's Intention*, 22.
10. Anscombe, *Intention*, 1.
11. Wiseman, *Anscombe's Intention*, 60.
12. Cavell, *Must We Mean*, 6.
13. Ross, *Right*, 3.
14. Saslow, *Rising*.
15. For Julia Annas, "'right' is a 'thin' ethical concept, lacking independent ethical content of its own, as opposed to 'thick' ethical concepts like the virtues"; Annas, *Intelligent Virtue*, 42. Whereas ethics based on the right often reduces the good to a question of motivation, Annas argues that "motivation" adds nothing to a virtue ethics. She states, "To ask how someone who thinks he should act bravely can *then* be motivated to be brave is a mistake"; Annas, 10. Likewise, John McDowell differentiates Aristotle and Kant on the relationship between the actor and the action. "Of course, Aristotle has nothing like a Kantian conception of the will. For Aristotle, what has the unconditioned value I want

to point to is *doing* well, and that is not something that is in place independently of what happens in the objective world"; McDowell, "Deliberation," 32.

16. MacIntyre, *Whose Justice?* ix.

17. Aquinas, *Summa Theologiae* (hereafter, *ST*), I.5.4, rep. obj. 1.

18. *ST*, I.5.1 resp.

19. Williams, "Point of View," 294.

20. Williams, 296.

21. MacIntyre, *Ethics*, 163–64, 220–31.

22. MacIntyre, 21–22.

23. Diamond, "Having a Rough Story," 160–61.

24. Blackburn, *Ethics*, 4.

25. By "modern moral philosophy," here I am referring explicitly to a dominant trend of teaching ethics that adopts these distinctions inherited from Sidgwick. Not all modern moral philosophy does so. One example, feminist philosophies of care, also refuses to teach ethics within these binaries; I draw on these philosophies in the second part of this book. Marxist ethics likewise often rejects them.

26. Safranski, *Martin Heidegger*, 90–91.

27. Poovey, *History*, 34.

28. O'Neil, *Weapons*, 161.

29. I am not referring to the complex "value theory" one finds in philosophy, with its distinctions such as objective or subjective value. As a theory, I do not find it that helpful, but the concern here has more to do with popular accounts of value as preference that most, if not all, moral philosophers seek to counter with some kind of objectivity.

30. Rawls, *Theory of Justice*, 587.

31. Frankena, *Ethics*, 112.

32. Whether Frankena is justified in finding Hume as an influence for the moral point of view has been called into question. Geoffrey Sayre-McCord makes a convincing case that Hume's general point of view is far from that of Frankena's ideal observer. For Hume, ethics begins in sentiments, giving rise to judgments of approbation or disapprobation toward persons and their actions. Such sentiments arise from a particular point of view and thus inevitably generate the problem that we might make judgments from our limited perspective. If we had the ability to adopt the position of an ideal observer, the problem of our limited perspective would never arise, but Hume rejects this ability. His general point of view assumes that we can learn to sympathize with others. He builds on the human character of communication, drawing upon it by learning to be self-critical, to react and respond to others, without ceasing to be human by abstracting from our subjective endowments; Sayre-McCord, "On Why Hume's," 214–18. If we were ideal observers, this sympathy would be impossible. I am indebted to Margaret Watkins and Rob Miner, who pointed me to the Sayre-McCord essay. Although I find Rawls's original position similar to that of an ideal observer, his reflective equilibrium surely has strong resonances with Hume's general point of view.

33. Crary, *Inside Ethics*, 44–49.

34. Rebanks, *Shepherd's Life*, 286.

35. Black's story is told by Saslow, *Rising*.

36. Hume, *Treatise*, 469.

37. Foot, *Virtues*, 100. Foot is not critical of Hume because of the is/ought distinction but because of his noncognitivism. Hume's noncognitivism distinguishes between a moral

judgement and its "ground." The judgment is based on an "attitude, feeling, or goal" and not "facts and concepts." Her ethics of natural goodness grounds "moral arguments" in "facts about human life"; Foot, 23–24. Anscombe did the same in her essay "On Brute Facts."

38. MacIntyre, "Hume," 452, 455, 459.

39. MacIntyre, *Ethics*, 91.

40. The eighteenth-century philosopher James MacKintosh held to an is/ought distinction before Sidgwick in his *Dissertation on the Progress of Ethical Philosophy Chiefly during the Seventeenth and Eighteenth Centuries*. It is discussed in part II.

41. Annas, *Intelligent Virtue*, 21.

42. Annas, 22.

43. Annas, 21.

44. Skidelsky, *Money*, 386.

45. Skidelsky, 387.

46. Skidelsky.

47. Rawls denies that this is an implication of his theory of justice. See his *Lectures on Moral Philosophy*, where he sides with Hegel's criticism of Kant concerning "the deep social rootedness of people" as necessary for a political framework. His *Theory of Justice* agrees with Hegel because "the basic structure of society" is the "*first* subject of justice"; Rawls, *Theory of Justice*, 366. Many critics are unsatisfied that this is adequate to correct his method of abstraction. See Nichole M. Flores's criticism of Rawls, which draws on the work of Eric Gregory, Jeffrey Stout, and Cathleen Kaveny; Flores, *Aesthetics*, 57–60.

48. We should not forget that Rawls emphasizes the place of imagination positively in ethics by supplementing Sidgwick's "time-related principles," in which no particular time is privileged over another with the importance of imagination. He writes, "In these remarks about the devices of deliberation and time-related principles I have tried to fill in Sidgwick's notion of a person's good. In brief, our good is determined by the plan of life that we would adopt with full deliberative rationality if the future were accurately foreseen and adequately realized in imagination"; Rawls, *Theory of Justice*, 370.

49. Saslow, *Rising*, 76.

50. I am indebted to Karen Kilby, who raised this question in a chapter examining the theology of F. D. Maurice and Dallas Gingles, who, in a discussion of an early version of this manuscript, found that it lacked an adequate account of the Fall.

51. Maurice, *Social Morality*, 136.

52. Maurice, 407.

PART II

TEACHING MORAL THEOLOGY IN CONVERSATION WITH MORAL PHILOSOPHY

INTRODUCTION

Sketching the Maurician Landscape

In April 1872, while visiting Bournemouth on the south coast of England, Henry Sidgwick heard of F. D. Maurice's death. Sidgwick was only thirty-three years old. In a letter to his mother, he expressed his surprise: "Poor Maurice's death was startling; I knew he had been very ill, but thought that he was out of danger just when I got the news of his death." He then expressed his hesitancy to apply for the now "vacant Professorship" of the Knightbridge Chair. He was not convinced that it would do much except give him a broader audience for his work.[1] He decided not to stand for the chair, which went to the theologian T. R. Birks. Eleven years later in 1883, when Birks died, Sidgwick applied and became the chair's thirteenth holder. Maurice held it for six years, and Sidgwick for seventeen. Two years after Maurice's death and before Sidgwick took the chair, he published his *Methods*. Maurice never had occasion to respond to the changes his younger colleague brought about in the discipline of ethics. Having already discussed that direction and its ongoing significance in part I of this work, this part II sets forth Maurice's moral theology to explore what was left behind and how it might yet contribute to the teaching and learning of ethics.

Maurice's and Sidgwick's lives were intertwined. They stood together against subscription to the Church's Thirty-Nine Articles. They supported women's education. Maurice enlisted Sidgwick into the working men's cooperatives. They were both members of the Apostles, attended the Grote Society for moral philosophy, taught the same subject, and held the Knightbridge Chair. But their lives also diverged. Maurice moved away from his Unitarian upbringing to become a priest in the Church of England. Sidgwick moved away from his Church of England upbringing to become the leader and organizer of Cambridge ethical societies. Sidgwick sought rigor and precision in teaching ethics that focused on methods. Maurice eschewed systems and methods and found the subject matter of ethics to be "life." It was too broad to be brought into a coherent system. While Sidgwick wrote careful, plodding, analyses of ethical methods, Maurice's voluminous corpus was composed primarily of occasional pieces that arose from sermons and lectures. Yet there were exceptions. Throughout his life, he worked on his massive two-volume *Moral and Metaphysical Philosophy*, a work that he thought would be his legacy but has been, like much of his work, forgotten and neglected. If Anscombe had engaged with his work, she might have realized how mistaken she was in her interpretation of Protestantism. Maurice never surrendered living the divine law, and he understood the theological virtues of faith, hope, and charity as the heart of it. He also recognized the importance of language for ethics, he rejected systems and methods because they abstracted from life, and he refused to divide moral philosophy from theology, literature, metaphysics, and much more. Like Anscombe, he affirmed much in Aristotle and Thomas Aquinas but also found them inadequate if they became mere authorities.

Maurice's work lacked the precision of either Sidgwick or Anscombe, and that could be a reason for its neglect. As Benjamin Jowett stated, his work could be "misty and confused."[2] In his insightful work *The Theology of F. D. Maurice*, Alec R. Vidler, the mid-twentieth-century Anglican theologian and dean of King's College, suggested that this impression of Maurice is mistaken. It arose because he is not "satisfactorily classified." He was a thoroughly orthodox Anglican dismissed from his teaching position for heresy and his radical, socialist politics despite the fact that he was an antidemocratic monarchist. His work can be enigmatic, but perhaps that should not be reason for dismissing him as a theologian. As Saint Paul reminds us, we see in a mirror enigmatically. To suggest otherwise might be to falsely clarify what cannot yet be plainly seen.

The point of part II of this book is not to retrieve a Maurician school of theology, which would have clearly horrified him.[3] Nor is there a pressing need for someone to put together the collected works of Maurice. The point is not to study Maurice but to study what Maurice studied. He gives us a way to go on in teaching and learning ethics that opens up possibilities that Sidgwick and his inheritors closed down. Maurice, like Wittgenstein in his *Investigations*, should not be read for a system, or to construct a method, or to accumulate arguments for this or that doctrine. As Wittgenstein after the *Tractatus* gave us "sketches of landscape," so Maurice guides us to know where to put a shovel and dig for what is there but can be difficult to see, and even when seen easily forgotten or neglected, especially life as a gift to be received.

Maurice held to an ethics of perfection, but it is not one that can be achieved solely through immanent, human powers. Human creatures are ordered to an end that surpasses their autonomous agency, and yet it does not contradict nor evacuate those powers but fulfills them. To receive powers from another to fulfill an end beyond one's individual grasp is to be fully human. Vidler found resonances between Maurice's work and mid-twentieth-century Catholic theologians like the Jesuit Henri de Lubac that led to the Second Vatican Council. Against more strictly observant forms of Thomism that divided nature and supernature, de Lubac taught that we are by nature oriented to an end, friendship with God, that we cannot achieve on our own. Vidler stated that after de Lubac's work, "Maurice's teaching may receive a more sympathetic and favourable hearing than it did in his own time."[4] Maurice, like de Lubac, refuses a "sharp differentiation between nature and grace, or between the natural and the supernatural, or between humanity and the redeemed humanity, that seems to underlie much received theology."[5] De Lubac recognized this natural desire for God confused neo-Thomistic categories that were well entrenched in Catholic moral theology, leading to the antimodernist oath. He paid a price for challenging those categories and was silenced by his order. Maurice recognized this natural desire for God intrinsic to creaturely being before Thomas Aquinas was turned into a philosopher and used to counter and correct modern philosophical and cultural trends. Pope Leo XIII published *Aeterni Patris* in 1879. Maurice died seven years earlier. His reflections on Aquinas's moral theology were not for the purpose of a reactionary antimodernism, a use that continues to flare up against the gains of theologians like de Lubac and the second Vatican Council.

Maurice critically appropriated Aquinas's moral theology by identifying what he thought was a tension, if not a contradiction, in his approach. Aquinas affirms natural, acquired virtues, and then suddenly refers to them as imperfect, contrasting them with the perfect theological and infused virtues. Maurice questions this contrast, finding both the acquired and infused virtues to be foundational, but they are so because of his Christological understanding of human agency. Because all things are created in and through Christ, his life of sacrificial love is the foundation for creaturely being. Dig deep enough, Maurice suggests, and something like this foundation will be unearthed in every religion, culture, morality, and nation.[6] Reversing the ancient virtue tradition, Maurice explicitly refers to the theological virtues as "cardinal," the hinge upon which all things move, leaving the acquired virtues to be subordinate to them. This shifts the understanding of the subject of the infused virtues.[7] They are not *in* persons as much as persons are *in* them.

Creation is an infusion of charitable being by the Triune God that cannot but give rise to faith and hope. Theology and ethics begin and end there, just as his own controversial *Theological Essays* did.

Theological Essays contained the controversial teachings that resulted in King's College dismissing Maurice. Chapter 1 is titled "On Charity." The next is "On Sin." Maurice worried that nineteenth-century theology focused too much on sin and the Fall, a proclivity he found especially among Methodists and evangelicals.[8] Sin was a derivative category that only came to the fore after the foundation of creation in charity was established. Maurice moved theology away from a preoccupation with avoiding hell and damnation to a desire for the realization of life, in all its dimensions, lived in charity both now and in the future. Charity is also the final word in *Theological Essays*. In his concluding chapter, "On the Trinity in Unity," he writes, "My first Essay was on *Charity*; this will also be on Charity."[9] Theology and ethics begin with the confidence that charity is God's first and last word for us.

Michael Ramsey judged *Theological Essays* to be "one of the weakest of Maurice's books." He found it too "exclusively Johannine-Platonist."[10] Kelly Brown Douglas offers a similar criticism. She recognizes that Maurice's theological methodology challenges social injustice, but he was incapable of deconstructing the "English society's class hierarchy." She does not use the term "Platonism" but faults Maurice's methodology for beginning from "above" and diminishing the role of human experience.[11] Although Maurice would have balked at having a methodology, her criticism is warranted, as we will see below in discussing Maurice's paternalism. The question is if Maurice's commitment to the pre-Incarnate Christ as his method for theology is the source of that paternalism. His placing the infused virtues as cardinal offers a corrective to the argument that he begins from above or was too Platonist in his theology. H. Richard Niebuhr suggests as much in a positive interpretation of Maurice's Johannine emphasis. He wrote, "He is above all a Johannine thinker, who begins with the fact that the Christ who comes into the world comes into his own, and that it is Christ himself who exercises his kingship over men, not a viceregent—whether pope, Scripture, Christian religion, church, or inner light—separate from the incarnate Word."[12] For Niebuhr, Maurice was the exemplar of Christ transforming culture: "In Maurice the conversionist idea is more clearly expressed than in any other modern Christian thinker and leader. His attitude toward culture is affirmative throughout, because he takes most seriously the conviction that nothing exists without the Word."[13] Niebuhr saw the benefits of Maurice's theology. Yet Maurice rejected the idea that we are to form culture or politics or ethics. His metaphor of digging suggests that discovery is the best approach to moral theology and philosophy. To see what Maurice meant by such a metaphor, and to discern the strengths and limits of his approach, the next two chapters discuss his life and moral theology. Chapter 4 discusses his theological vocation by tracing some key moments in his life. Because casuistry for Maurice is the examination if a life can embody its professed ethics, such a chapter fits well with his approach to ethics. Chapter 5 discusses more fully the content of Maurice's moral theology. Maurice seeks to unify nature and grace, acquired and infused virtues. Chapter 6 shows why and how he attempts this unification. Chapter 7 places his ethics of infusing virtue in conversation with contemporary moral and political philosophy. One strength of Maurice's approach, I argue, is that he does not lead to a reactionary posture toward modernity nor against antiquity. Niebuhr's and Vidler's insights into the importance of his work and how it might assist us in our own era prove fruitful.

NOTES

1. Sidgwick and Sidgwick, *Henry Sidgwick*, 261.
2. Quoted by Vidler, *Theology*, 10.
3. Vidler, 9. Michael Ramsey, the archbishop of Canterbury from 1961 to 1974, offers similar counsel in his 1948 Maurice Lectures when he concludes, "But to learn from Maurice puts us in no danger of creating a Maurice-cult or of enrolling ourselves as Maurice's disciples. We are prevented from this, sometimes by the difficult idiom of his writings, always by his horror at gathering disciples around himself"; Ramsey, *F. D. Maurice*, 114.
4. Vidler, *Theology*, 51.
5. Vidler, 79.
6. The extent to which this "colonizes" other religions, cultures, moralities, and peoples is discussed below.
7. Chapter 6 of this book addresses whether it makes sense to consider the infused virtues as cardinal. For Thomas Aquinas, charity and the form of the acquired virtues justice, temperance, prudence, and courage endure into the next life but not hope, because it is for those *in via*. Once beatitude comes, hope is no longer necessary. Faith for Aquinas is more complicated.
8. See Maurice, *Theological Essays*, 37; and Vidler, *Theology*, 37–43.
9. Maurice, *Theological Essays*, 281.
10. Ramsey, *F. D. Maurice*, 48, 54.
11. Brown Douglas, "Theological Methodology," 20.
12. Niebuhr, *Christ*, 220.
13. Niebuhr, 229.

4

F. D. MAURICE'S THEOLOGICAL VOCATION

MAURICE AND SIDGWICK

In part I, I stated that Maurice, Sidgwick, and their different approaches to ethics formed the structure of this book's overall argument. Even when they are not being discussed, they are always in the background. Having examined Sidgwick's ethics at length, we now turn to Maurice's. Maurice's and Sidgwick's approaches are not in direct opposition. How they went about their work bears similarities. For instance, their audiences overlapped. They shared the university context, and both addressed the working class at the Working Men's College. Maurice established the Working Men's College, and he served as its principal without pay after being fired from King's College. Each made significant advances in women's education. Maurice launched one of the first educational institutions for women, Queen's College. Sidgwick and his wife, Eleanor, were the force behind the establishment of Newnham College for women at Cambridge. Sidgwick followed Maurice in affirming women's education, and for a time so did the economist Alfred Marshall, whose life overlapped those of Maurice, Sidgwick, and Maurice's great-granddaughter Joan Robinson, one of the first women to be granted a degree from Cambridge, who went on to become an influential and controversial economist. Marshall and Sidgwick are often identified as the two sources originating the Cambridge School of Economics—Sidgwick affirmed its placement within the moral science tripos; Marshall did not.

When Marshall was elected professor of political economy in 1884, economics was still taught within the moral science tripos, which is why Sidgwick explained Marshall's tasks to him, much to his chagrin. One year later, Marshall shifted from his affirmation of women's education to rejecting it on social Darwinian grounds, arguing that it would damage women's natural endowments. He opposed granting women academic degrees at Cambridge. When Robinson entered Girton College at Cambridge in 1922, Marshall's influence still held sway. The previous year, Cambridge students voted down a proposal to give women rights comparable to those of other students. Nonetheless, Robinson persisted in her studies. Women were not permitted to serve in "teaching posts" and on "faculty boards" until 1925, the year she graduated.[1] She became a lecturer in economics in 1937 and a fellow of Newnham in 1962. Maurice and Sidgwick's work on behalf of women's education had significant consequences for Maurice's family, consequences about which he had no knowledge. Robinson was born thirty-one years after his death.

Maurice and Sidgwick shared ethical commitments other than the affirmation of women's education. They both, for a time and under Maurice's leadership, worked with the workers' cooperative movement, although Sidgwick was more ambiguous about socialism. They both opposed subscription, Maurice doing so as a devout Anglican, Sidgwick as someone who reacted against his Anglican upbringing. They both, with some qualifications, defended British colonialism. Sidgwick defended democracy while moving more toward Tory politics. Maurice defended the aristocracy while at the same time rejecting most Tory politics. He was wary of democracy because he thought it exacerbated the US slavocracy; public opinion took precedence over truth and goodness, and it subordinated spiritual concerns to material interests.[2] As is shown below, he defined his politics as aristocratic, democratic, and radical at the same time. Maurice published much more and in more intellectual disciplines than did Sidgwick, but without Sidgwick's close, careful argumentation.

Most importantly, Maurice differed from Sidgwick on the nature of ethical agency and the domain for ethics. Of course, he did not oppose the importance of voluntary acts, but for him they did not constitute a domain that a discipline called ethics with properly trained professionals could oversee. Maurice held to an ecstatic agency. An agent was most themselves when they were called out of themselves and given more than they could accomplish on their own. Maurice's moral theology returned again and again to the infusing of virtue by the Triune God as the basis for moral action, both inside and outside the Church. Finding the source of this gift outside the Church meant that he could affirm both ancient and modern moral philosophy without sacrificing one to the other. He refused to distinguish moral theology from moral philosophy and could be criticized by theologians for reducing the former to the latter and by philosophers for sneaking theological premises into philosophy. To the latter, he admitted his guilt.

Maurice was adamantly opposed to the development of any "system" in moral theology or philosophy, and any strong demarcation between them.

The ethical life did not proceed by way of a method but through a casuistry rooted in social locations such as the home, the nation, the Church, and creation. Casuistry asked if the theory promulgated by a philosopher or theologian bore any relation to their life or to a life that could possibly be lived. He was less concerned, then, to ask the question "What should we do?" and more to discern who we are, if we should be content with who we are, and, if not—which he assumed would almost always be the right answer—how we might become whom we should be. The next section begins with a brief history of Maurice's vocation as a theologian, and then discusses how he affirms the importance of life over system, relates moral theology and philosophy, draws on both ancient and modern moral philosophy, construes agency, and works with an ethics of perfection.

MAURICE'S THEOLOGICAL VOCATION

Maurice grew up in a Quaker and Unitarian village. His father was a Unitarian minister, who would nonetheless baptize his parishioners in the name of the Father, Son, and Holy Spirit.[3] His three sisters and mother converted to Calvinism, much to their father's chagrin, creating tension within the family. As was the case with almost any theology or philosophy he investigated, Maurice found both good and bad in Calvinism. As a young man, he was sent to live with the Hardcastle family before college. While there, a "lady friend" convinced him that the Calvinist God was a "tyrant," and throughout his writings he rejected any suggestion that power defined God.[4] Yet he affirmed the place for God as the initiator of all that is good in human actions. In 1844, he wrote, "In Supralapsarian Calvinism there lies a deep recognition of God, as a Living Being, an Originating Will, which the feeble frittering of Arminianism can provide no substitute for."[5] As we shall see, his account of human agency always begins with God's prior movement. If resources for agency are not given to us, action would not be possible. While Calvinism affirmed this in part, and more so for Maurice than Arminianism, it made the horrible mistake of conceiving this prior movement in terms of power rather than goodness. Maurice continued, "The great misery of the Calvinist is his constant substitution of the idea of sovereignty for that of righteousness."[6]

Maurice assisted his father in his Unitarian church, especially during Sunday school, by "teaching, reading, writing and kindred matters to the poor children of the neighbourhood."[7] In October of 1823, he entered Trinity College, Cambridge, and became the thirtieth member of the "Apostles' Club," the same club that had a marked influence on Henry Sidgwick, who was its one hundred and thirty-eighth member. Unlike Sidgwick, Maurice opposed utilitarianism, although he was friends with J. S. Mill, who wrote to Maurice's son and affirmed his father's work as editor for the *Metropolitan Quarterly Magazine*, especially his criticism of Bentham. As his son put it, Maurice's work with the magazine showed his "inveterate opposition to the principle of Utilitarianism," which was the one subject that his parents agreed upon. One does good because "conscience demands" and not for the "greatest happiness of the greatest number."[8]

In 1829 he entered Oxford to study for the priesthood, anticipating that his novel, *Eustace Conway*, would pay for his "necessary expenses."[9] In 1831 he was baptized into the Church of England and was ordained deacon in 1834 and priest in 1835, the same year that he published *Subscription No Bondage: Or the Practical Advantages Afforded by the Thirty-Nine Articles as Guides in All the Branches of Academical Education*. He defended requiring students to subscribe to the Thirty-Nine Articles upon matriculation. He would later change his mind, not on his adherence to the Articles but on the requirement that students should be required to subscribe to them. He joined with Sidgwick to overturn this requirement. Sidgwick, of course, rejected both the Articles and subscription. Maurice affirmed the Articles and found the doctrines of the Trinity and the Incarnation to be the basis for moral theology and moral philosophy.

In his magisterial biography of Sidgwick, Schultz recognizes the influence Maurice had on the younger Apostle Sidgwick, but he finds too much continuity with Sidgwick's post-Christian ethics, assuming that Maurice was more heterodox than he was. Schultz misstates the case when he claims this about Maurice: "After an unusual undergraduate career at both Cambridge and Oxford, when his religious heterodoxy had pushed him in directions allowing him to avoid subscription, he eventually quelled his doubts sufficiently to be ordained and become a chaplain of Guy's Hospital and Lincoln's Inn."[10] Because Schultz interprets Maurice as hiding his doubts, he cites him as an influence on Sidgwick's controversial statement about "esoteric morality." Sidgwick, Schultz states, involved himself in "Maurician subterfuges." Schultz claims that one source for Sidgwick's desire to keep utilitarian morality from those not yet able to handle it is "Maurician paternalism."[11] These judgments are misplaced, both in terms of history and of Maurice's character. Although the charge of paternalism could readily be defended, it could not be used to defend Sidgwick's claim that, on occasion, ethics must be reserved for an elite, a claim that Bernard Williams rightly interpreted as "Government House Utilitarianism."[12] Schultz seems to interpret Maurice too much in the vein of Sidgwick. For Schultz, Sidgwick, unlike Maurice, refused to equivocate and sign the Thirty-Nine Articles, whereas Maurice contorted his conscience so that he could. This gets things wrong.

While at Cambridge, Maurice refused to subscribe to the Articles, but not because he had doubts about them. He considered himself a "full believer in Christianity."[13] He had doubts about forcing students to adhere to teachings against their conscience. At Oxford, however, he claimed that they were a "defense of liberty."[14] The difference, according to Maurice, was this: Cambridge required subscription upon graduation, which meant that one had to subscribe to beliefs in order to get one's diploma, whether one held those beliefs. It was coercive. Oxford required subscription upon matriculation, which he suggested was not coercive because it served the purpose of letting the student know the framework within which their education would proceed. (Notice the subtitle to *Subscription No Bondage* given above.) Maurice, like Sidgwick, was consistently concerned with arguments that did not stand on their own, did not entail free consent, and thus rested on coercive authority. God did not operate this way; nor should creatures. He and Sidgwick made common cause in questioning coercive authority; but when it came to theological convictions, they went in different directions. Maurice defended subscription in the Oxford sense as not being a form of bondage, but he later came to reject it altogether, largely because the persons who affirmed his 1835 publication on subscription alarmed him.

One year after he published his defense of subscription, Maurice was asked to apply for the professorship of political economy at Oxford. The Oxford Movement, a High Church movement within the Anglican Church that sought to restore ancient Christian liturgical doctrine and practices, was behind his application, in a bid "to obtain possession for their party of the chief chairs in the University," because the members of the movement thought that he was on their side. Maurice agreed to apply because he envisioned himself challenging the discipline of economics from within. He wrote, "If the University can do anything to save us from being a nation of money-getters, it should surely try, and I should feel it no dishonourable office to be a hewer of wood to it while it was so engaged."[15] Edward Pusey was one of the leaders in the Oxford Movement who originally supported Maurice. However, when Maurice read Pusey's tract on baptism, he was alarmed and wrote his own tract, which was critical of Pusey's. Pusey reacted angrily, and the Oxford party realized that "they had mistaken their man." They decided to vote against him.[16] Maurice never became professor of political economy.

Maurice's life and work does not readily fall into distinct academic disciplines. His voluminous publications include novels, sermons, biblical commentary, philosophy, literary reviews, theology, and more. He published the novel *Eustace Conway* in 1834. His first academic position at King's College in 1840 was as professor of English literature. Literature was a lifelong pursuit. In 1873, a collection of his essays was published posthumously from earlier lectures titled *The Friendship of Books and Other Lectures*. Maurice expressed concern that books too often become mere "books of letters" rather than "books of life." The latter invite friendship with authors and readers; the former do not. Books invite friendship when they are read not to compete for prizes or to show one's cleverness but to discern the life the author seeks to show the reader, and then the reader judges the merit of that life. Such judgments connect readers across space and time because no book stands in isolation from others; it is their interconnection that allows readers to render judgment. All books, like words, fit within a nexus of other books and words that draw the reader ever more in and toward perfection. For Maurice, this leads to a theological interpretation of the terms "word" and "book."

Any book could be a book of life because every book, like language itself, participates in the Book of books, the Bible. He writes, "I believe all books may do that for us, because there is one Book which, besides bringing into clearness and distinctness a number of men of different ages from the creation downwards, brings before us one Friend, the chief and centre of all, who is called there *The Son of Man*."[17] Such a statement could be read, and dismissed, as a merely pious assertion, but to understand it rightly requires attention to Maurice's perfectionist ethics. Why do we use words in all their multiplicity? We seek to communicate; but when done well, it serves a purpose other than to demonstrate our cleverness. We seek to communicate something about life. The words assume more than the words themselves; we are looking for something that is both in the text and beyond the text: text as oral and written language. Perhaps it is truth, goodness, joy. Our desire to communicate has multiple purposes, and Maurice thinks that these multiple purposes produce discontent unless they can find rest in a final purpose, one for which we can only hope in faith, but one that gives life, so that it makes us truly human.[18]

Life rather than method or system, Maurice will consistently state, is what teaching and learning should be about. *The Friendship of Books* includes a lecture "On Words" that was given to the students of Guy's Hospital early in Maurice's vocation, around 1838. He began by suggesting that it might be a "waste" to discuss words because they have a simple function to "express meaning"—but to assume that this is all words do is mistaken. He states, "If we know how to use them aright, they will not only supply us with convenient forms for communicating our thoughts to others, but they will actually teach us what our thoughts are, and how to think."[19] In using words, we discover ourselves. For this to happen, however, the author of words must be attentive to how words point beyond themselves to something more. Two dominant ways of thinking about words—by the "lexicographer" and the "etymologist"—limit them because they fail to refer to the "life" of words and instead attend only to the words themselves.[20]

Samuel Johnson's dictionary represents the lexicographer. Maurice admits its usefulness, but when Johnson seeks to limit words to their definition, he finds it "distressing." It will not let us discover who we are. Maurice writes,

> You can no more reach the life of a word by means of a definition than you can reach the life of a chemical substance by means of a definition; that they are good and useful landmarks for the mind, while it is engaged in investigating the meaning of a word, but that they are not in any sense the meaning of it; and that he who, because he has got the definition, fancies he knows and understands that word, is practicing as great a fraud upon himself as the old schoolmen practiced upon themselves, when they fancied that by their endless speculations and definition of nature they were attaining a knowledge of nature.[21]

Horne Tooke represents the etymological approach. The meaning of a word is found by "knowing its origin" and then referring the word to its origin. Maurice takes as an example Tooke's use of "right" as that which is "ordered or ordained."[22] It can mean that, but it is too reductive. Maurice then uses the term "right" in different statements—such as "I have a right to that horse" or "you have no right to put me in prison" or "right hand"—and finds the etymological approach incapable of accounting for these different uses. Both Tooke and Johnson, he concludes, "deny the living, germinating power of words."[23] Rather than tracing a word back to its origin, its meaning is found in following it "up to its highest sense."[24] For Maurice, words can be inexhaustibly traced to others because they are made possible by the Word in John 1 from whom all words "proceed." He writes, "You find there that which is at once the ground and the pinnacle of all discourse, that which transfigures even ordinary converse into a mystery, and enables us to hear in the lispings of infancy the first notes of that harmony which is perfected in the songs of the Seraphim."[25]

Maurice never uses the term "projectability," as Cavell and Mulhall do, but his understanding of how language works is similar. He assumes words, like all creatures, accomplish more than what their definition or origin permit because they participate in perfection, in the Triune God who creates all things. He returns to this theme consistently. It is present in his *Theological Essays*, a work that, as noted above, begins with the theological virtue of charity and ends in an essay on the Trinity in which he writes, "For the Trinity is, as I believe, the grounds on which the Church stands and on which Humanity stands; Prayer and Sacrifice are, I believe, the means whereby the Trinity is made known to us; in the Trinity I find the Love for which I have been seeking; in Prayer and Sacrifice I hope that we may become partakers of it."[26] A similar theme is found in *Moral and Metaphysical Philosophy*. In that work, as elsewhere, Maurice can be both critical and affirming of Aristotle and Aquinas, especially when it comes to the virtues. He is critical when the virtues become like Tooke's understanding of words—something too settled that insufficiently takes us out of ourselves.

For Maurice, focusing on the acquired virtues alone misleads agents to imagine that they are too much in control of their life. They fail to discover themselves by losing themselves. The human person becomes like a mere book or word that neglects the "living, germinating power" that exceeds the word, book, and person. When Thomas Aquinas repeats Aristotle on the acquired virtues, Maurice is skeptical. When he turns to how the acquired virtues are perfected by the theological virtues, he is appreciative. First, he states, "But since man is intended to be perfect as his Father in Heaven is perfect, these properly human virtues must be connected with the divine or exemplary virtues." No part of the *Summa*, he then writes, "brings out more clearly than this his sense of the connection between Ethics and Theology, of their distinction, and of the subordination of the one to the other."[27] Below, we will explore more fully Maurice's insightful critique and affirmation of Aquinas on the infused virtues.

Six years after Maurice was hired as a professor of English literature, King's College established a theology department and he became a professor of theology.[28] His tenure was fraught with controversy brought on by his economics and his theology. The problems began with a series of letters in the conservative religious newspaper *The Record* in 1850–51 that accused him of Jacobinism.[29] The conservative J. W. Croker denounced Maurice and the journal he started by writing, "Mr. Maurice, we understand is considered the founder and head of the school [of Christian Socialism], and it certainly adds to our surprise to find the reputed editor of 'Politics for the People' and the avowed author of other works, theological as well as political, of a still more heterodox character, occupying the professorial chair of divinity in *King's College, London.*" Croker was troubled that Maurice would be allowed to teach theology; he was particularly galled by Maurice's avowal of socialism.[30] Croker's editorial troubled the principal of King's, Richard William Jelf, who wrote to Maurice and expressed his concern about Christian Socialism. He took issue with Maurice's association with Charles Kingsley, whose writings, he stated, "set the poor against the rich" and are "occasionally almost insurrectionary."

In 1852, Kingsley preached a sermon in London titled "Message of the Church to Laboring Men." It took Luke 4:16–21 as its text, in which Jesus, citing Isaiah, proclaims "good news to the poor" and "liberty to the captives and oppressed." Kingsley's first line chastised the Church for refusing to take up "liberty, equality, and brotherhood." He stated, "The notion of the Christian Church is associated in the minds of many, with the notion of priestcraft and kingcraft; of the slavery of the intellect, persecution, and tyranny; and it would be ridiculous to deny that they have cause enough for connecting the thought of it with those fearful sins of man against man." He asks if siding with the wealthy against the poor fits with, or against, the "spirit of the church," and argues that it works counter to the central text of Jesus's ministry in Luke 4. He explicitly connects "the acceptable year of the Lord" in Luke 4 with the Jubilee Year in Leviticus 25 and says, "If I wanted one proof above all others of the inspired wisdom of Moses, I should choose this unparalleled contrivance for preventing the accumulation of large estates, and the reduction of the people into the state of serfs and day-laborers." Scripture shows that "all systems of society" that "favor the accumulation of capital in a few hands" are "contrary to the Kingdom of God" and "to the church." In a statement that shows Maurice's influence on Kingsley, he proclaims that the "Bible, Baptism, and the Supper of the Lord—will witness against them [the 'tyrannical, luxurious, bigoted, ignorant, careless'], and witness for the people." Baptism places the "child of the queen and the child of the beggar" on the same plane, and the Lord's Supper is a "pledge that all men are equal. . . . One table, one reverential posture, one bread, one wine, for high and low, for wise and foolish."

A leading liberal paper, *The Monthly Religious Magazine*, published the sermon. The editor praised Kingsley for his sermon and coupled him with Maurice, informing readers that their "kind of preaching" had more adherents than the "powers" acknowledged. He wrote, "Nor are such men as Mr. Maurice and Mr. Kingsley, however watched and suspected by the 'powers,' by any means alone there in their progressive, humane, and liberal spirit."[31] But not everyone was happy with Kingsley's sermon. Kingsley preached at the request of the parish priest, Mr. Drew, who then publicly denounced him, suggesting that he had been misled. Kingsley appealed to Maurice to determine if he preached his sermon under false pretenses. Maurice testified that Drew had extended the invitation, that he had given Kingsley the title for the sermon, that Kingsley had shared the sermon with Drew before preaching it, and that Drew "intimated the most cordial approval of it." Maurice also reminded *The Monthly*'s readers that Drew was aware of Kingsley's work, so he had to know what Kingsley would say. He also revealed that Kingsley told Drew that he would submit his manuscript beforehand for his review, and that he would make changes at Drew's request. Maurice disagreed with Kingsley's willingness to submit a manuscript to Drew for possible revisions. Drew declined to take up Kingsley's offer and protested only after the sermon was delivered. Drew had no place to stand to object to Kingsley's sermon, and Maurice unequivocally and publicly endorsed it.

Maurice's very public support for Kingsley worsened his situation at King's. Jelf asked Maurice to disavow Kingsley and his connections with the communist *Leader* or "to resign your office without delay." Maurice replied that he would not disavow Kingsley, that Croker's charges were inaccurate, and that he would not resign. Instead, he wrote, "I ask for a full examination of anything I have ever written or uttered in any way." Jelf backed down and informed Maurice that he was satisfied with his response; Maurice need not resign.[32] But matters were not settled. Jelf admonished him that his silence on such matters would have served the college better, that he should pledge to do nothing to "compromise" the college, and that his refusal to do so made him appear "proud and obstinate." Maurice replied that he would take such a pledge if the words had any "definite meaning," but they did not, so no such pledge could be taken.[33]

The controversy continued until 1853, when the council of King's College met and dismissed Maurice. His opponents were persons in the disciplines of political economy and theology. The political heterodoxy of Christian Socialism and the perceived theological heterodoxy of rejecting eternal divine punishment were too much for them. On August 24 of that year, Maurice knew what was coming and he wrote this to his friend, fellow Christian Socialist, and coeditor of *Politics for the People* J. M. Ludlow: "The King's College business is nearly concluded. The only question is now whether I shall resign or wait for dismissal. Jelf, of course, urges the first course as most convenient to him and to the college, and I am well inclined for my own sake to adopt it. But the question is, which is the right thing to do for the sake of the Church and of the great principle which I am certain is at stake."[34] The theological issues for Jelf were "eternal life" and the importance of "the notion of rewards and punishment" for morality.[35] If there were no eternal punishment for evil, then, somehow, the distinction between good and evil in this life would become meaningless. Maurice rejected this teaching and pointed out that the Church of England contained no such teaching in its Articles; nor did the Creeds.

Maurice held to a simple, yet profound, argument that the term "eternal" characterized only the divine life and therefore could not be applied to punishment for evil. It made evil coextensive with God, and that flew in the face of the Church's teachings on divine perfection. Biblical references to eternal misery referred to the loss of the fullness of life intended by God for creatures, a misery that was brought about by creatures' acts of moral evil; it had nothing to do with eternal pain and punishment inflicted by God. Moral evil is self-inflicted punishment. "Pain," he stated, "did not make amends for sin." Painful punishment for sin, like the doctrine of penance, was a Catholic error that Luther had rightly protested. Maurice saw a pecuniary motive in the teaching of an eternal punishment that could be alleviated through penance.[36]

Maurice's teaching was too much for Jelf and the King's College Council. An "Extract from the Minutes of Meeting of the Council"—held on Friday, October 14, 1853—lays out the council's decision and reasons for Maurice's dismissal:

> 1. That in their judgment the options set forth and the doubts expressed in the said essay, and re-stated in the said answer as to the certain points of belief regarding the future punishment of the wicked and the final issues of the divine judgment, are of dangerous tendency, and calculated to unsettle the minds of the theological students of King's College.
>
> 2. That the council feel it to be their painful duty to declare that the continuance of Professor Maurice's connection to the college as one of its professors would be seriously detrimental to its usefulness.

The council added a third resolution, affirming "the zealous and able manner in which he has discharged the duties of the two offices which he has held," but this did not outweigh the council's perception that continuing Maurice in his role as professor of theology would damage King's students.[37]

The bishop of London was the primary instigator behind Maurice's dismissal, stating that he was "preaching dangerous doctrines." Not everyone was happy about this. W. E. Gladstone, later prime minister of the United Kingdom in 1868, was a party to the proceedings and proposed that a panel of competent theological judges should have been assembled to adjudicate the matter rather than the college council. The council's decision, he stated, was "a dangerous way of proceeding." He also expressed his vexation with Maurice for bringing them to this point, stating that "it would have been very much better if he had avoided connecting himself with the Christian Socialists, and discuss questions on which it was plain that persons having great influence in the college would be at variance with him." Maurice's only "blame" is a lack of "worldly wisdom" that is necessary "to do good in this world." Another member of the council, Sir Benjamin Brodie, backed Gladstone's call for a council of theologians, but it went unheeded. Later, Gladstone wrote to Brodie, thanking him for his support and stating that he "sorrowfully agreed" that the result of this decision would be "prolonged mischief." Brodie wrote to Archdeacon Hare, lamenting the decision and the Bishop of London's "unwise" actions.[38]

The mischief may have been more "prolonged" than Gladstone and Brodie could have recognized. If, as Schultz suggests, Sidgwick initiates a post-Christian approach to ethics, then the mischief that such unwise actions promulgated lived well beyond the immediate mischief done to Maurice. Given the assertion of ecclesial authority against reasonable arguments, is it any wonder that Maurice was the last significant moral theologian to hold the Knightbridge Chair? In an effort to save theology for ethics through the doctrine of eternal divine punishment, Jelf and others exacerbated theology's abandonment. If we are to have morality, then divine judgment and eternal punishment are necessary. Sidgwick will demonstrate that it need not be so. The mischief, however, was less prolonged in Maurice's life. There were immediate repercussions. After being removed from King's, Maurice considered it necessary to resign from Queen's College, the institution for educating women that he had initiated in 1848. The Working Men's College invited him to be principal (without pay); he accepted.[39] Despite these immediate setbacks, a little more than a decade later, he was vindicated by being named to the Knightbridge Chair at Cambridge.

Upon the death of John Grote in August 1866, the Knightbridge Professorship came open at Cambridge. Charles Kingsley urged Maurice to stand for it. Maurice hesitated and worried that his Oxford degree would make him ineligible. Kingsley convinced him otherwise, and so he applied. Maurice wrote to Kingsley, "At sixty-one I am perhaps past such work, yet I do think I might be able to do it if it were entrusted to me." He presented his publications—*Theological Essay, What Is Revelation, Sequel to What Is Revelation,* and *Moral and Metaphysical Philosophy*—for his application. Seven electors determined the holder of the Knightbridge Chair—including the vice chancellor, Regius Professor of Greek, master of Peterhouse, Regius Professor of Divinity, Margaret Professor of Divinity, public orator, and Regius Professor of Modern History, who happened to be Kingsley. Four voted for Maurice, one for a different candidate, and two abstained but supported him.[40]

The works submitted for his application convey something of Maurice's character and show how far he was from any duplicity or esoteric morality.

Rather than presenting safe works, he gave them his most controversial ones. His *Theological Essays* contained the teaching against eternal punishment that led the authorities at King's College to remove him from his teaching position. The two works on revelation were his response to Henry Longueville Mansel's 1858 Bampton lectures, "The Limits of Religious Thought." Influenced by Kant, Mansel sought clear lines of demarcation between theology and philosophy. The former was based on revelation and the latter on reason. Mansel's position is found in this statement from his first lecture: "If the tendency of Dogmatism is to endanger the interests of religious truth, by placing that which is divine and unquestionable in too close an alliance with that which is human and doubtful, Rationalism, on the other hand, tends to destroy revealed religion altogether, by obliterating the whole distinction between the human and the divine."[41] Maurice's entire body of work sought to show how religious truth was always closely allied with that which is most human, and that philosophy and theology were not so easily divided, so he held strong objections to Mansel. He viewed his lectures as akin to atheism because they denied knowledge of God other than in revelation. Knowledge of God was limited to a select few, outside whom God could not be found. He referred to his disagreement with Mansel as "the most important controversy of his life." It marked his work from then on because it fit with trends to "set 'religion' against God." Mansel's so-called orthodoxy, he suggested, only required a doctrine of revelation and a strong notion of judgment.[42] In that sense, his controversy with Mansel continued what his *Theological Essays* had provoked.

The works Maurice provided to the committee demonstrate the error that Schultz makes about his character and theology. Although he was in most respects a traditional Christian, he used the tradition against popular and conventional teachings that he found objectionable, such as eternal punishment and identifying power as one of God's attributes. Of course, he was correct that neither of these teachings was found in the Thirty-Nine Articles. He also rejected any foundation of ethics in divine punishment or a command stemming solely from power. Charity is the basis for ethics because creatures are made in the image of God, and this image reflects the gift and reception that identify God as Triune. It is also thus the basis for moral theology.

After being named to the Knightbridge Chair, Maurice decided to do a threefold series of lectures on what he termed the "magniloquent name" that his predecessor, William Whewell, gave to it: conscience for "casuistry," social morality for "moral philosophy," and moral theology.[43] He gave the first two series and published them under the titles *The Conscience: Lectures on Casuistry* and *Social Morality*. Because moral theology influenced everything he did, he decided that no reason existed to give a separate course of lectures. If he had, presenting his moral theology would have been easier, but it would also have been misleading—for two reasons. First, he would reject the idea that "moral theology" can be the object of a possessive like "Maurice's." If "Maurice's Moral Theology" made sense, it could not be Maurice's moral theology. "Kantian constructivism" makes sense (perhaps), but for Maurice neither moral philosophy nor theology are constructed; they are discovered and received. That is why he referred to himself as a "digger":

> My business, because I am a theologian, and have no vocation except for theology, is not to build, but to dig, to show that economy and politics . . . must have a ground beneath themselves, that society is not to be made anew by arrangements of ours, but is to be regenerated by finding the law and ground of its order, and harmony, the only secret of its existence, in God. . . . The Kingdom of Heaven is to me the great practical existing reality which is to renew the earth and make it a habitation for blessed spirits instead of for demons.[44]

Although moral theology is not a construct but a human act, to dig requires human agency. What is discovered, if Maurice is correct, is fully human.

Second, he insists that the ethical life cannot be systematized without significant loss; he consistently emphasizes "life" over any system or dogma, an emphasis that he associates with the task of casuistry. Casuistry considers conscience from an agent, an "I," who exists within nature, society, and a divine economy and is confronted with an "ought." The "ought" cannot be divided from this "I." "I and the ought," he states, "are twin words."[45] Because life takes precedence over system, Maurice refuses any sharp distinction between moral theology and moral philosophy. Both deal with the same matter, the human person in society and history seeking wisdom, goodness, and truth; they are there to be discovered in each generation and among all peoples. For this reason, he does not set modern and ancient philosophy against each other. Wherever wisdom is found, it should be embraced. What hinders it should be discarded. He is both for and against Aristotle, for and against Aquinas, and for and against most modern philosophers, depending on whether he considers them to have discovered Wisdom. It is always available and can be difficult to miss; for this reason, he finds something positive in nearly every religious and moral teaching that has existed.

Maurice's *Moral and Metaphysical Philosophy* shows this approach to moral theology. It begins with "Hebrew Philosophy" and moves to Egyptian, Phoenician, Assyrian, Hindu, Chinese, and Persian philosophy before discussing the Greeks. Philosophy has a unique origin with the Greeks, he observes, but because philosophy is a way of life rather than speculation or systematic construction, philosophy does not begin with them; it is found among every people. Practicing some way of life is inescapable, and thus so is philosophy. Maurice did not avoid privileging a European view, and he could be blind to the damage colonialism was doing even as he criticized colonialists. Yet he had a remarkable appreciation for the diverse peoples of the world in their search for wisdom, goodness, and truth. His 1871 preface to *Moral and Metaphysical Philosophy* imagines a dialogue with an undergraduate philosophy student, who objects to his theology, his affirmation of the election of the Jews, and his willingness to find wisdom in all peoples. Maurice's response shows how these affirmations were not an exception to his Christian theology but a consequence of it.

The student begins by informing Maurice that his generation will not accept Maurice's work because "[you have] felt as a theologian, thought as a theologian, written as a theologian; that all other subjects in your mind are connected with theology and are subordinate to it." Maurice admits this. He will be viewed as someone who belongs to the twelfth rather than the nineteenth century, not only because he "connects" theology and philosophy but even more because he gives theology "supremacy."[46] He then explains what he means. Theology has too often been approached as a "discourse or system about God" that seeks to move from the finite to the infinite. This places the theologian too much in control of the discourse. Theology is better understood as "God speaking . . . by a Word," and this takes the discourse out of the hands of theologians. Theology is not about controlling the discourse, but about listening, being attentive to what has been, is, and will be spoken. Because the Word that is spoken is Christological and thus a creaturely word, it could be heard by any people attentive to the finite "goodness and wisdom" of everyday life that is "grounded" in "the Infinite." This is because the Wisdom that speaks does so by "guiding men by various processes, in various regions and ages, into the apprehension of that which by their constitution they were created to apprehend. The history of Moral and Metaphysical Philosophy is, as I think, the History of this Education." The same theology that lets him find wisdom among diverse peoples also permits him to affirm the election of Israel and view it as a pattern for other nations. Because Wisdom works in "various regions and ages," the "same selector who called the Jews to be a family and a nation" also "forms the political life among Hindoos, Chinese, Persians, Greeks."[47] Judaism, and the Old Testament, provide the pattern for national life, and not just European national life but also life for all nations.[48]

If the Old Testament is the pattern for national life, the New Testament is the basis for a central theological idea that he holds: the Kingdom–Church ideal. It is related to yet different from national forms. They are "Protestant," but it is "Catholic." The nation is Protestant because it has no authority over it, such as the papacy. The Church is Catholic because it is found in every nation but also transcends them. Maurice's early work, *The Kingdom of Christ* (1838) established the Kingdom–Church ideal as the social context for the moral life. His lectures on the Epistles of Saint John, delivered to the students at the Working Men's College fifteen years later, are, as his son stated, "his clearest and simplest setting for the thought on the subject of morals."[49] Maurice begins these lectures not with Scripture but with Aristotle. He taught that everyone "aims at some End," and he defined the end as "*eudaimonia* or happiness." Without rejecting Aristotle, Maurice shifts the end from happiness to perfection by bringing in Augustine without mentioning him by name. He writes, "Man cannot be satisfied with anything short of what is Perfect. He must have perpetual 'unrest' till he finds what is Perfect."[50] This clearly paraphrases Augustine, who said "Our hearts are restless until they rest in Thee." It is the desire for the Perfect that sparks unrest and provokes searching for Wisdom. That our final end must give us rest and help us achieve the perfection of our nature is consistent with Aristotle; where Maurice differs is that this perfection is not found in some "condition" of our own "mind." The end does not arise from acquired virtues that are primarily a "quality of the mind (or soul)." Perfection is not achieved by our immanent sources but through a restlessness that calls us out of our self to receive it from another. As is shown below, being called out does not evacuate our agency but makes it possible.

NOTES

1. Aslanbeigui and Oakes, *Provocative Joan Robinson*, 26–28.
2. Maurice, *Life*, vol. 2, 130.
3. Maurice, *Life*, vol. 1, 122.
4. Maurice, 43.
5. Maurice, 376.
6. Maurice.
7. Maurice, 37.
8. Maurice, 61–62, 66.
9. Maurice, 110.
10. Schultz, *Henry Sidgwick*, 47.
11. Schultz, 268, 271.

12. As noted in part I of this book, Schultz goes to great length to justify Sidgwick against Bernard Williams's claim that his ethics served the colonialist enterprise, but in the end acknowledges that "Williams gets closer to the heart of the matter" than Schneewind; Schultz, *Henry Sidgwick*, 272.
13. Maurice, *Life*, vol. 1, 72.
14. Maurice, 168.
15. Maurice, 210–13.
16. Maurice, 221–22.
17. Maurice, *Friendship of Books*, 32.
18. His argument is similar to Aquinas's use of Aristotle's "deliberation" in the *prima secundae* as evidence that sources for ethics can be external to us; Aquinas, *Summa Theologaie*, I–II, 109.2.
19. Maurice, *Friendship of Books*, 33–34.
20. Maurice, 41–42.
21. Maurice, 46.
22. Quoted by Maurice.
23. Maurice, 51.
24. Maurice, 56.
25. Maurice, 59.
26. Maurice, *Theological Essays*, 302.
27. Maurice, *Moral and Metaphysical Philosophy: Volume 1*, 624.
28. Morris, *F. D. Maurice and the Crisis*, 131.
29. Maurice, *Life*, vol. 2, 69–70.
30. Maurice, 72–73.
31. Kingsley, "Message."
32. Maurice, *Life*, vol. 2, 79–83.
33. Maurice, 98–99.
34. Maurice, 176; Norman, *Victorian Christian Socialists*, 76.
35. Maurice, *Life*, vol. 2, 180.
36. Maurice, *Theological Essays*, 305–13.
37. Maurice, *Life*, vol. 2, 191–92.
38. Maurice, 198–99.
39. Maurice, 218–22; Morris, *F. D. Maurice and the Crisis*, 161.
40. Maurice, *Life*, vol. 2, 542–45.
41. Mansel, *Limits*, 11.
42. Maurice, *Life*, vol. 2, 333–34.
43. Maurice, 552; Wondra, "Introduction," xix.
44. Cited by Wondra, "Introduction," xii.
45. Maurice, *Conscience*, 33.
46. Maurice, *Moral and Metaphysical Philosophy: Volume 1*, xv–xvi.
47. Maurice, xxxix–xl.
48. Below, I discuss Willie J. Jennings's important thesis that the migration of the election of the Jews to European nations is a distorted Christian imagination that gives rise to white supremacy.
49. Maurice, *Life*, vol. 2, 310.
50. Maurice, *Epistles of St. John*, 339.

5

MAURICE'S MORAL THEOLOGY

The previous chapter concluded by offering a general description of Maurice's moral theology. This chapter fills in the details by discussing more fully these four themes: (1) Moral theology and philosophy should attend to life more than system. (2) Attention to life will discover that there is a ground or foundation, the Kingdom of God–Church ideal, that generates a cooperative social morality. It is primarily present in the Church, but because it reflects the Triune image in which everything is created, it is present in every nation. It is not only future but also can and should be exhibited in the present. Maurice's politics and economics emerge out of this theological ground. It leads him to advocate for the abolition of slavery and competitive economics, and on occasion, it causes some hesitation about colonialism, albeit insufficiently. It did not lead him to question paternalism. (3) Moral philosophy and theology cannot be firmly distinguished because they have the same ground in the Trinity and its social manifestation in the Kingdom of God. (4) The task of both is the full realization of the end to which each individual and society is called—perfection. The vocation to perfection requires more than virtue oriented toward an immanent human flourishing; it requires reception of a gifted agency through the theological and infused virtues, fashioning one to be truly human. This fourth point is alluded to in the conclusion to this chapter and is taken up in the next one.

LIFE VERSUS SYSTEM

Sidgwick sought to narrow the domain for ethics. Maurice widened it as far as possible. Ethics includes every aspect of life; such a totality could not be brought within a system. The differences between them are present in their orienting questions. Sidgwick began ethics asking, "What ought I to do?" Maurice began with something more fundamental, "What am I?"[1] If we did not know what constitutes the agent, then we could not ask what they ought to do. He gave multiple answers to his question: a person with a conscience who acts; a creature made in the image of the Triune God; a seeker after wisdom; an "I" ensconced in histories that raise practical problems that need resolution; an "I" capable of transcending history; an "I" situated in, and unintelligible from, a diversity of social contexts: family, nation, and a universal society. His question and answers also shaped what he means by "philosophy," "morals," and "metaphysics." They provide it with its form. Once this form can be seen, its overlap with theology will be obvious.

How Maurice uses "philosophy," "morals," and "metaphysics" is indicated in the introduction to *Moral and Metaphysical Philosophy*. Philosophy "is the love of a hidden treasure" that has no weight nor quantity that permit it to be measured. The treasure is "Wisdom." Maurice capitalizes the term because it has a twofold meaning. The first is theological. Wisdom is the second Person of the Trinity, the "divine humanity" that is the ground for any adequate answer to the question "What am I?" Such a "divine humanity" is present "in all ages."[2] The second meaning is philosophical. Wisdom is discovered in the "ways, habits, and manners" of peoples. Ways, habits, and manners define morality; they differ among peoples, but the Wisdom that unites them is common. Searching for this Wisdom through and beyond ways, habits, and manners constitutes metaphysics.[3] A "*Metaphysical* philosopher," he writes, is one "who seeks for an object which is not of the same kind with the things around him." This search does not abstract from one's situatedness because ways, habits, and manners are the means to discover the underlying Wisdom.[4] One digs for it through them. As the basis for creation, this Wisdom is present not only in the Church but also in every people. If Christians refuse the search, something that they often do when they prioritize dogma or system to life, it will still be found elsewhere. Wisdom expresses itself in creation; creatures will witness to that expression.

A central thesis throughout *Moral and Metaphysical Philosophy* is that every culture, philosophy, and religion discloses aspects of Wisdom. Maurice's reflections on the first-century Jewish philosopher Philo illustrate well this approach to moral and metaphysical philosophy. He is for and against Philo, depending on how well he expresses and witnesses to Wisdom. For Philo, Wisdom is "the I AM who spoke to Moses in the bush—the Instructor and Inspirer of all the prophets—He who gave the law on Sinai."[5] Wisdom addressing Moses in and through the burning bush is an example of what Maurice meant by metaphysics. Moses and Philo were "led, so far as they were led, out of the pursuit of visible and sensible things, by One who is seeking to bring man's spirit into communion with Himself." Metaphysics includes an exodus; it involves being led through the ordinary to glimpse the extraordinary, which is also how Maurice interprets the Christian Eucharist. Philo maintained "the profoundest reverence" for the revelation to Moses. He did not turn it into a dogma that should be protected, and thus Philo witnesses to it as a life-giving activity that opened him up to find something similar in "the Indian Gymnosophist, the Greek philosopher, the Egyptian symbolizer."[6] Maurice encourages his readers to have a similar approach to Wisdom. Yet Maurice faults Philo for a perceived elitism and for separating philosophy from ordinary life. Philo, like Seneca but unlike Epictetus, cordoned philosophy off from the ordinary person. He sets himself above "common men" and their "feelings, interests, hopes." Philo gets seduced by philosophy from "the principles upon which the commonwealth of Israel stood."[7] If moral philosophy cannot address ordinary persons, it has not fulfilled its task well. Ethical wisdom is never for an elite; nor should it be esoteric. It is found among ordinary persons and speaks to them.

Moral and Metaphysical Philosophy was not a work of Christian ethics. His lectures to the students at the Working Men's College were published in 1857 as *The Epistles of St. John: A Series of Lectures on Christian Ethics*. Both works share an emphasis on everyday life as the site to discover Wisdom. Maurice chose the Johannine epistles to explain Christian ethics because they eschewed "startling events" and "miracles" and attended to the ordinary. He writes, "There was a craving in the earlier ages, as there has been since, for stories of startling events," but instead these letters "of the simplest, most commonplace kind" found their way into the canon. The first epistle addresses a "society," the "elect lady" and her children, and repeatedly uses the expression that the author "loves them in truth" because the truth "dwells" or "abides" in them. Maurice uses these expressions to guide his students away from considering truth to be a property of propositions. He states, "We are frequently told—and told by persons to whose authority on many subjects I defer—that truth belongs to Propositions." One such person was his friend J. S. Mill, but Saint John could not agree, because applying his expression that truth "dwelleth in us" to propositions would be nonsense. Truth, like conscience, dwells in lives, not statements, properties, or faculties. The Incarnation provides warrant for this emphasis on life. The "perfect life" is the Incarnate One, who as "the Truth which dwelleth in us, and will dwell in us for ever, is He Who is, and was, and is to come, that true God whose life eternal Jesus came to manifest, that we might be partakers of it and might show it forth in our acts."[8] The terms "abideth" and "dwelleth" permeate Maurice's work. The Spirit infuses in us goodness and truth, which order us to a life we could not otherwise achieve; yet this infusion results in life abiding in us.

After being elected to the Knightbridge Chair, Maurice never published a specifically Christian ethics, as he did in 1857; yet this emphasis on life over dogma remained in his lectures and publications and especially the first series on casuistry. It begins with Lord McCauley's statement that a maker of shoes deserves "more gratitude" than authors of books on virtues and vices. Maurice raises this as a possible objection to his subject, one that he appears to find compelling. In a later lecture, he returns to this objection and states that the casuist

> is to be testifying in season and out of season, that the subject which he speaks of is a subject for books only because it is a subject for men and women, and that it would remain the same if all the books that ever have been written were burnt to ashes. But for this very reason he must mingle in the battle of the books; he cannot overlook the systems which philosophers are constructing, and sending forth into the world.[9]

Books have their place, but only as they convey something of life that requires focus "on the "word 'I,'" which is the title of Maurice's first lecture on casuistry. Unlike Whewell, who disliked the term "casuistry," Maurice begins with it and then moves to moral philosophy. Casuistry comes first because persons act from conscience; only if we understand "person" and "conscience" can Maurice's casuistry make sense. He writes, "First make it clear what you mean by a Person; that you will do when you make it clear what you mean by a Conscience; then treat these Persons as if they did form real bodies, and tell us out of history, not out of your own fancy, what these bodies are.'"[10]

Maurice's lectures were an explicit critique of Whewell's privileging moral philosophy over casuistry: "The illustrious man who thirty years ago restored this chair to dignity and efficiency, and began to endow it with some of his vast intellectual treasures, abandoned that title [casuistry] for his lectures, deeming Moral Philosophy a more suitable one in this age."[11] If casuistry is strictly defined as the adjudication of cases of conscience, Whewell might be correct. Yet Maurice retrieves "casuistry" by exploring how it relates persons to "conscious" and "conscientious," asking his readers to consider how these terms are used in everyday life: "And so I would lead you to reflect a little on the grandeur and power of words; of those words which we repeat most frequently, which we trifle the most." Through attention to "daily usage," we discover that "in them lies a wealth of meaning which each age has helped to extract, but which will contain something for every fresh digger." Consciousness and conscience are used with respect to "I," and they are a "class of words" that "rebels against arbitrary definition."[12] Butler and Whewell debated the definition of conscience, Butler defining it as a "faculty" and Whewell as an "exercise of reason." For Maurice, both miss something about the everyday use of the term. If it is referred to as a "faculty," Maurice states that he can give no meaning to the words. Nor does he side with Whewell and define it as an exercise of reason. He refuses to engage in the debate because it would incline him to neglect what matters most about the use of the term "conscience," which is "its adherence to the singular pronoun."[13] It is less helpful, he suggests, to ask if conscience is "in human nature" than in the "persons to whom this nature is attributed."[14]

Maurice eschews abstractions that would locate conscience in something like a faculty or an exercise of reason, and then falsely imagine that we have said something significant. The term, like its correlative "conscientious," poses a question to persons, not asking them if they have some faculty but if they have a conscience. Or, as he puts it in his most extensive statement of what he means by casuistry, how does the world appear to them and how do they appear to the world:

> I have told you in this lecture that I dread the temptation to lay down a general scheme of moral or of human nature. The examples of eminent men in former days who have adopted that course—the craving for facts, the impatience of mere opinion, which I welcome as some of the most helpful signs of our time—alike lead me to desire, as my immediate predecessor did [Grote], a more egotistical kind of study. Casuistry, it seems to me, is such a study. It brings us face to face with the internal life of each one of us. The world without, it leaves to the examination of other enquirers. The Casuist's business is with him who looks into that world, who receives impressions from it, and compels it to receive impressions from him.[15]

The statement that the "world without" is the domain of other inquiries could mislead readers into thinking that Maurice affirms an is/ought distinction. He explicitly raises and then rejects the distinction because ethics is about life.

Maurice was well aware of the is/ought distinction from the eighteenth-century jurist and philosopher James MacKintosh. His *Dissertation on the*

Progress of Ethical Philosophy Chiefly during the Seventeenth and Eighteenth Centuries, with a preface from Whewell, states,

> The purpose of the Physical Sciences, throughout all their provinces is to answer the question *What is?* They consist only of facts arranged according to their likeness and expressed by general names given to every class of similar facts. The purpose of the Moral Sciences is to answer the question *What ought to be?* They aim at ascertaining the rules which ought to govern voluntary action, and to which those habitual dispositions of mind which are the sources of voluntary actions *ought* to be adapted.[16]

MacKintosh's definition of ethics is strikingly similar to Sidgwick's. Maurice disagrees with it, claiming, "Ethics seemed transferred from the real world in which we dwell to some other imaginary world."[17] But his critique of this is/ought distinction is not due to some ethical naturalism per se; it is due to his emphasis on life over system. The good is not found "in things" but is "linked inseparable to me," to the life of an I who acts in the world as it is.[18] This is what he and Grote meant by egotism; ethics is personally encumbering. Inasmuch as Whewell adopts this distinction, Maurice also disagrees with him. He also departs from him at another point: "He avowedly endeavoured to construct a system of Morality. I have declared that I have no such object, that I shall even strive diligently against the wish to pursue such an object."[19] If Whewell was Sidgwick's negative example of intuitionism, he was Maurice's negative example of system. But Maurice rejected what Sidgwick affirmed from Whewell, system building based on an is/ought distinction—rather than focusing our attention on what mattered most for ethics, human lives lived well; it distracted from it to an "imaginary world."

Learning and teaching ethics require attending to real lives in their ordinary situations. It refuses the temptation to construct a system but asks how persons negotiate the world as it is while also being called to participate in the Wisdom found in that world. This Wisdom results in an ecstatic agency if learners approach the world in faith and confidence. Returning to Maurice's interpretation of Philo points to a crucial distinction that he draws between an ethics born out of fear and one from confidence that shows both his ecstatic agency and how persons of faith should approach the world. An ethics born out of fear seeks to "defend a certain religion against a certain other religion." It situates opponents of the Church only as "asserters of falsehood." Their wisdom will be viewed as a threat and neglected. Nothing will be learned of the Wisdom through whom all things were made.[20] An ethics of confidence is born out of faith, hope, and charity. It places faith in the "witness of the true constitution of all human beings" that prompts two dispositions. First, no one is trapped solely within an internal, immanent source. Because everyone, to some extent, receives Wisdom, it draws everyone out of themselves. An ecstatic agency constitutes human being. Second, Wisdom's excess prepares receivers to find it anywhere. Their approach to the world is to "rejoice to acknowledge its members to be what they could not embrace or comprehend, of which they often perceived only small portion, but which, through their lives and deaths, as well as through the right and wrong acts, the true and false words of those who understand them least, was to manifest and prove itself."[21] A life lived well points to something beyond that life without which it is unintelligible.

Wisdom's excess leads to a nonreactionary approach to antiquity and modernity. They need not be played off each other, as if we were to retreat to ancient sources for ethics to counter modern errors or to abandon ancient sources because of a supposed irreproachable modern progress. Wisdom also breaks down any dividing wall between theology and philosophy. No enforceable boundary between faith and wisdom can prevail. They transgress any such border.

MORAL THEOLOGY AND MORAL PHILOSOPHY: ANCIENT AND MODERN

For Maurice, the domain for moral philosophy did not differ from that for moral theology; both concern "life." It is too broad and general for the scientific precision Sidgwick desired, but that only restates Maurice's point. He did not think ethics could be systematized, as Sidgwick's *Methods* attempted. Schultz claims that Sidgwick inherited from Maurice "the fear of premature system building, and the effect that it might have on the pursuit of truth."[22] Something is to be said for this; Sidgwick was methodical in his approach, and that led him to admit that his system lacked completeness. Ethics could not be completely rational. Yet Maurice's opposition to system is much deeper than "*premature* system building." He eschewed it altogether and never attempted an ethical method that could guide action.

It was not, however, life in general that interested Maurice, but a life lived well, or what he would refer to as a "true human being." Such a domain for ethics meant that no single study or discipline oversees it; nor does it require privileging modern approaches over ancient or ancient over modern. What makes Maurice important for doing moral theology after the conflicts of modernity is that he provides a way to retrieve what is ancient without being reactionary and to adopt what is modern without assuming that change or progress requires the obsolescence of everything that came before. He held a place for ancient and modern thought based on the key question: What promotes life lived well, and what hinders it? Recognizing this important point makes sense of Maurice's affirmations and criticisms of creedal Christianity. For instance, he affirmed Athanasius, Basil, and Gregory of Nazianzus because doctrine served "as a foundation for human life." The "vigorous followers" of the same doctrine under Emperor Justinian, however, sought only to defend dogma and "reduced living truths into abstractions."[23] As his mixed evaluation of Philo shows, this distinction can exist within the same philosopher or theologian. The distinction was the basis for his criticism of Bentham, something for which Mill thanked him. Maurice wrote this critique with Bentham's utilitarianism in mind: "Here, as I have told you, my business is not with ideals, but with the questions, What am I? what has this word 'ought' to do with me? These questions can never be answered whilst we are busy about numbers, whilst we are losing ourselves in a crowd."[24] Quantifying and aggregating utility contribute little to a well-lived life.

When Maurice turns to modern philosophers in *Moral and Metaphysical Philosophy*, he reemphasizes the connection between ethics and life. His purpose is "to trace the progress of the thoughts that have contributed to form these schools and systems; to connect them with the lives of the men in whom they have originated; to note the influence which they have exerted upon their times, and the influence which their times have exerted upon them." The connection between their theories and lives leads him to "deduce those lessons" that serve his primary interest: "practical life; for which the man demands a solution even more than the professional philosopher."[25] The lessons he deduced from modern moral philosophy were both positive and negative. Positively, modern philosophers approached the same subject matter as the ancients with the new tool of science and an unwavering commitment to see the facts. Negatively, they unnecessarily narrowed the questions that were posed, imagining that they could focus on morality without attending to metaphysics.

Maurice worries that his criticism of modern philosophers might misrepresent them, and he warns the reader that if he does, it is due to his atheism and not his faith. Faith requires that he "dare not refuse to see the good, and the struggle after good" in every philosopher.[26] One good aspect of modern philosophy is the central place that morality occupies in it; but Maurice questions if modern philosophy's emphasis on experience, sentiment, and utility locates morality in "outward conditions" alone and misses the Wisdom upon which it depends. The result is a division of disciplines into morality, metaphysics, and political economy that become independent of each other.

By "outward conditions," Maurice meant sense impressions. Adam Smith and David Hume associate ideas with them for the sake of "political economy." Maurice write,

> We might conclude that political economy, in the form which it took at this time both in England and France, would destroy metaphysics, and would make morals entirely dependent upon the outward conditions of man. In that way Adam Smith would be a co-operator with Hume; the *Wealth of Nations* would be a kind of pendant to the *Principles of Morals*; it would be an additional weight in the scale that was making experience the one standard by which all acts and all principles were to be tied.[27]

To be satisfied with the single standard of experience is to stop digging and to miss what matters most. It failed to ask the question of what the conditions for experience were and assumed that political economy could be pursued without moral philosophy or metaphysics. For Maurice, the "laws" of economics "are not and cannot be at variance with moral and metaphysical laws," and yet this variance was what Hume and Smith suggested by dividing them from metaphysics.[28] It took time for the division of academic labor to divide what Maurice held together. As noted above, economics was taught under the moral science tripos at Cambridge until 1903, but Maurice saw what was coming, or rather coming apart.

Modern philosophers also erred in distinguishing their inquiries too decisively from theology. Maurice argued that before the fourteenth century, philosophers and theologians could not easily be differentiated. Most philosophers in the first thirteen centuries were "in some sense, or other, theologians." They had the same subject matter, and equally assumed that metaphysics was a necessary feature for discovering it. Modern philosophers share this subject matter, but they too often dispense with metaphysics, or at least imagine that they have. Kant was an exception. He understood that morality and metaphysics needed each other, but Hume and the Christian utilitarian Paley did not. The three began their philosophy at the same place—morality. They permitted "speculation, philosophical or theological, as important only for moral ends." But it was Kant who departed from them in a "radical and fundamental sense," because of his "strong conviction that there is an authority over him, which does not suspend his liberty, but without obedience to which he cannot enjoy his liberty."[29] Maurice interpreted

Kant along the lines of Allen Wood or Christopher Insole, more so than Rawls and Korsgaard. Morality has its "eternal grounds... in an Eternal Being; that conformity with them is the condition of man's eternal blessedness." For that reason, Kant's "reputation as a destroyer even of the metaphysics and psychology of his predecessors has been greatly exaggerated."[30] Yet Maurice's interpretation of Kant was mixed. Metaphysics serves the end of morality alone, and thus he had "no dealing with theology" and restricted the questions metaphysics pursued.[31] Morality rendered metaphysics intelligible rather than vice versa, and it rendered theology adiaphora.

The ordinary person, that is the nonphilosopher, cannot render asunder what these philosophers attempted to divide. Maurice shows the problem with the effort to abandon metaphysics in the first half of the eighteenth century in his discussion of Locke. He begins with a quotation from Locke's *Essay on the Human Understanding* about the need to "take a survey of our own understanding" so that we do not "begin at the wrong end, and in vain sought for satisfaction in a quiet and secure possession of the truth which most concerned us, whilst we let loose our thoughts into the vast ocean of *Being*."[32] From Locke on, the "vast ocean of *Being*" was perceived to be a temptation, the temptation of metaphysics that philosophers should avoid. Philosophers from Locke through Kant "laboured hard to overthrow metaphysics" and thought that studying their "own understanding" would suffice for morality; but it could not work. As much as they attempted to keep the "ocean of *Being*" away from morality, or seek to direct it only to serve morality, they failed. Nature alone, nature detached from *Being*, could not satisfy the questions life raised for the ordinary person: "Nature did not satisfy men if it satisfied philosophers. They must have something above nature. And that which was above nature must speak to them, must seek to raise them above its oppressions. They could become responsible beings only upon that condition."[33] The statement that questioning the sufficiency of nature raises people above oppressions is a theological claim that God continues to liberate, as God did in Exodus. The "ocean of being" can never be kept safely away; it inevitably returns. Maurice thought it was returning in his own day: "Being and Not Being, Being and Becoming are, as in the days of Plato, the watchwords which will be run in our ears; to which we may shut our ears if we please, but which will encounter us when we least expect them."[34]

Readers should not misunderstand Maurice's argument. It is not special pleading for a religious outlook at the expense of ethics. Nor is it a rejection of modern philosophy. Despite his criticism of Hume, for instance, Maurice claims that he has much to teach us. His critical "investigations" into morality do "a service to truth and to mankind." His failure, states Maurice, is when, as happens often in this treatise, he declines investigation, laughs at the effort to make it as useless and ridiculous, flings himself into his arm chair, becomes as indolently and contemptuously acquiescent as any priest ever wished his disciples to be; it is then that he exhibits the state of mind to which we are all tempted, and against which, whatever others do, the believer in a God of truth must wrestle to the death.[35]

Hume dismissed the "facts" that lead ordinary persons to "earnest reflection" on the invisible world. It cannot be so easily dismissed as, in Hume's dismissive phrase, "abstract" philosophy.[36] Philosophers and theologians fail when they quit digging. Because the domain of ethics is life, the theologian, or religious person, has no "study" of ethics that differentiates them from the place "which other men occupy."[37] The common subject matter means that the theologian cannot exclude the philosopher from investigating it but also that the philosopher has no basis to assume that the "ground" upon which they worked was different from that of "the Christian Church."[38] Ethics was neither the special province of the philosopher nor the theologian.

Maurice refused two possibilities for moral theology. The first is to adopt moral philosophy without theology; it abstracts from the content of Christian teaching into something putatively more universal, such as natural law, human dignity, utility, and so forth. The second is to retreat to moral theology without philosophy, as if Wisdom were found only within Christianity. Either abstraction or withdrawal will fail to find Wisdom. Maurice eschewed both, on the assumption that the deeper he went into the mysteries of the Trinity and the Incarnation, the more universal he discovered their significance to be. Two implications follow from his approach; the first is salutary, the second less so. First, it opened him to the possibility of finding Wisdom among every nation and people, giving his work the virtue of liberality or generosity. Second, the Wisdom he found there could be a priori prescribed as Christian dogma and colonize other cultures and nations.

Learning and teaching ethics requires attending to real lives. It refuses to construct a system or method that guides action but seeks to discover the Wisdom in every culture and nation. Its presence in each culture and nation is a gift that makes possible an ecstatic agency. Look for it, he suggests, and you may find it. This requires a wide search that refuses sharp disciplinary divisions or focusing on only one time period or one thinker. It also led him to consider nations as bearing a unique ethos that should be honored and protected, resulting in some of his most interesting and unsatisfying ethical claims.

NATIONS AND THE KINGDOM OF GOD–CHURCH IDEAL

Maurice's lectures on social morality set "ways, habits, and manners" within the "ἦθος of a Society." The term ἦθος, he writes, "is specially an Aristotelian word." An individual possesses a conscience that allows them to act, but that conscience is present within an ἦθος that gets "developed" in a society.[39] Each nation has its identifiable characteristics. His understanding of agency is Aristotelian, emphasizing character and habit rather than "outward acts" or "formal maxims." Although he draws on Aristotelian terms, he is also critical of Aristotle; he could be a "dogmatist" concerned more with teaching about life than life itself, but he was better than the scholastics because virtues were not abstractions. They are embodied in human lives. As is also shown below, he was highly critical of the retrieval of Aristotle by slavocrats who used his work to argue that modern slavery was a domestic society. Yet Maurice's emphasis on the uniqueness of each national morality had its own unsavory consequence.[40]

One of Maurice's undergraduate students, C. H. Pearson, was a strong and influential advocate for white supremacy. Pearson adopted the concept of "national life" for his white nationalist project. The historian Marilyn Lake finds more references to "white men" in English-speaking nations after the US Civil War, when Reconstruction briefly generated the possibility that Blacks might gain access to political and economic power, a possibility that prompted whites' reaction. She writes, "It was in identification with white Americans in the decades following the Civil War, that many English and Australians came to think of themselves as white men."[41] A concerted effort arose that influenced powerful men—such as Gladstone in the United Kingdom, Theodore Roosevelt in the United States, and Edmund Barton and Alfred Deakin in Australia—that gave rise to the idea of the "white man under siege."[42] It led to the "White Australia Policy," restricting immigration to whites, and to Roosevelt's efforts to increase white fertility and advocate imperial expansion so that whites would have a place to exercise their superiority. One source for these racist policies was the liberal reformer Pearson's influential book *National Life and Characteristics*.[43]

Pearson had studied at King's College and came under Maurice's influence when he was teaching there. As we saw in part I of this book, Henry Sidgwick was his friend and supporter. He echoed some of the teachings in Pearson's influential book. After Maurice was terminated, Pearson was given the teaching position in 1855 that Maurice had once held. Pearson was an abolitionist, a supporter of women's education, and a defender of secularization, and he argued that decolonization was inevitable. Yet despite his commitment to liberal reform, he could only be described as a white suprem-acist. He classified whites as the "superior race," and races from the "black and yellow belt" as inferior. The latter were advancing largely due to their prox-imity to the superior white race, but a consequence of their advancement was that "the higher may be assimilating to the moral and mental depression of the lower."[44] Rather than the inferior races being raised to the level of the superior, the latter were being reduced to that of the former. For Pearson, this raised a problem. Whites were incapable of the rigorous labor that people from the "black and yellow belt" could accomplish. Moreover, whites could not flourish in tropical climates. Thus, they were being squeezed out of their lands and no longer had recourse to colonial expansion. Their future was, for Pearson, not promising. Coupled with this was the fact that England and other "white" nations were approaching the "stationary state" (a clear refer-ence to J. S. Mill's economics), such that "State Socialism" was dissipating the energy from owners and producers. China would soon take over mar-kets with cheap labor, and England's shift to "State Socialism" would require protections that "if there be any truth in Free Trade, would be financially disastrous to England herself in the long run."[45] Did Maurice's influence exac-erbate Pearson's teaching of white supremacy?

The language of the superiority of the white race is not found in Maurice's work as it is in Pearson's. Maurice held a more positive understanding of socialism and would have rejected Pearson's secularism. Maurice affirmed the established Church. Any influence by Maurice on Pearson is most likely found in Maurice's insistence that a nation has a distinct characteristic or ethos that should guide its citizens. Oddly, the distinctiveness of every nation led Maurice both to affirm independence for every nation and the unique role of British colonialism. God, he wrote,

> has seen fit to bestow on us an empire on which the sun does not set. He has committed to our care some hundreds of millions of human beings, who have certainly the same flesh and blood with us, and who show by the strange speculations which their sages (often rich in the gifts we are deficient in) express in words, and which are for the people embodied in acts, that they are spiritual beings, and that they know they are.[46]

Maurice finds wisdom in colonized people, a wisdom that reveals itself in their own ecstatic agency. Yet the colonizers failed to affirm this wisdom and agency or to connect it with compelling wisdom from their own cul-ture: The result, he states, is that "the natives have only derived from their [colonialists'] presence a vague impression, that all they have had held themselves is false; and, that we could offer them in exchange the choice of some twenty different religions, manufactured in Europe, and belonging to white men."[47] Here is one of his few references to "white men." It is in the context of colonialization, but it is not positive. It bears no similarity to Pearson's use of the term. He does not reject colonialization, but he does reject the kind of colonialization that white men have "manufactured in Europe" and sought to impose on other nations. Such an imposition neglects the distinct ἦθος found in each nation through divine Wisdom. Maurice's emphasis upon the distinctive ethos of every nation may have influenced Pearson's "national characteristics," but they significantly differ in its use. Nonetheless, Pearson's development of the term should cause alarm, and it demonstrates how a liberal, secular view could produce white supremacy as much as a conservative, reactionary one. Being modern in that sense was no guarantee of progress toward a more just society.

For Maurice, national characteristics fit within the Kingdom of God–Church ideal, and it provides a critique of distorted national ends. Ethics may begin with a person located in a family and nation, but it also exists within a longing for the universal binding of community that is the Kingdom of God. These overlapping communities, with their distinct characteristics, provide the structure for his moral philosophy. It begins with conscience, moves to social morality, and assumes theology throughout. Although this approach to agency and action is Aristotelian, Maurice quickly adds that this structure is also present in the New Testament:

> The New Testament I scarcely tell you is occupied from first to last—specially in the Sermon on the Mount—in shewing that acts are nothing except as they are fruits of a state, except as they indicate what the man is; that words are nothing except as they express a mind or purpose. Not need I add that it is a Society—a Human Society—in which the preacher of that Sermon assumes that this ἦθος is to be exhibited.[48]

The society could be that of family (domestic morality), nation (national morality), or "a Human Society" (universal morality); these are the three parts to Maurice's lectures on social morality. He finds this ordering not only in the Greeks and the New Testament but also in the entire Scripture, from the call of Abraham and Sarah (domestic) to the establishment of Israel (national) to the expansion of the covenant to Gentiles through the Church and the proclamation of the Kingdom of God (universal).[49]

Maurice held to a complex social morality, in which the domestic, national, and universal are distinct and yet overlapping. Ethical and political problems arose when one sought to replace another or when one usurped the work of the other. For instance, the universal society could seek to take on the characteristics of a nation, something he viewed the Medieval Church as doing. The Protestant Reformation restored the legitimate but different sovereignties of the nation and Church. The Kingdom of God, with its temporal first fruits in the Church, was the true universal community. As such, it did not seek to do away with national or domestic moralities but to provide limits on their respective roles. The French Revolution is an example of the nation usurping the universal society; it wrongly attempted to generate a universal society based on individual rights that destroyed both the nation and the family. It was marked by the "substitution of a universal polity for national polities," and that led to its "monstrous absurdities."[50] This is why he affirms Coleridge in his preface to *Social Morality*. Coleridge came to understand "the unspeakable importance of a distinct National life" over and against a universal society after the French Revolution.[51] Yet a distinct national life by itself was insufficient. The French revolutionaries were not wrong in longing for the universal society; they erred in looking for it within the state. The nineteenth century's "attempt to create" a universal society were "very abortive" because too many attempted to turn the state into it. The local usurped the role of the universal.[52] Plato's communism attempted something similar. Neither the domestic nor the national morality could or should escape the influence, correction, or guidance of the universal community; nor should they seek to replace it. Although present in the Church, the purpose of the universal community was to bring nations into a common human family. Slavery, economic materialism, and unjust violence arose when this correction and guidance were rejected.

Maurice's domestic morality was undoubtedly patriarchal. As I mentioned above, Maurice led the way in advocating for women's education, putting institutions and reforms in place that had a lasting influence. When his great-granddaughter passed her two exams in the economics tripos at Cambridge in 1924 and 1925, she still could not be granted a degree. This was not available to women until 1948, fifteen years after she published her momentous *The Economics of Imperfect Competition*.[53] Maurice was also an early advocate for women's right to own property. Yet he rejected the expression "*independence* of women." It was an "attempt to deny the physical order, under pretence of asserting a moral order." Domestic morality assumed a "dependence" of the sexes on each other. Each has something to teach the other from their respective position. Men should have "the desire to learn from women what they can teach much better than man," and women should possess "always a willingness to receive from men what they better than women can impart."[54] This could be harmless, except that what each held was placed in a hierarchy of paternal authority and obedience. Domestic morality is defined by "the authority of fathers and the obedience of sons, the trust of husbands and wives, the respect of brothers and sisters for each other, the honour of the master for the servant, of the servant for the master."[55] Maurice adamantly opposed slavery but had no difficulty with a domestic morality composed of masters and servants.[56]

Despite his paternalism, Maurice recognized that placing women on pedestals did not advance their cause, stating that this was one of the main problems of the domestic morality that Christianity promulgated in the Middle Ages. It "degraded" women "by making them idols."[57] Nor did he accept the argument made by many that slavery was consistent with the master–servant domestic morality that he otherwise affirmed. He acknowledged that slavery was called a "domestic institution" in the Southern United States, but he rejected this claim unequivocally.[58] He wrote, "All relations of father and child, of husband and wife, of brother and sister were thrown into the wildest confusion by the practice which that tenet sanctioned. It was no question of colour or race. The white was more degraded by the presence of this anomaly in his household than the black."[59] This latter claim cannot be passed over. That slavery degraded white slaveowners raises no questions. It is an important insight. That it did so more than Blacks needs explanation. If Maurice means that the practice resulted in the *moral* degradation of whites rather than Blacks, and I think that is his meaning, the claim seems just. If it overlooks the humiliation and degradation laid upon Blacks by whites, it would be unjust. It could be another version of Pearson's "white man under siege." Yet Maurice's claim is as far from that as it could be. By stating that it was not a question of color or race, Maurice meant that it was not a question of a putative superior white race over a putative inferior Black one. Modern slavery results from a retrieval of Aristotle's teaching that transformed domestic relations into property ones. White supremacy was inextricable from economics. Maurice did not know the term "racialized capitalism," but it illumines his understanding of racism.[60]

Maurice identifies a source of the deformation of domestic morality brought about by slavery with Aristotle's *Politics*. That work began with the family but then mistakenly defended Greek slavery based on the superiority of the Greeks over other races. Aristotle's arguments, Maurice argued, had returned in his day with vehemence: "It has never been more vigorously asserted than in our own day. I am not aware that Aristotle's reasonings have ever been improved, that anything has been added to them, except a little violence of temper into which he was seldom betrayed." What had returned was an abhorrent doctrine that reduces people to "instruments, organs, through which certain other men effect their purposes."[61] Familial relations were reduced to property ones. Roman slavery was only minimally better because slaves could be "emancipated into the family," but it too reflected the worship of Mammon. The "Jewish Commonwealth" was unique in its domestic morality because it was called to bless "all the families of the earth." Israel had been delivered from slavery; that deliverance was essential to its mission and became the basis for the true universal community, the human family. It meant that "captives in war, all slaves purchased with money, came into the circle of the children of the Covenant."[62] Yet no race or nation had yet fulfilled this promise, because each had succumbed to "the maxims of property." Religion had also succumbed, becoming little more than "a calculation of profits and losses; Mammon was worshipped in the temple and in the corners of streets as the true Lord of Heaven and Earth."[63] Thus, apologists for modern slavery could unfortunately claim an "unquestionable right" to trace it back to "a Latin, and Hellenic, or a Hebrew ancestry," but only because it reflected a "disorder" of the domestic and national society common to both antiquity and modernity.[64]

Although it had this ancient lineage, modern colonial slavery was also distinct. Neither European "serfdom" nor "papalism" gave it its disordered character. Maurice wrote, "It is of Protestant birth; it belongs to the Trade age. . . . The spirit of trade, the desire for property, must be credited with the origin of the traffic, with the maintenance of it, with the resistance to every proposal for abolishing or even mitigating it"; and for him, those arguments remained in force in postabolitionist economics.[65] The abolition of slavery did not do away with its form. It continued to manifest itself in wages determined solely by market relations. Maurice saw it continued in employers who said, "I have paid the fellow for his services; what more can he ask of me?"[66] He feared that despite the "noble protests" that individuals and nations brought against the Church for its "money-worship," they were unable to construct society on any other basis: "But individuals and nations are the conservators of property; *they* cannot shew us any *human* basis for Society which can prevent property from being accepted as the basis of it. Where is this human basis to be sought for?"[67] Here is where the "universal society" and the virtues of charity, hope, and faith are necessary. They offer a basis for society other than property relations.

Domestic and national societies based on competition and ownership were likewise disordered. Maurice was convinced that laborers were not receiving the full value of their labor, something about which Sidgwick disagreed. This difference can be found in their basic understanding of ethics. For Sidgwick, ethics is constituted, like wages, through voluntary contract. For Maurice, this never sufficed. He thought workers were mistreated. He inherited this sentiment from his family, especially his mother. Early in his studies at Oxford, she wrote to him about a labor uprising in their village and expressed that her sympathies lay with the workers. She criticized the local minister, whose only concern was with "sabbath breakers" and not economic justice.[68] Maurice was deeply affected by his mother's observations and sided with labor against the ownership class throughout his life. Ownership had become a means for dominion that was destroying domestic, national, and universal morality. Concerning the first, he wrote, "The craving for ownership, for dominion, is that which distracts the household."[69] The Church was complicit in this craving, refusing to see that socialists were motivated, as his friend Ludlow put it, by "higher human instincts." Ludlow wrote this to Maurice from France in 1848, during a year of revolution: "Socialism was a real and a very great power which had acquired an unmistakable hold, not merely on the fancies but on the consciences of the Parisian workmen, and that it must be Christianized or it would shake Christianity to its foundation, precisely because it appealed to the higher and not the lower instincts of the men."[70] The term "Christian Socialism" emerged from Ludlow's influence on Maurice. On one hand, it sought to introduce Christian theology into the socialist movement. On the other hand, it introduced socialist approaches to ownership and profit distribution to Christianity.

In 1850, Maurice wrote two letters to Ludlow about their idea for a series of "Tracts on Christian Socialism." Maurice thought the term was "the only title which will define our object, and will commit us at once to the conflict we must engage in sooner or later with the unsocial Christians and the unchristian Socialists." To the charge by Christians that they are "socialists in disguise," it would allow them to respond, "'In disguise?' not a bit of it. There it is staring you in the face upon the title page!" To socialists who might accuse them "to want to thrust so much priestcraft under a good revolutionary name," they could respond, "Well, did not we warn you of it? Did we not profess that our intended something was quite different from what your Owenish lecturers meant"?[71] Just as he criticized Adam Smith's and Hume's capitalist political economy for discarding metaphysics, so he did the same for the socialists, with this significant difference. The metaphysics and theology that he held to sided with socialism because it more than capitalism recognized that the ocean of being that could not be contained promoted cooperation and not competition. Maurice held that "competition, which some deem the great sign of social advancement, the great help of modern learning, is threatening the existence of Society, is undermining knowledge." Its antidote cannot be "artificial" but is found in "brotherly love."[72] If creation occurs through the Triune God, then competition could not be the basis for society.

Maurice also challenged the Church's complicity with the ownership class. On this point, he was highly critical of the aristocracy:

> Or does the Churchman I am supposing find himself in one of our awful manufacturing districts? Of course, the sense of his own utter inadequacy to deal with the mass of evil which he meets there is the first which will take hold of him, and will grow stronger every day. Yet he is there, and he knows that there is One who cares for this mass of living beings infinitely more than he does. . . . A Church which was looked upon, and almost looked upon itself, as a tool of the aristocracy, which compared its own orders with the ranks in civil society, and forgot that it existed to testify that man as man is the object of his Creator's sympathy; such a Church had no voice which could reach the hearts of these multitudes.[73]

A Church content with the hierarchical ordering of classes could not fulfill its vocation.

Maurice's conflicting statement on the aristocracy can be confusing. He affirms it for the British nation but not for the Church. It should be democratic. He explains these confusing statements, perhaps, in an 1848 letter to Ludlow, noting the difference in his starting point from Ludlow and Thomas Carlyle's. They "start from the Radical or popular ground" and hope through "anarchy and in opposition to authority to create law." Carlyle looks for a "great man" to arise, which Ludlow rejects, but all three of them "reverence order and believe in God." Maurice, however, begins with "acknowledgement of divine sovereignty; thence I come to the Tory idea of kings reigning by the grace of God," but he differs from the Tory by affirming the "Whig idea of Constitutional Government," and he differs from both Whig and Tory by affirming the "radical idea of the distinct rights and privileges of each man as latent in their two truths and as necessarily developed out of them in its due season."[74] How does one put together kingship by grace, Whig constitutional government, and the radicalism of "distinct rights and privileges"? It remained confusing in his work, but some clarity is gained in his reactions to the Chartist Movement.

The Chartist Movement was a democratic reform of British politics led by the working class. Kingsley, Ludlow, and Maurice affirmed it, with the qualification that the Chartists should not agitate or riot. They held meetings of the "working men" involved in it. In June 1849, Kingsley addressed a meeting in London that had been called by "the Christian Socialists," and stated, "I am a parson and a Chartist."[75] Ludlow and Maurice began and edited the newspaper *Politics for the People* in 1848 that intended to advance the Chartist cause, but it did not last long. It ran from May 6 to July 29, and it did little to promote Chartism since it had already been defeated as a national movement. They followed this with *Tracts on Christian Socialism*.[76] The summer of 1848 saw little more than some "minor uprisings."[77] Kingsley and Maurice opposed them; Maurice even offered his service as a constable. His son writes, "Then and always throughout his life he looked upon it as essential to the cause of the poor, that they should learn the impotence of lawlessness and riot."[78] Maurice did not have much of a place for rage or anger in his politics.[79] Yet Maurice and Kingsley did gather working men and listen to their complaints. His brother-in-law, Julius Hare, promoted the idea of the newspaper but was not pleased with Kingsley's "Second Letter to the Chartists" in *Politics for the People* and let Maurice know. He responded that he would not have suppressed Kingsley's letter even if he could, and that most of the Chartists consider "the clergy as preachers of mere slavery out of the Bible." The Chartists thought the newspaper might be "a capitalist's trick to deceive them by false promises." Maurice tried to convince them otherwise; and on April 23, 1849, he met with "a set of Chartists at a coffee-house, in the hope of organising some regular meetings with them at some other place." The proposal for the meetings, he stated, came from them. The original meeting went well and led to others.[80]

Maurice's desire for a cooperative economics depended upon a harmonious nation bound together by an established Church. He thought it should be Protestant, Christian, and entrusted with education. The established Church would not, however, exclude non-Christians from citizenship. Although nothing is found in his writings like Pearson's white supremacist rhetoric, some of his statements on Jews can be troubling, despite his support for admitting Jews to Parliament. Two years before marrying Georgina Hare in 1849 (his first wife, Anna Barton, died in 1845), they had a letter exchange about his "firm support" for Jews. She thought he was "inconsistent," given that they lived in a "nation constituted by Christ," and yet he advocated for Jewish admission to full citizenship. If Jews are admitted, some will say, he writes, that "it is all over with us." He then responds:

It is not over with us at all, but it will be over with us if, instead of acknowledging Christ to be the root of our national stability, we make the declaration—the weak declaration—of our legislators that He is the root of it. Then you deny Christ, you who call yourselves by His name, which is more than all the Jewish denials in the world; you say that you do not think *He* is the Lord and bulwark of the nation.[81]

The crucial distinction in this paragraph is between acknowledging and declaring. If Christ is the root of the nation, then anxiety about declaring this tacitly denies it. It is governed by an ethics of fear rather than confidence. For this reason, Jewish emancipation poses no threat, but bears witness to the nation-state's Christological foundation. As interesting an argument as this is, it lacks concern for Jewish emancipation in itself.

Maurice's brother-in-law, Julius Hare, opposed admission to Jews in Parliament; and in 1847, Maurice wrote Kingsley about it stating that "nearly all his friends," and especially Hare, "are at war with me on this Jewish question." He repeated his argument that the truth should not be confused with the belief about the truth, so securing the former upon the latter by requiring Christian profession for members of Parliament denied the truth for something less. He then makes a troubling confession: "The feeling that the Jews are aliens used to be decisive with me, till I perceived that it ought only to be decisive as to my own conduct, and is no foundation for a law to deprive the aliens of their ordinary privilege."[82] Despite his advocacy for emancipation, Maurice still considered Jews "aliens" and repeated all-too-common myths that they were only concerned with money. In a letter to Ludlow in 1849, he claimed that the state could not be "communist" because "it is by nature and law Conservative of individual rights, individual possessions," but the Church could only be "communist in principle." The "union" between the two "should accomplish the fusion of the principles of Communism and property. A Church without a State must proclaim Proudhon's doctrine if it is consistent with itself; a State without a Church is merely supported by Jew brokers and must ultimately become only a stock exchange."[83] Sadly, despite Maurice's many positive arguments for Jewish emancipation, and his insistence on the doctrine of election, Jews represented a threat to the union of Church and state because Maurice could only imagine that they would establish it on competitive, economic exchange. Despite his many affirmations of the election of the Jews, he traded in old stereotypes.

Maurice never resolved how the state's defense of private property and the Church's communism could be unified. He had grown up with Quakers and knew their challenges to both private property and war based on Jesus's teachings. They challenged his "national creed," but because they appealed to Scripture, he thought their criticism had to be heard and answered. He wrote, "If it can be shown that these, or any portion of our national creed, are denounced in the New Testament, we, of course, must abandon them, even though by doing so we involve ourselves in the most painful perplexities respecting the nature and the permanence of moral principles." His response turns to a defense of capital punishment and war as establishing the Jewish nation, and by analogy every other nation as well.[84] Maurice's defense of war and capital punishment knew limits. They could not be used against heresy or for "pecuniary profit."[85] But pacifism resulted in a loss of the national spirit, a rise in a commercial society, and the "loss of moral fibre" through "laziness, luxury, self-seeking, slavery."[86] Intrinsic to being a nation is to defend the nation with arms. He is not advocating "*Si vis pacem para bellum.*" "The defense of a nation," he writes, "should have another ground. Every nation should be an armed nation, not because it regards any other with hostility, not because it imagines that any other has an interest in assaulting it, but because its own soil, its own language, its own laws, its own government are given to it, and are beyond all measure precious to it." There is no nation without arms.[87] Politics and religion share a common concern with "law," "language," "government," and "battles." Without all four, faith would be rendered apolitical, and it would not be "faith in a righteous Being, a distinguisher of Right and Wrong."[88]

The foundation for this national morality was in the exclusive nature of the Jewish polity: "The national polity of the Jews was in its essence exclusive. . . . But every *nation*, as such, is exclusive."[89] By locating Judaism within "national morality" and turning it into a form that can be embodied by any nation, has Maurice subordinated the election of Israel to a national form available to any nation? Willie Jennings finds in this move the origins of a "Christian imagination," whereby European whiteness replaces Israel's election. In fact, he finds evidence for a "colonialist relation" in one of Maurice's students who became an Anglican bishop in South Africa, John William Colenso.[90] Colenso was a religious liberal, whom Jennings argues "naturalizes Christianity, domesticating it by making Christianity the architecture of religious experience." Once it becomes a universal form, other religions are no longer "manifestations of the demonic" but "affirmations of racial character and indicators of civilization and human development." For all its advantages, this more liberal understanding of religion, its "modern invention," maintains the colonialist gaze because it comes with a ready-made, putatively universal template that lets it situate other religions, cultures, and nations within a civilized "white British identity."[91]

Maurice's relationship to Colenso's project, which Jennings defines so aptly, is mixed. On one hand, he offers a colonialist theology that fits well with Colenso's project and Jennings's critique. On the other hand, he offers a critique of colonialism that does not. In *The Kingdom of Christ*, he writes,

> The lessons which we have derived from the history of our connexion with Scotland and Ireland (I have spoken before of those which are suggested by the circumstances of our old colonies in North America) cannot surely be lost upon us when we go forth to plant new settlements on the other side of the globe, or when we are inquiring how we are to deal with those which we possess already. Every circumstance of their position and of ours seems to say, "See that you do not merely establish an English kingdom in those soils; if you do, that kingdom will not be a blessing to the colonists, to the natives, or to the mother country."[92]

While this appears more generous than many defenses of colonialist theology, such generosity is misleading. Maurice still finds the colonialist enterprise worth engaging. He has no qualms about "going forth" to establish colonial kingdoms. They are not to be "English" kingdoms, but this fits well what Maurice means when he says that nations are "Protestant," but the Church is "Catholic." Each nation is charged with developing its own identity according to Protestant principles of freedom, and each has the obligation to protect that identity with arms.

Yet there is another sense in which Maurice's theology does not fit nearly as well into Jennings's critique as does Colenso's. Maurice distanced himself from his former student, and did so for an interesting reason. Colenso rejected the historicity of the Exodus. In abandoning it, or what Maurice called the "Jewish economy," Colenso lost the condition for "the emancipation of women" and the "abolition of slavery." His son explains what Maurice meant by this: "It seemed to him that the emancipation of women, the abolition of slavery, the gradual substitution of law for arbitrary will, were all as much parts of the work of God the Deliverer, as the Exodus, but that the history of the Exodus was necessary to explain the central fact of the later history."[93] If God were not the agent at work in the world delivering Israel from slavery and oppression, then God could not be conceived to be at work in Maurice's day abolishing slavery and emancipating women. If God were not the deliverer, then, Maurice argued, little stood in the way of the worship of Mammon: "Our English theology, popular as well as systematic, has been gradually reconstructing itself on the commercial or material bases" and the "creeds" are the "perpetual witnesses" against it. The "most conspicuous and flagrant instance of the adoption in a money-worshipping community of a religion based on the acknowledgement of a God who is the enemy of Mammon into its service" was the argument that slavery was a divine institution.[94] Only by forgetting the Exodus could the latter be affirmed. While his colonialist inclinations should not be overlooked, Maurice recognized and criticized a key aspect of colonialism, its "commercial and material bases," and this should be credited to him. Pearson and Sidgwick did not consider it objectionable.

Maurice originally had high hopes for Colenso and his ministry. He wrote this about Colenso to a South African clergyman: "I remember the delight with which I contemplated the establishment of such a fatherly authority in our colonies. It seemed to me just what was wanted to check the wild craving for gain; to show that the Gospel unites instead of dividing, to balance the rigidness of mere law. At present, all looks as confused as possible." He then noted his disappointment when Colenso "set himself at war with the Jewish economy." Colenso's biblical interpretation stood in opposition to Maurice, who held that "the great hope of every nation lay in asserting the maxim of the Old Testament that God is Himself the Deliverer, that His name is the ground of national liberty." He then encourages the South African priest to claim the above for an "independent nation in South Africa—that you look upon the Church as that universal body consisting of kindreds and nations and tongues, which is to be far *more* extensive than the nation."[95]

Maurice was critical of colonialist practices. Ruling by "force" was rejected, and he recognized that force was the illegitimate basis for the conquest in Peru and Mexico. He referred to it as the "trade wars" that "were mainly enterprises to satisfy the intense hunger for gold."[96] Such "imperial lust" revealed the inadequacy of modern Christian morality. God had revealed "new regions of men" to "sailors of Spain or Holland or England," and the result was "crimes and brutality." They were "treated with unbridled ferocity." Rather than witnessing to the universal society, colonialism "set up a Western standard of morals against an Eastern" and claimed that its own "civilization" and "religion" was better. Such a claim was its own refutation, a denial of the wisdom and freedom God gave to each nation.[97]

That each nation should take the freedom to be independent meant for Maurice that each should be armed. Yet Maurice also claimed, "The glory of God revealing itself, not in a leader of armies, a philosopher, a poet, but in a carpenter—could anything be more revolting?"[98] The nonviolence assumed in this last sentence, however, is concerned with the universal rather than the national society. It also explains why Maurice argued that the nation-state should be Protestant and the Church Catholic. The Reformation prevented the Catholic states from acting like an empire ruling the nations of Europe through force. Maurice writes,

If we consider the subject calmly and solemnly, not omitting repentance for our sins nor thankfulness for our mercies, we shall, I believe, perceive, that but for the Reformation in the sixteenth century, European society must have sunk into the condition of an infidel world, nominally ruled by the intriguing head of a little Italian principality; really divided into a number of warring states, each aiming at the most selfish objects, each only looking to religion as the means of accomplishing them.[99]

Roman Catholicism, for Maurice, "undervalued the Church" because it neglects that the Church exists in Christ in the Holy Trinity and instead "asserts itself" as a "mysterious spirituality" that "delegates" authority to a "vicar" and then "forces" people to "assent to its opinions."[100] This distortion of authority was also why he was critical of Newman and the Oxford Movement. Newman's *Theory of Development* is "clever" but "much more calculated to make sceptics than Romanists" and possesses an "exceeding hollowness." Newman encouraged Anglicans to flee to Rome for the sake of ecclesiastical authority rather than to find "the living God." Ecclesiastical authority is a poor substitute. Taking refuge in it was a sign of a lack of faith.[101]

Maurice's book *Social Morality* assumed the Kingdom of God–Church ideal as the pattern for social morality. Maurice referred to the Kingdom as a "universal family" and contrasted it with an "empire." Drawing on the book of *Revelation*, he noted that what differentiates them is the use of "persecution and bloodshed." Empires use them; the Church must refuse. *Revelation*, he wrote, "promised victory to patience; they who followed Christ must conquer as He did, by giving up themselves to die, not by seeking power to kill."[102] The "Universal or Human Society," to which he appeals, also has a "certain ἦθος" that characterizes its life. On this point, he states, "the old doctrine of Cardinal Virtues . . . is a sound one." From the Latin *cardo*, the cardinal virtues were the ancient, acquired virtues of courage, justice, temperance, and prudence that formed the hinge by which one lived a good life. In his fifteenth lecture on social morality, when he affirms the cardinal virtues, he states, "I may have something to say about them hereafter. Here I will only repeat the sentence, 'And now abideth Faith, Hope, Charity, these three; but the greatest of these is Charity.'"[103] He then has more to say about the "hinge" upon which everyday life turns in his twentieth lecture: "There is in some a notion that Cardinal Virtues mean certain specially grand and exceptional virtues which entitle certain men to specially grand and exceptional reward hereafter." They are "counsels of perfection" for an elite group. He rejects this understanding because he cannot "associate them with

Universal Morality," and he offers a different definition. The cardinal virtues are the

> hinge on which other virtues turn, without which they would have no coherence, no vitality. If that force is given to the phrase, there can be no doubt that the Sermon on the Mount does set forth the Cardinal Virtue. Self-sacrifice is that upon which all its precepts hinge. Without this the faith, hope, and charity of the Apostle would be mere idle names, they would have no relation to the practice of life.[104]

Because Christ's self-giving love is the basis for creation and reconciliation, the infused virtues of faith, hope, and love are the hinge upon which everything turns.[105]

Maurice's correlation between the cardinal virtues and the theological virtues revises, or retrieves, the virtue tradition in significant ways. The acquired virtues are not cordoned off to some natural realm that can be achieved by internal principles alone, free from the Wisdom that makes creation possible. Nor are the theological virtues only for a religious elite, as if charity, faith, and hope were not intrinsic to ordinary life for all creatures. Both have their source in the Wisdom that creates, sustains, and redeems. This Wisdom is manifest in the Kingdom–Church as the ideal upon which creation exists. In other words, the theological virtues are not add-ons to acquired virtues or a second tier of grace upon an otherwise-completed pure nature by which human agents can acquire virtue without gifts from outside that agency. The theological virtues are in the Church; and because of that, they are also present in creation—they have become the hinge by which everything moves. For this reason, cooperation rather than competition will be found in all facets of human existence. The virtues are not individual possessions but participations in a life that exceeds the individual, both as a participation in God and in the divine realm God establishes. It must be exhibited in a present city and not merely a future "celestial" realm:

> The world to come whereof the Epistle speaks, cannot then, I conceive, answer to our ordinary notion of a future state; it must denote some kind of order established among human beings even here; one which was not yet shewn to be the divine order of the universe, but of which Christ's coming was to all who understood its meaning, the clear indication, the corner-stone. In that sense it will accord perfectly with the idea of a city or kingdom, to which the Jew had been trained by his long course of discipline. For he had never been taught to look

at the invisible world as altogether separate and remote from that in which he was living.[106]

Ethics, as Aristotle taught, is inseparable from politics. Ethics and politics, as Thomas Aquinas taught, require theology for their intelligibility.

Teaching and learning ethics, for Maurice, focused on actual lives embedded in social contexts, family, nations, villages, global communities, economic exchanges, military battles, the Church and other religious institutions, and a longing for universal community. To teach it well requires attention to this "whirl of organism" or "texture to being" that resists systematization. Situating ethical deliberation in such a context requires judgments about family relations, economics, war and peace, and much more. It does not begin by abstracting from these contexts to find a method that can bring consensus before the messy judgments that must be set forth. If ethics is about actual lives, then judgments must be risked, and this requires a vulnerability on the part of teachers and learners to attend to those judgments, deliberate, evaluate, and venture their own in return. This section has traced Maurice's judgments, offering positive and negative evaluations in confidence that such evaluations help us learn from the past as we offer judgments in our present. We have no rule that will let us go on without reproach. Pearson's secular, cosmopolitan ethics should be given no privileged hearing over Maurice's. What Maurice still had that Pearson and Sidgwick did not was this longing for a universal community whose ethos is found in his theological convictions: faith, hope, and love as the cardinal virtues drawing us into perfection.

A PERFECTIONIST ETHIC

Perfection is not our property; it belongs to another. The "perfect life," Maurice stated, is the Incarnate One, who as "the Truth which dwelleth in us, and will dwell in us forever, is He Who is, and was, and is to come." Perfection is rooted in ecstatic agency. We become most ourselves when taken out of ourselves and discover that our agency depends on another. Although, for Maurice, the Other is the Incarnate One, this ecstatic agency takes on a form illuminating human action. It arises not from a secure self-possession or achievement but from external sources that call us beyond ourselves. We are perfected from "without," even as what flows in us from outside us fills us with the powers necessary for our agency. As Michael Ramsey put it, Maurice's theology is a call to "become what you are."[107] Created in the image of the Triune God, and through the Incarnate One who is self-giving, this perfect life cannot but already dwell in us, even as marred and broken as we are. It formed us in our creation and will bring that form to completion. Baptism initiates this completion, but this way of life is not for a select few while the mass of humanity awaits damnation and relentless, eternal punishment. Maurice's moral theology moved away from an emphasis on evil and how to avoid it. Evil is not dismissed, but it is not given priority. It is not motivating. All creation longs for perfection. It generates our dissatisfaction with injustice, along with the faith and hope that justice will prevail.

Perfection generates longing. The way the world is, the way that we are, is found wanting. We desire something more, and from this we are moved to act, even when we do not see clearly what that perfection is. We are called beyond ourselves to inhabit a way of life that is only enigmatically glimpsed; we see through a glass darkly (1 Cor. 13:12). Perfection summons us to the constant clarification of vision that allows us to act and live well.

For Maurice, the Christological form of perfection grounds the life of virtue in sacrificial love. Sacrifice is, like every concept, potentially dangerous and subject to deleterious uses. To dismiss it for that reason, however, and seek to find some concept not potentially subject to abuse, is to seek to avoid the frailty and contingency of human communication and judgment. Neither the Triune God nor the Incarnate One lose themselves in giving; they are who they are. The Holy Trinity is "constituted" by gift and reception. The sacrificial character here is not that of asking ourselves or others to surrender their agency, but to discover it. What are sacrificed are competitive acquisition and all the concomitant vices that go along with it. Such vices turn virtue itself into an acquisition or an achievement solely through our own powers.

Maurice's emphasis on the infusing of virtue guards against this. Virtues are acquired; he never rejected Aristotle. But acquiring them is consenting to their infusing by the Spirit. In that sense, they are less in us than we are in them. They come to us, and we receive them as active recipients. We neither construct nor form them; they are there before we were; they are there to be discovered, which is an active metaphor. Discovery involves hope. We look for what we expect to see. The search occurs in faith that brings confidence rather than fear and produces love that casts away fears and insecurities. Perfection, oddly enough, frees us to acknowledge our failures, and others', without condemnation. Because it is not our achievement, we can be patient with our own and others' failures. Because the gift of perfection requires our active reception, it also demands that we call out injustice and our complicity in it.

Revisiting Maurice's moral theology accomplishes several purposes. First, it shows how moral theology and philosophy were approached before his younger colleague Sidgwick's reorientation, if not invention, of ethics as a scientific discipline seeking precision. The discussion above unearths what was left behind after Sidgwick, with its attendant losses and gains. The losses, I would submit, are the attention to the broader context within which ethics makes sense; it is inevitably situated in metaphysical, theological, and social contexts. Perhaps it is not too much of a stretch to say that Maurice's work on behalf of women's education makes possible a rediscovery of his work because the closest thing to it is found in the four women—Anscombe, Murdoch, Midgley, and Foot—who "brought philosophy back to life."[108] Their work was no repetition of Maurice's. It contained more precision in analysis, and that is a gain that should be credited to Sidgwick's influence on the discipline of ethics. As noted above, he also was an early supporter of women's education. Murdoch, Midgley, and Foot did not share Maurice or Anscombe's theological convictions, but the questions that they began ethics with had more in common with Maurice than with Sidgwick. As Mac Cumhaill and Wiseman state, they brought back questions that empirical methods had neglected, including, "What sort of animal is a human being? What do we need to live well? Is philosophy of any use?" The method or approach assumed to be best to address these questions was much wider than Sidgwick's and closer to Maurice's *Moral and Metaphysical Philosophy*. Mac Cumhaill and Wiseman, once again, point out the similarity by noting the "new picture" that arose from these women's philosophy: "We are *metaphysical animals*. We make and shape pictures, stories, theories, words, signs and artworks that help us to navigate our lives together. These creations are immensely powerful, because they at once show us what is and was the case, and at the same time suggest new ways of going on."[109] Ethics requires constant discovery and navigation. No method or rule, as helpful as they may be, provides secure precision as to what should be done. As Anscombe noted, "I think it is even safe to say that (except in doing arithmetic or dancing, i.e., in skills or arts—what Aristotle would call τέχναι) there is no general positive rule of the form 'Always do X' or 'Doing X is always good-required-convenient, a useful-suitable-etc.—thing' (where the 'X' describes some specific action) which a sane person will accept as a starting point for reasoning out what to do in a particular case."[110] Practical reasoning is "highly situation dependent," so that even something like "never tell a lie," if taken as a universal major premise, will work against "acting or doing or living well."[111] To provide resources to know how to go on, to separate nonsense from wisdom, and to discover and discern what is needed for a life lived well form a more reasonable approach to ethics.

This approach fits better the perfectionist ethic present in Aristotle, Aquinas, Maurice, Anscombe, Cavell, and Mulhall. Ethics is less about determining an object of study and more about naming the activities and criteria that help us attend to excellence or perfection that involves the pursuit of a good human life and provides resources to know how our lives fall short. Maurice's life, like Sidgwick's, fell short of perfection. We look back and see failures—paternalism, colonialism, his confusion about democracy. His confusion arose from a valid concern. He feared democracy would lead to mere opinion, the greatest beliefs of the greatest number holding sway whether they supported a good life or not. What happens when the greatest number holds the belief that slavery is a valid "domestic economy" or that competitive economics generates well-being? Monarchy is not exempt from such questioning. What happens when monarchs consider what is good for them is good for all, that nothing stands over them? No political form accomplished by us ensures the just society. Each one can, and has, been abused; but Maurice did not see the promise of enfranchisement as clearly as he should have. He lived during the Civil War and Reconstruction in the United States. While he was teaching and researching Christian ethics, Harriett Jacobs was hiding in an attic for seven years to escape slavery; and Frederick Douglass and Harriet Tubman escaped slavery and led movements for abolition. Maurice was keenly interested in abolition but failed to see the possibilities that Black enfranchisement could bring about. It was challenged by the ownership class during Reconstruction. As W. E. B. Du Bois noted, "The sudden enfranchisement of laborers threatens fundamental and far-reaching change no matter what their race or color."[112] What if Maurice, with his abolitionist convictions, would have asked, "How might politics change if enslaved Blacks were enfranchised, or women were enfranchised?" Given his convictions, those questions could have arisen, but they did not. What if the perfection he saw in the Kingdom–Church ideal has been projected into these contexts? His work has the possibility of showing how to go on in such contexts, even when his life did not (yet) measure up. The Christian Socialism that Maurice, Ludlow, Kingsley, and then Headlam envisioned cannot be realized without the extension of democracy. It is a moral tradition worth preserving and extending.

For Mulhall, philosophy projects perfection terms in new contexts through evaluative appraisals that open new possibilities for the relationship between philosophy and theology. He writes, "If it is of the essence of words to be projectible, and of perfection terms and transcendental terms to be open to indefinite ranges of new contexts in which they might find legitimate habitation without succumbing to equivocity, then it can never be legitimate to dismiss any attempts to project perfections and transcendentals into theological contexts as *necessarily* abusive of their meaning."[113] In other words, once the term "good" is invoked, we cannot a priori rule out its projection into new contexts unless it is used with such a completely different meaning that it becomes unintelligible. To say, "good tree" or "good knife" or "good human being" or "good God" does not require a univocal meaning to "good," as if we could give its properties such as "it cuts well" and then deny its appropriateness for the others because it lacks those properties. That is not how language or ethics works. Such precision would come at the expense of the ability to communicate.

In stating that words are "projectible," Mulhall draws upon Cavell. To learn a word is not to learn a definition, as helpful as it might be, but to learn the "whirl of organism" within which the word makes sense and how it can be projected without equivocation into new contexts. It would be to ask, What are the forms of life that allow us to use good in all these contexts? Philosophy is tempted, Cavell suggests, to abstract from the "whirl of organism" and appeal to a universal, to imagine that there is a universal concept or category that can be specified by its properties or by some rule and then all instances of that term either placed within that category or rule and rendered intelligible. Yet all attempts to establish meaning based on such a universal category or rule ultimately fail. They do not help us to distinguish between the proper projection of "feed the kitty" to "feed the meter" and the improper projection to "feed the quadratic equation." What allows for projection is a form of life or whirl of organism. We have no hard-and-fast rules, but we do have criteria. We discover that kittens and meters can be fed but quadratic equations cannot. Likewise, trees, knives, human beings, and God can be good. A certain kind of rigorous philosopher or theologian, perhaps of an analytic or empiricist persuasion, might find this use of words unsatisfying. It is why they might ask that we use "feed" or "good" with a precise meaning in every context. If we cannot, then perhaps we need different terms for each expression.[114] Let us call this the "univocity requirement" for philosophical discourse. If philosophers demand such a requirement, explicitly or implicitly, an artificial rule is imposed on language that can never be successful because of language's projectability. They abandon Maurice's claim that language is germinative.

What has this to do with teaching moral theology in conversation with moral philosophy? Perhaps it would help theologians convince philosophers that while their work is not identical, what they do bears a family resemblance. They seek the projection of terms into new contexts based on criteria that provide meaning for those terms. If that is true, then when philosophers dismiss theology, they also dismiss something tacitly present in their own work—the projectability of perfection terms based on reasonable criteria. A philosopher who rules out the theological use of terms, especially ethical ones, must show why they have violated their appropriate projectability; otherwise, they are not acting like philosophers but police. As Mulhall notes, a priori prohibitions and restrictions that prevent the projection of terms into new contexts are not just unreasonable; they are arbitrary exercises of power.

Mulhall refuses to prohibit theology because philosophy, like theology, also projects perfection terms into new contexts through "evaluative appraisals." It is what philosophy does, or at least what it is supposed to do. It loves wisdom. When philosophers reject this, they become something less than philosophers.[115] Love and wisdom, like goodness and beauty, are perfection terms. They have "transcategorical" uses. We use "good," "wise," "beautiful," and other such terms in diverse contexts: in beautiful activities, such as solving Fermat's last theorem; in making a catch in baseball; or in performing a symphony. Things can also be beautiful: a person, mountain, bicycle, a sunset. We seldom speak of perfection terms as having arrived at a limit; they are always perfectible. There are degrees to them. For theologians, perfection terms apply most properly to God. For Aquinas, the degree of perfectibility in things tacitly assumes a measure of the perfected; it is his fourth way to God.[116]

If philosophers retrieve perfection terms, or if philosophers pursue the love of wisdom, then an openness to theology and/or to antique philosophy inevitably results. Perfection is an inevitable feature of good human action, for it cannot occur without something like Mulhall's evaluative appraisals. Perfectionism assumes that the rational ordering of desire serves some end. It may be inchoate, or it may be obvious, but without some end no adequate answer to "Why did you do this rather than that" would make sense. "Why are you advocating for a just wage?" "Just because" or "For no particular reason" is an unintelligible response. "Inequality needs addressed" makes sense. But why should inequality be addressed? "Because a just society cannot tolerate it." "Why be concerned about a just society?" and so on. Some end helps rationally order desires. An end, whether explicit or implicit, assumes movement toward completion or perfection. It requires the projection of perfection terms across disciplines, bringing them into conversation. It requires attention to the "germinating" character of our language and to the infusing of virtues from the source(s) of perfection.

NOTES

1. Maurice, *Conscience*, 58.
2. Maurice, *Life*, vol. 2, 16.
3. Maurice, *Moral and Metaphysical Philosophy: Volume 1*, xliv, xliii.
4. Maurice, xliv.

5. Maurice, 257.

6. Maurice.

7. Maurice, 276.

8. Maurice, *Epistles of St. John*, 318, 320–22.

9. Maurice, *Conscience*, 198.

10. Maurice, 202.

11. Maurice, 20.

12. Maurice, 16, 18–19.

13. Maurice, 30.

14. Maurice, 31.

15. Maurice, 17–18.

16. MacKintosh, *Dissertation*, 8.

17. Maurice, *Conscience*, 52.

18. Maurice.

19. Maurice, 26.

20. An ethics of confidence led him to favor Jewish emancipation in England, as is seen below in the text.

21. Maurice, *Moral and Metaphysical Philosophy: Volume 1*, 299.

22. Schultz, *Henry Sidgwick*, 49.

23. Maurice, *Moral and Metaphysical Philosophy: Volume 1*, 409.

24. Maurice, *Conscience*, 58.

25. Maurice, *Moral and Metaphysical Philosophy: Volume 2*, vii–viii.

26. Maurice, ix.

27. Maurice, *Moral and Metaphysical Philosophy: Volume 2*, 578.

28. Maurice, 579.

29. Maurice, 634.

30. Maurice, 635.

31. Maurice, 636.

32. Maurice, 434.

33. Maurice, 654.

34. Maurice, 656.

35. Maurice, 567.

36. Maurice, 571.

37. Maurice, *Kingdom of Christ*, 340.

38. Maurice, *Moral and Metaphysical Philosophy: Volume 1*, 278.

39. Maurice, *Social Morality*, 18.

40. Philip Turner is rightly critical of Maurice's use of "nation." If by nation he meant nothing more than the "peoples" of the world, it fits well with divine providential ordering, but when it means "nation-state" it is more problematic and "highly doubtful"; Turner, *Christian Socialism*, 101. Maurice used it with both meanings and the problems with the second can be found in his establishment Christianity and its commitment to war.

41. Lake, "White Man," 48.

42. Lake, 51.

43. Pearson, *National Life*.

44. Pearson, 101.

45. Pearson, 134.

46. Maurice, *Epistles of St. John*, 201.

47. Maurice.

48. Maurice, *Social Morality*, 20.

49. The division of Scripture into a "national morality" for the Hebrew Bible and a "universal morality" for the New Testament clearly had a negative side. It refused to see the inextricable link between Judaism and Christianity, making the latter universal in the way the former supposedly was not. Maurice wrote, "I do not expect to find the principles of the universal society developed in the Old Testament, nor the principles of the national society in the New. I do expect to find each illustrating and sustaining the other"; Maurice, *Kingdom of Christ*, 237. Maurice failed to see the Kingdom of God–Church ideal as flowing from the call of Abraham and Sarah not to be like the other nations for the sake of the nations.

50. Maurice, *Kingdom of Christ*, 216.

51. Maurice, xxiii–iv.

52. Maurice, 235.

53. Harcourt and Kerr, *Joan Robinson*, 8.

54. Maurice, *Social Morality*, 56.

55. Maurice, 103.

56. This, too, had a lingering influence. After Joan's marriage to Austin Robinson in June 1926, he took a position as teacher to the ten-year-old maharajah of Gwalior. The Robinsons "occupied a villa staffed by fifteen servants, including kitchen help, housekeepers, maids, gardeners, and chauffeurs"; Aslanbeigui and Oakes, *Provocative Joan Robinson*, 15. Such a family situation would not have been at odds with F. D. Maurice's domestic morality. (We have no evidence that it troubled her Marxist sympathies.) Nor would her stated desire to her husband that she earn her own money, hold her own property, and pursue her vocation as a Cambridge economist.

57. Maurice, *Social Morality*, 282.

58. Maurice divested holdings in the State of Maryland because it passed a proslavery law; Maurice, *Life*, vol. 2, 378.

59. Maurice, *Social Morality*, 74.

60. See Tran, *Asian Americans*.

61. Maurice, *Social Morality*, 76–77.

62. Maurice, 81.

63. Maurice, 82.

64. Maurice.

65. Maurice, 82–83.

66. Maurice, 84.

67. Maurice, 319.

68. Maurice, *Life*, vol. 2, 139.

69. Maurice, *Social Morality*, 73.

70. Quoted by Maurice, *Life*, vol. 2, 458.

71. Maurice, 35.

72. Maurice, *Social Morality*, 72.

73. Maurice, *Kingdom of Christ*, 417–18.

74. Maurice, *Life*, vol. 2, 485.

75. Norman, *Victorian Christian Socialists*, 39.

76. Norman, 76; Morris, *F. D. Maurice and the Crisis*, 14.

77. Klaver, *Apostle*, 139–40.

78. Maurice, *Life*, vol. 2, 472.

79. For a defense of "Black rage" and its importance for politics, see Lloyd, *Black Dignity*, 38–56.

80. Maurice, *Life*, vol. 2, 476, 482, 536–38.

81. Maurice, 449–50.

82. Maurice, 455.

83. Maurice, 9.

84. Maurice, *Kingdom of Christ*, 233–36.

85. Maurice, *Social Morality*, 183.

86. Maurice, 181.

87. Maurice, 190–91. Maurice's son and grandson were military generals. His grandson, General Sir Frederick Barton Maurice, was in the British Legion and had been tasked by Chamberlain to resolve the Czech crisis. The legion "offered to place ten thousand legionnaires at the disposal of the German government as neutral observers and supervisors of the Sudeten territory." It was a controversial proposal that never materialized. See Aslanbeigui and Oakes, *Provocative Joan Robinson*, 76.

88. Maurice, *Social Morality*, 208.

89. Maurice, *Kingdom of Christ*, 278.

90. Jennings, *Christian Imagination*, 120.

91. Jennings, 134.

92. Maurice, *Kingdom of Christ*, 426.

93. Maurice, 453.

94. Maurice, 460.

95. Maurice, 489–91.

96. Maurice, *Social Morality*, 178.

97. Maurice, 373–75.

98. Maurice, *Theological Essays*, 87.

99. Maurice, *Kingdom of Christ*, 325.

100. Maurice, *Theological Essays*, 173–74.

101. Maurice, *Life*, vol. 2, 422–23.

102. Maurice, *Social Morality*, 249.

103. Maurice, 250.

104. Maurice, 396.

105. Aquinas made a similar claim. He did not state that the theological virtues are the cardinal, but he did state that they are "prior to" them; *Summa Theologiae*, II.II, 10.1 rep. obj. 3. And he crafted his discussion of the three theological and four acquired virtues accordingly; *Summa Theologiae*, II.II, 1–167.

106. Maurice, *Epistle to the Hebrews*, 67–68.

107. Ramsey, *F. D. Maurice*, 35.

108. This is the subtitle to Claire Mac Cumhaill and Rachael Wiseman's *Metaphysical Animals: How Four Women Brought Philosophy Back to Life*.

109. Mac Cumhaill and Wiseman, *Metaphysical Animals*, xii–xiii.

110. Anscombe, *Intention*, 62; cited by Campbell, "On Anscombe," 16n19.

111. Campbell, "On Anscombe," 16.

112. Du Bois, *Black Reconstruction*, 709.

113. Mulhall, *Great Riddle*, 109.

114. Cavell, *Claim*, 31.

115. Mulhall, *Great Riddle*, 85.

116. Aquinas, *Summa Theologiae*, I.2.3. Once this is understood, Hurka's criticism that "theological perfectionists" like Aquinas "do not derive the perfectionist ideal from claims about God; they apply it to him" loses its force; Hurka, *British Ethical Theorists*, 33. Of course, human language can only be projected onto God by way of analogy. But that it does not speak well of God because it is projected or applied by creatures does not logically follow unless a dogmatic prohibition is in place that knows a priori that such speech is impossible.

6

INFUSING VIRTUE
AND THOMISTIC TENSIONS

In June 1832, at the age of twenty-seven, F. D. Maurice wrote to his sister, "How strongly have I been convinced lately that we spend half our time in thinking of faith, hope and love, instead of in believing, hoping, and loving! How utterly we forget that the very meaning of the words implies that we should forget ourselves and themselves (the acts I mean) in the objects to which they refer."[1] This sentiment captures well the project of moral theology as Maurice develops it over the next forty years. Central to this project are the theological virtues. They are not mere doctrines to be reflected upon but activities to be inhabited and lived. Maurice was on to something significant here, not only for his day but also for ours. Much of the discussion on the theological and infused virtues focuses on interpreting Thomas Aquinas and interminable debates on the relationship between the acquired and the infused virtues. The relationship between them is confusing in the writing of Aquinas. Maurice recognized this confusion and pointed in an intriguing direction to reconcile the acquired and infused virtues that was never taken up, for at least two reasons. First, Sidgwick and the subsequent tradition of moral philosophy abandoned theology and the questions it poses about human agency. They were not answered; they were neglected, bracketed out because they troubled the methods of ethics. Second, Aquinas's work was used by reactionary forces in the latter part of the nineteenth century, throughout much of the twentieth century, and has made a powerful return in the twenty-first century, primarily to combat modernity and especially its understanding of human agency. Sidetracking a more theological use of Aquinas, the reactionary reading primarily interprets Aquinas as a philosopher who has the answers to counter errors in modern philosophy. The *nouvelle théologie* generated a fruitful correction that, as Vidler noted, lets us see Maurice, and his sympathetic criticism of Aquinas, in a new light. If Maurice had the Thomism of de Lubac before him, perhaps he would have found less tension in Aquinas's teaching on the acquired and infused virtues, or recognized, as I attempt to do below, that this tension is salutary. It resists fitting ethics within a complete system.

This chapter examines Maurice's appreciative criticism of Aquinas and how he anticipated debates that are still very much with us today. The next chapter traces reactionary uses of Aquinas; they are not the only way to retrieve his important work for learning and teaching ethics. Alasdair MacIntyre's ethics of resistance offers an alternative to it. Because Maurice worked before the reactionary use, he too charts a different way to receive Aquinas, which brings the acquired and infused virtues together through an ecstatic agency that is more resolutely theological than that of MacIntyre. Aquinas offers something similar in the *Tertia pars*, but it is too often neglected in discussions of the virtues.

MAURICE'S ECSTATIC ANTHROPOLOGY AS INFUSING VIRTUE

We find ourselves in losing ourselves; but in losing ourselves, we discover the possibility of receiving ourselves. This Augustinian anthropology was constant for Maurice; we most fully come to be who we are when we are least preoccupied with ourselves. Nor was it unique to him; it is a common "ecstatic" agency in the Christian theological tradition. Only by being drawn out from oneself toward something that is more do we receive agency. For Maurice, this occurs by "walking *secundum Deum*."[2] He looked to the Trinity and the Incarnation as foundational for this ecstatic agency. Because persons are made in the image of the Triune God, their being is grounded not in themselves but in the life of another.

Shortly after the death of his first wife, Maurice wrote to his sister on May 17, 1845, her birthday, about his idea of the Trinity as foundational for ethics and politics: "The idea of the unity of the Father and the Son in the Holy Spirit, as the basis of all unity amongst men, as the groundwork of all human society and of all thought, as belonging to little children, and as the highest fruition of the saints in glory, has been haunting me for a longer time than I can easily look back to."[3] This idea remained with him, and he interpreted it as he did the theological virtues and Christian doctrine by comparing a use of the Trinitarian doctrine that confidently gives life with one that fearfully takes it. For instance, he contrasts Emperor Justinian with Pope Gregory I. Both sought to restore unity to Europe, but they had different starting points. Justinian attempted it with law and compulsion. Gregory I attempted it through worship. In so doing, he set forth the Trinity as "the starting-point for all the metaphysical and all the moral philosophy of modern Europe." The result was a very different politics than Justinian's. Maurice writes, "What we say further is, that the mystery which lay beneath his desire for uniformity, because he believed it [Trinity] the basis of unity among men, acted as a counterbalancing power to the Latin love of rules, forms, dogmas, and compelled him to ask with as much ardour as the Greek had ever done, what constitutes right, order, obligation, among men."[4] Worship directs our gaze to something beyond us. It sets forth an object of desire that exceeds human grasping, making possible an order among persons that is first received before it can be enacted. What constitutes right order is charity.

Charity was the highest virtue because, as Saint Paul teaches, it alone remains. Maurice offers a different hierarchical order of the virtues from the Protestant Reformers. Their insistence on justification by faith set faith above charity. He reverses this because the Trinity is charity. Faith directs us to God as its end or object, but charity is that end. He acknowledges that placing charity above faith could, unfortunately, fit the nondogmatic age in which he lives as if what matters most is ethics and not doctrine, but he disagrees that emphasizing faith above charity correlates with doctrine better than charity, which is why he states that charity is "the key to unlock the secrets of Divinity as well as of Humanity."[5] Charity is Trinity; Trinity is Charity. "Writers" in the patristic and Medieval era "speak continually of the Trinity as the 'Eternal Charity,' and as the foundation of all human life."[6] As the foundation for metaphysics and morals, the Trinity has a contemplative and "practical form." The latter is that "Christ dwells in us by faith and strengthened by the Holy Spirit—being rooted and grounded in love."[7]

The Incarnation is the manifestation of the Triune life in creaturely existence and the basis for human agency and its perfection. It is a "paradox of divinity," Maurice states, that our perfection is in "the acknowledgment of [the creature's] whole moral and spiritual life and being as in another."[8] The practical form of the Trinity is the Incarnate One as an object of desire that makes ecstatic agency possible. The Trinity comes to us in the Incarnate One, mediating through his humanity new possibilities for ours. Because of this anthropology, Maurice was both for and against Aristotle, Aquinas, and Luther. Aristotle's virtue ethics reflected the goodness of the Wisdom that made them possible, but they secured rather than lost the self. It lacked the ecstatic agency faith, hope, and love required. Maurice affirms acquiring virtue, but if we conceive them as our achievements, we lose their gifted character in the theological virtues that are a participation in the divine nature, something we cannot achieve. In his lectures on Christian ethics, Maurice begins by telling the students that the ethics text he studied at Oxford was Aristotle's *Nicomachean Ethics*. He applauds the university for putting it "into his hands"; he could not "have received a greater service from any university or any teacher." Aristotle taught him that ethics "must belong to all times," and that it cannot be learned "by reading a book, or learning a set of maxims by heart" because its subject matter "belongs to life, and must be learnt in the daily practice of life." He taught that ethics is about the "worth of habits, acts, and moral purposes." Yet, in the end, Aristotle was unsatisfying because he could not provide "the standard of my habits and acts and moral purposes."[9] Maurice does not cite Aristotle's definition of virtue at this point; but given what he states, he must have been thinking about it. Aristotle's standard is the prudent person. For Maurice, this is helpful but inadequate. He agrees in part: "The standard must be a LIFE. It must be set forth in a living Person." But he also adds this: "If it is to do me any good, his life must in some way act upon my life."[10] Because Christ can so act, he becomes the standard to whom Aristotle pointed but was unable to identify. His life acts upon ours, making our actions possible by infusing them with charity. In this sense, it is ecstatic.

Maurice returns to this central idea later in his lectures by contrasting the "world's ethics" with "Christian ethics": "Has he made himself God's child by some services which he has rendered to Him? No! these are the world's ethics; in these lies that self-righteousness which the Bible denounces, and which the conscience in us revolts against. Christian ethics proceed on the opposite principle. We do not attach ourselves to Christ by performing righteous acts. We are able to perform righteous acts because we are attached to Him."[11]

The contrast between Christian ethics and the world's ethics could be read as a contradiction to Maurice's repeated theme, also stated in these lectures, that "Christian ethics" does not differ from "human ethics."[12] He did not think it was a contradiction because the ecstatic agency found in Christianity is not supernatural versus natural; it is both. He justified this on the doctrine of the Incarnation: Christ reveals true divinity *and humanity*. Christ gives to humanity "its true position and glory. Therefore, our ethics are in the strictest sense Christian; but they are also in the strictest sense human."[13] Locating our agency in Christ's life qualifies, but does not deny, a role for the acquired virtues. Maurice worked this out in his nuanced but critical interpretation of Aquinas on the relationship between the acquired and infused virtues.

Aquinas begins his discussion of human action by first affirming that we are the source of our action through internal principles and then leads his reader to conclude that this can be true without denying that God and other external agents are equally sources for our action. He begins the *prima secundae* with the distinction, which was influential for Anscombe's *Intention*, between human action (*actiones humanae*) and the acts of a human (*hominis actiones*). The latter are done without deliberation, such as nonreflexive jerking, hair growing, thoughtlessly tapping. When asked "Why?" about such actions, a reasonable answer would be "for no reason" or "I was unaware that I was." Such action is known only through observation, so it cannot be intentional. A human action, conversely, is an act by reason and will that is the person's own action (*suorum actuum dominus*[14]). In the question on the necessity of grace for acting well, Aquinas returns to his claim that a person is *suorum actuum dominus*. If grace is necessary to act well, he argues, then how can our actions properly be our own? His response is not particularly theological. He looks to Aristotle and everyday life. To act is to own one's deliberations, but deliberation always presumes some "previous deliberation," so that it fits within an ongoing history of deliberations that cannot go on infinitely. In other words, human agents are the sources of their own deliberations, but only as they participate in deliberations that they did not originate and will not terminate. Deliberation assumes that the agent is part of an ongoing conversation that comes before and continues after the agent. His argument resembles Maurice's claim about how words and texts work, always inviting us into the lives of others. For Aquinas, like Maurice, deliberations must have an origin that is something other than the one deliberating, even though their deliberations are their own. Aquinas calls this origin "God." That deliberation requires a first cause to avoid an infinite regress is not the strongest argument, but that every deliberation assumes a previous context of deliberation outside it for its plausibility is convincing. (Think of Wittgenstein's "An 'inner process' stands in need of outward criteria.") This relates to his second, more convincing, argument on the role friendship plays in human agency. He cites Aristotle to explain the necessity of grace: "What we can do through our friends, we can do in some sense, by ourselves." This fact, he suggests, is why we know that "what we can do with the Divine assistance is not altogether impossible to us."[15] Friendship is, like grace, a source for living well that is "external" to us and yet makes possible the sources for our good actions because we act in concert with our friends. Aquinas draws on Jesus's pronouncement that he calls us friends and interprets the theological virtue of charity as friendship with God, a friendship that also makes us friends with all whom God befriends.

Aquinas's theory of human action assumes both internal and external sources working noncompetitively. It culminates in his confusing discussion of the relationship between the acquired and infused virtues that continues to perplex Thomists. This perplexity arises as to what happens to the acquired virtues once they are infused by the Holy Spirit. If the acquired virtues do not remain after the infused ones, then why be concerned with moral formation? If the acquired virtues do remain after the infused ones, how do we make sense of two sources of moral agency? F. D. Maurice recognized this confusion. For Maurice, Aquinas "carries" Aristotelianism "to its highest point" and lapses into Platonism as he does.[16] These are not criticisms. They prove his "master's prophecy": the Ox has bellowed and been heard throughout the world.[17] The "echo" in his own day, however, can be less than salutary. Aquinas's guidance has become an impediment in Maurice's time. He does not explain why he makes this judgment but suggests something very similar to Anscombe's hesitancy in citing Aquinas. Aquinas has become a mere authority without attention to what exceeds him. What exceeds him is what matters most in his ethics, so Maurice considers that a future era may be able to retrieve Aquinas to good effect: "A time may be coming when it will be possible to derive more good from Aquinas than any age has owed to him, because we are free from his trammels and have learned to walk at liberty under higher guidance."[18]

Why he considers Aquinas to be restricting at present and hopeful for the future is found in his criticism that Aquinas and the Thomists divide ethics from theology. Aquinas gets "frustrated by the complicated machinery" of Aristotle in discussing whether habit is a quality or quantity and with the distinction between intrinsic and extrinsic principles.[19] He does not reject Aristotle's language of habits; it is useful and makes a "very natural transition . . . to the language of Saint Paul concerning the putting off of the old man, and the putting on of the new." The difficulty arises when Aquinas and Aristotle "draw a line between habits considered as *in* us and habits considered as put upon us, which is so sharp and deep that we lose all feeling of the relation between them."[20] Aquinas and the Thomists never unify the two sources for ethics, and in turn they shift between affirming acquired virtues without God and viewing the infused virtues as the only perfect virtues, failing to give the acquired ones their due. Here is the heart of the tension Maurice identified. Given his anthropology, this division is obviously problematic. Habits considered in us resemble what Maurice called "the world's ethics," while those "put upon us" fit better as an ecstatic agency. Both are to be affirmed, which requires their integration.

Aquinas, Maurice argues, has the potential to integrate what he has divided because his ethics, unlike morality in modern philosophy, require theology. Maurice, like de Lubac, looks to Aquinas the theologian to unite what a sharp distinction between nature and grace, or creation and redemption, too decisively divides. In fact, he argues, Aquinas will be misunderstood by anyone "who tries to contemplate the ethical questions upon which he enters, apart from the subject which gives its title to the whole work."[21] At his best, Aquinas recognizes that ethics cannot be divided from theology. The basis for this recognition is the common teaching shared by Aristotle and Aquinas that acts always occur "with reference to some End." What constitutes the end so radically differs from Aristotle that his ethics has no need for theology. Aquinas's does. For him, the end is the "Blessedness" found in the "vision of the Divine Essence"; Aristotle "never soared" toward that end, which is charity.[22] Maurice then offers what he takes to be Aquinas's definition of virtue, bringing Aristotle and Augustine together: "Virtue is determined to be a Habit; to be an operative Habit; to be a Habit operative of good. A good definition of it is at length worked out. Virtue is a good quality or habit of mind; upon which right living depends; which cannot be turned to evil use; and which God without us, works in us. The Aristotelian Energy is here subjected to the Christian Law 'He worketh in us to will and do of his good pleasure.'" Maurice affirms Aquinas's formulation but also claims that it is "overloaded and clumsy."[23]

Given Maurice's revision of the infused virtues as the cardinal ones, what makes it clumsy is surprising. Maurice objects to Aquinas's insistence that only the infused virtues, and not those "acquired by human industry, . . . possess the proper conditions of virtue." He finds Aquinas inconsistent. How could he expend so much effort in the *Summa* positively explicating Aristotle on the virtues only to arrive at the conclusion that the acquired virtues are only virtues imperfectly considered? Yet the problem is not just with Aquinas or Catholics but has become endemic to Protestantism. Maurice writes, "We rejoice to expose this inconsistency, because in doing so we are gratifying no party animosity or predilection. Protestants have inherited the contradiction from the Schoolman."[24]

The tension is found in these three assumptions, all which Maurice rejects: First, natural virtues are not true virtues but only splendid vices. Second, virtue can be acquired without God. And third, only the infused virtues are true virtues. The first assumption denies the goodness of creation. Natural virtues found among the nations are not vices; they are true virtues. Scripture and the creeds "refute" this option because it would suggest that "the world, . . . with the exception of one little corner of it, was a Christless and a Fatherless world."[25] The second assumption assumes atheism. True virtues cannot be acquired without God. No virtue, natural or infused, has only immanent natural powers as its source. Virtue does not arrive from some pure nature because no such thing exists. The Wisdom by which all things were created cannot but be reflected in the moral and metaphysical philosophy of every nation. And the third assumption denies that the infused and acquired virtues cohere; it rejects their common foundation in divine Wisdom.

INTERPRETING AQUINAS ON THE ACQUIRED AND INFUSED VIRTUES

Several questions follow from Maurice's interpretation and criticism of Aquinas. First, has he interpreted Aquinas well; is the tension that he identifies there? Second, if the acquired and infused virtues cohere, how do they do so? The next section is a technical discussion of the ongoing difficulties among contemporary Thomists on interpreting Aquinas on the relationship between the acquired and infused virtues. Its purpose is not to resolve the difficulty but to illustrate that the tension Maurice discovered is present in Thomas, but for a good reason. It leads to the kind of ecstatic agency that Maurice envisioned. Affirming both natural, acquired virtue and infused theological and moral virtue requires affirming both human and divine agency in the moral life without competition or division. As is shown in the next section, turning to a Christological understanding of agency helps make sense of the tension. Here is a case where analytic precision would mislead us because bringing together divine and human agency without contradiction could not logically be construed in analytical terms. If God exists, God could not be an object in the world that can be indicated. That the tension exists is salutary because it reminds us that we are speaking of God, a mystery to be inhabited and not an "object" to be mastered. What the tension points to is twofold. First, any adequate discussion of the relationship between the acquired and infused virtues needs something like a Christological account of agency for it not to collapse into nonsense. Second, the infused virtues, and by implication the acquired virtues they make possible, are less in us, less our possessions, than we are in them. I will return to these claims after the technical discussion on contemporary interpretations of Aquinas.

The tension Maurice found in Aquinas is present in this statement on the relationship between the infused and acquired virtues:

Thus, it is clear from what has been said that only the infused virtues are perfect virtues, and only the infused virtues should be called virtues absolutely speaking, since they order a man in the right way, absolutely speaking, toward his ultimate end. The other virtues, i.e., the acquired virtues, are virtues in a certain respect and not virtues absolutely speaking (*secundum quid virtutes, non autem simpliciter*), since they order a man in the right way with respect to the ultimate end in a certain genus, but not with respect to the ultimate end absolutely speaking.[26]

This passage could be interpreted as suggesting that the acquired virtues are in a genus that differs in kind from the ultimate end. In other words, God is not the direct source for these virtues, because they achieve a purely natural end that does not require grace. For Maurice, if the acquired virtues result solely from natural, internal principles, then theology makes no difference for them. They would also be less than the infused virtues, which are possible only with divine assistance. Maurice suggests that Aquinas's theology rescues him from such an interpretation, and claims that his heirs—both Catholic and Protestant—have neglected it, rendering Aquinas little more than an Aristotelian philosopher. Maurice does not then offer a theological interpretation of Aquinas. However, his emphasis on the Incarnate One as the practical application of the Trinity in creaturely life points the way forward. It is a way that would challenge any Thomistic idea that nature and grace differ in kind rather than degree.

For Aquinas, even though grace is a "quality of the soul," and thus has the same definition as a virtue, it is not a virtue but the source of the infused virtues. Acquired virtues, however, do not appear to have this source. They "are dispositions by which a man is appropriately disposed in relation to the nature by which he is a man." The infused virtues "dispose" someone "in a higher mode," not by their nature but by grace. Aquinas, of course, would acknowledge that human nature is itself a creaturely gift. Creation is a grace, but it is not redemption. If, as Maurice suggests, the theological virtues are cardinal virtues, given with creation, then several problems could arise. Our creaturely nature could be considered sufficient for not only acquired virtues but also infused ones. That would call into question the role of the work of Christ, the Church, and the sacraments. It would not fit with Maurice's emphasis on baptism. It would render it unnecessary. Yet if a disposition in relation to human nature requires no grace, then Maurice's concern about a tacit underlying atheism for teaching and learning ethics might be warranted. His concern is that Aquinas has not resolved the tension between these two positions.

How Aquinas is interpreted depends on the lens through which he is read. He can be interpreted through an Aristotelian lens. Then the emphasis on what human industry achieves foregrounds the virtues. Practices, habituation, actualization of potentialities, internal principles, and an immanent telos of human flourishing will be the focus. God may be present as Creator, but the Trinity or Incarnation need not be invoked. He can also be interpreted through an Augustinian lens. Grace, the sacraments, infusion, divine agency, and a transcendent telos of beatitude will be the focus. Then he cannot be interpreted well without the Trinity or Incarnation. Thomistic theologies of action can swing between these two foci. Before discussing how moral theologians interpret Aquinas, caricatures should be rejected. First, no serious moral theologian seeks to collapse grace completely into nature, rendering the sacraments or Christian teaching irrelevant for virtue. Second, none seek to deny God's role in the entirety of the moral life, in both the acquired and infused virtues. The difference is whether a doctrine of Providence alone suffices or, with Maurice, whether the two mysteries of the Trinity and the Incarnation are necessary for the acquired as well as the infused virtues.

A STRICTLY ARISTOTELIAN THOMISM: THE SUFFICIENCY OF NATURE

Some philosophers and theologians claim that a strict Aristotelian Thomism is necessary to preserve the gratuity of grace. Nature can be known with precision apart from grace. The argument goes like this: If nature is not known apart from grace, then nature runs the risk of collapsing into grace. Once the single desire for beatitude, for friendship with God, defines our nature, then grace would be owed to creatures, making it something other than God's free gift. If God creates us with a desire for God but does not satisfy this desire, then God is unjust. If God creates us with such a desire and does satisfy it, then little or no role exists for the redemptive economy. Jesus's life, death, resurrection, ascension, sending of the Spirit, and forming the Church are rendered moot.

A correlate of this teaching is the sufficiency of nature to achieve moral ends, albeit always qualified by placing it in a providential order. Lawrence Feingold explains the sufficiency of nature in his defense of the Catholic doctrine of pure nature. This doctrine is based on two Aristotelian axioms. The first is that "a natural passive potency in a genus never expends beyond the active power of that genus" and the second is that a "natural desire is never in vain."[27] In other words, if a potency is natural, the power to actuate this potency, which is what constitutes a virtue, would also be natural. If the desire to do so is natural, then likewise the creature contains what is necessary internal to its being to satisfy that desire. Otherwise, we would have desires that could be frustrated not because of our own doing but because we *naturally* desire something that exceeds our nature, such as friendship with God, and how could that be a natural desire? Yet Catholic theologians like Henri de Lubac and Hans Urs von Balthasar, whose work contributed to the retrieval of a different Thomism at Vatican II, challenged the doctrine of pure nature, teaching that human creatures had a natural desire for God.

Steven A. Long agrees with Feingold against de Lubac and Balthasar, whom he thinks misled Catholic teaching, especially given their influence in the way Vatican II was interpreted. For him, the Catholic doctrine of pure nature is necessary if the "enormous complication and confusion following the Second Vatican Council" are to be overcome. To do so, it is necessary to recover and return to the classical doctrine of pure nature in Thomas Aquinas, as set forth in Vatican I and *Aeterna patris*.[28] He acknowledges that if his "analysis is true, then critical aspects of the systematic contemplation, and of the prudence, of a generation and more of theologians is rendered suspect and in need of corrective mediation in order to serve the tradition.[29] He primarily has in mind de Lubac, Balthasar, and those influenced by them. De Lubac comes off better than Balthasar in Long's analysis, but the judgment against him is nonetheless severe: "It is not the first time that a physician unintentionally has communicated the plague he nobly sought to resist."[30] De Lubac's work plagues modern Catholic theology not because of his opposition to extrinsicism, which is the idea that grace is completely external to nature and comes to it as something alien that nature could not recognize. Here, Long would agree with him; he faults de Lubac for failing to understand "obediential potency," especially "specific obediential potency."[31] It is an "aptness" of nature to its proportionate end imprinted upon a creature, which occurs always within the context of God's providential action. It is, nonetheless, a natural end that need not refer to any supernatural one for its intelligibility. The neglect of this, he argues, has had dire consequences for Catholic moral theology, especially in the work of Balthasar, who failed to uphold the certainty of natural law teachings on marriage, politics, and more.

Balthasar went horribly wrong on nature and grace in his book on Barth because he rejected the claim that nature could be known in "precision from the order of grace."[32] The offending paragraph from Balthasar is this:

Now common sense claims to know what nature is. But the more exactly it tries to grasp it, the more difficult—nay impossible—it becomes to isolate it neatly from the other dimension: supernatural grace. But it is equally difficult to espy the negative effects on the realm of nature of the loss of grace. The questions, for example, of how far "ignorance and hardship belong to natural existence," how much concupiscence, disease, death (and the form that death takes) are the result of sin or in part of the definition of being human and animal; but also questions about marriage, community, the State, our relation to a God who might not have revealed himself in his personal, interior life, the necessity for prayer in a natural state (which many people deny, for good reasons), the eschatological fate of the soul, resurrection of the body, Last Judgment, eternal bliss: all such questions addressed to pure nature are simply unanswerable.[33]

These questions may be unanswerable for Balthasar, but they are not for Aristotelian Thomists once nature is known in its "precision" from grace.[34]

Maurice suggested that this strictly Aristotelian interpretation of the virtues was a form of atheism because it could set forth the moral life without any attention to God. De Lubac worried that it led to a secular politics and ethics, which makes Vidler's claim that Maurice's work makes more sense after de Lubac's all the more compelling. These may be unfair judgments. Such Thomists emphasize that while nature is known with precision from grace, it is not known apart from divine providence. What is lacking in this interpretation, however, is any consequential affirmation of the Trinity and the Incarnation as its practical form. We can understand marriage, politics, economics, sex, gender, reproduction, and even death from nature qua nature. Christ, the Church, and the sacraments have little role to play. Those who do not agree with the ethical judgments known from nature by precision can only be understood as irrational, ignorant, or recalcitrant. As the next chapter seeks to show, this emphasis on a purely natural ethics has reactionary political consequences.

A STRICTLY AUGUSTINIAN THOMISM: GOD WORKING IN US WITHOUT US

Thomas Aquinas introduces his discussion of virtue with Augustine's definition rather than Aristotle's, and this has led some interpreters to question how Aristotelian Aquinas is.[35] Mark Jordan argues that "Aquinas attempts to resolve the tension" between Aristotle and Augustine's definitions of virtue and "succeeds in the attempt but only by subordinating Aristotle to Augustine."[36] Bonnie Kent points to Aquinas's praise of Augustine's definition.[37] Aquinas states, "The definition in question captures completely the whole nature of virtue. For the complete definition of any given thing is gathered together from its causes, and the definition stated above includes all the causes of virtue."[38] Robert Miner cites the same passage and notes that Aquinas begins with Augustine's definition and then explains virtue as a *"habitus operativus bonus,"* God works it in us, *and* it becomes a *"habitus"* operative within us. He argues that the infused virtue is virtue simply given, but this does not make it any less something that works "in" us.[39] Nicholas Austin concurs and notes that Aquinas affirms Augustine's definition because he is searching "for a properly theological definition and that applied strictly only to the 'infused' virtues that come to us as a gift from God." Aquinas explicitly states that Augustine's is best because it "embraces all its causes."[40] This constitutes a near consensus among contemporary Thomists. Yet this consensus also affirms, as Aquinas did, that what God works in us without us does not occur without our consent.[41] Beginning with Augustine's definition, then affirming human consent, and having at least some place for Aristotle's definition does not resolve the tension that was raised in part I of this book: If God's work depends on our consent, then how is it done without us? How would consent not be an intentional human act? How are these words something other than nonsense: God works virtue in us without us but not without our consent?

One way to render them sensible would be through a "hyper-Augustinianism," or "Augustinian passivity," that leaves little to no role for the acquired virtues. David Decosimo and Jennifer Herdt identify such a position and caution against it. For Decosimo, the crucial issue is whether charity is necessary for all virtue. If it is, then "pagan"—or, as he puts it, "outsider virtue"—could not be true virtue. He worries that some moral philosophers and theologians fail to appreciate outsider virtue because of their "hyper-Augustinianism"—these include Hauerwas, Milbank, MacIntyre, and James K. Smith. Decosimo explains the difference this way: "The human virtues are, in principle, attainable without charity by everyone because they perfect and are founded on the natural virtues. . . . In contrast, the virtues exclusive to Christians, infused virtues, are caused solely by God's grace and are not rooted in natural virtue. They are an entirely different species of virtue from those virtues Christians and non-Christians can share."[42] In seeking to affirm natural virtue, Decosimo sides with the more strictly Aristotelian Thomists by rendering natural, acquired, and infused virtues as different in kind.

The hyper-Augustinians appear to collapse all the virtues into the infused ones, and since the latter are the province of Christian faith, it leaves them incapable of recognizing virtue in "their non-Christian neighbors."[43] If only the infused virtues are virtues, then non-Christians cannot be virtuous. Decosimo resolves the tension between the two definitions by suggesting that Aquinas affirms Aristotle's virtues on Augustinian grounds by identifying Aristotle's transcendent good with Christ, but it is unclear what status "natural virtues" have once he interprets them via Augustine. They appear to be purely natural, and thus exist without charity, and at the same time are ordered to a transcendent good, who is Christ, which would make it difficult to understand them without charity. Decosimo does not consider Maurice's position that charity is a cardinal virtue.

Jennifer Herdt made a similar argument in 2008, but she was more circumspect in dismissing some whom Decosimo labels "hyper-Augustinian"— none of whom explicitly affirm that non-Christians lack virtue. Both Decosimo and Herdt take up Jeffrey Stout's critique of Hauerwas, Milbank, and MacIntyre as lending support to a reactionary traditionalism, a movement that undoubtedly exists and has only increased since Stout made his criticism in 2004. (This is discussed below, along with Hauerwas's and MacIntyre's relationship with it.) Herdt identifies three problems with the legacy of an Augustinian rejection of pagan virtue as splendid vice; each is related to the fundamental problem that pagan virtues are ordered to self rather than God. First, this legacy questions "ordinary habituation" because it "entrenches the vices of pride and self-love." Second, it takes a "foundation stance of pure passivity" because it fears false virtue, and habituation always has a gap when one is acting virtuous without being virtuous. Third, for the Augustinians, one's agency must depend solely on God, so even the effort to pursue God through one's own resources becomes "a problematic expression of self-love."[44] The acquired virtues become downright dangerous for the Christian life.

Herdt does not accuse MacIntyre and Hauerwas of Augustinian passivity; she locates it more within Reformed expressions of Christianity. Hauerwas, she writes, "is both more critical of the church and more appreciative of the world than Stout indicates."[45] Yet she thinks that his ecclesial vision of virtue inclines toward, and should resist, a "temptation: on the one hand, that of falsely idealizing the church and its practices and, on the other, that of denouncing secular modernity rather than discerning God at work within it. And Hauerwas's rhetoric does feed these tendencies at times." Hauerwas, and Charles Pinches, fail to give the acquired virtues their due because they associate them "with the world of sin."[46]

Hauerwas and Pinches acknowledge that Augustine is not far "off track" in his criticism of pagan virtues, but this is only the case when these virtues "appear as our own achievements." Then, righteousness would be something that we could accomplish without any assistance from God, the Church, or friends.[47] Sources internal to the agent suffice; an ecstatic agency and external sources would be irrelevant. While Decosimo and Herdt are concerned with the first aspect of the tension that Maurice identified, the acquired virtues are not treated as true virtues, Hauerwas and Pinches are concerned with the second; virtues cannot be understood well apart from God. Like Aquinas and Maurice, they seek a theological rendering of virtue. This does not require a rejection of habituation or the moral virtues. It requires reading them also as gifts, and like Aquinas, Hauerwas and Pinches see a convergence between the Augustinian and Aristotelian definitions of friendship.

Friendship is a central means whereby virtues are received. Christian charity differs from Aristotle's natural account of friendship, but it does not oppose it. Some of it must be denied, such as the claim that friendship primarily takes place with those most like us. Yet some of it is affirmed. Friendship reminds us that ethics is not a domain we master; rather, others are necessary to assist us in being better than we would otherwise be. Some of what Aristotle taught on friendship needs to be completed or perfected, and this occurs when we become what Aristotle never imagined—friends with God—the very definition of the virtue of charity. Such a friendship calls for a participation in God's infinite love, a love that cannot come to an end and brings encumbrances such as the demand to love one's enemies. Just as we receive this gift of love from others, we also become its source for others, as Augustine noted: "Blessed is the man who loves you, who loves his friend in you, and his enemy because of you."[48] For Hauerwas and Pinches, the infusion of virtue is necessary for friendship, and it is discovered and received through Christ's body: "The sign and substance of this infusion of the Christian virtues is always participation in the body of Christ."[49]

The "always" in this sentence is the kind of claim that concerns both Decosimo and Herdt.[50] If participation in Christ's body is necessary for infusing virtue, and infusion is necessary for virtues to be true virtues, then little recognition of virtues outside Christianity would seem to follow. The central question is what Hauerwas and Pinches mean by "participation in the body of Christ." If it means exclusively in the empirical churches one can point to, then it would be problematic. If it means, as the Creed states, "through him all things are made," then it would not differ considerably from Decosimo's or Herdt's position.[51] Maurice made the infused virtues cardinal because of the Creed. This leads to his conviction that virtue cannot be without charity.

Decosimo's and Herdt's concern is with any exclusive claim that virtue only arises from participation in Christ and that such participation is limited to the baptized. Such a position could only be maintained by denying what is obvious: Unbaptized persons have virtues, including charity, faith, and hope, and sometimes more so than the baptized. If, with Maurice, participation in Christ is understood as a necessary feature of the gift of creation—given that creation occurs through, in, and for, Christ—then its exclusivity may be less problematic. It makes theology necessary for the virtues, and that might still worry a philosopher like Kent. She does not share the Christological rendering of virtue that Hauerwas, Pinches, Decosimo, and Herdt do; but she shares Decosimo's and Herdt's concern that virtue should not become parochialized. If the infused virtues are understood as the true, perfect virtues and the acquired ones are dismissed, then the virtue tradition becomes defined by a Christian parochialism. For her, MacIntyre's virtues are too parochial because they require charity. For MacIntyre, she states, "Merely natural ends are morally virtuous only when sought from the charity, faith, and hope that, by definition, only Christians can have."[52] MacIntyre's Thomism is too "Augustinian" and "only superficially Aristotelian." Thus, he finds Aristotle's telos inadequate and in need of being informed by "*caritas*, which is a gift of grace."[53] She affirms a cosmopolitan version of the virtues that, like Decosimo's, does not require the infusion of charity. Moral virtues exist without charity.

If Kent accuses MacIntyre of being too Augustinian and insufficiently Aristotelian, Hauerwas and Pinches make the opposite charge. For them, Christianity inaugurates a "new tradition that sets the virtues within an entirely different telos in community."[54] Because of this new tradition, they are critical of MacIntyre: "We cannot, then, begin with Aristotle's virtues and fill in the gaps with Christianity, nor can we, as Christians, defend virtue first and Christianity later, the strategy we find prevalent in MacIntyre."[55] In a 2022 work, Hauerwas questions why MacIntyre has given insufficient attention to the infused virtues.[56]

The opposing interpretations of MacIntyre are curious. Does he side with Augustine against Aristotle, making charity and the infused virtues too essential? Or does he give insufficient attention to the transformation of the virtue tradition that Aquinas brings about by making the acquired virtues too essential? The answer depends on whether we read MacIntyre primarily through his 1988 *Whose Justice? Which Rationality?* or his 2016 *Ethics in the Conflicts of Modernity*. The latter draws on Aristotle, Aquinas, and Marx; Augustine disappears, not even warranting an entry in the index. In *Whose Justice? Which Rationality?* MacIntyre refers to his Augustinian Christianity and interprets Augustine as setting forth a "new account both of the nature of justice and of the genesis of human action." Faith is prior to understanding, and charity becomes the form of the virtues. This new account differs from that of Aristotle, who had "no place for any human *telos* beyond that to be attained by mortals before death."[57] For MacIntyre, Aquinas's genius is to bring together the traditions of Aristotle and Augustine, such that his "account of the natural virtues in the *Secunda secundae* had to have as its prologue an inquiry into the supernatural virtues." Charity is a "gift of grace, flowing from the work of Christ through the office of the Holy Spirit."[58] Aquinas never abandons Aristotle, but he corrects his deficiencies with Augustine and gives concretion to Augustine's "generalizations" with Aristotle's particularistic rendering of the virtues.[59]

The central role that MacIntyre gives to the supernatural virtues, and especially charity, in *Whose Justice? Which Rationality?* all but disappears from his *Ethics in the Conflicts of Modernity*. Given that both are works on practical reasoning, it is difficult to understand why. If all we had was the 1988 work, Kent's criticism would seem compelling. If all we had were *After Virtue* and the 2016 work, Hauerwas and Pinches's criticism makes more sense. Perhaps the reason for the difference is that the 2016 work seeks to show how an account of natural human flourishing gives "resources for constructing a contemporary politics and ethics, one that enables and requires us to act against modernity from within modernity" more so than the 1988 one.[60] This natural flourishing remains open to divine agency and the infused virtues. It commits the virtuous person to a "belief in God" and "to a belief that if there is nothing beyond the finite, there is no final end, no ultimate human good, to be achieved."[61] The latter is necessary for deliberation borne out of desire. As is noted below, MacIntyre concludes *Ethics in the Conflicts of Modernity* with an openness to "natural theology." While this might still be too much for Kent, it is too little for Hauerwas. It lacks any appeal to participation in Christ.

Decosimo questions the hyper-Augustinians by denying that charity is necessary for virtue. However, to affirm that non-Christian virtues are virtues without charity raises its own problem. It could tempt someone to a doctrine of pure nature, which is not Decosimo's position. It also overlooks Aquinas's desire for a theological rendering of virtue that makes charity essential even for moral virtues, although his interpretation is confusing, as Maurice noted. For Aquinas, like Aristotle, the measure of virtue is the prudent person. In the *prima secundae*, he had stated that the infused moral virtues ordered to our supernatural end are "virtues perfectly and truly."[62] The moral virtues are connected by prudence, which orders the human creature to both the natural and supernatural end. For this reason, it must also be infused. Infused prudence does not exist without charity. The other moral virtues do not exist without prudence. Thus, the moral virtues require infused prudence, and it cannot exist without charity. Aquinas also asks in the *prima secundae* if the "moral virtues" exist "without charity."[63] They can, he states, if they are ordered to an end that does not exceed human nature and can be acquired through its works. The moral virtues can exist without charity, but charity cannot exist without the moral virtues: "All the moral virtues are infused simultaneously with charity. The reason for this is that God does not operate less perfectly in the works of grace than He does in the works of nature."[64] The question is how the works of nature and grace work together, if they do. If they differ in kind, the tension becomes a contradiction. If they differ in degree, grace perfects and does not contradict nature. The latter possibility assumes Maurice's stance that both the acquired and the infused virtues should be affirmed, but in a unified, ecstatic agency.

THE UNITY OR COEXISTENCE OF THE ACQUIRED AND INFUSED VIRTUES

Recall that for Maurice, the Incarnation is the "practical form" of the Triune life in creaturely existence and the basis for human agency and its perfection. Our participation in the divine life is by faith, is grounded in love, and issues in the hope that all creation might share in communion. Because of his Trinitarian theology, Maurice made the theological virtues cardinal ones and the acquired virtues derivative. Nonetheless, he, like Aquinas, still distinguished them. What ancient philosophers identified as acquired virtues were authentic. Maurice critiqued Aquinas and his heirs, including the Reformers, for failing to keep together three claims: (1) God is the source of all virtue, (2) true virtue is found among every people and culture, and (3) the priority of the theological virtues and their infusion do not render acquired virtue imperfect or less than true virtue. These three claims are not easily held together, and he thinks Aquinas failed to do so.

Contemporary interpreters of Aquinas acknowledge the tension Maurice noted, and they debate if Aquinas has the resources to resolve it. The tension is how to relate his careful exposition of Aristotle's acquired virtues to their rule in human reason and his affirmation of Augustine's and Lombard's infused virtues with their rule in God. He does not give us an explicit question on what happens to the acquired virtues once virtues are infused, although he addresses this indirectly in several places. The question is if he has given us enough.

Some think so. Peter Lumbreras, OP, offered a well-known coexistence model in the mid–twentieth century.[65] The acquired virtues exist with and without charity, as if the two sources for virtue, what we achieve and what God does within us, fail to touch each other. Nature and the cardinal virtues suffice for ethics and politics; grace and the infused virtues suffice for redemption. Lumbreras's interpretation requires a strong distinction between the human creature's proximate and ultimate ends, something that is common to what was once called the two-tiered interpretation of Aquinas. Although Lumbreras admits that the connection of the virtues had been "disputed and at times poorly elaborated," he was confident that "little more" needed to be said after his interpretation.[66] Given how much more has been said since his influential 1948 essay, it obviously did not suffice to resolve the difficulty.

Nicholas Austin is less confident that Aquinas provides an adequate account of how grace infuses virtues that are at the same time acquired. The infused virtues can appear to be a "discontinuous intervention," like God "flicking a light switch." Because Aquinas locates the infusion of the virtues with baptism, he is unable to explain how an infant can have the virtues. His account of the Holy Spirit is "unconvincing."[67] Jean Porter asks, "Can infused and acquired moral virtues co-exist in the same individual?" and acknowledges that Aquinas "does not address this question directly in the *Summa Theologia*." But he gives us "enough" for an answer: they cannot coexist.[68] Two sources of action cannot operate simultaneously. Once virtues are infused, the acquired cannot work. Angela McKay Knobel states that Aquinas is "unclear" on the relation.[69] On the question of whether grace transforms "our natural principles or simply exists alongside them," she notes that Aquinas "says virtually nothing." There is "more ambiguity" on this question "than many scholars claim."[70] She also explains why this debate matters by looking at three main ways that the two strands are related: redirected, coexistence, and absorption. If the infused virtues are nothing but acquired virtues "redirected" to a supernatural end, then the "magnitude of the rebirth brought about by salvation is diminished." If they exist side by side, then grace and nature are "compartmentalized." If the natural or acquired virtues are "absorbed," then grace "supplants" rather than "perfects" nature.[71] This debate matters because how it gets reconciled says a great deal about the relationship between human and divine agency, which is the fundamental question about how moral philosophy and theology relate to each other for learning and teaching ethics.

William Mattison acknowledges that nearly every Thomist interpreter agrees on these two points:

> It is possible for people to possess virtues, variously called by St. Thomas "acquired," "natural," "political," or "social" virtues, which enable one to act in a manner oriented toward and indeed constitutive

of natural human flourishing as one's last end. All participants also agree that through God's grace people are oriented toward supernatural happiness as their last end, and God gives graced virtues to enable action oriented toward that end.[72]

The differences arise at two points. First is whether the acquired virtues remain once the infused ones are operative. Mattison agrees with Lumbreras's interpretation of Aquinas: that someone who lost the infused virtues through mortal sin still gives evidence of having the acquired ones. Yet he interprets the implications differently. If the infused virtues are lost through mortal sin, then the apparent presence of the acquired virtues is misleading. They are not virtues but customs.[73] Second, the coexistence model results in a bifurcated agency. For Mattison, this will not do. Christians no longer possess the acquired virtues once virtues are infused, for two reasons. First, the "singularity of the last end" requires that the acquired virtues be transformed. Aquinas categorizes virtues in a threefold form based on the distinctions of the last end, cause, and object: "infused (supernatural) theological virtues, infused (supernatural) cardinal virtues, and acquired (natural) cardinal virtues."[74] Mattison denies that someone in the state of grace still possesses the third category because of the singularity of the last end: "If a person has one last end, and 'wills all whatsoever he wills' toward that one last end, then it is not possible on Aquinas's terms to possess a set of acquired cardinal virtues that are not willed toward one's last end."[75] The second reason is the "difference in formal objects" between infused and acquired,[76] where Aquinas argues that they do not belong to the same species because acquired virtues take up a "rule of human reason" and the infused that of "divine rule."[77] If they are of different species, then their coexistence would deny a single last end.

Jean Porter's and Mattison's positions are similar. She states that "it is impossible on [Aquinas's] view that the infused and acquired virtues can coexist in the same individual." Her position opposes "a well-established line of interpretation that goes back at least to Cajetan": that Christians can possess the third category of virtue that Mattison identified above.[78] The infused virtues are, Porter notes, "operative habits."[79] She asks why the cardinal virtues "are necessarily infused together with charity" and suggests that one possible interpretation would be that they work "harmoniously to lead us to our final end of union with God." It is not, however, Aquinas's view, because "habits must be proportioned to the end towards which they are oriented." The acquired virtues arise from "natural capacities" and cannot order us to "supernatural beatitude."[80] They have different rules of "right reason" and "divine law."[81] These arguments explain why Aquinas cannot affirm a coexistence model, so what is the relationship between them?

Porter affirms a twofold happiness without adopting the Cajetanian two-tiered interpretation. Each set of virtues, acquired and supernatural, is proportioned to its end.[82] The "infused cardinal virtues" and the "acquired virtues" are not "two distinct, coeval and potentially competing sets of virtues" but "two distinct ways of perfecting natural human faculties."[83] They are not two different "sets," but they are two different "ways." Porter is concerned to maintain the integrity of nature so that grace is neither reduced to it nor evacuates it, and reading the two sets of virtues as "distinct ways" serves to protect nature's integrity. It also preserves the novelty of grace. She writes, "The transformation brought about through charity is profound and complete. Someone who receives the grace of God is a new creation, and this implies new moral virtues as well as a new set of beliefs, hopes, and desires. We cannot fully appreciate the significance of Aquinas's moral theology unless we take this point into account."[84] The acquired virtues do not coexist in the graced person, but they would seem to remain as distinct ways of perfecting. The conclusion appears to be that ungraced persons exercise acquired virtues to attain the natural good. Graced persons exercise infused virtues to attain natural and supernatural goods. Yet her question to Aquinas as to the role for the infused moral virtues remains open. What role does charity play in attaining the natural good?

Knobel interprets Aquinas beginning with Aristotle's structure for virtue. Thus, her own position assumes that Aquinas has (1) a "fulfillment proportionate to our created human nature" and (2) "our created human nature provides us with the resources (albeit impeded by original sin) to pursue that fulfillment." This structure sets forth the "framework" that is then used for "supernatural virtue."[85] It requires a "second gift" of grace beyond creation that is given freely. One result is "that it is coherent to discuss the virtues that order man to the perfection of what he 'is' prior to the gift of saving grace."[86] This second gift can be understood as "strengthening" or "completing" the acquired virtues. Or the acquired virtues can be interpreted as "facilitating" the infused virtues, which is how Anscombe understood them.[87] Yet Knobel denies that this prior order is one of pure nature. The difference that Aquinas adds with "supernatural virtues" to the Aristotelian structure is "that we are far more dependent on divine help at every stage of the process."[88] This claim is crucial to show how the moral life, for Aquinas, requires conversion and not just the completion of what can be acquired naturally. The difference between Aristotle and Aquinas runs deep: "The Aristotelian ethic of acquired virtue is an ethic centered around the notions of self-perfection and self-sufficiency. An ethic of infused virtue is an ethic of humility and dependence."[89]

Knobel discusses more fully how this difference relates to the acquired virtues. Two main views are possible, and both have evidence in Aquinas's work. The first is the "unification view." Like Mattison's view, as noted above, it sees "natural principles" as "transformed by grace."[90] This view has three different versions based on where the change occurs—the agent, the form of the virtues, or the act accomplished. The first understands the agent as being transformed, such that the "same virtues" before their graced transformation change because the agent has changed and has been given a "new perspective."[91] A stronger account of transformation emphasizes that the "form" of the virtues themselves changes, as Mattison suggests.[92] A more cooperative view of unification is that both the acquired and infused virtues contribute "to a single act," which is how Knobel interprets Decosimo.[93] This view slightly differs from the coexistence view. The coexistence view interprets the "new principles given in the gift of grace" not as transforming or unifying but coexisting with natural principles. Both are sources for "two different kinds of virtuous action." It is this latter that she finds best represents Aquinas's position. She writes, "The best we can say is that Aquinas appears to lean toward the view that the Christian possesses and cultivates both infused and acquired moral virtues and that both are operative in distinct arenas of the Christian moral life."[94] The problem with this view is why, if there are two kinds of virtue from which one could act, would one not act from the infused all the time?[95]

In many ways, Knobel restates the difficulty in the relationship between the acquired and infused virtues that Maurice identified and finds it much more difficult to resolve than previous interpreters. She admonishes humility. The "habits of the theological virtues" are never perfectly present in wayfarers. Her own proposal is to understand "previously acquired habits" as inclinations rather than as virtues, post the "infusion of grace."[96] Maurice critiqued Aquinas and the Thomists for failing to hold together these two claims: (1) the acquired or moral virtues are true virtues and (2) all virtues, even those considered imperfect, have God as their source. The coexistence model affirms that the acquired ones are true virtues but has no substantive way of explaining God's role in their acquisition. The unification models deny acquired virtue in graced persons. They may still be virtues in the ungraced, but for the graced they are customs or inclinations.

The previous discussion looks to some of the best contemporary Thomist commentators to address the tension that Maurice recognized in the nineteenth century. Their interpretation is insightful but inconclusive. The relationship between the acquired and infused virtues is not easily unified, but this lack of completeness explains better the moral life than a system that tidies everything up. Perhaps Aquinas is trying to show us something that is not easily said. We strive to achieve what we cannot, and in that failure recognize that we often receive more than we deserve or have earned through our own resources. Aquinas goes to great lengths to set forth the acquired virtues in the *Prima secundae*, but when he explicates the content of the virtues in the *Secunda secundae*, much of that earlier discussion is ignored. The earlier discussion might best be interpreted as a ladder that leads us to what matters most: the theological virtues of faith, hope, and charity that now frame the discussion of the infused moral virtues of prudence, justice, fortitude, and temperance.[97] The "imperfect" virtues are not imperfect because they are the semblance of virtue but because, separate from the theological virtues infusing them with the ultimate end, they cannot come into their own. The infused virtues make the acquired virtues what they can and should be. In terms of agency, all virtue participates in the gift of divine agency. In terms of natures, they are human and divine without confusing the two. The relationship between the two sets of virtues is viewed under two different aspects. Viewed through the prism of human nature, they appear to be achievements. Viewed through the prism of divine grace, they are gifts. To see them in their unity requires a virtue of theological imagination, one that ignores a quasi-Nestorian dual agency on one hand and a quasi-Apollinarian loss of natures on the other hand. Like teaching or learning the doctrine of the Incarnation, setting forth human agency once God is affirmed is less solving a problem through the use of analytic skills, as important as they are, and more an aesthetic that seeks to inhabit a mystery.

That Maurice makes the theological virtues cardinal ones finds a resonance in Aquinas. In Aquinas's discussion of faith in the *Secunda secundae*, he asks if an angel or human creature had faith in their "original [i.e., pre-Fall] condition." If they were created in a "purely natural state," then faith would not be present, but he holds that no such state exists. Both angels and humans "were created with the gift of grace," and thus "there existed in them the beginnings of the beatitude which was hoped for and which, as was explained above,[98] begins in the will through hope and charity, and in the intellect through faith."[99] This remarkable passage seems to align Aquinas and Maurice: the theological virtues are endemic to creation. They are distorted in the Fall, but they must remain to some extent because the ultimate end initiates action. Aquinas states, "Faith is per se the first among all the virtues. For since, as was explained above,[100] the end is the principle in the case of things to be done, the theological virtues, whose object is the ultimate end, have to be prior to the other virtues."[101] The last end comes first in the intellect, by way of faith, and issues hope and charity in the will.

If faith is per se first among all virtues, it seems impossible for any virtue to be without it. The desire for an end, any end, brings forth action to achieve that end born out of faith. The end that we do not yet have is held by faith as its realization is sought. If the end is arduous, not easily seen or attained, faith must be accompanied by hope. As we saw in part I, Rawls, following Kant, used the term "faith" for his aspirational political ethics. He would, I think, according to Aquinas, be using it improperly or *secundum quid*. It is not yet ordered to its proper object. In this sense, the *matter* of faith would be lacking; but its *form* still points in the right direction. The faith, charity, and hope intrinsic to creaturely being makes possible the moral virtues, which can then remove material difficulties from practicing the theological virtues. In turn, these moral virtues become what they are intended to be: virtues that make possible life in the City of God. In the *Prima secundae*, Aquinas asks which virtues endure into the next life. An objection states that the moral virtues cannot endure because they are associated with the body.[102] Aquinas agrees that the dependence of moral virtues on a corruptible body cannot endure, but both the moral and intellectual virtues "do exist in the future life, but in a different mode," not in their material but in their formal mode, which is "determined by reason."[103] Faith and hope, however, do not. Faith is an imperfection, in that those who have it do not clearly see that in which they believe. Once a person attains beatitude, faith disappears.[104] Likewise, hope disappears, because that which is longed for has arrived.[105] Faith and hope serve as the source for the infused moral and intellectual virtues that transform wayfarers into heavenly citizens, but they are only for us while we are on the way to the city constituted by charity. As Paul teaches in 1 Corinthians 13:8, "Charity never passes away."[106] Infused moral virtues become more necessary for life in the City of God than the theological virtues of faith and hope. Yet these infused moral virtues cannot be had without the theological virtues. They geminate and develop the moral virtues so that they are appropriate for the City that is coming, that we long for, and that we acknowledge is not yet here.

The endurance of the virtues also assumes that they are gifts. Gifts and virtues, Aquinas states, have the same function. They perfect human agents "with respect to acting well." The difference between them is that gifts arise from an external source, the Holy Spirit, and virtues come from an internal source, reason. The gifts, like virtues, are habits that perfect persons to their proper ends. Yet God has also given fruits and beatitudes for perfection. They are not habits. Fruits are the acts that proceed from either reason or "a higher virtue, i.e., a virtue of the Holy Spirit." These fruits arise from seeds that then come to full fruition. Aquinas uses everyday imagery to explain the fruits. Someone watching a tree while its leaves are green hopes for its fruit. Once it begins to bear fruit, "a different hope" arises. He does not tell us if this hope differs by degree or kind, but it makes more sense to see it as degree. The fruit does not arise without the previous green leaves.

Aquinas's reflections on the relationships between gifts, fruits, beatitudes, and virtues, as well as his account of which of these endures, show us more than they say. The infused virtues are both the source of the seeds that dispose persons to their perfection and the means by which they can be perfected, and once perfect, only Charity and the form of the infused moral and intellectual virtues remain. A picture cannot capture such a dynamic agency. An infusing source gives dispositions and brings them to fruition. That Source, the Holy Spirit, perfects persons to be friends with God. To see it well is to look to Christ for our understanding of agency.

A CHRISTOLOGICAL AGENCY

Maurice criticizes the Scholastics for affirming acquired virtues without a theological grounding. Ethics trumps theology: God becomes unnecessary for the moral life. At his best, for Maurice, Aquinas avoided this, but Aquinas was misinterpreted by those who thought they could address his "ethical questions" without attending to "the subject which gives its title to the whole work," *theology*.[107] An emphasis on acquired virtues that requires no reference to God working them in us without us leads to atheism (or secularism). Aquinas was innocent of such an accusation, as long as his affirmation of Aristotle's virtues was placed within the theology that structured the *Summa*. Maurice did not explicitly note the importance of the *Tertia pars* and Aquinas's Christology for the virtues, but his emphasis on the Incarnation as the basis for a paradoxical agency fits well with Aquinas's own understanding. Without Christology, the two rules of human virtue, human and divine, can only stand in contradiction to each other. Either we affirm human virtue as virtue but deny its measure in God or we affirm that the "proper conditions" for virtue are only divine and thus deny that human virtue is virtue. Neither of these options works. The acquired virtues cannot stand alone without faith, charity, and hope; but neither can they be rejected, as if those outside Christianity lacked virtue. Maurice revised the virtue tradition by making the theological virtues cardinal to avoid these unpalatable options, and then he grounded them Christologically, both in creation and in redemption. He also shifted what we mean by redemption.

If the theological and infused virtues are only necessary to save individuals after death, then they have limited relevance. Charity's rule is relegated to the City that is coming and not to cities and nations that exist now. For Maurice, avoiding hell was not the purpose of salvation, nor of the virtues. Salvation results from God's desire to bring persons into communion, a communion that entails new forms of liberation and abolition—abolishing slavery, liberating women for education, drawing excluded persons into politics, and socializing economics. These ethical and political movements are not the Kingdom of God built by human hands; they always come as gifts. But they are places where the Kingdom's first fruits can be seen because they are embodiments of the righteousness and charity that define the Trinity, and its practical manifestation in the Incarnation, who forms the basis for creation and redemption. God is not an absolute power over creatures who must be obeyed or else; God seeks to infuse us with the charity that the Trinity is. This infusion permits participation in the divine life that calls into question the sufficiency of creaturely powers. In a sense, the power to act is always "external." There is no secure interiority that suffices to achieve the good.[108]

Maurice was preoccupied with the relationship between divine and human agency. In 1841, he writes that "I have been thinking much about the will these last two days, and how much the power of God is to be realized in it, how much a constant recollection of the words 'I believe in the Holy Ghost,' is the energy we want to enable us to resolve and to act."[109] Notice how the power of the Holy Ghost becomes the "energy" that enables human agency. God works directly on the human will via the Holy Spirit, but God does so to enable the human will to act. Maurice's concern with the relationship between divine and human agency led to doctrinal criticisms of Calvinism and Islam and found its practical application in worship, especially baptism and the Eucharist.

Rightly or wrongly, Maurice accuses Islam and Calvinism of a "fatalism," in which the divine will becomes so absolute that it opposes rather than establishes the human will. He finds this teaching not in the early Calvinists but in the Synod of Dort, where "the Calvinists began to set up the idea of the Absoluteness of the Divine Will against the idea of a will in man."[110] If God becomes conceived as absolute power, then it skews both divine and human agency. An emphasis on divine sovereignty at the expense of Triune Charity exacerbates this distortion. He writes, "The notion of a sovereign Necessity has taken the place of a Will of absolute truth and goodness; the notion of a capricious Power to be made placable by some agency of ours has superseded the belief in a Father, whose will Christ came on earth to manifest and to fulfil."[111] Maurice found that the proper relationship between divine and human agency had been distorted, in different ways, from William of Ockham (1285/7–1347) through Augustus Comte (1798–1857). The former obliterated the human for the sake of the divine. The latter obliterated the divine for the sake of the human. The central question was how to account for setting "what is human" in "what is divine" by being attentive to these two questions: "How are we to avoid sinking the divine in the human? How are we to avoid the crushing of the human under the divine?"[112] The answer is found in the Incarnation as the ground of our ethical agency. Humanity and divinity act as one without the loss of either. One acting subject acts non-competitively in two natures.

Our agency is not Christ's. We are not hypostatically united to God, such that we are a single subject acting in both divine and human natures. Yet Jesus invites us to be his friends and shares his life so that we can participate in the unity of his action. Baptism initiates us into this unified agency.[113] In opposition to Comte, who argued that his new religion of humanity should replace the "infantine worship" of Christianity, Maurice defends the Christian Eucharist as making "it possible to have communication with a Will such as I have been speaking of—one which is good, and is seeking to make us all like itself, . . . and so that we may become reasonable members of a Society—in the real sense of the word, fellow-creatures." Such a worship must "emphatically" be a "Eucharist, a thanksgiving for a transcendent gift making all common things look beautiful and amazing, giving a divine character to the earth which they trod, to the food which they ate."[114] Only Christ makes possible free acts.[115] But Christ's agency does not compete with ours; it makes our free acts *our* free acts.

For Maurice, moral theology takes the infusing of the virtues of faith, hope, and love as its beginning, middle, and end. Faith, he writes, "is the act of going out of self, the act of entering into union with another from whom all our graces are to be derived."[116] Placing faith in another is the essential practice for his ecstatic agency. It is the way to charity, just as charity is the way to faith: "A Being who shows that he cares for me, and in whom all love dwells, proposes himself to me as an object of my trust; I trust him, and so enter into a knowledge and participation of his love."[117] A participation in love will demonstrate itself in works. Scripture relates faith and works, in what could appear to be a contradiction. Paul teaches that faith with works cannot save, and James says that faith without works cannot. The contradiction arises only when faith "is contemplated simply as a property in ourselves." If it is, then it is an individual possession that will not achieve its end, the generation of "a kingdom of righteousness, peace, and joy, because a kingdom grounded upon fellowship with a righteous and perfect Being, the notion that that righteousness can ever belong to any man in himself, and the notion that everyone is not to exhibit the fruits of it in himself would seem to be equally contradictions."[118] Faith is not in us any more than hope and charity are. We are in them.

Because faith is a participation in a "righteous and perfect Being" outside us, it leads to hope. The society of righteousness, peace, and joy we seek cannot be brought about unless we are taken beyond ourselves in faith; but this very act infuses hope. Our failures to produce such a society do not have the last word. The very fact that we strive for such a society, and are restless when it does not materialize, assumes the hope present in a perfectionist ethics. The "imperfect hope of the philosopher," he boldly states, depends upon this "idea of a perfect Being united to man, inspiring him with prayer, and hearing his prayers." Lose it, and the imperfect hope will soon die as well.[119] Otherwise, all that remains is that false hope of an always-receding horizon of expectation, "like the end of the rainbow of the boy who is in chase of it."[120]

Without hope, creaturely being is unsustainable, but its sustenance cannot be based on illusory hope. It eventually loses its luster. The ethics in the Epistles to Saint John offer an alternative: "The blessedness which is to be, has a ground in the blessedness that is. *Now are we the sons of God,* is the revelation of that ground. That is the true glory of man, the glory which Christ has vindicated for him by taking his nature."[121] Here we return to something like Irenaeus's claim that the glory of God is the human person fully alive. For Maurice, this is hope: that someday we will rise as true human beings.[122] Becoming truly human, or fully alive, requires love. It is the "law of the universe" that beckons us to itself. Because it is such a law, our natural, creaturely being finds its place in the world by submitting to it. Charity is not a work of "supererogation"; it arises when we cease resisting. Love abides in letting oneself go in order to become what one was always intended to be. Worship is an act of hope, an expectation that the divine reign will come to Earth as it is in heaven. It perfects because it is "union with God":

> To the perfection of love it is necessary that it should be both in the lover and in the object beloved. St. John tells us that *herein,* i.e., in this union of ourselves with God *is our love,* [more strictly, the love that is *with us,*] *perfected.* This is the completest idea of love, the only complete idea we can have. And he shows, at the same time that it is the only practical idea of love; that no other will stand the great test of all.[123]

Paul is correct that love is greater than faith, because if this love did not exist, faith would have no object in which it could place hope.[124]

Maurice was on to something when he refused to divide Aquinas's ethics from his theology. The infusing of virtue is a work of the Holy Spirit effected by Jesus, who makes creatures friends with God, which is how Aquinas defines the virtue of charity. The first *sed contra* in his treatise on charity cites Jesus's words at John 15:15, "Now I will no longer call you servants, but my friends."[125] A second cites Romans 5:5: "The charity of God is poured forth into our hearts by the Holy Spirit, who is given to us."[126] These two passages set the context for understanding the infusing of virtue. Aquinas returns to the role of Jesus and the Holy Spirit in the concluding question to the treatise on charity and the gift of Wisdom. He refers to the Holy Spirit as giving us a "likeness" to the Son, who is "Wisdom begotten."[127] The Spirit, through the infused virtue of charity, its attendant gift of Wisdom and the beatitude of peace, makes us like the Son. This is how we become friends with God. The rule of reason, Wisdom, has become the divine rule.

Because Jesus is one person, fully human and divine, friendship with him is complicated. It might seem as though such a friendship would not fit with any natural understanding of it. Although the two passages cited above frame the context for understanding the virtue of charity as friendship, Aquinas begins his discussion with three possible objections from Aristotle, which he then answers. First, friendship requires "living together" (*convivere*), and that would be impossible between creatures with a "sensible and bodily nature" and God. Yet Aquinas argues that such converse is possible, even in this life "*secundum mentem*" (according to mind). It will be incomplete for creatures *in via* but complete when we see God face-to-face. Second, friendship requires the possibility of reciprocity or mutual return, but charity as friendship entails love of enemies, and no such return should be expected from them. The mutuality that Aristotle sets forth, Aquinas states, includes not just friendship with a reciprocating friend but also all those whom the friend befriends. Because God loves all creatures, the friendship of charity extends to enemies. Charity is not sentimental or easy; it is demanding. Finally, Aristotle's friendships of pleasure, utility, and nobility appear to differ from friendship as charity. Aquinas places charity as friendship within nobility because God is the virtuous other with whom we share friendship, and even though the enemies we love may be less than noble, we love them "on account of God."

Aquinas goes to great lengths to show how charity as friendship fits within Aristotle's understanding. This is surprising because Aristotle's friendship is natural and needs no divine infusion. Why would charity as friendship require infusing rather than acquiring virtue? Aquinas's answer is consistent: "Charity's act exceeds the nature of the will's power" because its object is friendship with God, and such friendship cannot be attained by our natural sources.[128]

Nonetheless, the infused virtue of charity cannot displace our natural sources, so it makes sense to understand charity as arising from both external and internal sources at the same time, which calls into question any firm division between them. The rule of wisdom in Aristotle's prudence is the Wisdom that the Spirit forms in us. Aquinas addresses this when he disagrees with Lombard that charity is the Holy Spirit. If it were the Holy Spirit working in us and not a created virtue, then "the human mind" would only be moved and not be "the principle of this motion." Likewise, the will's act would be neither voluntary nor meritorious if it played no role. Thus, Aquinas states, "Rather, it is necessary that the will be moved by the Holy Spirit toward loving in this way—that the will itself also bring about this act [of loving]" (*Sed oportet quod sic voluntas moveatur a spiritu sancto ad diligendum quod etiam ipsa sit efficiens hunc actum*). The movement matters here. The Spirit moves the will toward loving so that the will is enabled to act toward the object of love, who will be God and all creatures related to God. An object elicits love, such that it also enables the one loving to act. The will brings about this act because of a "habitual form" given to it by God. Without this form "superadded," the will would not be able to exercise charity as friendship.

The infusion of charity does not occur as if it were some kind of quantity that fills up an empty space or overpowers that space with an alien force, removing what was there. It is not natural but intensifies what is natural. Because of its twofold aspect, as both moved by the Spirit and self-moved, the concept of a person infused by charity is difficult to set forth in words.

Aquinas's teaching on the virtues reflects, on one hand, Aristotle's teaching that "a natural effect does not transcend its cause" and, on the other hand, Augustine's teaching that all virtues require infusion because "charity itself surpasses the power of nature"[129] Charity can be both natural and infused. A kind of charity is found in the sharing of natural goods. Dionysius teaches as much, and Aquinas does not disagree. He states, "Dionysius is speaking of the love of God (*de dilectione Dei*) that is founded upon a sharing of natural goods, and so is in us naturally. But charity (*caritas*) is founded upon a certain supernatural sharing. So there is no similar reasoning [about the two]."[130] Aquinas reiterates this claim: "But charity and nature do not belong to the same genus. And so there is no similar reasoning [about the two]."[131] The reader should take note that here Aquinas denies any "similar reasoning" between natural and infused love. He also uses different terms for them, and this difference matters.

Aquinas explained diverse kinds of love in his treatise on the passions in the *Prima secundae*.[132] He states, "There are four names that in one way or another point to the same thing (*ad idem quodammodo pertinentia*): 'love' (*amor*), 'elective love' (*dilectio*), 'charity' (*caritas*), and 'friendship' (*amicitia*)." They are differentiated as follows: *amicitia* is a "habit," *amor* and *dilectio* are an "act or passion." *Caritas* can be either a habit or an act or passion. *Amor* is "common" to all the terms. "For love is common to the three of them, since every act of elective love or act of charity is an act of love, but not vice versa." Here Aquinas seems to be arguing that an act of charity can be understood as an act of love, but that not every act of love, such as loving wine or horses, is an act of charity. He clarifies this, somewhat, in the *Secunda secundae*, where he associates the virtue of charity with friendship with God. Despite this clarification, the use of these terms remains confusing, because he claims in the *Prima secundae* that they "belong to the same thing," but in the *Secunda secundae* that they are differentiated by their object, and that any "similar reasoning" between them is denied.

Robert Miner recognizes that the four terms for love are not "interchangeable." *Dilectio* has a lesser role than *amor* and *caritas* because it requires a judgment from the immanent sources of human reason. *Dilectio* adds "a preceding choice, *electio*" and is only "in rational nature." *Dilectio* and *amor* (including *caritas*) have different directionalities. *Dilectio* moves from the deliberation of human reason to its object. *Amor* is drawn by the object. The result of this different directionality helps make sense of the difference between natural and infused love. Miner puts it well: "The power of God to draw creatures to himself by sensible means exceeds the power of human reason."[133] Aquinas returns to this conviction when he explains why God can be loved but not known without mediation. He differentiates between the completion of a cognitive power, in which "the thing known is in the knower," and the completion of an appetitive power, in which "the appetite is inclined to the thing itself." Cognitive powers begin with sense and move outward toward what is more remote. Appetitive powers have a different movement. Love as "an act of the appetitive power, tends first to God, even in the wayfaring state, and from God is drawn to other things." Aquinas explains this succinctly in a reply: "While knowledge begins from creatures and tends toward God, love begins from God as from an ultimate end and is drawn toward creatures."[134]

What, then, happens to *dilectio* that moves from creaturely reason to its object? In his response to this question, Aquinas discusses whether we should love God above ourselves.[135] He distinguishes the "twofold good" creatures "can receive from God": the "good of nature" and the "good of grace." The first makes possible "natural love" (*amor naturalis*). This natural love includes, within "integral" nature, that we "love God above all things, more than one's self and also any creature in its own way." Natural love expresses itself in loving God (*diligent Deum*). Once again, it is found in the sharing of natural goods and the "inclination" to set the common good above one's private goods. It is present in "political virtues, according to which citizens sometimes sustain losses to their property and persons for the common good."

Aquinas identifies how natural love is present through a political and economic ethic through sharing natural goods. Despite telling us that there is no "similar reasoning" between natural and infused love, he then analogizes from "natural love" to the "friendship of charity" (*amicitia caritatis*). He states, "Much more is this verified in the friendship of charity, which is founded on a sharing of the gifts of grace. And so out of charity a man should love God, who is the common good of everything, more than himself, since blessedness is in God as in the common and original principle of everything that is able to participate in blessedness."[136] Aquinas offers other analogies from nature to depict the infusing of virtue, such as "light flowing in" (*influere*),[137] the growth of the human body,[138] and fire.[139]

Aquinas's teaching on the relation between natural love and infused charity is often unconvincing. Perhaps it is so because he is trying to show us something difficult to put into finite words. On one hand, he tells us that not every act of love has this peculiar character of requiring a superadded form. For instance, "love of wine or horses" does not need to be infused. On the other hand, the peculiar character of charity as friendship requires receiving and acting upon an infused habitual form. This charity exceeds our natural powers because, as Aquinas has already put it, it involves loving God and loving all things in God, including our enemies. Creatures cannot accomplish this act without "a certain participation in divine charity" that "brings about an infinite act as it joins the soul to God."[140] Charity as friendship requires a communication of the infinite and finite without losing either. Lombard, Aquinas feared, lost the finite because it was replaced with the infinite Spirit. Aristotle, of course, lacked the infinite. Yet Aristotle's finite friendship fits within the Augustinian/Lombardian view, so that charity as friendship is an act of an internal principle, an operative habit, infused in creatures by an external source. The boundary for human agency is always permeable.

How can the finite and infinite work cooperatively and finite human creatures still be free? A fuller answer to this question is found in the *Tertia pars*, where Aquinas turns his attention to who Jesus is and what he has done. Seldom do discussions of the infused virtues look to them as the culmination of his teaching on infusing virtue, but Aquinas returns to the subject there, and I suggest that his teaching on the virtues makes little sense without attention to Christ's person and work. It runs through the background of all Aquinas's ethics, proving Maurice's point that those who seek to extract an ethics from Aquinas without the theology will miss the whole point of the *Summa Theologiae*.

Aquinas gives an explanation on the commanding of love by Jesus in his question on the "precepts of charity" that points to the role law, grace, Christ, and the Spirit play in the infused virtues. He begins with an obvious objection that charity cannot be commanded. Charity infused by the Spirit makes us free; obligation appears to "oppose freedom."[141] His response is that the infusing of charity does not happen without a person's "free decision," but it can be commanded.[142] For Aquinas, two external sources for virtue are law and grace. He reminds us of this in the *sed contra* to the question of whether the order of charity should fall under a precept: "Whatever God brings about in us by grace, he teaches us by the precepts of the law, according to Jeremiah 31: 'I will give my law in their hearts.'"[143] Grace and the law, including precepts, do not oppose freedom but enable it. Only for someone who keeps the precepts "out of fear" would it appear to stand in opposition to freedom. The very fact that love can be commanded, that it is a precept, presumes that it "cannot be fulfilled except by one's own will."[144] Aquinas does not argue that a command brings with it its own fulfillment. Nor is fulfillment an all-or-nothing affair. It is fulfilled in degrees, incompletely *in via* and perfectly *in patria*.[145] The precepts are found in the Old Testament and are summarized by Jesus: "And he said to him, 'You shall love the Lord your God with all your heart, and with all your soul, and with all your mind. This is the great and first commandment. And a second is like it, You shall love your neighbor as yourself.' On these two commandments depend all the law and the prophets" (Matt. 22:37–40).

What renders Aquinas's seemingly confusing and inconsistent account of the infused and natural virtues coherent is the Christological locus for the infused virtues. Aquinas's teaching on the virtues, like Maurice's, finds its culmination in an agency that participates in divinity because of Christ's work. His prologue to the *Tertia pars* brings together Christ, the creature's ultimate end, and the virtues and vices. He stated,

Forasmuch as our Saviour the Lord Jesus Christ in order to save His people from their sins (Matt i. 21), as the angel announced, showed unto us in His own Person the way of truth (*viam veritatis nobis in seipso demonstravit*), whereby we may attain to the bliss of eternal life (*ad beatitudinem immortalis*) by rising again, it is necessary, in order to complete the last end of human life, and the virtues and vices, there should follow the consideration of the Saviour of all, and of the benefits bestowed by Him on the human race.[146]

Aquinas's first question addresses the "fitness" of the Incarnation. God is perfect goodness without being found in human flesh. Human flesh adds nothing to God, so it seems that taking on human flesh is neither fitting nor necessary. What makes the Incarnation fitting is the fact that "what belongs to the essence of goodness befits God."[147] Goodness, as Dionysius teaches, communicates itself. As perfect goodness, then, it is fitting for God to communicate the divine goodness to others. There is, in this sense, no necessity to it; it is pure gift. The Incarnation and moral science are linked right away in Aquinas's discussion.

Aquinas then explains how the Incarnation was, and was not, necessary for salvation. It is not necessary to an end in the sense that *"sine quo aliquid esse not potest"* (without it, something would not be able to be). His example would be food for the conservation of life. The Incarnation is not necessary in that sense. In other words, God was not bound out of some kind of necessity to become incarnate and direct human creatures to their ultimate end, charity as friendship. It is necessary, however, *"per quod melius et convenientius pervenitur ad finem"* (by which the end is attained better and more fittingly). His example is the use of a horse for a journey. One could make the journey and arrive at the end in other ways, but the horse makes possible a "better and more fitting" way to take the journey and arrive at the end.

The Incarnation is necessary in this sense because it leads to the "furtherance of good." It does so, Aquinas states, through the theological virtues. First, with respect to faith, it furthers the human journey to its ultimate end because in Jesus, God's own speech makes faith more certain. Second, it does so with respect to hope; by God's speech, it is *"maxime erigitur"* (greatly strengthened). Third, it does so with respect to charity, which is *"maxime excitatur"* (greatly excited). He adds two more reasons: fourth, *"quantum ad rectam operationem"* (with respect to right or proper operations/actions); and fifty, *"quantum ad plenam particpationem divinitatis"* (with respect to the full participation in divinity). Here Aquinas's teaching on the virtues is completed by relating it to Christ, who is both an example in his humanity of how one should act and a source for that action through his communicable human participation in divinity. Created human agency, itself a gift from another, finds its proper ordering to its ultimate end by participating in that which exceeds without displacing created human agency. Robert Miner puts this well: "I would hazard that Thomas's deepest intention in the *ST* is to produce a rational ecstasy, an elevation of the reason beyond its connatural apprehension that does not destroy its rational character, but perfects it."[148]

If we teach the virtues without attention to theology, we can easily lose this ecstatic agency and the giftedness of the moral life. Rowan Williams claims that the language of Christology "holds together a set of intractably complex questions in a way that offers a coherent context for human language." Central to these questions is that of human agency. How is it that human agents can be the source of their actions, when "every limited finite state of affairs" has God as its source?[149] In Christ, we see perfect humanity and divinity in one acting subject, a single *esse*, revealing that the glory of God is, as Irenaeus taught us, reflecting on Mount Tabor, "a human being fully alive." Our agency is not evacuated when infused with virtues; it is actuated. It comes into its own—*suorum actuum dominus*. Christology is the theological basis for finite and infinite cooperative action that acknowledges our ability to act comes as a gift. As Williams puts it, "The supernatural is not something inserted into the natural and breaking its integrity; it is never 'cut off from its natural base.' Its distinctiveness is not in some sort of 'territorial' difference from finite acts and substances, but is simply to do with the degree to which the unconditioned is allowed to transform the finite from within."[150] Creation and redemption find their home in the divine gift that is the Incarnation and the Trinity: "For Christ to live in the believer is for the believer to be caught up into the self-abandoning love both of the Son for the Father and of God for creation. In both creation and incarnation, God has elected to live within the created order without ceasing to be what God eternally is."[151]

Both acquired and infused virtues are created acts, as is everything that is not God. Thus, we should not separate and divide them decisively. In neither case does God force virtue upon us. The infused virtues are only "infused" by the Holy Spirit via human consent. They do not stand over and against human freedom. Likewise, the acquired virtues are, like everything in creation, gifts. And both are "according to human nature." Can there be virtue without faith, hope, and charity for people *in via*? In part I, I sided with Terry Eagleton against Peter Geach on hope. Eagleton questioned if someone's hope to be sustained with the necessities of everyday life could only be rendered intelligible by the Christian Gospel. Surely one would be hard pressed to defend such a truncated view of hope. Hope does not define one thing, of course. We hope for our daily needs to be met. We hope for peace. We hope for the reign of God to come to Earth as it is in heaven. We project the term toward diverse objects without assuming it can only be used univocally. If no family resemblances exist with the use of the term, we would require different senses of the term "hope" each time it is projected in a new context. The same would be the case for faith and charity. These terms are with us; they are used in everyday language in diverse ways. No one has exclusive possession over them or can limit who gets to use them to make sense of the desires and fears humans share. Sometimes they are projected in ways that are contradictory. When faith and charity become enacted through the execution of heretics, as Aquinas taught and Rawls rightly recoiled against, the use of the terms undoes what they otherwise should do. Likewise, the terms even if known in their particulars through Christian teaching can be projected into other contexts which in turn show Christians something about them that they were missing.

In a powerful essay on the life and death of the Jewish thinker Etty Hillesum who died at Auschwitz and left us her profound diaries, William McDonough claims that her life and thought reveal that "no human being has actually lived a life of acquired virtue only." Instead, "all actual virtue in the world may be infused virtue."[152] He seeks not to baptize her postmortem, or to "sentimentalize" the horrors that she endured but asks what gave her calm resolve to love and find delight amid such horror. God is there all along, "infusing the lives of people without respect to religion (or the lack of it)."[153] It is basic to everyone who finds themselves receiving life over and over again.

If virtues are primarily gifts received from others, then less attention will be given to the immanent powers as conditions for virtue and more to the relational bonds that make virtue possible. The focus will be less on achievement and more on reception. Reception is not mere passivity; it requires action. However, the action turns us away from ourselves to something that exists beyond us. It assumes an ecstatic agency, not a self-constituted one. If we think of ethics less as a theoretical puzzle to be solved and more of a mystery to be inhabited, it issues in an exciting summons to display in practice what can only be hinted at in theory. This returns us to Maurice's important statement to his sister in 1832 that set him on his quest to dig for the Wisdom in moral and metaphysical philosophy: "How strongly have I been convinced lately that we spend half our time in thinking of faith, hope and love, instead of in believing, hoping, and loving! How utterly we forget that the very meaning of the words implies that we should forget ourselves and themselves (the acts I mean) in the objects to which they refer."[154]

Infusing virtue should be a practice of receiving and giving gifts. It offers no precise science of ethics. Nor will teaching it ensure that everyone lives life well. Like all contingent, fragile human realities, teaching and learning it can go horribly awry and used to establish ourselves, our people, our Church, and our faith, especially as a power unleashed to dominate others rather than as a source of communion.

NOTES

1. Maurice, *Moral and Metaphysical Philosophy: Volume 1*, 139.
2. Maurice, *Life*, vol. 2, 166.

3. Maurice, 414.

4. Maurice, *Moral and Metaphysical Philosophy: Volume 1*, 416.

5. Maurice, *Theological Essays*, 22–24.

6. Maurice, *Life*, vol. 2, 416.

7. Maurice, *Life*, vol. 1, 349.

8. Maurice, *Kingdom of Christ*, 85.

9. Maurice, *Epistles of St. John*, 3–5.

10. Maurice, 5.

11. Maurice, 174.

12. Maurice, 14.

13. Maurice, 66–67.

14. Aquinas, *Summa Theologiae* (hereafter *ST*), I–II, 1.1.

15. *ST*, I–II, 109.2.

16. Maurice, *Moral and Metaphysical Philosophy: Volume 1*, 616.

17. Maurice, 606.

18. Maurice, 616.

19. Maurice, 621–22.

20. Maurice, 622.

21. Maurice, 620.

22. Maurice, 621.

23. Maurice, 623.

24. Maurice, 626.

25. Maurice.

26. *ST*, I.II, 65.2.

27. Feingold, *Natural Desire*, 128, 135.

28. Long, *Natura Pura*, 211.

29. Long, 199.

30. Long, 44.

31. Long, 28–32.

32. Long, 61.

33. Balthasar, *Theology*, 283.

34. Some seventy years before Long's criticism, Balthasar's book on Barth was denied publication by ecclesial censors for the same reason. After its publication, Engelbert Gutwenger, SJ, reviewed it in 1953 and stated that Balthasar was misled by Barth to deny the sufficiency of nature for ethical matters. He cited the exact same passage that Long did. Gutwenger, "Natur."

35. *ST*, I–II, 55.4. Aquinas does not refer to the definition as Augustine's in *ST*, I–II, 55, but as the "customary definition."

36. Jordan, "Theology," 237.

37. Kent, "Augustine's *On the Good of Marriage*," 117.

38. *ST*, I–II, 55.4.

39. Miner, "Infused Virtue," 414.

40. Austin, *Aquinas*, 60–61.

41. *ST*, I–II, 55.4 ad 6.

42. *ST*, I.II, 63.4; Decosimo, *Ethics*, 103.

43. Decosimo, *Ethics*, 255.

44. Herdt, *Putting on Virtue*, 2.

45. Herdt, 347.

46. Herdt, 347–48.

47. Hauerwas and Pinches, *Christians*, 27.

48. Augustine, *Confessions*, IV, 9; Hauerwas and Pinches, *Christians*, 187n11.

49. Hauerwas and Pinches, *Christians*, 69.

50. Hauerwas's essay "The Good Life" takes for its exemplar James Rebank's life as a shepherd. It draws on a concrete, material practice that has at most indirect theological implications. In that sense, I do not see why his emphasis on the Christological and ecclesial rejects outsider virtue or differs significantly from Decosimo, who gives the following reason why Aquinas claims that everyone needs the cardinal virtues: "We all must do something about our appetites for food, sex and so on, and our anger and fear. Everyone has to live with and relate to others. And everyone has to consider what ends to pursue and how to go about pursuing them. These are, respectively, the matters of moderation, courage, justice and prudence"; Decosimo, *Ethics*, 162. Yes, but can they be had without God as if in a state of pure nature? For Decosimo, Aquinas's perfectionist ethics works with a transcendent good that results in "a capacious and generous recognition of pagan virtue." He does this "on the basis of an irreducibly theological ethics" because seeking that transcendent good is also seeking Christ; Decosimo, 4, 41. How does this not restate Hauerwas's "Good Life"?

51. Herdt's concern to contest Augustinian passivity and its emphases on virtue as what God does in us without us led some to find in her a reduction of the infused to the acquired. Herdt has been interpreted as assuming "divine/human cooperation in achieving perfect virtue," and this leads to an overemphasis on acquired virtue. She denies such an interpretation: "I do not think, then, that there is any real danger that my insistence that our own active participation is necessarily involved in our arriving at our final good spells the reduction of infused to acquired virtue.... That God brings us to our ultimate good *through our own agency* does not render us any less utterly dependent on God." She admonishes theologians not to be "overly confident" in their ability to distinguish acquired from infused virtue; Herdt, "Redeeming," 735.

52. Kent, "Moral Provincialism," 271.

53. Kent, 276. Kent's criticism was written before MacIntyre's *Ethics in the Conflicts of Modernity*, so it did not consider that work. She primarily draws on MacIntyre, *Whose Justice?*

54. Hauerwas and Pinches, *Christians*, 63.

55. Hauerwas and Pinches, 68.

56. Hauerwas, *Fully Alive*, 83n5.

57. MacIntyre, *Whose Justice?*, 157–58, 163.

58. *ST*, II1–IIae, 23 to 44.

59. MacIntyre, *Whose Justice?*, 205.

60. MacIntyre, "Irrelevance," xi.

61. MacIntyre, 56.

62. *ST*, I–II, 65.2 resp.

63. *ST*, I.II, 65.2.

64. *ST*, I.II, 65.3.

65. Lumbreras begins his interpretation with a threefold division of virtue followed by nine succinct claims concerning their relations. He first distinguishes real and apparent virtue. The latter is not ordered to the good, so it has little significance. Real virtue can be further divided between perfect and imperfect. Perfect virtue attains the natural or supernatural

good and connects the virtues together. He further divides perfect virtue between "philosophical" and "theological." Philosophical perfect virtue achieves "good acts within the limits of the natural order" and theological perfect virtue attains the good of the supernatural order. The connections between the moral and theological virtues depend on whether they are perfect or imperfect. Imperfect moral virtues lack connection; perfect moral virtues are connected through prudence. Their connection to the theological virtues likewise depends on their status as perfect or imperfect. "True natural imperfect virtues" are "without charity" and charity without them because charity is not given by nature. For instance, baptized infants have charity but do not have habituated natural virtues. Natural virtues without charity can be perfect without any connection to the theological virtues "philosophically speaking." He admits that this is a contested position. He bases his interpretation on the fact that for Aquinas acquired virtue remains after an act of mortal sin, but charity does not; see *ST*, II–II, 24.12. Thus, moral virtue can exist without charity. The acquired virtues are political or social and are connected by prudence. Infused moral virtues, however, cannot be without charity. The perfected moral virtues are connected by infused prudence and charity; both give them their form. Charity is also the form of faith and hope, but they can exist without it. Without charity, faith is still "infallibly" ordered to the true and hope to the good. To say otherwise was anathematized at the Council of Trent. Yet for a wayfarer, charity is "impossible" without faith and hope. See Lumbreras, "Notes," 220–40.
66. Lumbreras, "Notes," 240.
67. Austin, "Spirituality," 208–9.
68. Porter, "Moral Virtues," 41.
69. Knobel, *Aquinas*, 1–2.
70. Knobel, 83–84.
71. Knobel, "Elevated Virtue?" 25.
72. Mattison, "Aquinas," 3.
73. He states, "I claim that a person may possess a disposition to consistent action, even quite stable such action, which is nonetheless not a habit properly understood, and therefore not a virtue"; Mattison, 5.
74. Mattison, "Can Christians Possess?" 560, 563.
75. Mattison, 565.
76. *ST*, I–II, 63.4.
77. Mattison, "Can Christians Possess?" 565.
78. Bowlin's, Decosimo's, and Herdt's defenses of acquired virtues might appear to stand in that established line, although they do not explicitly say so, and there is much in their discussion that complicates such an interpretation. In 2008, before the explicit discussion of the relationship between the acquired and the infused by Porter, "Moral Virtues," Herdt expressed concern that Porter's insistence on the integrity of nature and "assertion of the mysteriousness" of the "virtues infused by grace" led to the "danger . . . that the natural virtues take over, since at least we can talk about these"; Herdt, *Putting on Virtue*, 96. Porter's later work addresses this danger.
79. Porter, "Moral Virtues," 43.
80. Porter, 45, 49.
81. Porter, 51.
82. Porter.
83. Porter, 63.

84. Porter, 66.

85. Knobel, *Aquinas*, 8.

86. Knobel, 17.

87. Knobel, 84.

88. Knobel, 48.

89. Knobel, 178.

90. Knobel, 83.

91. Knobel, 129.

92. Knobel, 134.

93. Knobel, 141.

94. Knobel, 105.

95. Knobel, 106.

96. Knobel, 166.

97. I owe this suggestion to conversations with Robert Miner.

98. I.e., at q. 4, a. 7.

99. *ST*, II–II, 5.1.

100. *ST*, 1–2, q. 13, a. 5, and q. 57, a. 4.

101. *ST*, II–II, 4.7.

102. *ST*, I–II, 67.1, obj. 3.

103. *ST*, I.II, 67.1 ad 2.

104. *ST*, I–II, 67.3.

105. *ST*, I–II, 67.4.

106. *ST*, I–II, 67.6.

107. Maurice, *Moral and Metaphysical Philosophy: Volume 1*, 620.

108. Maurice could be wrongly interpreted as embodying the Augustinian passivity that Jennifer Herdt attributes to Martin Luther that was noted in the previous section. Maurice affirms Luther's teaching that the divine will acts "directly upon" the creature and interprets favorably Luther's attack on Aristotle's ethics as a "necessary prelude to the war with the Pope"; Maurice, *Moral and Metaphysical Philosophy: Volume 2*, 114. The problem with Aristotle's ethics, however, was not with the acquired virtues; it was when it became coupled with penitential practices that correlated the work of virtue with avoiding punishment. Luther "denounced the Aristotelian moralists because he desired to assert the essential dependence of moral *doing* upon moral *being*" and Tetzel's penitential practices reversed this. Moral being depended on doing because the acquisition of virtue served the end of avoiding punishment rather than overcoming evil; Maurice, 121. Maurice affirmed Luther "without assenting to [his] sweeping condemnation either of the Greek sage or of the Mediaeval sages, who had, we conceive an honour of their own which we are bound to render them, though he did not and could not"; Maurice, 114. Moreover, the Peasants' war showed the limits to Luther's theology. "They cried out for a *social* revolution" and he was unable to offer it; Maurice, 120. Maurice's ecstatic agency fits better Herdt's understanding of it in the Bildung tradition: "We are not so much achieving ourselves as receiving ourselves from one another, and insofar as we grant that consummation can only be eschatological and hence beyond our ability to secure. It is in mutual recognition of one another in all of our socially embedded particularity, and in the shared life, the friendship, that this recognition makes possible, that we become more fully human. We are in one another's hands"; Herdt, *Forming Humanity*, 251.

109. Maurice, *Life*, vol. 1, 324.

110. Maurice, *Kingdom of Christ*, 122.

111. Maurice, *Theological Essays*, 287.

112. Maurice, *Moral and Metaphysical Philosophy: Volume 2*, 3.

113. Maurice, *Kingdom of Christ*, 337.

114. Maurice, *Social Morality*, 405–7.

115. Maurice, *Theological Essays*, 75–76.

116. Maurice, *Kingdom of Christ*, 90.

117. Maurice, 91.

118. Maurice, 299.

119. Maurice, 51.

120. Maurice, *Epistles of St. John*, 178.

121. Maurice, 179.

122. Maurice, 181.

123. Maurice, 242–43.

124. Maurice, 257.

125. *ST*, II–II, 23.1.

126. *ST*, II–II, 24.2. Translations of the questions on charity come from Miner, *Questions*.

127. *ST*, II–II, 45.6, rep. obj. 2.

128. *ST*, II–II, 32.2 resp.

129. *ST*, II–II, 24.1 resp.

130. *ST*, II–II, 24.2, rep obj. 1.

131. *ST*, II–II, 24.3, rep obj. 2.

132. *ST*, I–II, 26.

133. Miner, *Thomas Aquinas*, 95, 120.

134. *ST*, II–II, 27.4 resp and rep obj. 2.

135. *ST*, II–II, 26.3.

136. *ST*, II–II, 26.3 resp.

137. *ST*, II–II, 24.5, rep obj. 2.

138. *ST*, II–II, 24.9 resp.

139. *ST*, II–II, 24.10 sc. One of his more troubling is the order of charity found in nature that involves loving God, parents, neighbors, and self. It bears a resemblance to Augustine's patriarchal tranquility of order. Aquinas's order of charity includes loving fathers more than mothers. Both "are loved as a certain principle of natural origin," but the father has a "more excellent aspect than the mother" because the father is "the principle in the mode of an agent" and the mother "in the mode of a patient and matter." In this case, nature putatively known in precision from grace went wildly astray. This putatively natural order of charity is not confined to creatures *in via* but will remain *in patria* because "nature is not destroyed by glory, but perfected" and the order of charity is from "nature"; *ST*, II–II, 26.10, 13 sc and resp. Of course, Aquinas did not know the biology of reproduction as we do because of advances of modern science. His patriarchal order depends on a faulty understanding of nature that infused charity could have but did not challenge. While Aquinas moves from the natural order of charity to a graced order within a patriarchal view of relationships, he rejects any movement from a natural peace present among pagans to the beatitude of peace associated with infused charity. Peace is the beatitude associated with the gift of wisdom present in infused charity. His first objection to peace as a "proper effect of charity" is that "pagans sometimes have peace." Rather than invoking the principle that grace perfects nature and affirm the pagans, Aquinas denies that

pagans, who lack grace, can have "true peace." They have "only apparent peace"; *ST*, II–II, 29.3, rep obj. 1. The different kind rather than degree of the virtues of a graced and natural charity lead to the inability to affirm the beatitude of peace present among those outside the Christian faith.

140. *ST*, II–II, 23, rep. objs. 1, 3.
141. *ST*, II–II, 44.1, obj. 2.
142. *ST*, II–II, 24.10, rep. obj. 3.
143. *ST*, II–II, 44.8.
144. *ST*, II–II, 44.1, rep. obj. 2.
145. *ST*, II–II, 44.6.
146. *ST*, III, pro; English Dominicans.
147. *ST*, III.1 resp.
148. Miner, *Thomas Aquinas*, 136.
149. Williams, *Christ*, xi–xii.
150. Williams, 226–27.
151. Williams, 107.
152. McDonough, "Etty Hillesum's Learning," 193.
153. McDonough, 194.
154. Maurice, *Life*, vol. 1, 139.

7

RETRIEVING THOMAS AQUINAS'S MORAL SCIENCE WITH CAUTION

Thomas Aquinas's treatise on faith begins with nine questions that display well how faith connects people with God and one another. Unfortunately, it then takes a negative turn, focusing on unbelief and asking if nonbelievers can have political power. Some of Aquinas's worst teaching is present within this discussion on faith, including that the Church does not err when it "disposes of Jews' belongings,"[1] when it executes heretics,[2] and when it punishes apostates and blasphemers. The theological virtues of faith and charity become the basis for domination. If salvation is fleeing damnation understood as eternal punishment, then there is a logic, albeit a twisted one, that executing heretics serves the common good more than executing counterfeiters.[3] These teachings should be abandoned, and it was remarkable progress when they were. They are an illiberal politics that cannot provide an ethics for people to live together in pluralist societies in solidarity or communion. That they were supposedly consistent with infusing virtue should be a reminder that how even what is good can be twisted to serve wicked ends.

F. D. Maurice represents a significant achievement in theology. Salvation is not fleeing punishment. The threat of damnation or the reward of heaven is not the basis for ethics. Discerning the Wisdom by which a good and charitable God creates and redeems, participating in this wisdom and extending it through the means appropriate to it, becomes the task of moral philosophy and theology. Not believing in the wrong god can be the first act of faith; a god who requires the sacrifices of those who disbelieve is a god not worthy of our reasonable desires. We have come to see that it is irrational to execute heretics and that is a progressive achievement worth sustaining. Any retrieval of Aquinas ought to take cognizance of the errors that an illiberal politics can generate. Retrieving infusing virtue in learning and teaching ethics does not provide an error-proof method that cannot go astray. No such method is available.

Aquinas died in 1274 and was canonized in 1324. His work was appreciated in the subsequent centuries but became used in the latter part of the nineteenth century to combat philosophical shifts in the modern era. Aquinas, of course, knew nothing of these shifts, but his work became the basis for the "Oath against Modernism," which was promulgated by Pius X in 1910 and was not revoked until shortly after Vatican II by Paul VI in 1967. Vatican II retrieved a different Aquinas who was something other than a philosophical bulwark against the perceived threats to faith and authority raised by modernity. Maurice hoped for a day when "it will be possible to derive more good from Aquinas than any age has owed to him, because we are free from his trammels." Vatican II delivered on this hope. This version of Thomism was and is always available to us, but not when he is primarily used as a bludgeon against perceived modern threats.

The perceived threats were, surprisingly, not that philosophers from the modern era elevated human rationality to a promethean dominance, an all-too-common but mistaken criticism of modernity; the perceived threats were that modern philosophers diminished what human reason, in its speculative and practical roles, could achieve, especially in metaphysics and morals. The First Vatican Council in 1870, under the papacy of Pius IX, emphasized the role of "natural reason" in knowing God. The dogmatic constitution *Dei filius* stated that God "may be known for certain by the natural light of human reason by means of created things."[4] Any who rejected this were to be anathematized. The oddness, and importance, of this claim should be acknowledged. The council affirmed what natural, human reason could achieve on its own and then drew on magisterial authority to damn anyone who disagreed. As Maurice noted in his defense of Jewish emancipation, if a "declaration" grounded in authority supports a conviction, the confidence placed in the conviction is questioned. Those who hold the conviction lack faith. In that sense, Vatican II was much more confident in its convictions because it made no declaration of damnation to any who disagreed.

REACTIONARY THOMISM

Less than a decade after the First Vatican Council in 1879, Leo XIII issued the encyclical *Aeterni patris*, or "On the Restoration of Christian Philosophy," that used Aquinas to oppose what he considered to be "false conclusions" from modern philosophy. He stated that "false conclusions concerning divine and human things, which originated in the schools of philosophy, have now crept into all the orders of the State, and have been accepted by the common consent of the masses." He spent little time explaining these false conclusions, but one of them was that the Church was not an authority in philosophical matters, in matters of reason, or in political and moral philosophy. The Church, he stated, is the "common and supreme teacher of all peoples," and its role is "to teach religion and contend forever against its errors." These include forms of philosophy that relegate the Church's authority to matters of faith alone. Leo XIII called upon everyone to retrieve and restore philosophy, especially that of Thomas Aquinas, to its proper place. Philosophy, as Augustine taught, "generates," "nourishes," and "defends" faith. Citing *Dei filius*, Leo XIII affirms philosophy's ability to demonstrate that God exists as one way it generates faith, "for the greatness of the beauty and of the creature the Creator of them may be seen so as to be known thereby." Philosophy "nourishes" and "defends" faith, but obviously not all philosophy does this, for Leo XIII is writing against modern philosophy's errors. A retrieval of Aquinas is necessary to counter these modern errors, and it will include a retrieval of "Greek philosophy." Leo XIII juxtaposes the riches of Scholastic philosophy against the "novel system of philosophy" that emerged from the sixteenth century, when philosophers began to philosophize without attention to faith. He concludes with an exhortation: "We exhort you, venerable brethren, in all earnestness to restore the golden wisdom of St. Thomas, and to spread it far and wide for the defense and beauty of the Catholic faith, for the good of society, and for the advantage of all the sciences." Aquinas became central for teaching and learning a countermodern metaphysics and moral philosophy.

Pius X took the next step in using Thomism against modernity by initiating an "oath against modernism" that placed all religious under obedience to the retrieval of the role of natural reason to generate, nourish, and defend faith. Religious were required, by the power of magisterial authority, to vow:

> I . . . firmly embrace and accept each and every definition that has been set forth and declared by the unerring teaching authority of the Church, especially those principal truths which are directly opposed to the errors of this day. And first of all, I profess that God, the origin and end of all things, can be known with certainty by the natural light of reason from the created world (see Rom. 1:19), that is, from the visible works of creation, as a cause from its effects, and that, therefore, his existence can also be demonstrated.

Fergus Kerr notes the tension between the claims for reason and authority that this oath generated.[5] The hierarchical authority of magisterial declarations promulgates natural reason.

In 1914 Pius X decreed twenty-four theses that set forth Aquinas's basic teaching and required that they be affirmed by Catholic religious to combat modernism. The first thesis drew on Aristotle's distinction between act and potency and stated, "Potency and act are a complete division of being. Hence, whatever is must be either pure act or a unit composed of potency and act as its primary and intrinsic principles."[6] In the Thomist tradition, potency gets divided between active potency (the "capacity to bring about an effect") and passive potency (the "capacity to be affected"). Passive potencies are then further divided based on a distinction between natural and supernatural or obediential passive potencies. Natural passive potencies are actualized by creaturely agents with their "natural capacities." Supernatural or obediential passive potencies require something more than natural capacities; they require the elevation of the human person by grace normally acquired in baptism and brought about by divine agency.[7]

The countermodern use of Aquinas had its benefits. Modern philosophy, of course, is not without error. I have defended Anscombe's criticisms in "Modern Moral Philosophy." To identify and correct errors is one aspect of what philosophers and theologians do. In that sense, this use of Aquinas brings with it much that is illuminating. Catholicism consistently upholds the "grandeur of reason." Retrieving Aquinas against Ayer's logical positivism gave new life to moral philosophy among persons of faith like Anscombe and even an atheist like her friend Philippa Foot.[8] Alasdair MacIntyre gets faulted or credited with a reactionary traditionalism for working within this tradition, but that neglects his "politics of resistance," as is shown below. He teaches us how to discern errors in modernity without abandoning its strengths. He does not affirm tradition qua tradition, but facile criticisms of it as if everything, including our agency, was made *modo*—"just now." He writes, "the conception of tradition is so little at home in modern culture—and when it does seem to appear, it is usually in the bastardized form given it by modern conservatism—that they find it difficult to come to terms with Aquinas's metaphysical theology."[9]

The kind of modern conservatism that affirms tradition with insufficient attention to Aquinas's metaphysical theology would be found in the work of Edmund Burke, to whom postliberal philosophers often point. In contrast, for MacIntyre, Aquinas's metaphysics is found in the "ultimate unity of the good" that provides politics with a "singleness of purpose." It contrasts with Rawls's political liberalism, which eschews such a unity; he was convinced that it would lead to oppression.[10] If practical reasoning assumes an account of desire that requires the wise person to ask if their desires are worthy of their life, then Rawls could only give a nonpublic version of practical reasoning that would make it nonpolitical. However, antiliberal philosophers and theologians who appropriate Aquinas as an important ally and affirm a conservative view of tradition warrant Rawls's concern. The reactionary reading is present and has made something of a return, co-opting any disease with modernity by failing to distinguish its genuine advances from its distortions.

Anscombe titled her criticism of Henry Sidgwick "Modern Moral Philosophy," and one possible interpretation of her work is that she set ancient ethics, particularly Aristotle and Aquinas, against the moderns, finding the latter thoroughly corrupt and the former the antidote. Anscombe was no Aquinas sycophant. Mary Geach stated that she did little "expounding" him and was wary to cite him because of the positive and negative reactions to him rather than his philosophy.[11] Nor did she seek an uncritical retrieval of Aristotle. She once wrote, "We are now in a position to read Aristotle critically and at the same time with sympathy—without either servility or hostility."[12] The same could be said of her reading of Aquinas. What she retrieved was not a loyalty to Aquinas per se but to his theory of human action and to the practical knowledge and practical reasoning that modern moral philosophy neglected or misunderstood. This brought her into conflict with Sidgwick's theory. Aquinas's theory, dependent as it is on the infused virtues, holds forth promise for an alternative to Sidgwick's, but there are dangers in retrieving Aquinas, as if everything post-Descartes was a fall from an original purity.

Faulting modern ethics for restricting its domain; privileging right over good; emphasizing theory, method, or procedure; neglecting practical reasoning and virtue; and shifting the questions ethics ask could lead, and has led, to a reactionary traditionalism. Take, for instance, Sanford's *Before Virtue*. My work and his share common criticisms. He also sides with Anscombe and Aristotle against modern moral philosophy. Aristotle's ethics opposes modern moral philosophy because he asks these questions: "What is a human being? What is the end of human life?"[13] But he rejects contemporary proponents of virtue because they lack a key element that he finds essential to Anscombe, that of "moral absolutes."[14] He pits virtue categorically against liberalism, and thus finds the democratic theory in Rawls objectionable. Rawls's contractualism distributes "goods" by political "institutions" rather than by "nature," "God," or "members of society." It is unclear how "members of society" significantly differ from "institutions" in Rawls's thought, but we do not find a careful assessment of Rawls's work. It is also unclear what it would mean to leave the distribution of goods up to nature or God; but Sanford seems convinced that only such a distribution permits a natural telos whereby the human person can be perfected. What opposes this natural telos is known without hesitation. No analysis of its patriarchal origins is undertaken. The focus of the virtues then becomes achieving this natural telos by subscribing to absolute prohibitions against abortion, contraception, homosexual acts, and divorce.[15] For Sanford, nothing good seems to have come from these practices; nor were reasons for their adoption in modernity addressed. Surprisingly, these absolute prohibitions appear disconnected from specific virtues that would render the actions opposing or affirming them intentional. The prohibitions seem to be divinely instituted and the virtues result from the commands not to transgress them, rather than the commands being rendered intelligible by the virtues.

Sanford's affirmation of ethics before virtue's eclipse—that is, before all things modern or liberal—leads him to be highly critical of Rosalind Hursthouse's neo-Aristotelian account of virtue. He acknowledges that her Aristotelianism is "neo" for both negative and positive reasons. The negative reason is because Aristotle is, as Hursthouse states, "just plain wrong on slaves and women." The positive reason is that his list of virtues excludes ones that most types of virtue ethics now affirm, such as "charity or benevolence."[16] Sanford criticizes her negative reason. He wants to know precisely why she finds his teachings on slavery and gender wrong, and he asks,

> Does she mean she disagrees with Aristotle's view in the *Politics* that slaves are capable of virtue, or his view in the *Nicomachean Ethics* that a free person can be a friend of a slave insofar as a slave is a human being? Should we presume that she means that she disagrees with Aristotle's claim that there is such a thing as natural slavery insofar as it allows for treating as tools those who are fit for self-rule? Are we to think contrary to Aristotle, that friendship between a wife and her husband is not possible? Aristotle's views on slavery and women are multifaceted and yet they are treated by Hursthouse as one-dimensional.[17]

Sanford then admits that one might "disagree wholeheartedly" with Aristotle's biology that women are "incomplete men," but not that men are hairier and women smaller.

These questions betray a tone-deafness to Hursthouse's criticisms of Aristotle that highlights one of the serious problems with antiliberal (or postliberal) defenses of the virtues. Sanford does not pause and denounce slavery or recognize the advances brought about by progressive movements like abolition. I assume that he would, and of course anyone who does is in some sense a "liberal," but he appears to find Aristotle's take on friendship between masters and slaves and men and women sufficient to challenge Hursthouse's liberalism, and then he launches this criticism: "The sort of qualification Hursthouse most likely means to imply is that she disagrees with Aristotle's views on slaves and women *insofar* as his views conflict with what Hursthouse would characterize as her ethical outlook, an outlook that is, one gathers from her judgments on particular points of ethical dispute, identifiable with a version of liberalism."[18] To these points, Hursthouse might rightly acclaim, "Yes, of course." The version of liberalism that rejects the morality of master–slave relations and patriarchal male–female relations is an advance in ethics that calls into question one of the ways antimodern virtue ethics goes horribly awry through a reactionary traditionalism. Any retrieval of Aquinas that is inattentive to the progress that modernity has made through abolitionism and against patriarchy should be abandoned.

Patrick Deneen and Adrian Vermeule likewise draw on Aristotle and Aquinas to counter modernity, especially what they label "liberalism." Deneen understands it as "three basic revolutions of thought, redefining liberty as the liberation of humans from established authority, emancipation from arbitrary culture and tradition, and the expansion of human power and dominion over nature through advancing scientific discovery and economic prosperity." The result of these revolutions is the "loosening of social bonds in nearly every aspect of life."[19] Liberalism's "two foundational beliefs," states Deneen, are first its "anthropological individualism and the voluntarist conception of choice" and second "human separation from and opposition to nature." The two are related through autonomy. Through "the unfettered and autonomous choice of individuals," moderns will to master and then overcome the limits of their nature, especially their biology but also the natural foundations of political society, jurisprudence, and morality.[20] This agent knows no limits to its willfulness. It consumes economic resources, sexual partners, and every traditional bond in service to its false view of freedom.

Early Christianity as well as the abolitionist tradition could certainly be understood as liberating us from "established authority" and opposing "arbitrary culture and tradition." It is unclear that modernity has a monopoly on, to my mind, such worthwhile aims, but when Deneen discusses economics, he has something to offer. His criticisms could be read in a way similar to Marx's critique that under capitalism "all that is solid melts into air." Marx and Marxists also critique what passes for "liberty" in modern, capitalist societies. Like the criticism of politics as consent found in the work of Mulhall, Deneen rejects what he identifies as "one of liberalism's most damaging fictions: . . . an imaginary scenario in which autonomous, rational calculators formed an abstract contract to establish a government whose sole purpose was to 'secure rights.'"[21] He rightly acknowledges that politics should aim for more than a negative version of liberty. It should be ordered to what is good. A crucial difference, however, is how "nature" functions for Deneen and how it can be known with certainty that can order ethics and politics without attention to infusing virtue. Liberalism is a war against nature that Aristotle and Aquinas remedy. For Aristotle, human creatures "have a *telos*, a fixed end, given by nature and unalterable." Liberalism refuses to acknowledge this fixed end in politics, marriage, and culture.

For Deneen, retrieving Aristotle and Aquinas is an attempt "to educate man about how best to live within those [natural] limits through the practice of virtues, to achieve a condition of human flourishing."[22] As an example, he points to liberalism's attempted "emancipation from [women's] biology." By freeing them from "the household," it has placed them, along with men, "into a far more encompassing bondage." Men and women are fated to work for "'corporate' America."[23] He looks to cultivating local communities—to Rod Dreher's "Benedict Option," Wendell Berry's farming practices, and Shannon Hayes's "Radical Homemakers"—as the best that might be done to resist the corrosive effects of liberalism. His criticism that modernity wrongly emancipates women from their biology is as tone-deaf to significant moral advances in modernity as is Sanford, but his constructive position has something to be said for it. Eugene McCarraher's affirmation of a Christian Socialism that affirms local cooperatives might look similar, but Deneen does not raise the question of socialism.

While Deneen is critical of the liberal state, its role in educating the citizenry in the proper limits that nature sets forth is unclear. Take, for instance, this claim:

> And while "progressive" liberals declaim the expansive state as the ultimate protector of individual liberty, they insist that it must be limited when it comes to enforcement of "manners and morals," preferring the open marketplace of individual "buyers and sellers," especially in matters of sexual practice and infinitely fluid sexual identity, the definition of family, and individual choices over ending one's life.[24]

This statement could be read in several ways. One suggests that progressive liberals are wrong in their support for the state's expansion to protect liberty and should seek a more limited state altogether. A second suggests that progressives should be consistent and seek the state's protection also in "manners and morals." A third is that the liberal state's role is to protect manners and morals, but the liberal state is incapable of it. Thus, we need a different understanding of the state that has the authority to regulate economics and manners and morals. I do not know which interpretation he would affirm, if any; but this third one fits well with his affirmation of Adrian Vermeule's "common good constitutionalism," which, as Deneen states, "charts a new and better path . . . grounded in the classical tradition but repurposed for the revitalization of a declining but redeemable republic."[25]

Similar to the arguments in this work, Vermeule affirms happiness or human flourishing as the common good to which constitutionalism and the state should be ordered. Dissimilarly, he rejects that it requires any relation to a supernatural end. He quotes Walter Farrell, OP, on the natural law as that which concerns not a supernatural happiness but a "natural or temporal" one, and he cites Steven A. Long on the common good. He concludes that he "must limit his account to the secondary ends of the political community, to temporal felicity" and that "nothing" in his account "depends" on "ultimate ends."[26] Nature suffices. It bears no relation to infused virtues.

Vermeule's common good constitutionalism draws on Aquinas to explain his alternative to originalism and living constitutionalism, both of which reject the natural law.[27] He states, "In the classical tradition, law is seen as—in Aquinas's definition—an ordinance of reason for the common good, promulgated by a public authority who has charge of the community."[28] Vermeule understands progressivism as a tradition with an "account of human flourishing" that is different from common good constitutionalism. He defines progressivism as "liberating individuals from the unchosen bonds of tradition, family, religion, economic circumstances, and even biology," and he judges it to be a "wildly implausible account."[29] One example of its implausibility is found in Justice Kennedy's "notorious passage" in *Planned Parenthood v. Casey*: "At the heart of liberty is the right to define one's own concept of existence, of meaning, of the universe, and of the mystery of human life. Beliefs about these matters could not define the attributes of personhood were they formed under compulsion of the State." Vermeule then states that this "should be not only rejected but stamped as abominable, beyond the realm of the acceptable forever after."[30]

Kennedy's "notorious passage" is troubling. Theologically and morally, existence, meaning, the universe, and the mystery of human life are not matters for individual definition. If they were, then each person could determine such matters for themselves and there would be no way of making evaluative appraisals. The work of the famous quartet—Anscombe, Foot, Midgley, and Murdoch—called this approach to teaching and learning ethics into question.[31] Perhaps I am not alone in dissuading students from thinking that their individual definition of such matters is adequate as a normative conviction, and in fact I would go so far as to say it is corrupting, if that is what *Planned Parenthood v. Casey* teaches. What comes after the quotation that Vermeule cites makes it more complicated: "These considerations begin our analysis of the woman's interest in terminating her pregnancy but cannot end it, for this reason: though the abortion decision may originate within the zone of conscience and belief, it is more than a philosophic exercise. Abortion is a unique act. It is an act fraught with consequences for others."

The decision here depends upon the autonomous right to *define* these matters for oneself but not to act upon them. It acknowledges that their definition is a "philosophic exercise," but the act itself cannot have the same autonomous right because it is "fraught with consequences for others." The decision makes clear that it affirms the right to define without suggesting that once it is so defined, one can then act upon that definition and have those consequences exculpated based on autonomous choice. But should we deny the legal right to make such definitions? Should those who offer unpalatable definitions be denied the right to their definition? Is it the role of the executive authority to protect the common good by denying this right? Vermeule seems to say yes. Unlike Rawls, he is willing to ally the coercive forces of the state with the right definitions of existence, meaning, universe, and the mystery of human life, which are known from nature alone.

The US Constitution, says Vermeule, has developed into a "powerful presidency" and a "powerful bureaucracy," and it "will be seen not as an enemy, but as the strong hand of legitimate rule." Examples of legitimate rule include the denial of any autonomous right to refuse vaccination and of businesses to disenfranchise unions or guilds, and the promotion of the "traditional multigenerational family."[32] The executive authority has the duty, and should have the authority and power, to promote the common, *natural* good in each of these cases. He advocates for a "police power framework," in which the federal government has the duty and authority to regulate the common good for the purpose of "justice, peace, and abundance" and their "modern corollaries."[33] Common good constitutionalism should provide "latitude" for "public authorities" to "promote these ends" This is a perfectionist, strongly Aristotelian, image of a political ethic. Key is "respect for legitimate authority" and "legitimate hierarchy." Citing Aquinas's question on the usefulness of human law,[34] he understands the purpose of law "to promote good rule" that "can encourage those subject to the law to form desires, habits, and beliefs that better track and promote communal well-being."[35]

One of the most troubling aspects of Vermeule's perfectionist political ethic is that he logically connects Catholic social thought, American constitutional law, and Carl Schmitt's state of exception. For him, the Catholic principle of subsidiarity fits Schmitt's state of exception, which gives the executive power to intervene against other agencies with their regulations and laws for the sake of the common good. He explains how these come together by beginning with Isabella's "exclamation" in Shakespeare's *Measure for Measure*:

> O, it is excellent
> To have a giant's strength, but it is tyrannous
> To use it like a giant.

The giant's strength is the "state of exception." Drawing upon the Catholic principle of subsidiarity, he acknowledges that the normal functioning of political society occurs when "subsidiarity institutions" perform their functions well and promote the common good. When they fail, however, the principle of subsidiarity "requires extraordinary intervention by the highest level of public authority in the juridical order, for the purpose of helping those subsidiary institutions function correctly in an overall scheme that conduces to the common good."[36] The congruence between this Catholic social teaching and the emergence of the "powerful presidency" and a "powerful bureaucracy" in the US Constitution constitutes the conditions for common good constitutionalism. He does not hesitate, citing Messner, to refer to this as a possible "dictatorship," "where the will to moral responsibility in a society shrinks. . . . In such cases, even dictatorship may be compatible with the principle of subsidiarity."[37] Knowing that this will raise eyebrows, he then seeks to reassure his readers: "This sounds alarming, of course, but we should understand that Messner with his massive classical erudition is certainly best understood as speaking not at all of the modern strongman or junta, but rather within the tradition of the carefully cabined Roman model of dictatorship."[38] Here is an example of countermodern Thomism adhering to a sufficiency-of-nature thesis founded upon a perfectionist political ethics that should raise considerable hesitations about its retrieval. What is more than ironic is that given the sufficiency of nature thesis, these rightist postliberals interpret Aquinas through a strong Aristotelian insistence on nature's sufficiency that looks quite similar to the modern liberal agent that they otherwise despise. It is a secular subject. There is little to no infusing of virtue in their political ethic—little charity, faith, or hope. Biological nature does most of the work. What matters most is properly engaging sex for the sake of good order.

MACINTYRE'S POLITICS OF RESISTANCE: CHALLENGING MODERNITY WITHIN

The difficulty with postliberals is not only that they ignore infusing virtue, although I think that matters, but that they also trade on reasonable critiques of modernity and liberalism and convert them to an authoritarian politics that would inevitably lead to domination. The intriguing intervention in ethics by Anscombe, MacIntyre, and others, with its retrieval of virtue, is put to use for an antiliberal or postliberal ethics and politics. Dreher's "Benedict Option" took MacIntyre's work in a direction that led Dreher to look to Hungary's prime minister, Viktor Orbán, for a postliberal politics. MacIntyre rejected this use of his work.[39] Yet his use of traditioned-based rationality and his conversion to Catholicism led many to dismiss him as a conservative if not a reactionary.[40] Jeffrey Stout draws on Okin's delineation of two kinds of tradition in MacIntyre's work to identify one possible source of reactionary traditionalism. On one hand, tradition is an ongoing historical debate about what constitutes the good life for human persons. Tradition emphasizes history, social context, desire, and rational deliberation. On the other hand, tradition is institutions, as defined by authoritative texts and interpreters. It requires "deferential submission" to authority.[41] If a tradition-dependent rationality requires the latter, it can lend itself to the kind of reactionary politics that has authoritarian leanings that was outlined in the previous section. Yet Kelvin Knight, Paul Blackledge, and Jason Hannan offer a very different interpretation of MacIntyre.

MacIntyre was a member of the Communist Party and the Church of England throughout the late 1940s and early 1950s.[42] He became disenchanted with the proletariat—the perceived revolutionary subject of capitalism. Marxism wrongly assumed that economic crises would give rise to it and downplayed the way capitalism "fragmented workers" rather than bringing them into solidarity.[43] Knight finds the criticisms of MacIntyre as a conservative to be based on a faulty syllogism that equates giving any account of tradition with being a conservative.[44] The place for tradition in the work of MacIntyre is not some authoritative elite who demand submission but the opposite. He looks to MacIntyre's early Marxism and his criticism of Leninism as a revolutionary elite that instructs the working classes because their practices were insufficient without their guidance.[45] Neither was Anscombe's considerable influence on him reactionary. Knight states, "MacIntyre shares Anscombe's conviction that our ends should be determined by reason, not custom, and that our institutional order now provides us with no ethically compelling reasons for action."[46]

Anscombe found Oxford moral philosophy too conventional, and thus incapable of challenging societal customs. MacIntyre, like Anscombe, is not setting forth an ethics that asks persons to obey tradition because it is tradition, Aquinas because he is Aquinas, Aristotle because he is Aristotle. They are looking for reasons for ethical action, which the market state no longer provides, for reasons that recognize the inextricable relationship between reason and desire. Blackledge disagrees with Knight's interpretation of Lenin but agrees with his reading of MacIntyre.[47] He also affirms Anscombe for her critique of consequentialism: "The idea that our unmediated desires can act as a basis for the good life is fundamentally problematic."[48] MacIntyre looks to tradition for a philosophy of revolutionary desire that mediates it historically without "Stalinist determinism" or any version of "mechanical Marxism" that resists ethics such as Althusser's. He seeks those places where historical practices resist the domination of an ethics of unmediated desire.[49]

Hannan argues that the dismissal of MacIntyre as a reactionary did not prepare us for the relationship between liberal democracy and the reactionary politics found in Trumpism. He states, "They labeled [MacIntyre] a reactionary. They reasserted their faith in liberal democracy. There is no crisis, they assured us. All is well. Yet here we are in the Upside Down, with Donald Trump in the White House. . . . MacIntyre was right all along."[50] Hannan finds MacIntyre setting forth a deliberative democracy in which "communication" and rational deliberation allow the pursuit of something other than power or "shared traditions and values." The former defines liberal democracy because it "locates political legitimacy in numbers." The latter defines Republican democracy. Chantal Mouffe's agonistic pluralism eschews rational deliberation altogether. MacIntyre avoids the "false universalism" of Rawls and Jürgen Habermas and the "antirationalism" of Mouffe.[51]

MacIntyre's *Ethics in the Conflicts of Modernity* offers a politics of resistance, an ethics of freedom grounded in rational desire. Unlike many antiliberals or postliberals, he does not reject modernity or seek to return to an era before virtue, as if that were something other than nostalgia born out of a politics of grievance. MacIntyre seeks a better way "after virtue" that refuses to dismiss gains in modernity. The "history of modernity," he notes, consists of liberation from various forms of oppression along with artistic and scientific achievements that show "genuine and admirable progress," albeit with new forms of inequality.[52] His criticisms come consciously from within modernity. He writes, "It is only from a Thomistic Aristotelian perspective that we are able to characterize adequately some key features of the social order of advanced modernity and that Thomistic Aristotelianism, when informed by Marx's insights, is able to provide us with the resources for constructing a contemporary politics and ethics, one that enables and requires us to act against modernity from within modernity."[53] Inequality drives MacIntyre's ethics of resistance. Politics and ethics should serve the ends of human flourishing that answer the question of a good life. A good human life is characterized by "good health," freedom "from destitution," "good family relationships," "sufficient education," "productive and rewarding work," friendships, leisure, and "learn[ing] from one's mistakes."[54] For MacIntyre, asking "What is a good life?" and offering substantive answers is a basic feature of teaching and learning ethics. It does not inevitably lead to a reactionary politics or the fact of oppression.

Perhaps MacIntyre's 2016 work answers Peter Dula's insightful criticism of his work. Dula pits Cavell against MacIntyre.[55] For Dula, MacIntyre elides Cavell's distinction between "must" and "ought." A must is a necessary rule for going on as one would find in a game. An "ought" is a claim for how one should go on that requires acknowledgment from another. It does not close down conversation but risks it. For Cavell, the moral life does not function like rules in a game, but with criteria. MacIntyre's practices, Dula states, are "musts" that sought to silence the conversation because of his "confidence that he knows all there is to know about us."[56] Cavell acknowledges that we never know the other, or ourselves, with this level of confidence. If practical reasoning seeks to overcome the proper skepticism attendant on the contingency of human interaction, it can only do so by shutting down what is necessary for morality, ongoing communication. Such closure inclines toward authoritarianism, denying the possibility of self-determining agents, what Aquinas referred to as "*suorum actuum dominus.*"[57] The "carefully cabined Roman dictator" knows best. Yet MacIntyre points to our desires and how they are and are not satisfied in ways that make his work closer to Cavell's "oughts" than "musts." There is an openness to his philosophy that avoids the kind of authoritarian closure that rightly worries Dula.

MacIntyre, like Mulhall, argues that perfectionism opens philosophy to theology. He concludes *Ethics in the Conflicts of Modernity* with this: "So there is presupposed some further good, an object of desire beyond all particular and finite goods, a good toward which desire tends insofar as it remains unsatisfied by even the most desirable of finite goods, as in good lives, it does. But here the enquiries of politics and ethics end. Here natural theology begins."[58]

Ethics is the rational ordering of desire to good ends, but those finite ends always require yet another rational ordering of desire because they lack completion. The movement of desire, suggests MacIntyre, leads to theology, but natural theology. Why natural? This reflects his sharp philosophy/theology distinction. Natural theology could be secular, another name for Aristotle's metaphysics, or it could be Catholic. It is a minimal theological perfection.[59]

Rational desire's dissatisfaction with finite objects points in the direction of a more substantive theological perfection with attention to the infused virtues. Maurice's ecstatic agency fits it well. A similar account of agency has been with MacIntyre throughout his work, albeit theologically undeveloped, and it brings his Marxism and Thomism together. In a 1960 essay, "Freedom and Revolution," he stated that individuals who seek "most to live as individuals" become the most dependent on others, while an individual who recognizes their "dependence on others has taken a path which can lead to an authentic dependence."[60] No one can reasonably satisfy their desires and needs without the assistance of others. Infusing virtue assumes such assistance. Natural, acquired virtues without the infused misdescribe the moral life, overlooking too much that should be obvious.

Stanley Hauerwas critiques MacIntyre for his sharp philosophy/theology distinction and draws on Aquinas's virtue of charity to challenge it. He writes, "At the very least, Aquinas's emphasis on charity as the form of the virtues, which admittedly makes the status of the moral virtues ambiguous, would seem to make a strong distinction between philosophy and theology problematic. Charity is not just the form of the virtues; it is the transformation of our knowledge of the way things are." Hauerwas once asked MacIntyre about the infused virtues and why they did not have more of a place in his work. MacIntyre told him that he "tries not to think about them."[61] Maurice thought moral philosophy could not be done well, or perhaps at all, without making them central. He did so with a sympathetic critique of Aquinas that avoided any reactionary use that set his work against modernity, but he also gave us means to critique modernity while affirming what is good about it. He offered the beginning of a Christian Socialism informed by Aristotle, Aquinas, and Saint Paul—one that awaits completion.

MAURICE'S CHRISTIAN SOCIALISM

Like MacIntyre, Gary Dorrien criticizes elements of Marx and Marxism while appreciating its "creative and sophisticated tradition of anticapitalist criticism."[62] He critiques Marxism's proletarian subject, any economic determinism, its "catastrophic mentality," and the "denigration" of morality.[63] That Marx offers a morality, as Blackledge and Knight affirm, does not take away from Dorrien's important insight that democratic socialism arose in Britain well before Marx had much influence on it. The Christian Socialism originated by Maurice—which was taken up by Kingsley, Ludlow, and then Headlam—offered a more democratic socialism than some of that which emerged from Marxism. It lacked the sense of economic determinism and catastrophe that affirmed violence, and it holds a place for morality. It also offered a political theology before Carl Schmitt and his state of exception found in the work of Vermeule and many others. For Dorrien, Maurice was at the heart of this tradition.

Sidgwick's ethics distanced it not only from theology but also from socialism. His ethics serves well the emerging dominance of capitalist economics. He is often critical of "orthodox political economy," which would be a kind of laissez-faire approach without any governmental regulations, but the regulations on markets that he sets forth are little more than what Adam Smith advocated. Sidgwick assisted in the marginalist revolution in economics through Edgeworth and would most likely have found Keynesianism congenial. J. M. Keynes's father, John Keynes, was Sidgwick's student, but placing Sidgwick on the side of the socialists is difficult to defend.[64] If Maurice's moral theology served the Church and a version of socialism, Sidgwick's served the market and liberalism's emphasis on individuals.

Much like the political economists who came before him, Sidgwick worried that charity harmed the poor, stating that "the motives to industry and thrift are impaired by the indiscriminate relief of the idle and improvident."[65] In a telling judgment about the difference in charity from Bishop Butler's age to his own, Sidgwick wrote, "The plain man of Butler's time knew that when he heard the cry of distress he ought to put his hand in his pocket and relieve it; but now he has learnt from newspapers and magazines that indiscriminate almsgiving aggravates in the long run the evils that it attempts to cure."[66] The advance of ethics and economics complexified charity not only against Butler but, although he does not name him, also Maurice. Maurice was unconcerned with the negative effects that charity provided. Because of his utilitarianism, Sidgwick was. For this reason, he took a much more cautious approach to socialism. He adopted Mill's distinction between production and distribution. Wealth was best produced by allowing private ownership, market wages, the disciplining of labor by capital, and limiting government "the protection of person, property, and reputation, and the enforcement of contracts not obtained by force or fraud." No socialist reformer, he stated, set forth an "adequate substitute" for Adam Smith's self-interest and natural liberty.[67] Socialism made little contribution to economics: "All modern Socialism has been based on *some* theory of the effects of the production of wealth that would follow from the total or partial abolition of private property, and none, I conceive, has been based on a *sound* theory. So far as I know, no positive contribution of importance has been made to Economic Science by any Socialist writer throughout the century."[68] This judgment included Maurice and Ludlow.

Benthamite laissez-faire economics was the rule for production, with some important exceptions, such as education, child labor, "sanitary regulations," combating "infectious diseases," some necessary environmental regulations, and the provision of some utilities, such as lighthouses and water.[69] Yet on one point Sidgwick sided with socialism, or what he referred to as semisocialism: Remunerating owners for their employment of capital based on delayed consumption had no logical relation to production. If the profits were given to workers instead, it should have no effect on production. On this point, Sidgwick was following and defending Mill's posthumously published *Chapters on Socialism*. The problem, of course, is how distribution can occur on socialist grounds when production remains in the hands of owners who can use it against workers' calls for just and equitable distribution. Sidgwick never reconsidered private ownership, and he stated that Marx contributed nothing positive to economics.[70] Given their different ethics, it should come as no surprise that Maurice's moral theology leads more to socialism than Sidgwick's utilitarianism.

For Maurice, Christian Socialism did not begin with Marx but with the Church, with its doctrines and liturgy. His *Kingdom of Christ* looks to a spiritual constitution that binds persons in cooperation rather than competition. It reflects the Trinitarian love that is the basis for creation and is found in baptism, the common creed, the Eucharist, the ministry, and Scripture. Despite his suspicions about democracy, he suggests that this spiritual constitution is "more democratical, than any which you can create; but it is a fellowship of mutual love, not mutual selfishness."[71] Although the spiritual constitution is located in the Church and its practices, it is never confined to them, for creation occurs within the Kingdom of God and its instantiation in the Church. It is the ideal upon which God patterns creation.

Maurice's reflections on baptism led him to this conclusion: "In this way there rose up before me the idea of a Church Universal, not built upon human inventions or human faith, but upon the very nature of God himself, and upon the union which he has formed with His creatures: a Church revealed to man as a fixed and eternal reality by means which infinite wisdom had itself devised."[72]

Much as the tabernacle in Exodus is the pattern for creation, so Maurice sees the Church as the blueprint whereby infinite Wisdom creates. Jeremy Morris refers to this as "realized ecclesiology."[73] Dorrien interprets this as the basis for Maurice's socialism: "Socialism was a divine religious ideal, an expression of the Kingdom of God already existing on earth."[74] Because the Kingdom–Church is the ideal pattern for creation, cooperation and mutual love are more basic to existence than competition and acquisition—the two vices Maurice sees dominating economics and English culture in his day. Cooperation and mutual love will be found in everyday life, Maurice argued, not because humans will it into existence but because God wills existence through it.

Maurice's Christian Socialism was inextricably Christian and was often without much nuance. Morris finds the publications of *Politics for the People* and *Tracts on Christian Socialism* to be the first "phase of activity" for Christian Socialists. The meetings and organizing of workers into cooperatives were the second, and the establishment of the Working Men's College in the mid-1850s was the third.[75] It was, without a doubt, an odd account of socialism that dissipated once Chartism did so as well, only to return after Maurice's death in the 1880s through the "Anglo-Catholic priest" Stewart Headlam and Octavia Hill, who founded the Christian Social Union.[76] Headlam was a "protégé" of Maurice and the person responsible for a more thorough development of Christian Socialism. He once "posted bail for Oscar Wilde."[77] Headlam developed Maurice's Christian Socialism in a more radical political direction. Simple appeals to theological doctrines were insufficient. As Philip Turner notes, Maurice's claim that the Incarnation was the foundation for socialism was often presented "in a rather flat-footed way."[78] Turner's judgment is that Maurice was "remarkably conservative in respect of the reform of social institutions."[79] Maurice's confusing mix of aristocracy, Whig constitutionalism, and radicalism was short on social and political analysis, and it led to a defense of traditional institutions while at the same time generating new ones, such as the Working Men's Association, and education for women and the working-class. These contained implicit, if not explicit, criticisms of traditional institutions. Yet Turner rightly reminds us that the Christian Socialists still have much to show anyone who is concerned with a viable social ethic. Their "sacramental view of creation," coupled with the doctrine of the Incarnation, continues to be a powerful "inheritance."[80] Christian Socialists did not seek grand programs to be implemented at the level of the nation-state but ones focused on neighborhoods, churches, and local places.

Morris also acknowledges that interpreting Maurice as the originator of Christian Socialism is not without its problems. On one hand, those who came after him "elevated" his role without attending to the difficulties that his lack of political and economic analysis raised. On the other hand, Maurice's use of the term "socialism" had little in common with its later association with "state action and collective ownership."[81] Ludlow was better equipped at political and economic analysis, but no Christian Socialist advocated state ownership of property or a command economy. This common understanding of socialism, however, misses the diversity within it. Many socialists reject, and have rejected, socialism as primarily a state project focused on controlling, through the threat of violence, the means of production. For instance, in a fascinating chapter on "sewer socialism" in Milwaukee from 1910 to 1946, John Nichols explains how it was an attempt at "a legal and peaceable revolution" and opposed American militarism as much as it opposed the inequality that arose from the private control of vast amounts of capital.[82] Likewise, one of the more prominent contemporary socialist economists, Richard Wolff, writes, "The role of the state is no longer the central issue in dispute." Instead, "21st-century socialism focuses on and prioritizes something else—namely, the transformation of workplaces from capitalism's hierarchical internal structures to fully democratic worker cooperatives."[83] The problem with capitalism is the hierarchical structure of the corporation, the business, the university, and the like, which gives a few people maximum control over the labor of others with little accountability for their lives. Maurice's Christian Socialism focused on worker cooperatives nearly two centuries before Wolff's analysis; it arose from his theological convictions. One profound loss in the transition from Maurice's moral theology to Sidgwick's methods is that ethics began to serve a conventional capitalist economics and neglected Christian Socialism. Abandon theology in ethics and the infusing of virtue that requires authentic dependence gets supplanted by individuals voluntarily contracting with one another.

INFUSING VIRTUE IN TEACHING ETHICS

Christian Socialism brings together moral theology, philosophy, economics, and politics. It blurs any rigid boundaries among them, acknowledging that teaching or learning one of these disciplines inevitably leads to the others. Infusing virtue holds them together. The moral, economic, and political life are inseparable from gifts that come to us from the work of the Spirit in the Church and radiate into all creation. The political and social conditions in which we live can assist or hinder infusing virtue. Forced "consent" to external sources hinders; consensual conditions assist us to recognize and become habituated to these virtues. All of life is filled with the infusion of goodness. Our task is to see, consent, receive, and activate what is already there.

Consent is not a private, mental event but an intentional action that occurs within a nest of causes and reasons. When Thomas Aquinas affirms

Augustine's definition that virtue is what God works in us without us, he adds that it is a "complete" definition because it includes all the causes of virtue.[84] Causes include the reasons for intentional actions that the exercise of virtue requires. For Anscombe, however, first distinguishing cause from reason clarifies intentional action. When a tree falls because it was damaged in a storm (her example), it has a cause but no reason that could make for an intentional action. Human beings can be moved to act by similar causes. Force, coercion, manipulation, and other unjust acts of power are external sources of action that cannot infuse virtue because intentional action, like infused virtue, requires consent. Aquinas emphasizes this when he states, "Infused virtue is caused in us by God without our acting, but not without our consenting. And this is the way to understand the phrase 'which God works in us without us.' On the other hand, what is done by us is such that God causes it within us but not without our acting. For He operates in every act of will and every act of nature."[85] As the constant donating source of being (*semper eis esse dando*),[86] God not only gives us the conditions for willing and acting but also works in and through them. God is not their cause in the way that a storm causes a damaged tree to fall.

Having first distinguished a cause from a reason as a source for action, Anscombe then suggests that a cause can also be a reason for an intentional action. She asks us to consider a case when someone gives a command such as "Hang your hat on a peg and you do it." When asked "Why did you do it?" a reasonable reply could be "Because he told me to." She then asks "Is this cause or a reason?" and states,

> Roughly speaking—if one were forced to go with the distinction—
> the more the action is described as a mere response, the more inclined
> one would be to the word "cause"; while the more it is described as a
> response to something as *having a significance* that is dwelt on by the
> agent in his account, or as a response surrounded with thoughts and
> questions, the more inclined one would be to use the word "reason."
> But in very many cases the distinction would have no point. This,
> however, does not mean that it never has a point.[87]

The infused virtues can be understood well as a case in which the distinction has little "point." As the donating source of our being, God is both a cause and reason for intentional acts, because God is both their perfection and the means to move toward it. Infused virtues arise from without, flowing into us, summoning us toward goods, and the Good, who draws all goods into Triune communion. Consenting to this work is a practice that exists over time and requires ongoing deliberation. Consent has a form that gives shape to ordinary life. We learn to consent to our existence, our name, our sexuality, gender, family relations, political communities, friendships, baptisms, vows, and the like. Like intention, it requires a description that allows us to own the actions. God's infusion, and our consent, are the sources, simultaneously, for our intentional action.

These two statements distinguish between a mere cause that would prohibit free, deliberative human agency and a cause that not only permits but also works in and through it:

1. God made me do it.
2. God made me *to* do it.

The first appears to fit with the definition of virtue as what God works in us without us, but it has no consent and thus cannot constitute an intentional action. Thus, it hampers virtue. The second also fits that definition but includes the possibility of consent for an intentional action necessary for virtue. A paradigmatic case for Christian theology would be Mary's *fiat*. When the angel Gabriel announces that she will bear a child, her response is, "Let it be with me according to your word" (Luke 1:38). Without her consent, the scene is vicious. With her consent, her life receives the infusion of virtue that renders God present in the world. God, of course, is always already present; but her yes makes what is already present even more so, in surprising and unexpected ways. The infused virtues are like this.

The infused virtues assume a particular metaphysics of creation. While creation is a free act of God and is distinct from God, God's knowledge and will are the foundation for creation. This raises a perplexing difficulty. If what God wills is what God knows, and God is eternal, then in knowing and willing creation, creation appears to be eternal, an emanation of the divine will that would be necessary rather than free. Such a conclusion is difficult to avoid; but Judaism, Christianity, and Islam demand rejecting it because it denies creation as a free act of God that exists temporally. Can language express these convictions well? The priority of existence to essence assisted Medieval theologians from concluding that creation shares eternity with God.

According to this metaphysics, God does not think of all possible essences that could be created and then chooses among possibilities with some kind of libertarian freedom. Nothing intervenes between God's knowledge and will and creation; the power of divine freedom to create is consistent with God's nature. Divine freedom does not choose among possibilities to bring into existence because such essences would posit potentiality in God that were not actualized and God is pure act. For this reason, existence is not a predicate. (Kant's critique is correct, even if it misunderstands Anselm.) Existence is not a predicate because there is no subject or essence prior to existence to which it could be attributed.[88] God's freedom to create is that God cannot but create in a way consistent with God's nature, and it is perfectly good. Creation then is good. Every good thought, event, and action not only has its source but also its execution in God.

This metaphysics of creation assists us in understanding how adding "to" to "God made me to do it" renders intelligible, or as intelligible as it can be rendered, infusing virtue and the moral life as gift. Creatures can only exist within the perfection consistent with the divine nature God creates. There can be no other form of existence, neither neutral nor evil. To be is to be from and ordered to the perfectly good. For this reason, practical reasoning cannot but take place "under the aspect of some good." The good—real or apparent—is that which is desired. Without desire, no practical reasoning gets off the ground. This desire is not a universal premise for practical reasoning, but the form that practical reasoning takes. The form is the "manner of representation" the good takes as desired.[89]

In Christian theology, because God is charity, the formal aspect of the good will be equivalent to charity. Love is a desire for the good that wills what God wills. Charity is unavoidable and yet can be freely willed or unfreely rejected. Human creatures have the freedom to will what God wills, with God's help. Human creatures also have the choice (not freedom) to will against God; yet to will against God cannot but mean participating in the goodness/charity that being is, for being itself is good. Far from diminishing the brokenness of the world—its injustice, sinfulness, and fallenness—this metaphysics accentuates it. Such viciousness does not have to be, and yet it is. We have no excuse for it; nor can we render it intelligible. God is not its source, and if we ask for its source, we ask the wrong question. Evil interrupts the source, refusing to cooperate with, or participate in, it. Human creatures cannot thwart charity; but we can block streams of it, stand in its way, and hinder others from seeing what is there. We can look away. The virtues of faith and hope constitute the longing to live lives flowing in harmony with the source and end of creation. Because God is not only perfect but also infinite, there are innumerable ways to participate in divine goodness. Each finds their own, and in finding their own cannot but contribute to that of others. The glory of God is human beings fully alive.

Virtues, both infused and acquired, are found not in theories but in persons. Persons of virtue, especially the faith-infused prudent person, or the person of practical wisdom, who knows when, where, and how to identify and pursue what is good, is the measure of virtue. Such persons are found in ordinary life. They are certainly found in people who lived extraordinary lives in service to others but also in people such as my grandmother, who was abandoned by her spouse, raised five children with the help of her extended family, and worked in a factory to make ends meet. Hope, faith, and love sustained her; her life made no sense without them. Does any life?

NOTES

1. Aquinas, *Summa Theologiae* (hereafter, *ST*), II, 10.10 resp.
2. *ST*, II, 11.3 resp.
3. *ST*, II–II, 11.3.
4. How this gets interpreted is, of course, contested. Some emphasize the qualifier "may be known," but others emphasize the "for certain."
5. Kerr, *Twentieth-Century Catholic Theologians*, 223.
6. Feser, *Scholastic Metaphysics*, 31.
7. Feser, 39–41; see also Long, *Natura Pura*, 28–32.
8. Mac Cumhaill and Wiseman, *Metaphysical Animals*, 161.
9. MacIntyre, *Whose Justice?*, 165.
10. MacIntyre, 165–66.
11. Anscombe, *From Plato to Wittgenstein*, xix.
12. Diamond and Teichman, *Intention*, xv.
13. Sanford, *Before Virtue*, 17.
14. Sanford, 112.
15. Sanford, 229, 246.
16. Hursthouse, *On Virtue Ethics*, 8.
17. Sanford, *Before Virtue*, 146.
18. Sanford.
19. Deneen, *Why Liberalism Failed*, 27.
20. Deneen, 31.
21. Deneen, 188–89.
22. Deneen, 35.
23. Deneen, 187.
24. Deneen, 58.
25. Vermeule, *Constitutionalism*.
26. Vermeule, 29, 29n60.
27. Vermeule, 17.
28. Vermeule, 3.
29. Vermeule, 22–23.
30. Vermeule, 42.
31. Mac Cumhaill and Wiseman, *Metaphysical Animals*, 182–87.
32. Vermeule, *Constitutionalism*, 42.
33. Vermeule, 35–36.
34. *ST*, I–II, 95.1.
35. Vermeule, *Constitutionalism*, 38.

36. Vermeule, 154–55.

37. Vermeule, 156.

38. Vermeule, 157–58.

39. See Tradistae, "'New Set.'"

40. See Okin, *Justice*, 43–58; and Nussbaum, "Virtue Ethics," 200.

41. Stout, *Democracy*, 136.

42. Blackledge and Davidson, *Alasdair MacIntyre's Engagement*, xxi.

43. Blackledge and Davison, xxxviii.

44. Knight, *MacIntyre Reader*, 20.

45. Knight, *Aristotelian Philosophy*, 122.

46. Knight, 113.

47. Blackledge, *Marxism*, 121.

48. Blackledge, 26.

49. Blackledge and Davidson, *Alasdair MacIntyre's Engagement*, xlix.

50. Hannan, *Ethics*, xiv.

51. Hannan, 13, 108, 125.

52. MacIntyre, *Ethics*, 123.

53. MacIntyre, xi.

54. MacIntyre, 222.

55. I am indebted to Daniel Lightsey's presentation on MacIntyre's *Ethics in the Conflicts of Modernity* at a 2022 seminar on Historical Studies in Christian Ethics for reminding me of Dula's criticism and suggesting that MacIntyre's later work addresses it better than *After Virtue*.

56. Dula, *Cavell*, 56.

57. *ST*, I–II, 1.1.

58. MacIntyre, *Ethics*, 315.

59. Stephen Mulhall critiques MacIntyre and Taylor for this minimal theological perfection that inclines them toward too much narrative wholeness and a confusion between a narrative structure in which we are both author and character. See Mulhall, "*Theology and Narrative*." I am indebted to Tyler Womack for pointing out this important essay to me.

60. Blackledge and Davidson, *Alasdair MacIntyre's Engagement*, 133.

61. Hauerwas, *Fully Alive*, 83, 184n5.

62. Dorrien, *Social Democracy*, 114.

63. Dorrien, 4–5.

64. See Schultz, *Henry Sidgwick*, 530.

65. Sidgwick, *Miscellaneous Essays*, 185.

66. Sidgwick, *Practical Ethics*, 6.

67. Sidgwick, *Miscellaneous Essays*, 201–4.

68. Sidgwick, 237.

69. Sidgwick, 202–9.

70. Sidgwick, 236–37.

71. Maurice, *Kingdom of Christ*, 419–20.

72. Maurice, xxviii.

73. Morris, "F. D. Maurice," 8–9.

74. Dorrien, *Social Democracy*, 42.

75. Morris, *F. D. Maurice and the Crisis*, 143–45.

76. Morris, 159.

77. Dorrien, *Social Democracy*, 64.

78. Turner, *Christian Socialism*, 9. My argument above suggests that it may not be as flat-footed as Turner claims when Maurice turns to how divine and human agency cooperate; it is how he tries to make sense of the synthesis between Aristotle and Augustine's definitions of virtue in Aquinas.

79. Turner, 22.

80. Turner, 30.

81. Morris, "F. D. Maurice," 16.

82. Nichols, *"S" Word*, 101–39.

83. Wolff, *Understanding Socialism*, 51.

84. *ST*, I–II, 55.4.

85. *ST*, I–II, 55.4 rep. obj. 6.

86. *ST*, I, 9.2.

87. Anscombe, *Intention*, 23–24.

88. Burrell, *Aquinas*, 34.

89. Schwenkler, *Anscombe's Intention*, 15; Anscombe, *Intention*, 75.

CONCLUSION
Learning and Teaching Ethics

"What do you do for a living?" Well, it is complicated. Teaching, researching, and constantly learning and relearning theological ethics have taken me on a journey through moral theology, philosophy, economics, political science, and history. Let me offer a summary, restating some of the lessons that this journey teaches. Learning and teaching ethics requires attending to real lives in their ordinary situations. It refuses the temptation to construct a system but asks how persons negotiate the world as it is while also being called to participate in the Wisdom found in creation. Wisdom arrives as a gift in multiple forms. For this reason, learning and teaching ethics should be open to the gifted character of our agency. Infusing virtue is not a private Christian language that bears no public accountability; the Christian sacraments presume it but have no monopoly over it. It is basic to everyone who is born, gives birth, is fed, feeds others, eats, drinks, works, enjoys family and friends, learns, loves, receives medical care, dies, and entrusts their body to others in hope as one last gracious act of love. Faith, hope, and love are unavoidable to sustain life's basic activities.

The gift of agency is found in every creature because it is intrinsic to being. Without an authentic dependence that receives from others, no one can act in the world. Ethics and economics are inseparable. Gift makes possible an ecstatic agency; only as we are brought out of ourselves do we come to ourselves. The Wisdom we discover, in its multiple forms, enriches our agency. The more we find, the more human we become. This requires a wide search that refuses sharp disciplinary divisions or focusing only on one time period or one thinker. Yet to teach or learn ethics requires risking normative judgments that will generate opposition and counterclaims. Reflective equilibrium makes no sense without reflective judgments. If we remain at a metalevel, we can never teach or learn ethics; we will only teach or learn *about* ethics. Teaching and learning ethics involves telling and retelling the connections between people's lives, work, and normative convictions. It can go horribly awry. For that reason, to teach or learn it requires a generous charity that listens to and responds to others as they express their normative convictions. It invites them to do so in an ongoing scene of communication and instruction that cannot come to an end. Those persons who tell me that in teaching ethics I will always be employed are correct.

Teaching ethics has also taught me to be attentive to people's histories. History is not fate. Knowing what occurred, why it occurred, and how it could have been and might still be otherwise all allow us to own our past without being determined by it. We can reasonably deliberate about our moment without falling prey to narratives of progress or decline. The former considers the past as something from which we must escape. Everything before we arrived was bleak and wicked. Our task is to liberate, and be liberated, from the past for the sake of a future that never seems to arrive. Narratives of decline reverse the directionality. Everything was justice and light, truth and goodness prevailed, until William of Ockham, or the Reformation, or René Descartes, or Adam Smith, or the Mont Pèlerin Society.... If we retrieve Aristotle or Aquinas, then we can redeem the social, political, or moral order before it is too late. These are caricatures, of course. Seldom does any well-thinking person adopt wholesale a narrative of progress or decline. There is truth in both narratives. Bleak oppression and wickedness existed before us, and some of it has been successfully challenged. Progress has been made, and that progress is worth defending. The right for women to vote, receive an education, own property, hold academic and political office, and attend to their bodily needs without oversight from a patriarchy (including the right to ride a bicycle) are moments of progress.[1] If countless women had not marched, protested, and advocated in speech and writing, such progress would not have been made. Maurice and Sidgwick understood the moment; and unlike many, including Alfred Marshall, they met it, with some qualifications. It is somewhat ironic, and illuminating, that the four women philosophers Anscombe, Foot, Murdoch, and Midgley, who were the second generation permitted to earn academic degrees in the British university system, were the ones who found modern developments in ethics, especially in the work of Ayer and Hare, as a form of decline that could be revised by turning to Plato, Aristotle, and Aquinas. They also recognized, especially Midgley, that too many single, male philosophers were detached from ordinary life, and that makes a difference for what one sees and how one acts.

Women's education was not the only modern development about which Maurice and Sidgwick met the moment. They also affirmed the abolition of slavery. Maurice recognized that its economic form continued to some degree in wage labor. He was more skeptical of developments in economic science than was Sidgwick. Sidgwick saw them as an advance, Maurice as decline. His skepticism arose from his theological convictions. If creatures were made in the image of the Triune God, and the agency that redeemed them is found in the Incarnation, then cooperation, sharing, and especially charity should be the basis for the political and social order. Sidgwick's privileging of the right over the good, and his narrowing ethics to voluntary action directed to what ought to be done, opened him to new developments in economics with little critical resistance. Maurice's and Sidgwick's approaches to economics affected their ethics, and vice versa. My own judgment is that Bernard Williams is correct and that Sidgwick's economics led to "Government House Utilitarianism" and made the teaching of ethics for a professional class that, on occasion, should keep their lessons from ordinary persons who would not understand. Perhaps his support for homosexuality and an "epistemology of the closet" led him to his esoteric morality, but it also arose from his utilitarianism and professionalization of ethics. Neither Maurice nor Sidgwick was sufficiently attuned to the problems with British colonialism and nationalism. Nothing like Pearson's secular white supremacy is found in Maurice, but his emphasis on national characteristics was exploited by Pearson and should be a caution to us all. For all Sidgwick's insights into the moral and political issues of his day, his affirmation of aspects of Pearson's work should provoke a serious investigation into why, having stood on the right side of many issues, he missed this one so thoroughly. What Maurice had that Pearson and Sidgwick did not was something that limited the role of the nation, the Kingdom–Church ideal. Lose it, and one basis for recognizing the catholicity of all the peoples and nations of the world also gets abandoned. It is by no means the only such basis but one that should generate less opposition in the teaching and learning of ethics than what transpired post-Sidgwick. Ethics need not be post-Christian, or post–any religious tradition. They provide essential sources for addressing the good life.

More could be said about Maurice and Sidgwick's life, work, and normative convictions. I have tried to include similar analyses of Anscombe and Rawls. These four persons represent the streams of ethics known, respectively, as infused virtues, utilitarianism, virtue, and deontology. Theories become more interesting when we recognize their histories and embodiment in persons. If ethics has a method, it is more like what Maurice called casuistry, and the best way to teach or learn it is through its narrative display. It is not a rule or procedure that overcomes skepticism about the ambiguities of the moral life; it does not bring certainty. It is learning to go on the way with others (μετ' ὁδός). Other ways of journeying through the development of ethics—of the relationship between Maurice, Sidgwick, Anscombe, and Rawls—are always possible; no scientific precision exists in the living, teaching, or learning of ethics. If such precision did arise, it would be too technological, reductive, and most likely authoritarian to advance a life lived well.

To change metaphors, ethics is more like rowing a boat across an open sea than finding the right method that secures right action.[2] Good is the point toward which we are aiming. Sometimes, as in rowing, we look backward to gain our bearings. Sometimes, we look forward. Rawls's political and moral philosophy by no means rejects the past, but he begins with Sidgwick and looks forward. Faith is placed in the progress of constitutional democracies. As they are put under threat by postliberal, antiliberal, and authoritarian forces, such faith seems all the more necessary at the present moment. Constitutional democracies are not without errors—errors that reflect the problems with ethics that were identified in part I of this work. They too often fear any comprehensive good and thus privilege the right, assume voluntary consent without the means to acknowledge when or how it could be withdrawn, and place too much confidence in proper procedures based on principles without acknowledging the importance of reflective judgments. These convictions limit the questions that can be put to politics, such as "What are the good purposes government should serve?" Without this question, democracies become too subject to market forces. Then ethics becomes little more than amassing power through data and opinion rather than deliberating about good lives. The fear of any comprehensive good also engenders a bias against ancient sources of wisdom. As valid as I find these criticisms of liberalism to be, so is Rawls's fear of the "fact of oppression." A comprehensive religious or moral good allied with the violent power of the state, especially a well-cabined Roman dictator, is a danger against which all people of goodwill should remain vigilant. Yet this fear of the good can lead to such a minimal theory of goodness that we lose the possibility to critique constitutional governments. Reflective judgments on the good and perfect are cordoned off to nonpublic and apolitical spaces. Meanwhile, potential violence against external and internal enemies becomes an unquestionable basis for national life.

Anscombe looks back, and in so doing, she challenged the violence of modern nation-states more so than Rawls, and was more critical of modern economics than Sidgwick. While Sidgwick narrowed the domain of ethics, Anscombe expanded it. Ethics ran aground on Sidgwick and needed different currents to find its way into the world as it is and not simply how professional philosophers thought it ought to be. Those different currents are available, and Anscombe initiated a retrieval of Aristotle and Aquinas that was something other than the reactionary retrieval of antimodern Thomism. There are dangers here. Those two currents can run in tandem. Oddly enough, at the present moment, it is the strictly Aristotelian Thomism with its sufficiency of nature that poses more of a threat to the gains of constitutional democracies than an Augustinian Thomism that emphasizes the infusing of virtue, as Maurice's life and work demonstrated. For secular persons concerned with maintaining important modern gains, this might be counterintuitive. The infused virtues assume explicit theological teachings that lack the apparent universality of a natural law ethics. If ethics and democracy require universality and impartiality, then a natural law ethics that eschews the parochialism of the infused virtues might appear more open to outsider virtue, but that is not where we are. I have little doubt that a theory of the infused virtues can be put to oppressive ends. We must not forget that Aquinas advocated the execution of heretics as consistent with the virtues of faith and charity; but to imagine that this threat can be avoided by seeking an impartial and universal ethics is to ask for a rule, procedure, or precision that creatures like us do not have. It would require overcoming any skepticism about potential vicious uses of our virtues, rules, and principles, seeking certainty and transparency that elude us. Cavell helps us avoid the search for such certainty.

What we want, I think, is not impartiality and universality. It would be a very odd expression for someone to say, "I want to inhabit the universal position." The criteria that we possess to make sense of such a statement come with serious liabilities. "Do you want to be pope, emperor, divine? In what sense can you be universal?" "I want to be impartial" has better criteria for it. Perhaps you are a referee, judge, or police officer, but does it make sense for moral philosophers and theologians? Imagine someone who says, "I think that we should rethink the abolition of slavery." Any moral philosopher or theologian whose next response is, "Well, let me consider this impartially" would not help us know how to respond to someone whose life has become ruled, for whatever reason, by viciousness.

If we ask people "What do you want out of life?" very few, and perhaps only philosophers, would respond "impartiality and universality." Their answers would be more like "the freedom to live a good life in cooperation with others." We know how to go on from there. We can identify forms of oppression that prohibit it, and the daily conditions of food, shelter, health, education, and friendship that sustain it. We will disagree over the prohibitions and sustenance necessary for a good life; we will disagree over what we mean by that expression, but we will have a better conversation than if we begin by assuming that everyone must first answer with impartiality and universality. We will, inevitably, raise questions of faith, hope, and love. In what do you place your faith to live such a life? What are your hopes for it; is it only future, present, past? If it is future, what are the means by which it is brought about? And most importantly, What do you love? These questions, I venture to claim, are inevitable aspects of everyday life for creatures like us. They are more fundamental than "What ought I to do?" It is not irrelevant, but questions of faith, hope, and love come first. They are cardinal. First tell us what you love, in what you place faith, and for what you hope. In answering those questions, we can reasonably deliberate how to go on.

Questions of faith, hope, and love open ethics into discussions of economics and politics. Something as simple as hoping for our daily bread implicates us in numerous political and economic relationships. Faith in constitutional democracies may have its place, but we can ask if it is sufficient. How is such faith related to hope? Does it invite us to love well? Faith, hope, and love can be projected into a variety of contexts. Some of the uses would be nonsensical: "I only have faith in myself and hope for a future that I alone bring about." Showing that no criteria exist by which such a faith and hope could be embodied would, hopefully, inform someone that there is no way to go on in this life with such a conviction. Likewise, statements such as "I only have faith in, and love for, my white race" or "I only place hope in my nation and its leaders" lack criteria whereby people can seek to live a good life in cooperation with others.

Could not the same be said about Christian moral theology and its basic confession of faith: "I believe in God, the Father Almighty . . ."? Yes, it could, and such a danger ought to be kept in mind. Maurice noted as much when he warned against letting this confession be used to damn others rather than live into the charity that he claimed it named. No guarantee exists that what we place faith in, what we hope for, and what we love cannot generate vice rather than virtue. As with love for our family or nation, it can and has led to a wicked parochialism, a rejection of the outsider, even violence. Love is always partial, and that makes it potentially dangerous, but a life without love is not worth living. The question is how we love in all its glorious partiality— I love *this* person at *this* time in *this* way—without it leading to the fear and destruction of others.

Acknowledging that virtues have been, are, and will be infused by sources outside us helps. We are not alone or trapped in immanent sources; our agency is ecstatic. Such a moral philosophy and theology remind us that our life, like all lives, is a gift. If we consider all that we are and have as gift rather than achievement and possession, perhaps we will be less likely to view others as competitors against whom we must secure our lives. They are potential friends whose lives and loves are also the result of gifts. For Christian theology, the Triune God is charity, gift, and reception, whose image is indelibly printed in creation itself. This same God redeems by drawing us into the divine life, a life of charity, of sharing in natural and supernatural goods, of the reconciliation and unity of humanity and divinity in Christ. We hope for the full manifestation of such sharing in the future and are called to live into it as best we can "*in via.*" We find evidence in daily existence that this way of life, this whirl of organism and texture of being, is always present among us. Even the most basic materiality that constitutes who we are, the water and cells that give us our form, are constantly being replenished, being received as a gift when we are unaware of it. We also have criteria whereby we can make sense of this infusing.

Anyone who understands the words "here, have a drink of water" can understand the role of the infused virtues in the moral life. A parched, thirsty person receives from another person life-giving sustenance—"take, drink," "take, eat." The person who has known thirst or hunger knows best how life-giving a drink or food can be, something that in our ordinary, everyday drinking and eating we can easily forget but never fully escape. The perfection of this ordinary act is found in the recognition of its giving life. It infuses life. Drinking and eating, of course, are not the only instances of such an infused life. Unless we are bewitched by our language and assume that we are always the master of our words and thereby our world, rather than inhabiting a world that is always already worded, then ordinary life reveals how deeply we are sustained through acts of infusing goodness: the joy of communicating with others, drinking wine to celebrate with family and friends, ingesting food, the intimacy of sex, listening to music, attending to another's words, receiving medical care, even restoration through the infusion of blood and intravenous antibiotics, inhabiting familiar and social roles, walking or riding a bicycle with the wind at your back. A virtuous life, a good life, cannot be had without infusing virtues.

What does this mean for teaching and learning ethics? This book has suggested that it is unlike other disciplines. We assume (1) that everyone has some understanding and practice of ethics, so they can be held accountable for their actions, and (2) that they should be instructed in ethics. How we go about teaching and learning ethics should preserve both assumptions. A good starting place is to invite persons to address the questions "In what do you have faith? For what do you hope? What do you love?" A second task is to reflect on the sources that have led them to provide their answers, reflect on these sources, and consider their goodness. Theories of goodness will certainly be helpful at such a point; comparing the good in Plato, Aristotle, Aquinas, Sidgwick, Rawls, a feminist ethics of care, abolitionism, and more have their places. More important, however, will be examining lives that embody goodness, whether it be lives that have overcome serious moral failure or those that sustained a goodness received from others over a lifetime. Extraordinary lives and exemplars can be useful, but memoirs, novels, screenplays, and other means that depict the goodness of ordinary lives, both like and unlike our own, will be more beneficial.

A third task is to ask by what criteria, if there are any, people could pursue their named objects of faith, hope, and love. What do these objects ask of them, and are they worthy of pursuit? Adequate answers will venture beyond some narrow domain of ethics. They will require something other than constructing a method for decision-making. If ethics is about a well-lived life, then it engages most other disciplines. Ethics should not be construed narrowly as subordinate to other disciplines, such as engineering ethics, business ethics, legal ethics, medical ethics, clergy ethics. . . . Such restrictive professional ethics do little more than generate worthless codes of conduct that fail to make a difference because they set the good life within the context of professions rather than professions within the context of the good life. The moral science tripos in the mid–nineteenth century at Cambridge had this much right; economics should be pursued within the context of moral science and not vice versa. Its independence from questions of the good life has caused lasting damage. If ethics, as the question of the good life, were understood to be more basic than those of utility, value, return on investments, and doing one's duty, then it could help restore the *universus* (wholeness) of the university, which has too often, like Rawls's liberalism, so feared any comprehensive rendering of the good that it has lacked the resources to resist domination by market forces. Education thus becomes primarily about return on investment rather than seeking the good life and finding the means to attain it. Teaching and learning ethics, if it were to be a serious endeavor, requires restructuring the university, bringing its various departments and divisions under the overarching question of the good life. Institutions that maintain some connection with their religious or moral traditions are better suited for such restructuring because asking questions about the good life cannot help but ask questions about God. Until there is such restructuring, and it may be impossible, teaching and learning ethics can only be a marginal educational activity, accomplishing little more than laying out professional code of conduct or coming up with methods that, once drafted, are forgotten, often for good reason. Fortunately, universities are not the only place where we can learn and teach ethics. Its practice can be done well when we draw on the resources from those other places—families, villages, cities, religious institutions, artistic organizations, sports clubs, and other activities that assume and pursue socially cooperative forms of goodness.

Teaching and learning ethics begin by taking into account the particular histories that are present in the people gathered before us. They are the sources that have already constituted agency. They proceed by inquiring into those histories, bringing them into conversation with others, and asking them if what they desire, what they hope, what they place faith in, and what they love are worthy of human lives, individually and collectively. That will inevitably assume that there is such a thing as a way of being human, a perfection for which we are striving, as human beings fully alive. It is difficult to name—perfection, *eudaimonia*, blessedness, charitable cooperation, the common good, the freedom to live and love with others. We rightly fear that some authoritarian will impose their view of the good on us, and for that reason we ask the question and pose answers cautiously. But if the question is not posed and possible answers are not given, then there is no sense to teaching and learning ethics except to learn what others once thought it was but no longer can be. The result of that will not be liberation but an uncritical vulnerability to those societal forces that seek to keep us from asking "What is a life lived well?" Teaching and learning ethics done well, at a minimum, keeps this question alive.

NOTES

1. See Long, *Art of Cycling*, 20.
2. I owe this analogy to Gerhard Lohfink and to being born and raised, in part, on the banks of the Tippecanoe River.

BIBLIOGRAPHY

Annas, Julia. *Intelligent Virtue*. Oxford: Oxford University Press, 2011.

———. *The Morality of Happiness*. New York: Oxford University Press, 1993.

Anscombe, G. E. M. *Ethics, Religion and Politics: Collected Philosophical Papers*. Vol. 3. Oxford: Basil Blackwell, 1982.

———. *Faith in a Hard Ground: Essays on Religion, Philosophy and Ethics*. Edited by Mary Geach and Luke Gormally. Exeter, UK: Imprint Academic, 2008.

———. *From Plato to Wittgenstein: Essays by G. E. M. Anscombe*. Edited by Mary Geach and Luke Gormally. Exeter, UK: Imprint Academic, 2011.

———. *Human Life, Action and Ethics*. Edited by Mary Geach and Luke Gormally. Exeter, UK: Imprint Academic, 2005.

———. *Intention*. Cambridge, MA: Harvard University Press, 2000; orig. pub. 1957.

Aquinas, Thomas. *Questions on Love and Charity: Summa Theologiae, Secunda Secundae, Questions 23–46*. Edited by Robert Miner. New Haven, CT: Yale University Press, 2016.

Aristotle. *Nicomachean Ethics*. Translated by Terence Irwin. 2nd ed. Indianapolis: Hackett, 1999.

Aslanbeigui, Nahid, and Guy Oakes. *The Provocative Joan Robinson: The Making of a Cambridge Economist*. Durham, NC: Duke University Press, 2009.

Austin, Nicholas, SJ. *Aquinas on Virtue: A Causal Reading*. Washington, DC: Georgetown University Press, 2017.

———. "Spirituality and Virtue in Christian Formation: A Conversation between Thomistic and Ignatian Traditions." *New Blackfriars* 97, no. 1068 (2016): 202–17.

Balthasar, Hans Urs von. *The Theology of Karl Barth*. Translated by Edward T. Oakes, SJ. San Francisco: Ignatius Press, Communio Books, 1992.

Beck, Lewis White. "Translator's Introduction." In *Critique of Practical Reason*, by Immanuel Kant. New York: Macmillan, 1993.

Berkman, John. "Justice and Murder: The Backstory to Elizabeth Anscombe's 'Modern Moral Philosophy.'" In *Oxford Handbook to Elizabeth Anscombe*, edited by Roger Teichmann, 225–70. New York: Oxford University Press, 2022.

Bernstein, Jeffrey A. "Righteousness and Divine Love." In *Questions on Love and Charity: Summa Theologiae, Secunda Secundae, Questions 23–46*, edited by Robert Miner, 336–55. New Haven, CT: Yale University Press, 2016.

Blackburn, Simon. *Ethics: A Very Short Introduction*. Oxford: Oxford University Press, 2021.

Blackledge, Paul. *Marxism and Ethics: Freedom, Desire, and Revolution*. Albany: State University of New York Press, 2012.

Blackledge, Paul, and Neil Davidson. *Alasdair MacIntyre's Engagement with Marxism: Selected Writings, 1953–1974*. Chicago: Haymarket Books, 2009.

Bok, P. MacKenzie. "To the Mountaintop Again: The Early Rawls and Post-Protestant Ethics in America." *Modern Intellectual History* 14, no. 1 (2017): 153–85.

Bok, Sissela. Introduction to *Practical Ethics*, by Henry Sidgwick, v–xix.. New York. Oxford University Press, 1998.

Bradley, F. H. *Mr. Sidgwick's Hedonism: An Examination of the Main Argument of "The Methods of Ethics."* London: H. S. King, 1877.

Bretherton, Luke. *Christ and the Common Life: Political Theology and the Case for the Common Life*. Grand Rapids: William B. Eerdmans, 2019.

Brink, David O. "Introduction." In *Prolegomena to Ethics*, by T. H. Green. Oxford: Oxford University Press, 2003.

Broad, C. D. *Five Types of Ethical Theories*. London: Routledge, 2000.

Brown Douglas, Kelly. "Theological Methodology and the Jesus Movement through the Work of F. D. Maurice and Vida Scudder." *Anglican Theological Review* 102, no. 1 (2020): 7–30.

Burley, Mikel. "Wittgenstein and the Study of Religion: Beyond Fideism and Atheism." In *Wittgenstein, Religion and Ethics: New Perspectives from Philosophy and Theology*, edited by Mikel Burley. London: Bloomsbury, 2018.

Burrell, David. *Aquinas, God & Action*. London: Routledge & Kegan Paul, 1979.

———. *Toward a Jewish-Christian-Muslim Theology*. Malden, MA: Wiley Blackwell, 2014.

Campbell, Lucy. "On Anscombe on Practical Knowledge and Practical Truth." In *Oxford Handbook to Elizabeth Anscombe*, edited by Roger Teichmann. New York: Oxford University Press, 2022.

Cavanaugh, William. *Migrations of the Holy: God, State, and the Political Meaning of the Church*. Grand Rapids: William B. Eerdmans, 2011.

Cavell, Stanley. *The Claim of Reason*. Oxford: Oxford University Press, 1979.

———. *Conditions Handsome and Unhandsome: The Constitution of Emersonian Perfectionism—The Carus Lectures, 1988*. La Salle, IL: Open Court, 1990.

———. *Must We Mean What We Say?* Cambridge: Cambridge University Press, 2015; orig. pub. 1969.

Chapell, Sophie Grace. "Anscombe's Three Theses after Sixty Years: Modern Moral Philosophy, Polemic, and 'Modern Moral Philosophy.'" In *Oxford Handbook to Elizabeth Anscombe*, edited by Roger Teichmann. New York: Oxford University Press, 2022.

Coates, Ta-Nehisi. "A Rising Tide Lifts All Yachts: Why Class-Based Social Policy Doesn't Address African Americans' Problems." *Atlantic*, June 2013.

Colón-Emeric, Edgardo. *Oscar Romero's Theological Vision: Liberation and the Transfiguration of the Poor*. Notre Dame, IN: University of Notre Dame Press, 2018.

Conradi, Peter J. *Iris Murdoch: A Life*. New York: W. W. Norton, 2001.

Copjec, Joan. *Radical Evil*. London: Verso, 1996.

Crary, Alice. *Inside Ethics: On the Demands of Moral Thought*. Cambridge, MA: Harvard University Press, 2016.

Decosimo, David. *Ethics as a Work of Charity*. Stanford, CA: Stanford University Press, 2014.

Deneen, Patrick J. *Why Liberalism Failed*. New Haven, CT: Yale University Press, 2018.

Desmond, William. *Is There a Sabbatical for Thought? Between Religion and Philosophy*. New York: Fordham University Press, 2005.

Diamond, Cora. "Having a Rough Story About What Moral Philosophy Is." *New Literary History* 15, no. 1 (Autumn 1983): 155–69.

———. *Reading Wittgenstein with Anscombe, Going On to Ethics*. Cambridge, MA: Harvard University Press, 2019.

Diamond, Cora, and Jenny Teichman. *Intention and Intentionality: Essays in Honour of G. E. M. Anscombe*. Ithaca, NY: Cornell University Press, 1979.

Dorrien, Gary. *Social Democracy in The Making: Political & Religious Roots of European Socialism*. New Haven, CT: Yale University Press, 2019.

Doyle, Dominick. "The Dialectic Unfolding of the Theological Virtues: Tayloring Christian Identity to a Secular Age." *Gregorianum* 94, no. 4 (2011): 687–798.

Dubler, Joshua, and Vincent Lloyd W. *Break Every Yoke: Religion, Justice, and the Abolition of Prisons*. Oxford: Oxford University Press, 2019.

Du Bois, W. E. B. *Black Reconstruction: An Essay Toward a History of the Part Which Black Folk Played in the Attempt to Reconstruct Democracy in America, 1860–1880*. New York: Library of America, 2021.

Dula, Peter. *Cavell, Companionship, and Christian Theology*. Oxford: Oxford University Press, 2011.

Eagleton, Terry. *Hope without Optimism*. New Haven, CT: Yale University Press, 2017.

Edmundson, William A. *John Rawls: Reticent Socialist*. Cambridge: Cambridge University Press, 2017.

Engstrom, Stephen, and Jennifer Whiting, eds. *Aristotle, Kant, and the Stoics: Rethinking Happiness and Duty*. Cambridge: Cambridge University Press, 1996.

Feingold, Lawrence. *The Natural Desire to See God According to St. Thomas Aquinas and His Interpreters*. Ave Maria, FL: Sapientia Press, 2010.

Feser, Edward. *Scholastic Metaphysics: A Contemporary Introduction*. Neunkirchen-Seelscheid, Germany: Editiones Scholasticae, 2014.

Flores, Nichole M. *The Aesthetics of Solidarity: Our Lady of Guadalupe and American Democracy*. Washington, DC: Georgetown University Press, 2021.

Foot, Philippa. *Natural Goodness*. Oxford: Oxford University Press, 2001.

———. *Virtues and Vices and Other Essays in Moral Philosophy*. Berkeley: University of California Press, 1978.

Forrester, Katrina. *In the Shadow of Justice*. Princeton, NJ: Princeton University Press, 2019.

Foster, James J. S. "Patching Up Virtue: Overcoming the Emersonian/Augustinian Divide in Jennifer Herdt's *Putting on Virtue*." *Journal of Religious Ethics* 41, no. 4 (2013): 688–709.

Frankena, William K. *Ethics*. 2nd ed. Englewood Cliffs, NJ: Prentice Hall, 1973.

Freddoso, Alfred J. "New English Translations of St. Thomas Aquinas's *Summa Theologiae*." www3.nd.edu/~afreddos/summa-translation/TOC.htm.

Freeman, Samuel. "The Burdens of Public Justification." *Philosophy, Politics, and Economics* 6, no. 1 (February 2007): 5–43.

Gardner, Patrick M. "Thomas and Dante on the *Duo Ultima Hominis*." *The Thomist: A Speculative Quarterly Review* 75, no. 3 (July 2011): 4–59.

Geach, Peter T. "Good and Evil." *Analysis* 17, no. 2 (December 1956): 33–42.

———. *The Virtues*. Cambridge: Cambridge University Press, 1977.

Gorman, Michael J. *Participating in Christ: Explorations in Paul's Theology and Spirituality*. Grand Rapids: Baker Academic, 2019.

Gouldstone, Timothy Maxwell. *The Rise and Fall of Anglican Idealism in the Nineteenth Century.* New York: Palgrave Macmillan, 2005.

Green, T. H. *Prolegomena to Ethics.* Edited by David O. Brink. Oxford: Oxford University Press, 2003.

Gregory, Eric. "Before the Original Position: The Neo-Orthodox Theology of the Young John Rawls." *Journal of Religious Ethics* 35, no. 2 (June 2007): 179–206.

Grisez, Germain. *Christian Moral Principles, Volume 1: The Way of the Lord Jesus.* Staten Island: St. Pauls / Alba House, 1983.

Griswold, Charles L., Jr. *Adam Smith and the Virtues of Enlightenment.* Cambridge: Cambridge University Press, 1999.

Gutwenger, Engelbert. "Natur und übernature." *Zeitschrift für katholische Theologie* 75 (1953): 82–97.

Hall, Amy Laura. "Love: A Kinship of Affliction and Redemption." In *The Oxford Handbook of Theological Ethics*, edited by Gilbert Meilaender and William Werpehowski, 307–22. Oxford: Oxford University Press, 2007.

Hannan, Jason. *Ethics under Capital: MacIntyre, Communication, and the Culture Wars.* London: Bloomsbury Academic, 2020.

Harcourt, G. C., and Pure Kerr. *Joan Robinson.* London: Palgrave Macmillan, 2009.

Hare, John E. *The Moral Gap: Kantian Ethics, Human Limits, and God's Assistance.* Oxford: Clarendon Press, 1996.

Hare, R. M. "Geach: Good and Evil." *Analysis* 17, no. 5 (April 1957): 103–11.

Harms, Arielle. "Acquired and Infused Moral Virtue: A Distinction of Ends." *New Blackfriars* 95, no. 1055 (January 2014): 71–87.

Hauerwas, Stanley. *Fully Alive: The Apocalyptic Humanism of Karl Barth.* Charlottesville: University of Virginia Press, 2022.

———. "The Good Life: If Liberalism Failed to Deliver It, What Can?" *Plough*, October 13, 2021. www.plough.com/en/topics/life/work/the-good-life-hauerwas.

Hauerwas, Stanley, and Charles Pinches. *Christians among the Virtues: Theological Conversations with Ancient and Modern Ethics.* Notre Dame, IN: University of Notre Dame Press, 1997.

Hector, Kevin. *Theological Project of Modernism.* Oxford: Oxford University Press, 2015.

———. *Theology without Metaphysics: God, Language and the Spirit of Recognition.* Cambridge: Cambridge University Press, 2011.

Held, Virginia. *The Ethics of Care: Personal, Political, and Global.* Oxford: Oxford University Press, 2006.

Herdt, Jennifer A. *Forming Humanity: Redeeming the German* Bildung *Tradition.* Chicago: University of Chicago Press, 2019.

———. *Putting on Virtue: The Legacy of the Splendid Vices.* Chicago: University of Chicago Press, 2008.

———. "Redeeming the Acquired Virtues." *Journal of Religious Ethics* 41, no. 4 (2013): 727–40.

Herman, Barbara. "Editor's Foreword." In *Lectures on the History of Moral Philosophy*, by John Rawls. Cambridge, MA: Harvard University Press, 2000.

Hickel, Jason. *The Divide: Global Inequality from Conquest to Free Markets.* New York: W. W. Norton, 2017.

Hume, David. *A Treatise of Human Nature.* 2nd ed. Edited by L. A. Selby-Bigge and P. H. Nidditch. Oxford: Clarendon Press, 1978.

Hurka, Thomas. *British Ethical Theorists from Sidgwick to Ewing.* Oxford: Oxford University Press, 2015.

———. *Perfectionism*. New York: Oxford University Press, 1993.

Hursthouse, Rosalind. *On Virtue Ethics*. Oxford: Oxford University Press, 2010.

Insole, Christopher J. *Kant and the Creation of Freedom: A Theological Problem*. Oxford: Oxford University Press, 2013.

———. *Kant and the Divine: From Contemplation to the Moral Law*. Oxford: Oxford University Press, 2020.

Irwin, T. H. "Eminent Victorians and Greek Ethics: Sidgwick, Green, and Aristotle." In *Essays on Henry Sidgwick*. Edited by Bart Schultz. New York: Cambridge University Press, 1992.

Jennings, Willie. *The Christian Imagination: Theology and the Origins of Race*. New Haven, CT: Yale University Press, 2010.

John of St. Thomas (1589–1644). "The Gifts of the Holy Ghost." Translated by James M. Egan and Walter D. Hughes. *The Thomist: A Speculative Quarterly Review* 9, no. 2 (1946): 266–326.

Jordan, Mark D. "Theology and Philosophy." In *The Cambridge Companion to Aquinas*. Edited by Norman Kretzmann and Eleanore Stump. Cambridge: Cambridge University Press, 1993.

Kant, Immanuel. *Critique of Practical Reason*. Translated by Lewis White Beck. New York: Macmillan, 1993.

———. *The Metaphysics of Morals*. Translated by Mary Gregor. Cambridge: Cambridge University Press, 1991.

Kent, Bonnie. "Augustine's *On the Good of Marriage* and Infused Virtue in the Twelfth Century." *Journal of Religious Ethics* 41, no. 1 (2013): 112–36.

———. "Moral Provincialism." *Religious Studies* 30, no. 3 (1994): 365–85.

Kerr, Fergus. *Twentieth-Century Catholic Theologians: From Neoscholasticism to Nuptial Mysticism*. Malden, MA: Blackwell, 2007.

Kingsley, Charles. "The Message of the Church to Laboring Men." *Monthly Religious Magazine* (1844–56) 9, no. 2 (February 1852).

Klaver, J. M. I. *The Apostle of the Flesh: A Critical Life of Charles Kingsley*. Leiden: Brill, 2006.

Knight, Kelvin. *Aristotelian Philosophy: Ethics and Politics from Aristotle to MacIntyre*. Cambridge: Polity, 2007.

———, ed. *The MacIntyre Reader*. Notre Dame, IN: University of Notre Dame Press, 1998.

Knobel, Angela McKay. *Aquinas and the Infused Virtues*. Notre Dame, IN: University of Notre Dame Press, 2021.

———. "Can Aquinas's Infused and Acquired Virtues Coexist in the Christian Life?" *Studies in Christian Ethics* 23, no. 4 (2010): 381–96.

———. "Elevated Virtue? A Reply to Bowlin and Aquinas." *Journal of Moral Theology* 8, no. 2 (2019): 25–39.

———. "Insight, Experience and the Notion of 'Infused' Virtue." *American Catholic Philosophical Quarterly* 90, no. 4 (2016): 621–33.

———. "Prudence and Acquired Moral Virtue." *The Thomist: A Speculative Quarterly Review* 69, no. 4 (2005): 535–55.

Korsgaard, Christine M. *The Constitution of Agency: Essays on Practical Reason and Moral Psychology*. Oxford: Oxford University Press, 2008.

Kripke, Saul A. *Wittgenstein on Rules and Private Language*. Oxford: Blackwell, 1982.

Lake, Marilyn. "The White Man under Siege: New Histories of Race in the Nineteenth Century and the Advent of White Australia." *History Workshop Journal*, no. 58 (Autumn 2004): 41–62.

Lipscomb, Benjamin J. B. *The Women Are Up to Something: How Elizabeth Anscombe, Mary Midgley, and Iris Murdoch Revolutionized Ethics.* Oxford: Oxford University Press, 2022.

Lloyd, Vincent W. *Black Dignity: The Struggle against Domination.* New Haven, CT: Yale University Press, 2022.

———. *In Defense of Charisma.* New York: Columbia University Press, 2018.

Long, D. Stephen. *The Art of Cycling, Living and Dying: Moral Theology from Everyday Life.* Eugene, OR: Cascade Press, 2021.

———. *Augustinian and Ecclesial Christian Ethics.* Lanham, MD: Lexington Academic, 2018.

———. "Moral Theology." In *Oxford Handbook of Systematic Theology.* Edited by John B. Webster, Kathryn Tanner, and Iain Torrance. Oxford: Oxford University Press, 2009.

———. *Saving Karl Barth: Hans Urs von Balthasar's Preoccupation.* Minneapolis: Fortress Press, 2014.

———. *Speaking of God: Theology, Language, and Truth.* Grand Rapids: William B. Eerdmans, 2009.

Long, Steven A. *Natura Pura: On the Recovery of Nature in the Doctrine of Grace.* New York: Fordham University Press, 2010.

Lumbreras, Peter. "Notes on the Connection of the Virtues." *The Thomist: A Speculative Quarterly Review* 11, no. 2 (1948): 218–40.

Mac Cumhaill, Claire, and Rachael Wiseman. *Metaphysical Animals: How Four Women Brought Philosophy Back to Life.* New York: Doubleday, 2022.

MacIntyre, Alasdair. *Ethics in the Conflicts of Modernity: An Essay on Desire, Practical Reasoning, and Narrative.* Cambridge: Cambridge University Press, 2016.

———. "Hume on 'Is' and 'Ought.'" *Philosophical Review* 68, no. 4 (October 1959): 451–68.

———. "The Irrelevance of Ethics." In *Virtue and Economy: Essays on Morality and Markets.* Edited by Andrius Bielskis and Kelvin Knight. London: Routledge, 2016.

———. "Plain Persons and Moral Philosophy: Rules, Virtues and Goods." In *The MacIntyre Reader.* Edited by Kelvin Knight. Notre Dame, IN: University of Notre Dame Press, 1998; orig. pub. 1992.

———. *Three Rival Versions of Moral Enquiry: Encyclopedia, Genealogy, and Tradition.* Notre Dame, IN: University of Notre Dame Press, 1990.

———. *Whose Justice? Which Rationality?* Notre Dame, IN: University of Notre Dame Press, 1988.

MacKenzie, Catriona. "Feminist Innovation in Philosophy: Relational Autonomy and Social Justice." *Women's Studies International Forum* 72, no. 1 (2019): 144–51.

MacKintosh, James. *Dissertation on the Progress of Ethical Philosophy Chiefly during the Seventeenth and Eighteenth Centuries.* Edinburgh: Adam and Charles Black, 1862.

Mahoney, John. *The Making of Moral Theology: A Study of the Roman Catholic Tradition.* Oxford: Oxford University Press, 1987.

Mandle, Jon, and David A. Reidy. *A Companion to Rawls.* Malden, MA: Wiley Blackwell, 2016.

Mansel, Henry Longueville. *The Limits of Religious Thought Examined in Eight Lectures.* London: John Murray, 1867.

Martin, James, SJ. "Don't Call Me a Saint." *America: The Jesuit Review,* November 14, 2012. www.americamagazine.org/content/all-things/dont-call-me-saint.

Mattison, William C., III. "Aquinas, Custom, and the Coexistence of Infused and Acquired Cardinal Virtues." *Journal of Moral Theology* 8, no. 2 (2019): 1–24.

———. "Can Christians Possess the Acquired Cardinal Virtues?" *Theological Studies* 72, no. 3 (2011): 558–85.

————. "Thomas's Categorization of Virtue: Historical Background and Contemporary Significance." *The Thomist: A Speculative Quarterly Review* 74, no. 2 (2010): 189–235.

Maurice, Frederick, *The Life of Frederick Denison Maurice: Chiefly Told in His Letters by His Son.* Vols. 1–2. London: Macmillan, 1885.

Maurice, F. D. *The Conscience: Lectures on Casuistry.* London: Macmillan, 1868.

————. *The Epistle to the Hebrews: Being the Substance of Three Lectures Delivered in the Chapel of the Honourable Society of Lincoln's Inn.* London: John W. Parker, 1846.

————. *The Epistles of St. John: A Series of Lectures on Christian Ethics.* 1st ed. London: Macmillan, 1893; orig. pub. 1857.

————. *The Friendship of Books and Other Lectures.* Edited by T. Hughes, Q. C. London: Macmillan, 1904.

————. *The Kingdom of Christ or Hints to a Quaker Respecting the Principles, Constitution, and Ordinances of the Catholic Church.* 3rd ed. London: Macmillan, 1884.

————. *Moral and Metaphysical Philosophy: Volume 1, Ancient Philosophy from the First to the Thirteenth Centuries.* London: Macmillan, 1886.

————. *Moral and Metaphysical Philosophy: Volume 2, Fourteenth Century to the French Revolution with a Glimpse into the Nineteenth Century.* London: Macmillan, 1873.

————. *Social Morality: Twenty-One Lectures.* London: Macmillan, 1886.

————. *Theological Essays.* London: James Clarke & Co. Ltd., 1957; orig. pub. 1853.

McCarraher, Eugene. *The Enchantments of Mammon: How Capitalism Became the Religion of Modernity.* Cambridge, MA: Belknap Press of Harvard University Press, 2019.

McDonough, William. "Etty Hillesum's Learning to Live and Preparing to Die: *Complacentia Boni* as the Beginning of Acquired and Infused Virtue." *Journal of the Society of Christian Ethics* 25, no. 2 (2005): 179–202.

McDowell, John. "Deliberation and Moral Development in Aristotle's Ethics." In *Aristotle, Kant, and the Stoics: Rethinking Happiness and Duty.* Edited by Stephen Engstrom and Jennifer Whiting. Cambridge: Cambridge University Press, 1996.

McMinn, Mark R., Paul T. McLaughlin, Bradley C. Johnson, and Rosanna Shoup. "Psychotherapy and the Theological Virtues." *Open Theology* 2 (2016): 424–35.

Midgley, Mary. *Can't We Make Moral Judgments.* New York: Bloomsbury Academic, 2017.

Miner, Robert. "Infused Virtue as Virtue Simply: The Centrality of the Augustinian Definition in *Summa Theologiae* I/2.55–67." *Scottish Journal of Theology* 1, no. 4 (2018): 411–24.

————. *Thomas Aquinas on the Passions: A Study of* Summa Theologiae *Ia2ae 22–48.* Cambridge: Cambridge University Press, 2009.

Miner, Robert, ed. *Questions on Love and Charity: Summa Theologiae, Secunda Secundae, Questions 23–46.* New Haven, CT: Yale University Press, 2016.

Mirkes, Renée. "Aquinas's Doctrine of Moral Virtue and Its Significance for Theories of Facility." *The Thomist: A Speculative Quarterly Review* 61, no. 2 (1997): 189–218.

Morris, Jeremy. *F. D. Maurice and the Crisis of Authority.* Oxford: Oxford University Press, 2008.

————. "F. D. Maurice and the Christian Socialist Origins." In *Theology Reforming Society: Revisiting Anglican Social Theology.* Edited by Stephen Spencer. London: SCM Press, 2017.

Mouffe, Chantal. *The Democratic Paradox.* London: Verso, 2009.

Mulhall, Stephen. *The Great Riddle: Wittgenstein and Nonsense, Theology and Philosophy.* Oxford: Oxford University Press, 2015.

————. "Theology and Narrative: the self, the novel, the Bible," *International Journal for Philosophy of Religion,* Vol. 69, No. 1, (February 2011), pp. 29–43.

———. *Stanley Cavell: Philosophy's Recounting of the Ordinary*. Oxford: Clarendon Press, 1994.

Mulhall, Stephen, and Adam Swift. *Liberals & Communitarians*. 2nd ed. Oxford: Blackwell, 1997.

Neiman, Susan. *Evil in Modern Thought*. Princeton, NJ: Princeton University Press, 2002.

Nelson, Eric. *The Theology of Liberalism: Political Philosophy and the Justice of God*. Cambridge, MA: Belknap Press of Harvard University Press, 2019.

Nichols, John. *The "S" Word: A Short History of an American Tradition . . . Socialism*. London: Verso, 2015.

Niebuhr, H. Richard. *Christ and Culture*. New York: Harper Torchbooks, 1951.

Nietzsche, Friedrich. *Beyond Good and Evil*. New York: Modern Library, 1927.

Norman, Edward. *The Victorian Christian Socialists*. Cambridge: Cambridge University Press, 1987.

Nussbaum, Martha. "The Epistemology of the Closet." *Nation*, June 2005, 25–30.

———. "Virtue Ethics: A Misleading Category?" *Journal of Ethics* 3, no. 3 (1999): 163–201.

O'Donovan, Oliver. *Self, World, and Time: Ethics as Theology*. Vol. 1. Grand Rapids: William B. Eerdmans, 2013.

Okin, Susan Moller. *Justice, Gender, and the Family*. New York: Basic Books, 1989.

O'Neil, Cathy. *Weapons of Math Destruction: How Big Data Increases Inequality and Threatens Democracy*. New York: Broadway Books, 2017.

Osborne, Thomas M., Jr. "The Augustinianism of Thomas Aquinas's Moral Theory." *The Thomist: A Speculative Quarterly Review* 67, no. 2 (2003): 279–305.

———. "Perfect and Imperfect Virtues in Aquinas." *The Thomist: A Speculative Quarterly Review* 71, no. 1 (2007): 39–64.

———. "Thomas and Scotus on Prudence without All the Major Virtues: Imperfect or Merely Partial?" *The Thomist: A Speculative Quarterly Review* 74, no. 2 (2010): 165–88.

Osiander, Andreas. "Sovereignty, International Relations, and the Westphalian Myth." *International Organization* 55, no. 2 (Spring 2001): 251–87.

Overmyer, Sheryl. "Grace Perfected Nature: The Interior Effect of Charity in Joy, Peace, and Mercy." In *Questions on Love and Charity: Summa Theologiae, Secunda Secundae, Questions 23–46*. Edited by Robert Miner. New Haven, CT: Yale University Press, 2016.

Pearson, C. H. *National Life and Character: A Forecast*. London: Macmillan, 1893.

Phillips, Elizabeth. "Narrating Catastrophe, Cultivating Hope: Apocalyptic Practices and Theological Virtue." *Studies in Christian Ethics* 31, no. 1 (2018): 17–33.

Pogge, Thomas. *John Rawls: Life and Theory of Justice*. Oxford: Oxford University Press, 2007.

Poovey, Mary. *A History of the Modern Fact: Problems of Knowledge in the Sciences of Wealth and Society*. Chicago: University of Chicago Press, 1998.

Porter, Jean. *Moral Action and Christian Ethics*. Cambridge: Cambridge University Press, 1997.

———. "Moral Virtues, Charity, and Grace: Why the Infused and Acquired Virtues Cannot Co-Exist." *Journal of Moral Theology* 8, no. 2 (2019): 40–66.

———. "The Subversion of Virtue: Acquired and Infused Virtues in the *Summa Theologia*." *Annual of the Society of Christian Ethics* 12 (1992): 19–41.

Ramsey, Arthur Michael. *F. D. Maurice and the Conflicts of Modern Theology: The Maurice Lectures 1948*. London: Cambridge University Press, 1951.

Rawls, John. *Brief Inquiry into the Meaning of Sin and Faith (with "On My Religion")*. Edited by T. Nagel. Cambridge, MA: Harvard University Press, 2009.

———. "Foreword." In *The Methods of Ethics*, by Henry Sidgwick. 7th ed. Indianapolis: Hackett, 1981; orig. pub. 1907.

———. *Justice as Fairness: A Restatement.* Edited by Erin Kelly. Cambridge, MA: Harvard University Press, 2001.

———. "Kantian Constructivism in Moral Theory." *Journal of Philosophy* 77, no. 9 (September 1980): 515–72.

———. *The Law of Peoples.* Cambridge, MA: Harvard University Press, 1999.

———. *Lectures on the History of Moral Philosophy.* Edited by Barbara Herman. Cambridge, MA: Harvard University Press, 2000.

———. *Lectures on the History of Political Philosophy.* Edited by Samuel Freeman. Cambridge, MA: Belknap Press of Harvard University Press, 2007.

———. "Outline for a Decision Procedure for Ethics." *Philosophical Review* 60, no. 2 (April 1951): 177–97.

———. *Political Liberalism.* New York: Columbia University Press, 1996; orig. pub. 1993.

———. *A Theory of Justice.* Cambridge, MA: Harvard University Press, 1999; orig. pub. 1971.

Rebanks, James. *The Shepherd's Life.* New York: Flatiron Books, 2015.

Rehnman, Sebastian. "Virtue and Grace." *Studies in Christian Ethics* 25, no. 4 (2012): 473–93.

Reidy, David A. "From Philosophical Theology to Democratic Theory: Early Postcards from an Intellectual Journey." In *A Companion to Rawls.* Edited by Jon Mandle and David A. Reidy. Malden, MA: Wiley Blackwell, 2016.

———. "Rawls's Religion and Justice as Fairness." *History of Political Thought* 31, no. 2 (Summer 2010): 309–43.

Robin, Corey. *The Reactionary Mind: Conservatism from Edmund Burke to Donald Trump.* 2nd ed. Oxford: Oxford University Press, 2018.

Rose, Gillian. *Hegel Contra Sociology.* London: Verso, 2009; orig. pub. 1981.

Ross, W. D. *Aristotle.* 6th ed. London: Routledge, 1995; orig. pub. 1923.

———. *Kant's Ethical Theory: A Commentary on the* Grundlegung zur Metaphysik der Sitten. Oxford: Oxford University Press, 1954.

———. *The Right and the Good.* Indianapolis: Hackett, 1988; orig. pub. 1930.

Safranski, Rüdiger. *Martin Heidegger: Between Good and Evil.* Translated by Ewald Osers. Cambridge, MA: Harvard University Press, 1998.

Sanford, Jonathan. *Before Virtue: Assessing Contemporary Virtue Ethics.* Washington, DC: Catholic University Press, 2015.

Saslow, Eli. *Rising Out of Hatred: The Awakening of a Former White Nationalist.* New York: Doubleday, 2018.

Sayre-McCord, Geoffrey. "On Why Hume's 'General Point of View' Isn't Ideal—and Shouldn't Be." *Social Philosophy & Policy* 11, no. 1 (Winter 1994): 202–28.

Schneewind, J. B. *Sidgwick's Ethics and Victorian Moral Philosophy.* Oxford: Oxford University Press, 1977.

Schultz, Bart, ed. *Essays on Henry Sidgwick.* New York: Cambridge University Press, 1992.

Schultz, Barton. "Henry Sidgwick." In *The Stanford Encyclopedia of Philosophy.* Edited by Edward N. Zalta and Uri Nodelman. July 2019. https://plato.stanford.edu/archives/fall2019/entries/sidgwick/.

———. *Henry Sidgwick: Eye of the Universe.* Cambridge: Cambridge University Press, 2004.

Schwenkler, John. *Anscombe's Intention: A Guide.* New York: Oxford University Press, 2019.

Screpanti, Ernesto, and Stefano Zamagni. *An Outline of the History of Economic Thought.* Translated by David Field. Oxford: Clarendon Press, 1993.

Shanley, Brian. "Aquinas on Pagan Virtue." *Thomist: A Speculative Quarterly Review* 63, no. 4 (1999): 553–77.

Sherwin, Michael. "Infused Virtue and the Effects of Acquired Vice: A Test Case for the Thomistic Theory of Infused Cardinal Virtues." *The Thomist: A Speculative Quarterly Review* 73, no. 1 (2009): 29–52.

Sidgwick, Henry. *The Ethics of T. H. Green, Herbert Spencer, and J. Martineau.* London: Macmillan, 1902.

———. *History of Ethics.* London. Macmillan, 1962; orig. pub. 1886.

———. *Lectures on the Philosophy of Kant and Other Philosophical Lectures & Essays.* London: Forgotten Books, 2012; orig. pub. 1905.

———. *The Methods of Ethics.* 7th ed. Indianapolis: Hackett, 1981; orig. pub. 1874.

———. *Miscellaneous Essays and Addresses.* New York: Kraus Reprint Co., 1968.

———. *Practical Ethics.* New York: Oxford University Press, 1998; orig. pub. 1898.

———. *The Principles of Political Economy.* London: Macmillan, 1901; orig. pub. 1883. New York: Kraus Reprint Co., 1969.

Sidgwick, Arthur, and Eleanor Mildred Sidgwick. *Henry Sidgwick.* London: Macmillan, 1906.

Skelton, Anthony. "William David Ross." In *The Stanford Encyclopedia of Philosophy.* Edited by Edward N. Zalta and Uri Nodelman. Summer 2012. https://plato.stanford.edu/archives/sum2012/entries/william-david-ross/.

Skidelsky, Robert. *Money and Government: The Past and Future of Economics.* New Haven, CT: Yale University Press, 2018.

Smith, Adam. *An Inquiry into the Nature and Causes of the Wealth of Nations.* New York: Modern Library, 1965.

Solomon, David. "Virtue Ethics: Radical or Routine?" In *Intellectual Virtue: Perspectives from Ethics and Epistemology.* Edited by Michael Depaul and Linda Zagzebski. Oxford: Clarendon Press, 2003.

Stout, Jeffrey. *Democracy & Tradition.* Princeton, NJ: Princeton University Press, 2004.

Taylor, Charles. *Hegel.* Cambridge: Cambridge University Press, 1975.

———. *A Secular Age.* Cambridge, MA: Belknap Press of Harvard University Press, 2007.

Teichman, Jenny. "Gertrude Elizabeth Margaret Anscombe, 1919–2001." *Proceedings of the British Academy* 115 (2001): 31–50.

———. *Pacifism and Just War: A Study in Applied Philosophy.* Oxford: Blackwell, 1986.

Teichmann, Roger. *The Philosophy of Elizabeth Anscombe.* Oxford: Oxford University Press, 2008.

———, ed. *Oxford Handbook to Elizabeth Anscombe.* New York: Oxford University Press, 2022.

Todd, Robert B. "Henry Sidgwick, Cambridge Classics and the Study of Ancient Philosophy: The Decisive Years (1866–69)." In *Classics in 19th- and 20th-Century Cambridge: Curriculum, Culture, and Community.* Edited by Christopher Stray. Cambridge: Cambridge Philosophical Society, 1999.

Tradistae. "'A New Set of Social Forms': Alasdair MacIntyre on the 'Benedict Option.'" April 21, 2021, https://tradistae.com/2020/04/21/macintyre-benop/.

Tran, Jonathan. *Asian Americans and the Spirit of Racial Capitalism.* New York: Oxford University Press, 2021.

Turner, Philip. *Christian Socialism: The Promise of an Almost Forgotten Tradition.* Eugene, OR: Cascade Books, 2021.

Vergerio, Claire. "Beyond the Nation-State." *Boston Review: A Political and Literary Forum,* May 27, 2021. http://bostonreview.net/politics/claire-vergerio-beyond-nation-state.

Vermeule, Adrian. *Common Good Constitutionalism.* Cambridge: Polity, 2022.

Vidler, Alec R. *The Theology of F. D. Maurice*. London: SCM Press, 1948.

Vogler, Candace. "Turning to Aquinas on Virtue." In *The Oxford Handbook of Virtue*. Edited by Nancy E. Snow. Oxford: Oxford University Press, 2018.

Walzer, Michael. "Why Was This War Different?" *Philosophy & Public Affairs* 1, no. 1 (Autumn 1971): 3–21.

Ward, James. "Editorial Note." In *Lectures on the Philosophy of Kant and Other Philosophical Lectures & Essays*, by Henry Sidgwick. London: Forgotten Books, 2012; orig. pub. 1905.

Weithman, Paul. "Does Justice as Fairness Have a Religions Aspect?" In *A Companion to Rawls*. Edited by Jon Mandle and David A. Reidy. Malden, MA: Wiley Blackwell, 2016.

Wendt, Fabian. "Rescuing Public Justification from Public Reason Liberalism." In *Oxford Studies in Political Philosophy*. Vol. 5. Edited by D. Sobel, P. Vallentyne, and S. Wall. Oxford: Oxford University Press, 2019.

Whewell, William. *The Elements of Morality*. New York: Harper & Brothers, 1859.

Williams, Bernard. "A Mistrustful Animal: An Interview with Bernard Williams." *Harvard Review of Philosophy* 12, no. 1 (2004): 80–91.

———. "The Point of View of the Universe: Sidgwick and the Ambition of Ethics." In *The Sense of the Past: Essays in the History of Philosophy*. Edited by Bernard Williams and Myles Burnyeat. Princeton, NJ: Princeton University Press, 2006.

Williams, Rowan. *Christ: The Heart of Creation*. London: Bloomsbury, 2018.

Wiseman, Rachel. *Anscombe's Intention*. London: Routledge, 2016.

Wittgenstein, Ludwig. *Philosophical Investigations*. 3rd ed. Translated by G. E. M. Anscombe. New York: Macmillan, 1968.

Wolff, Richard D. *Understanding Socialism*. New York: Democracy at Work, 2019.

Wolin, Sheldon. *Politics and Vision: Continuity and Innovation in Western Political Thought*. Princeton, NJ: Princeton University Press. 2016.

Wondra, Ellen K. "Introduction." In *Reconstructing Christian Ethics: Selected Writings*, by F. D. Maurice. Edited by Ellen K. Wondra. Louisville: Westminster John Knox Press, 1995.

Wood, Allen W. *Kantian Ethics*. Cambridge: Cambridge University Press, 2008.

Zagzebski, Linda. *Virtues of the Mind: An Inquiry into the Nature of Virtue and the Ethical Foundations of Knowledge*. Cambridge: Cambridge University Press, 1996.

INDEX

abolition: in Aquinas 254–55; and Christianity, 80; and Maurice, 171, 187, 193, 200, 232, 275; of prisons, 73, 81; and Rawls, 73, 77

abortion, 118n37, 254, 258

abstract: and appeal to universal, 201; ethics, 4, 51n50, 131; ethics from theology, 12, 17; and Maurice, 172, 175, 178, 181; and Rawls, 146n47; and subjectivity, 137–38, 145n32, 110; and systems and methods, 135, 150, 197; virtue, 141, 182

action: and Anscombe, 6, 253; and ethics, ix, 9, 50n32, 50n50, 131–35, 141–43, 176–77, 181; foreseen consequences of, 33–34, 47–49; intentional, 61–65, 99–100, 105, 114–15, 123, 267–69; morally good, 71–72, 202; ordinary, 11, 22; philosophy of, 55–56, 109–10; and practical reasoning, 66; responsibility for 3, 134; right, 35, 39, 128–29; sources of human, 210–11, 216–17, 222, 240–42; and virtue, 36, 225–26, 228; voluntary human, 7, 25–27, 39–41, 101, 113, 124–27, 276–77

ancient ethics: and Christian theology, ix, 151, 224; and the good, 60–61, 130, 195, 277; and modern ethics, 9, 68, 124, 134, 155–56, 167, 177–78, 253; and Sidgwick, 26–27, 53n105, 76, 83n27–28, 83n31; and wisdom, 11–12, 36

Annas, Julia, 53n105, 123, 132, 140, 144n15

Anscombe, G. E. M.: and constructivism, 120n94; and criticism of Sidgwick, 5–6, 29, 47–49, 55–58, 122–23; on facts, 65–67; and hope, 115–16; and human action, 33, 61–64, 125–28, 211, 268; and killing the innocent, 51n66, 118n37; and Maurice, 150, 199, 212; and modern moral philosophy, 8, 40, 70, 84n57, 111–13, 118n34, 134, 140, 252–53, 275–77; and perfectionist ethics, 73, 100, 105 260–62; and philosophy and faith, 10, 86, 94–96, 109–10, 121n99; and practical reasoning, 77; and virtue, 227, 260; and war, 97–99, 106–7, 119n45–46. See also *Intention*

Anselm, 10, 270

antiliberalism. *See* authoritarian; post-liberalism; reactionary traditions

Aquinas, Thomas: and Aristotle, 3, 6, 16n3, 170n18; and good, 71–72, 90, 130, 280; and human action, 55, 211–13; and MacIntyre, 261, 263; and Maurice, 8, 107, 150–51, 167, 209–10; and moral theology, ix, 8–10, 197, 275; and perfection, 30, 199, 202, 206n116; reactionary reading of, 207–8, 249–53, 255–59, 277–78; and Sidgwick, 25–27, 123; and virtues, 142, 153n7, 161, 205n105, 214–31, 235–41, 244n50, 245n65, 247n139, 267–68, 273n78. See also *Summa Theologiae*

ABOUT THE AUTHOR

D. STEPHEN LONG is the Cary M. Maguire University Professor of Ethics at Southern Methodist University. Previously, he worked at Marquette University, Garrett-Evangelical Theological Seminary, Saint Joseph's University, and Duke Divinity School. He received his PhD from Duke University and is an ordained United Methodist minister in the Indiana Conference. He works at the intersection between theology and ethics, and he has published over fifty essays and nineteen books on theology and ethics, including *Divine Economy: Theology and the Market*; *Christian Ethics: Very Short Introduction*; *Augustinian and Ecclesial Christian Ethics: On Loving Enemies*; *Truth-Telling in a Post-Truth World*; and *The Art of Cycling, Living and Dying*; and he recently edited *The Routledge Companion to Christian Ethics* with Rebekah Miles. He has served as the president of the Society of Christian Ethics.